Robert Wodrow

Selections from Wodrow's biographical Collections

Divines of the north-east of Scotland

Robert Wodrow

Selections from Wodrow's biographical Collections
Divines of the north-east of Scotland

ISBN/EAN: 9783743345249

Manufactured in Europe, USA, Canada, Australia, Japa

Cover: Foto ©ninafisch / pixelio.de

Manufactured and distributed by brebook publishing software (www.brebook.com)

Robert Wodrow

Selections from Wodrow's biographical Collections

Selections

FROM

Wodrow's Biographical Collections

DIVINES
OF THE NORTH-EAST OF SCOTLAND

EDITED BY
THE REVEREND ROBERT LIPPE

ABERDEEN
Printed for the New Spalding Club
MDCCCXC

The New Spalding Club.

Founded 11th November, 1886.

Patroness:
HER MAJESTY THE QUEEN.

OFFICE-BEARERS FOR 1889-90.

President:
THE EARL OF ABERDEEN.

Vice-Presidents:

THE DUKE OF RICHMOND AND GORDON, K.G.
THE DUKE OF FIFE, K.T.
THE MARQUIS OF HUNTLY.
THE MARQUIS OF BUTE, K.T.
THE EARL OF STRATHMORE.
THE EARL OF SOUTHESK, K.T.
THE EARL OF KINTORE.
THE EARL OF ROSEBERY.

THE LORD FORBES.
THE LORD SALTOUN.
THE LORD PROVOST OF ABERDEEN.
THE PRINCIPAL OF THE UNIVERSITY OF ABERDEEN.
C. ELPHINSTONE-DALRYMPLE of Kinellar Lodge.
GEORGE GRUB, LL.D.
ALEXANDER FORBES IRVINE of Drum, LL.D.
JOHN WEBSTER of Edgehill, LL.D.

Ordinary Members of Council:

William Alexander, LL.D., Aberdeen.
Colonel James Allardyce, Aberdeen.
George Burnett, LL.D., Lyon King of Arms. *Deceased.*
James A. Campbell of Stracathro, LL.D., M.P.
The Rev. James Cooper, Aberdeen.
William Cramond, Cullen.
Peter M. Cran, City Chamberlain, Aberdeen.
John Crombie of Balgownie Lodge.
Alexander Davidson of Dess.
Charles B. Davidson, Aberdeen.
The Rev. John Davidson, D.D., Inverurie.
Thomas Dickson, LL.D., H.M. General Register House.
The Hon. and Right Rev. Bishop Douglas, D.D., Aberdeen.
Francis Edmond of Kingswells, LL.D.
John Philip Edmond, London.
Robert F. O. Farquharson of Haughton. *Deceased.*
James Ferguson, Edinburgh.
William Ferguson of Kinmundy.
James Murray Garden, Aberdeen.
Henry Wolrige-Gordon of Esslemont.
The Rev. Walter Gregor, LL.D., Pitsligo.
Alexander Kemlo, Aberdeen.

Colonel William Ross King of Tertowie. *Deceased.*
The Rev. William Forbes-Leith, S.J., Selkirk.
George Arbuthnot-Leslie of Warthill.
David Littlejohn, Sheriff-Clerk, Aberdeen.
James Matthews of Springhill.
The Rev. John G. Michie, Dinnet.
James Moir, Rector of the Grammar School, Aberdeen.
Arthur D. Morice, Aberdeen.
Charles Rampini, Sheriff-Substitute, Elgin.
Alexander Ramsay, Banff.
Major John Ramsay of Barra.
Professor William M. Ramsay, Aberdeen.
Alexander W. Robertson, Librarian, Public Library, Aberdeen.
William Forbes Skene, D.C.L., Ll.D., H.M. Historiographer for Scotland.
The Rev. William Temple, Forgue.
Alexander Walker, Aberdeen.
George Walker, Aberdeen.
Robert Walker, Aberdeen.
John Forbes White, LL.D., Dundee.
John Dove Wilson, LL.D., Aberdeen.
The Rev. John Woodward, Montrose.

Secretary:
PETER JOHN ANDERSON, 2 East Craibstone Street, Aberdeen.

Treasurer:
FARQUHARSON TAYLOR GARDEN, 13 Union Terrace, Aberdeen.

Auditors:
JAMES AUGUSTUS SINCLAIR, C.A., Aberdeen; and GEORGE COOPER, C.A., Aberdeen.

PREFACE.

It was originally intended that this volume should be edited by the late Professor Christie, D.D., an intention that was frustrated by his lamented death. In view of his editorial labours, Dr. Christie had collected a considerable number of dates and references, and these memoranda were considerately placed at the service of the Club by his representatives. The Editor, however, has been unable to make, with one exception, noticed in its proper place, the least use of these jottings, from their disjointed and fragmentary nature.

Except correcting manifest clerical errors and introducing such punctuation as seemed best fitted to educe the writer's meaning, the Editor has endeavoured to present Wodrow's text *verbatim et literatim*.

The thanks of the Club are hereby rendered to the Senatus of the University of Glasgow for allowing with courteous readiness the transcript of these Selections to be made from the Wodrow MSS. in the University Library; to the Senatus of the University of Aberdeen for granting leave to reproduce for this volume the portraits of Bishops Patrick and William Forbes in the University hall; and to the Town Council of Aberdeen for permitting fac-similes of these Bishops' signatures to be taken from documents preserved among the City Archives.

The Editor begs leave to record his grateful acknowledgments for extended privileges in the use of the Aberdeen University Library to Professor Fyfe, the Curator, to Mr. Walker, the Librarian and his obliging assistants; to Professor Story, D.D., of the University of Glasgow, for handsomely granting permission to make full use of his Lecture (unpublished) on John Craig; and specially to his friend William Walker, Esq., the accomplished author of the "Bards of Bon-Accord," who not only took an interest in the work, giving many valuable suggestions, but also spent much time in assisting to correct the proof sheets.

Use has also been freely made of the published works of many writers, but always when possible with due acknowledgment.

THE EDITOR.

CONTENTS.

	PAGE
Introduction	xi
Collections on Mr. John Craig	1
,, Bishop David Cunningham	57
,, Bishop Peter Blackburn	66
,, Bishop Patrick Forbes	80
,, Bishop Adam Bannantyne	106
,, Mr. John Durie	124
,, Bishop David Lindsay	165
,, Principal Alexander Arbuthnet	179
,, Sub-principal James Lawson	193
,, Principal Robert Howie	235
,, Principal and Bishop William Forbes	245
,, Principal Charles Ferme	270
,, Mr. John Johnstoun	282
Notes	297
Appendix	343
Index	351

ILLUSTRATIONS.

Bishop Patrick Forbes, *from the portrait in the possession of the University of Aberdeen* . . . . . . *Frontispiece.*

Principal and Bishop William Forbes, *from the portrait in the possession of the University of Aberdeen* . . . *Page* 244

b

INTRODUCTION.

I.

The history of the Church in Scotland may be conveniently divided into three distinct periods. The first may be said to extend from the introduction of Christianity to the arrival in Scotland of Margaret, who became Queen of Malcolm Canmore, and died in 1093. The second commenced with the changes introduced by that princess—the ecclesiastical division of the country into parishes and dioceses, the appointment of officials to minister to those, and the organisation of the Church in ritual and ecclesiastical polity into strict harmony with the Roman order—all which were effected by Margaret, and by her sons, especially David I. The close of this period is marked by the accession to the English throne of the Protestant Elizabeth, and her interference in the affairs of Scotland, which definitely turned the scale in favour of the Reformers. These, in the year 1560, formally repudiated the Catholic Church, and abrogated the jurisdiction of the Roman See over Scotland. The third and last period, in which we now live, was ushered in by the convulsive struggles of that wonderful religious revolution of the sixteenth century, generally known as the Reformation, and whose issues are still mightily affecting the destinies of the world. These three divisions may be with considerable propriety denominated the Celtic, the Mediæval, and the Modern.

THE CELTIC CHURCH.

Scotland, as Bishop Forbes has remarked in his Preface to the Arbuthnot Missal, has been evangelised by successive waves of Christian civilisation, which, century after century, and quite independently of each other, extended themselves over the country. Tertullian is the earliest writer who speaks of the conversion of the northern parts of our island, and says that places in Britain, inaccessible to the Roman arms, were brought under subjection to Christ. But this rhetorical statement may simply mean, that some knowledge of the Christian religion was brought into the remote fastnesses of the North by the captives carried away by the rude inhabitants in their savage incursions into the southern or Roman districts of the island. Be this, however, as it may, the Christianity introduced by direct contact with the Romans or their subjects seems never to have gained any footing in the country, and to have been utterly extinguished without leaving a solitary relic behind. The first Christian missionary of whom we have any definite notion was St. Ninian, who is said to have built in Galloway, about 397, the first stone and lime church in those parts. This structure, doubtless from its appearance, was styled Candida Casa, and afterwards, from its Saxon equivalent, Whiteherne or Whithorn. We have no trustworthy accounts of the life of St. Ninian or of his companions, though we have not a few legends regarding his labours and miracles.

The sphere of St. Ninian's labours seems to have been the South-East part of what now forms Scotland, for he is reported to have converted the southern Picts who dwelt between the Grampians and the Firth of Forth. The South-West regions, extending from Glasgow or Dumbarton as a centre, are said to have received a knowledge of the truth from the preaching of St. Kentigern and his companions, probably a little later than the time of St. Ninian. This district, forming part of the kingdom of Strathclyde, was the home of St. Patrick, who, passing thence to Ireland, became the great Christian missionary to that island, and was deservedly chosen as its patron saint.

In groping our way along these uncertain tracks amidst

almost midnight darkness we, however, obtain a more distinct path and clearer light to guide us, when we reach the times of St. Columba, the first missionary of whom we have, what may be called, authentic and distinct accounts. Columba, of royal parentage, and a native of the North of Ireland, was born about the year of our Lord 521. Being involved in the consequences of implication in civil feuds, Columba was forced to leave Ireland, and landed along with twelve companions at Iona, in the forty-second year of his age. There he founded a famous monastery, which became the centre whence the light of Christianity radiated all over the North and East of Scotland, and extended also over districts previously to some extent christianised, as far as to the Lothians and North-East parts of England, then embraced by the kingdom of Northumbria. Columba died in 597, and his Life was written by his successors in Iona, Cumin and Adamnan, who lived respectively about 60 and 90 years after their great predecessor and founder. These Lives, along with some notices in the subsequent History of Bede, afford us almost the whole authentic accounts we have concerning the ancient Celtic Church. Its doctrines seem to have been few, simple, and scriptural, and though at times tinged with heretical notions introduced by foreigners, generally orthodox. Of its ritual we have no means of forming a complete notion, the only remnant of it, so far as this country is concerned, being a fragment of an office for the visitation of the sick contained in the Book of Deer. The ecclesiastical polity was monastic, and generally tribal, there being no diocesan bishops with districts distinctly defined as their sees. The abbot, who generally held his office by heredity, was the supreme authority over the monastery. There were undoubtedly bishops, perhaps duly consecrated, who theoretically held a higher ecclesiastical rank than the abbot, and could discharge functions which he could not, but these were exercised in strict obedience to the abbot's orders. In the course of time, these abbots became to all intents and purposes territorial lords, performing in peace and war the duties of such, as circumstances required. Some persons, however, professing a stricter mode of life and a more rigid adherence to religious rites, retired into solitary places, and lived as hermits apart from the world, and came to be known afterwards by the name of Culdees, or more correctly Keledei, from Céli-Dé, servants of God. These religious recluses, abandoning their solitary habits and their vows of abject poverty, from time to time congregated in various parts of the country, and became possessed of much property; and, gradually yielding to the secularising influences around them, became so sunk in ignorance and corruption as to possess nothing but the name to distinguish them from the other monastic establishments of the Celtic Church. By inexact writers, the term Culdees is employed to denote the various churches planted by Columba and his companions and successors over the country, and by others, again, the whole Celtic Church in Scotland. It has, however, been established by Dr. Reeves, that the name Keledei occurs historically as a designation for a clerical body of monks, used in Scotland by writers, to denote a particular but numerous class of monastic bodies of the Irish type north of the Forth, as distinguished (1) from Columbite monasteries, and (2) from the special Augustinian, Benedictine, and other orders, subsequently introduced. Indeed, the Celtic Church has long been a battlefield between Anglicans and Presbyterians, both sides claiming in it a true example of their own ecclesiastical polity. The Anglican finds a Church ruled by duly consecrated bishops with the subordinate orders of presbyters and deacons, and constituting an Apostolic Church independent of the Roman See. The Presbyterian, on the other hand, finds the same Church constituted on strictly presbyterian principles—co-ordination of the presbyters or ministers, assisted in temporal matters by laymen, corresponding to the ruling elders or deacons, as they understand these terms. Both parties found on the same scanty and obscure statements in Bede. Without presuming to give an authoritative opinion, which must be no less incompetent than useless, we may merely remark that, from an impartial examination of the whole case, the historical student will probably come to the conclusion, that the Celtic Scottish Church was undoubtedly episcopal, but not strictly so in the modern sense of that term, and that it has not been clearly proved that the bishops alone, to the exclusion of abbots, ordained missionaries and other clerics; while it is certain that, in all matters of rule and discipline, the bishop was in strict subordination to the abbot. The Bishop of Rome, too, may be held to have had, perhaps from the introduction of Christianity, a certain moral superiority, if not something more, over the whole Celtic Church, which authority manifested itself in directing missionary effort and advising in doctrinal and especially in ritualistic matters. This Roman influence was at first weak and unable to enforce conformity from the Celts to the Roman Order in various respects, as for example, in the tonsure, the keeping of Easter, and organisation after the Roman model, but gradually increased in strength, till at last it became able to control the development of the Church according to the principles and practice of the Roman See.

For further information regarding the Celtic Church in this country, the reader is referred to Skene's Celtic Scotland, Adamnan's Life of St. Columba by Reeves, Robertson's Early Scotland, Warren's Ritual and Liturgy of the Celtic Church; and for authentic information regarding the Culdees, to Dr. Reeves's monograph on that subject. An abridgment of the last forms the Article on the Colidei, or Culdees, in the Dictionary of Christian Antiquities.

THE MEDIÆVAL CHURCH.

The Primitive Scottish Church, as we have hinted, gradually

sank into a state of corruption and decay. This was brought about by various causes besides the innate depravity of human nature. These were chiefly the Church's remote situation, cut off by distance and want of means of communication from the various centres of intellectual activity and Christian life and progress, her loose organisation without any controlling central authority, and above all, the possession of superfluous wealth, which, gradually accumulating, rendered the religious orders independent for their support on the gratitude and liberality of their people. A reformation of this state of matters was introduced by Queen Margaret, as soon as she became partner on the throne with Malcolm Canmore. In this good work she was not a little aided by the influx of Saxons and Normans from the South, who, for various reasons sought power and place among the less civilised inhabitants of the North. Margaret appears to have been a good and enlightened woman, and to have exercised the most beneficial influence on her husband and his subjects. She was enabled, in no small degree, to do this from her possessing and exercising all the qualities, then deemed peculiarly saintly, of humility, charity to the poor, and strict attention to all prescribed religious duties and observances. We have her Life, written by Turgot, who became Bishop of St. Andrews; and in this production, one would willingly exchange the accounts of her religious affections and of her methodical rounds of duty and devotion for some simple facts regarding her actual every-day life and secular surroundings. Her sons, who successively came to the throne, especially David, carried on, and, indeed in a measure, completed St. Margaret's work of reformation. Many of the ancient religious houses, and among them several occupied by Culdees, gave place to Cathedral churches with their attendant functionaries. The country was distributed into thirteen ecclesiastical divisions or dioceses, and a bishop, in strict dependence on the Holy See, appointed over each. These dioceses were gradually parcelled out into parishes, which theoretically contained at least one place of public worship, which all resident within the parochial bounds were entitled, and astricted to attend. Ample provision for the maintenance of the whole ecclesiastical system was found in the free-will offerings of the pious and religiously disposed. According to Dr. Lee [Church History, vol. I. p. 39,] "those possessions of the Church began to be called in the twelfth century *benefices*, because they originated chiefly from the beneficence of the devout, who consecrated part of their substance to the service of religion. Benefices were of two kinds : *regular*, belonging to the monastic orders, or regular clergy, and *secular*, which belonged to the bishops and the churchmen under their inspection. Each of these kinds of livings consisted of a *temporality* and a *spirituality*—the *temporality* including the lands and other civil rights, superiorities and jurisdictions—and the *spirituality* embracing the tithes, churches and churchyards, glebes and manses, which, according to the canonists, pertained to the church *jure divino*."

The clergy who held these benefices were consequently of two kinds : monastic or regular because bound by a certain rule (*regula*), and secular. The regulars were divided into several orders, the most numerous of which was the Augustinian. These were not restricted like the other regulars to the duties of their own monasteries, but often discharged the functions of parish priests. They were the richest of all the regulars in Scotland, and are said to have possessed twenty-eight monasteries, among which may be named as chief, St. Andrews, Scone, Holyrood House, and Cambus-Kenneth. One of the most ancient orders was the Benedictine. These were subdivided into several classes, many of whom were honourably distinguished by their devotion to learning and tuition. Their chief houses were Coldingham, Kelso, Paisley, Melrose, Arbroath and Kinloss. Besides these, there were about twenty other monasteries of various denominations, professing to belong to canons regular. The other great divisions of the monks was the mendicants, divided into four orders: Dominicans or Black Friars, the most considerable order—the Franciscans or Grey Friars—Carmelites or White Friars—and Hermits of St. Augustine.

All the monks were distinguished by a shaven crown or tonsure, in imitation of Christ's crown of thorns, or to denote their expectation of the heavenly crown; and all, on their admission, took the three vows of chastity, poverty, and obedience to their superiors. From their increasing riches, all these orders of monks became possessed of enormous power, and, from the same cause—and also from their exemption from episcopal jurisdiction, their pride and ambition became excessive. The head of the monastery was styled Abbot, and all the monasteries of the same order were subject to the same superior, called the Provincial. Next in station was the Prior, and under him was the sub-Prior. Some monasteries, however, were ruled by priors, independent of abbots, as, for example, the rich Augustinian Convent of St. Andrews, ruled by a prior, who claimed precedence over all the abbots and priors of the kingdom as well as independence of any bishop. This system of religious houses was the occasion of the great abuse of gifting a vast number of churches with their lands and tithes to different monasteries, who thus became patrons of a large proportion of the parish churches. Kelso had thirty-six churches annexed to it, Arbroath thirty-two, and Paisley twenty-eight. These houses drew the revenues, and served the cure of the parishes annexed by members of their own establishment, deputed for that purpose, and hence called vicars. The number of the various religious houses, abbeys, and monasteries exceeded an hundred. For female religious orders were established convents, but these were less numerous than the monasteries—amounting to about twenty. Some of them, however, contained a great number of inmates. Though we cannot now obtain an exact computation of the numbers of those men and women who devoted themselves to a monastic life, yet we may estimate them at several thousands.

The other great division of ecclesiastics was the secular clergy, also of various orders and dignities. The highest resident dignitaries in the Mediæval Church in Scotland were the bishops, some of whom were occasionally raised to the rank of cardinals, and two of whom, in the later stage of the Church's life, were promoted to the dignity of archbishops. Subordinate to the bishops were the three greater orders, priest, deacon, and sub-deacon, and inferior to these, the four minor orders, doorkeeper, reader, acolyte, and exorcist. The cathedral establishment consisted of dean, sub-dean, archdeacon, chanter, sub-chanter, chancellor, treasurer, and occasionally of other officials. The Council of the bishop was called the chapter, and was composed of the dean and several prebendaries and canons. The head of the chapter was the dean or *decanus*, so called from his being the chief of the ten prebendaries or canons, comprising the chapter—a number, however, not always maintained. Next to the dean was the archdeacon, originally the chief of those in deacon's orders; but the archdeacon in course of time increased in dignity, and became in certain cases the bishop's substitute, and was assisted in his functions by rural deans under him, enjoying a limited jurisdiction.

Next in dignity to the Cathedrals were the Collegiate churches, the government and regulation of which, though on a smaller scale, were similar to the Cathedrals. The head of a Collegiate church was called provost, or sometimes dean. There were at one time thirty-three such churches in this country. The prebendaries or canons attached to these varied in number; in some there were five or six, in others, they amounted to twelve, or even to sixteen. The Chapel Royal of Stirling was the most opulent, but Roslin far surpassed all others in point of architectural magnificence. These Collegiate Churches had generally superadded a great number of altars or chaplainries (St. Nicholas in Aberdeen had sixteen) more or less richly endowed. To the Cathedral and Collegiate churches were attached schools, which, through the munificence of the bishops, and with the express sanction of the Pope, eventually developed, as at St. Andrews, Glasgow, and Aberdeen, into universities; and all were of immense benefit to the country in maintaining and diffusing some learning and enlightenment in the midst of ignorance and barbarism. Indeed, the Mediæval Church in Scotland has not received her due meed of credit for the benefits she conferred in originating and maintaining the various grammar schools and colleges, which produced a body of men of no mean literary acquirements.

Such, then, is a rough outline of our Mediæval Church organisation, with, however, various local and temporary modifications and additions, which the space at our command prevents us from even mentioning.

In regard to ritual and liturgy, our Mediæval Church, as in other respects, became, after the abrogation of her Celtic peculiarities, an integral part of the Western or Catholic Church. Consequently the various old Celtic Ecclesiastical Uses and customs were rigidly suppressed, though not without a severe and protracted struggle. The service books, vestments, services, and festivals, were all in accordance with the Roman Order. So completely was every vestige of Scottish Church individuality swept away, and such was also the want of literary and liturgical acquirements among her clergy, that none of the Scottish bishops ever succeeded in originating and maintaining any peculiar diocesan uses, or service books, as we find was the case in several of the English bishoprics, as for example in Sarum, York, and Hereford, and to an infinitely greater extent on the continent, especially in the French and German dioceses. Scotland, in fact, all through the Mediæval period, was entirely dependent on England, and perhaps to a slight extent on Ireland, for her service books—especially to Sarum whose Breviary and Missal were in all but universal use. The only doubtful exception was the diocese of Aberdeen, which, about the close of this period, through the exertions of the patriotic James IV. and the enlightened Elphinstone, gave birth to the Aberdeen Breviary. This book, however, was just the Sarum Breviary adapted for Scottish use. Even it was but partially introduced or used by the country generally, notwithstanding the fond anticipations of king and bishop; for we find that only one edition was required during the whole remaining period—about fifty years—of Catholic supremacy.

For a complete account of this period, we beg to refer the reader to the historical works of Lee, Grub, and Cunningham; also to the Councils and relative documents of Wilkins, Dalrymple, Haddan and Stubbs, and especially to the Statuta Ecclesiæ Scoticanæ by Dr. Jos. Robertson. Much information, at first hand, may also be gleaned from the various chartularies which have been printed, often with valuable Introductions. An excellent abstract of the history of this period is contained in one of the St. Giles's Lectures, vol. I. by Dr. Campbell. He closes his lecture with a fair and candid appreciation of the benefits conferred on the country by the Mediæval Church, and a masterly summary of the causes of its declension and failure. Want of space forbids us from pursuing this part of our subject further than to refer the reader to that lecture, and to the succeeding one, in the volume mentioned, by Prof. Mitchell. A useful abstract of statistical and other information regarding this and other periods of Church history is contained in Dr. Rankin's Handbook of the Church of Scotland.

The Modern Church.

The Reformation, which ushered in the modern period of Church history, is second only to the birth of Christ in importance in the history of human progress. It closes the mediæval system, and introduces the modern with its manifold bearings—social, political, and religious. Like many other great national upheavals, the Reformation was the resultant of various forces, acting from various and often discordant motives and for as various ends. A potent factor in bringing it about in Scotland was the cupidity for the Church possessions, entertained by the greedy and turbulent nobles and barons. These not only coveted the Church lands, but were envious of the political influence wielded by the dignified clergy, who engrossed, and we readily admit often worthily engrossed, the chief offices in the State, as being the best scholars, the most capable statesmen, the most accomplished diplomatists, and the profoundest and acutest lawyers. Another was the fact that the religious man had long been hungering and thirsting after spiritual nourishment. Teaching by the religious orders had ceased; preaching, except by some of the mendicant friars, had died out. The Church services, which enshrined what was once the warmest and tenderest and most devout affections and aspirations of the human heart, were coldly mumbled over in a foreign tongue, and had become a piece of mere priestly acting, in which the pious worshipper had no share, and from which he could derive neither comfort nor strength. Even had the Church services been otherwise, their good effects would have been entirely neutralised by the scandalous lives of many of the clerical orders. Though we need not give literal credit to all the charges urged against the clergy by the poetical wrath of the satirists and the heated imagination of the reformers, yet, from what is recorded, we must conclude that the morality of the Scottish clergy then was probably the lowest in Christendom. Besides, the Church, in addition to her enormous wealth, had gradually foisted in several dues and exactions which pressed heavily on the poorer classes—the immense majority of the population. For example, we are told that "when death visited, a family, the violence of grief was scarcely allowed to subside till the parson came and carried off the best cow and the uppermost cloth".

But perhaps the most potential cause of the Reformation was the spread of light and learning—the first gropings of free thought that attended the revival of letters, consequent on the awakening of the intellect of Europe, after its long dark sleep and perverse employment, for many dreary centuries. To all these new ideas and new aspirations the Church in Scotland opposed dogged, unyielding opposition, not scrupling to employ every engine in her power to thwart and stamp out every movement, tending to advance and improve mankind, not only in their moral and religious, but even in their social and political progress. Scotland had never shown any backwardness in responding to the various movements for reformation in England and Germany. The followers of Wicliffe in England had their counterpart in the Lollards of Carrick, Kyle, and Cunningham; and, not to mention others, Patrick Hamilton, Luther's disciple and friend, testified to the reformed faith at the stake, in 1528, before the gate of St. Salvator's College in St. Andrews. This and several other cases of cruel martyrdom of pious and peaceable men produced a profound effect on the people of Scotland, and, perhaps more than all other causes together, served to instil into the popular mind a rooted aversion and hatred to everything Catholic, feelings possibly never to be eradicated. These and various other causes, such as the removal by death and otherwise of the chief supporters of Catholicism in Scotland, led to the downfall of the Mediæval Church. She, however, did not die without some faint struggles. Even in the throes of dissolution, she made some efforts at self-reformation. For this purpose, several provincial councils were held, which enacted various canons to regulate the dues of the clergy, and induce some improvement in their morals and attention to clerical duties. A catechism, too, was put forth under the auspices of the Archbishop of St. Andrews, chiefly, however, for the instruction of the clergy. This is called Hamilton's Catechism, and is one of the most interesting relics of the ancient Catholic Church in Scotland. Its merits as a manual of doctrine have been variously estimated, but the reader has ample means for forming his own conclusion on this point, as the work has been recently reproduced in two editions with valuable Introductions, the one by Prof. Mitchell, of St. Andrews; the other by Mr. Law, of the Signet Library, Edinburgh. All these efforts, however, proved powerless to save from ruin; and the Catholic Church in Scotland was subverted with a completeness to be found perhaps in no other Protestant country.

In the following few pages we propose to give a brief chronological synopsis of the chief events bearing on church life in Scotland from the Reformation, in 1560, down to what has been by some styled the Second Reformation, inaugurated by the Glasgow General Assembly, in 1638, and ending with the temporary suppression of episcopacy in Scotland; and to conclude with a glance at the ritual and polity of the Church during that period. We have chosen this halting place, because none of Wodrow's Lives in the present volume extend beyond that epoch.

In 1557, certain nobles and gentlemen, who afterwards came to be styled Lords of the Congregation, subscribed a "band" called the First Covenant, by which they pledged themselves to see certain reforms carried out in the Church, and to act in concert against all opposers. These reforming principles spread, and strengthened still more, after the martyrdom of Walter Milne, the aged priest of Lunan, and the accession of Elizabeth to the

English throne, and a second band was signed in 1559. The effect of this was more energetic action. A petition embodying the Reformers' demands was presented to the Regent by Sir James Sandilands, and a second invitation was sent to John Knox, then at Geneva, to return and assist in promoting and consolidating the new ecclesiastical order. This invitation Knox accepted, and returned to Scotland, in May, 1559. The previous movements of Knox at home, and in England, Germany, and Switzerland, are quite explicable on the grounds of common prudence and a common-sense regard to personal safety, but have hitherto proved an insoluble problem to those who feel bound to maintain that to Knox human fear was absolutely unknown, and that the progress and success of the Reformation in Scotland had always been his one object in life. Aided by Willock and Douglas, and shortly afterwards by Craig and others, Knox itinerated through the central parts of the country, inveighing against the principles and practices of Rome, and preaching the doctrines of the Calvinistic Reformation. In this he was eminently successful; truth was promulgated and waverers confirmed. Politicians secured the country from the presence of contending foreign soldiers, and a national parliament was called. This parliament met in August, 1560, and though wanting the commission of the Queen, then in France, did not hesitate to set about the transaction of the most important business. So far as regarded the Church the outcome was this: a new Confession of Faith, drawn up in four days by a Committee of the Reformers, was approved and sanctioned, the celebration of the Mass was declared illegal and penal, and all Papal jurisdiction over Scotland was abolished. It was thus, on the 24th August, 1560, that the Scottish Reformation was consummated by the Scottish Parliament. But though Protestantism was thus established, its organisation was in a very chaotic state, and there was still some fear of the country slipping back to Catholicism. To guard against and counteract any such tendency, as well as to imbue the mass of the people with sound Protestant and evangelical principles was the great work of Knox and his coadjutors. What for a time seemed to give some impetus to this tendency was the return of the widowed Mary to her native kingdom. Though, for a brief period, Mary seemed to count for a factor in the reactionary tendency, and as such, was heartily opposed and denounced by Knox, yet Mary had little real influence in the country, surrounded and thwarted as she was by turbulent nobles and treacherous friends—including her illegitimate half-brother, Moray—who were all in the pay of England. Mary, in fact, had difficulty in obtaining liberty to enjoy the exercise of her own religious rites in opposition to the ferocious bigotry of Knox and his party, who were for putting to death all who in any way took part in the celebration of Mass. Besides, what little chance of influence Mary might have succeeded in building up, was entirely lost by her subsequent domestic life and all its resulting disasters. Seven years after her return to her native land saw her a fugitive and a prisoner in a foreign and hostile country. The government of Scotland, during the minority of Mary's infant son, James, now for several years became the prize to be schemed for, and secured by the selfish and greedy nobles. Moray naturally held the prize first, and he zealously forwarded the Reformation on evangelical principles so far as they did not clash with his own material interest. Knox's honesty and sagacity enabled him to detect Moray's interested motives and rising ambition, and a temporary estrangement was the result, but, though a reconciliation was afterwards effected, Knox never succeeded in obtaining any suitable legislative enactment, securing a due maintenance for the ministers of the Reformed Faith. Knox had done his work in helping to pull down the ancient ecclesiastical edifice, but his principles of reconstruction did not suit the greedy nobles, and so his further services were dispensed with.

After Moray's assassination, in 1570, the regency was successively held by the Earls of Lennox, Mar, and Morton. The last held the reins of government from 1572 to 1578, and proved himself an energetic ruler, though cruel, and utterly unscrupulous in advancing his own interest, a course in which he was aided and imitated by the other Scottish nobles and barons. When the Catholic Church had been overthrown, the Parliament, in 1562, enacted that the bishops of the old Church should enjoy for life two thirds of their episcopal revenues, and that the remaining third should go to the support of the reformed ministers. Now, as it was the case that ecclesiastical revenues could be legally enjoyed only by ecclesiastical persons, the question arose as to the disposal of these episcopal revenues, on the decease of the existing bishops. To provide for this case was the object of the Concordat of Leith, which met, in 1572, under the direction of the Regent Morton, during a period of civil war and religious chaos. Who actually convened the meeting is unknown. It was not a regular Assembly, but it illegally assumed to itself the functions that belong to a legal General Assembly. The business transacted was in point of fact the work of a committee of six chosen by the members to meet another committee of six representing the Privy Council. By those twelve it was enacted " that the names and titles of archbishops and bishops are not to be altered or inovate, nor yet the bounds of the dioceses confounded ; but to stand and continue as they did before the reformation of religion, at least to the King's Majesty's majority, or consent of Parliament". It was further provided, " that there be a certain assembly or chapter of learned ministers annexed to every metropolitan or cathedral seat," and further, "that all archbishops and bishops be subject to the Kirk and General Assembly thereof *in spiritualibus*, as they are to the King *in temporalibus*". These arrangements were not meant for the establishment of episcopacy so much as for the creation of a medium through which, by a legal fiction, the episcopal revenues could be conveyed to laymen. The method of operation was to appoint clerical creatures to the vacant sees who were willing to allow the chief share of the income to be appropriated by the patron, or other, who had procured the appointment. The new class of bishops, who were bishops only in name, were in derision called Tulchan bishops. John Knox saw through the whole arrangement, and denounced it as a simoniacal paction. But he was powerless to do more, and soon after died of premature old age. The Church had meanwhile given a hesitating and temporary adherence to the Concordat, stipulating that the names, archbishop, dean, &c., " slanderous and offensive to the ears of many," should be changed into others, and that the whole arrangement be only interim. The struggle against episcopacy went on from the date of the Concordat, increasing in virulence year by year, until the year 1580, when the Assembly, in which Andrew Melville, since his return to Scotland in 1574, had acquired paramount influence, declared the office of bishop to be unlawful, having neither foundation nor warrant in the Word of God. The Assembly at the same time, in pursuance of this finding, ordained all persons holding the office of bishop to demit the same, and to cease from preaching the word and administering the sacraments till they should be admitted anew by the General Assembly, under pain of excommunication.

About this time there arose a new disturbing element in the affairs of the Church. James, since 1578, had nominally assumed the government, but he was still, as in fact he remained all his lifetime, under the direction of favourites. Under their direction, and from his own inordinate conceit and high notions of kingly prerogative, James gradually took an increasing share in ecclesiastical matters—an interference troublesome to himself—pernicious to the best interests of the Church, and eventually disastrous and fatal to his family and name.

Under a temporary Popish scare and to gain popularity, the King, his nobles, and others, signed a document drawn up by Craig, variously denominated the King's Confession, the Second Confession, the Negative Confession, or First Covenant, chiefly directed against Roman Catholicism. The sympathy, if not active support, of the Presbyterian leaders with the abettors of the Ruthven Raid, alienated James from Presbyterianism. He and his supporters, styled by Wodrow the Court party, having the ascendency in Parliament, destroyed the freedom of the Church, which, since 1560, she had enjoyed; and by five enactments, called the Black Acts of 1584, set up Episcopacy and secured it by penal sanctions. These Acts have been thus summarised:—
"(1) The ancient jurisdiction of the three estates was ratified (one of the three being the bishops) and to speak evil of any of them is treason. (2) The king was supreme in all causes and over all persons, and to decline his judgment is treason. (3) All convocations, not specially licensed by the king, are unlawful. (The calling of General Assemblies and other church courts was thus made to depend on the King's will.) (4) The chief jurisdiction of the Church lies with the bishops. (These thus took the place of the Church Courts.) (5) None shall presume *publickly* or *privately*, in sermons, declamations, or familiar conferences, to utter any false, untrue, or slanderous speeches, to the reproach of his Majesty or Council, or meddle with the affairs of his Highness and Estate, under the pains contained in the Acts of Parliament made against the makers and reporters of lies" [Rankin]. That these Acts should not remain inoperative, Parliament met soon again, and added an Act to the effect, that all ministers, readers, and masters of colleges, should compear within forty days, and subscribe the Acts concerning the King's jurisdiction over all estates, temporal and spiritual, and promise to submit themselves to the bishops, their ordinaries, under pains of being deprived of their stipends. The enforcement of these Acts led

to the imprisonment, banishment, and flight of most of the Presbyterian leaders, but, under the moderate guidance of John Craig, a compromise was effected, and the stringency of subscription was gradually relaxed, so that the fugitives, and those under restraint, were enabled to return to their accustomed charges. But, though a modified Episcopacy was now established with a sort of half consent of the General Assembly, an Act was passed by the Parliament, in 1587, which practically uprooted it, without leaving the means for any future planting of Episcopacy taking root in the country. This was the Act annexing the temporalities of the various bishoprics to the Crown. This proceeding left to the bishops mere titles without corresponding means for their maintenance. Dr. Cunningham notices that various causes concurred to the passing of this Act, so fatal to Episcopacy in Scotland. The royal revenues were very scanty, and James, always impecunious, was persuaded that in this way his funds could be largely augmented without the necessity of imposing hateful taxation. The bishops in possession were made to believe that their episcopal palaces, and the tithes annexed to their respective sees, would support them in affluence; and it is probable that these, if paid, would amount to more than their present uncertain incomes. The ministers, no doubt, had always resisted the secularisation of Church property, but they hated the bishops more than they loved their benefices, and they let the one go that the other might go with them. Every acre of ecclesiastical patrimony now passed into laymen's hands, and the Church herself henceforward became a pensioner of the State, receiving a small dole grudgingly of what had once been her own. Nor was the Crown much enriched by this sacrilegious spoliation. James soon squandered away the plunder among his greedy courtiers and favourites, who grew great upon the spoils of the bishops; and he had nothing left to himself but regret at his double folly in first plundering the Church and then squandering the booty.

The King's thoughts were now for a time diverted from Church politics to matrimonial projects. With a lover's ardour he had lost patience with his ambassadors' slowness, and set out to Denmark to wed the King's daughter, leaving affairs at home to be guided chiefly by the Presbyterian leaders. Returning home in May, 1590, with his bride, he found the state of the country to be to his entire satisfaction, and gave utterance to his gratitude and good humour in some extravagant speeches, laudatory of the Presbyterian Church of Scotland—speeches which now read curiously in the light of his after conduct. During the continuance of this good understanding between the King and the Presbyterians, the General Assembly met in May, 1592, at Edinburgh, with Robert Bruce, the King's favourite, as Moderator. Under Bruce's guidance, a petition to the King was drawn up embodying the Church's requirements. His Majesty was compliant, and Parliament, which met shortly after the Assembly's meeting, ratified the demands of the Church by passing an Act, which has been styled the Magna Charta of the Presbyterian Church of Scotland. By this Act legal jurisdiction was granted to Church Courts, the Black Acts of 1584 were abrogated, so far as they trenched on her authority in matters of religion, heresy, excommunication, or collation, and provision was made that presentations to vacant churches should henceforth be directed not to the bishops, but to the presbyteries within whose bounds the vacant charges lay. This Act was sent by the King as a great gift to the General Assembly, which met in April, the year following, and the good understanding between the King and the Assembly lasted four years.

James had not seldom shown a latent hankering after the Catholic religion by adopting, as his favourites, some who were adherents of the ancient faith. He had shown a wonderful readiness to be reconciled to the Catholic Earls, Huntly, Errol, and Angus, even after the two former had defeated his own lieutenant, the Earl of Argyll, at the battle of Glenlivat. He in particular showed an anxious desire to pave the way for Huntly's release from excommunication on the easiest terms, and sought to influence the Church to that end. The Church became jealous and alarmed, and a sermon by Black of St. Andrews increased the excitement. The Secret Council interfered to put some check on the unbridled license of clerical agitators, but the Council's authority was denounced as incompetent to interfere in spiritual affairs. A riot in Edinburgh, arising from this collision between the civil and ecclesiastical powers, led to the King's quitting Edinburgh for Stirling in real or pretended terror. But, a reaction setting in, the King was enabled to return to Edinburgh in triumph. The magistrates met him, and upon their bended knees protested their innocence, offered to do their best to discover the ringleaders in the riot, and promised in future to consult his Majesty in the appointment of their ministers. A sermon was preached in the High Church, and after it was done, his Majesty made an oration to the people, declaring his devotion to the reformed faith and his indignation at the conduct of the reformed ministers. Parliament supported the King, and declared the rioters guilty of treason. The King was invested with power to interdict ministers from preaching, or Church Courts from meeting, when he saw cause ; and the Edinburgh clergy, who had been particularly forward, were deprived of their official residences, which were bestowed on the Crown.

The year 1597 is an important era in the history of the Church in Scotland. From this date, James definitely entered upon his policy of entirely subverting Presbyterianism and introducing Episcopacy. "He had come to the conclusion that Presbytery was essentially anarchical and foul-mouthed—a conclusion natural in the circumstances, but which a larger experience in its working has sufficiently refuted" [Cunningham]. This course was uninterruptedly pursued by the King and his successor during the whole period of Church history now under our review. The methods of procedure have been variously estimated by historians according to their principles or their prejudices. The General Assemblies of the Presbyterian Church were so managed as to be the means of gradually introducing a system, which superseded their own authority, and, under court influence, they ceased to represent the national will. James proceeded with singular caution and address, gradually unfolding his designs, which he succeeded in carrying out by playing off one part of the Assembly against the other. The King's accession, in 1603, to the throne of England intensified his Episcopal tendencies, and furnished him with a plausible reason for them in a laudable desire to promote the uniformity of the English and Scottish Churches. The General Assemblies, which the King exercised the right of calling, became more and more mere conventions to ratify the royal decrees. The last one for many years that was deemed valid in after times was held at Aberdeen, in 1605, with John Forbes, Minister of Alford, Moderator. The few members, who constituted this Assembly in opposition to the King's injunctions, and who simply met and adjourned, were subjected to the severest penalties. Forbes and some of his coadjutors were banished, and all were made to feel the heaviest weight of the King's displeasure. In 1610, true Episcopacy was introduced into Scotland by the consecration in London of Spottiswoode (Glasgow), Lamb (Brechin), and Hamilton (Galloway), who, on their return home, consecrated bishops for the vacant sees. The old Presbyterian spirit in the country, however, was perhaps as strong as ever, and probably more intense the more it was strictly suppressed, and it showed itself whenever an opportunity was afforded. This was emphatically the case, when certain proposals were introduced into the Assembly, held at Perth, in August, 1618. It required all the exertions of the bishops and court party to obtain a majority of the Assembly in favour of them, but by the

e

profuse employment of threats and promises these propositions were passed, and they became part of the ecclesiastical law of the land. These are known as the Five Articles of Perth, and were shortly these:—"(1) Enjoining kneeling at Communion; (2) Permitting Communion in private houses in case of sickness; (3) Permitting private baptism on necessary cause; (4) Enjoining the confirmation by the bishop of children eight years old; (5) Orders for observing as holy days Christmas Day, Good Friday, Easter Day, Ascension, and Whitsunday, with abstinence from business and attendance on worship. Afterwards ministers refused to read the order about them from the pulpit, people avoided the churches where they were observed, and the terrors of the High Commission were used to enforce obedience" [Rankin]. The death of James, in 1625, and the succession of his son, Charles I., introduced no break nor change in the ecclesiastical policy of Scotland. The only difference in carrying out this policy was that Charles, being more ignorant of Scotland and Scottish tastes than his father, adopted more unworkable plans for carrying out his designs. He alienated the Scottish nobles and barons by his proposal to resume the grants of tithes and benefices so wastefully squandered by his father upon his favourites; he alienated almost the entire body of the people by seeking to impose upon the country, by his own authority, a Service Book not in accordance with the national religious tastes. These and other ill-judged acts of interference led to such an outburst of national feeling, that the obnoxious books—the Book of Common Prayer, and the book containing the canons—were rejected with every mark of derision and contempt, and the tide of popular feeling rising still higher, a free General Assembly, one representing the national mind and will, was demanded. This Assembly met, in 1638, in Glasgow, and overturned at once the whole edifice of Episcopacy, which had for long been laboriously a-building at such a cost. But we forbear to enter upon, or characterise, this great national uprising; and with a glance at the ritual and polity of the Church during this period, must conclude this part of our Introduction.

Mankind, in performing their acts of devotion to the Supreme Being by prayer, naturally fall into two classes or types. The one, realising the infinite distance between themselves and the Being they address and the awful solemnity of the occasion, feel that their words should then be few and well chosen, and consequently shrink from addressing the Almighty otherwise than in terms, either drawn from His own Word, or sanctioned by the long usage of eminent saints. To the other, this infinity of distance is lost in the urgent, agonising feeling of need, the intense longing after a closer communion with their Heavenly Father, and a passionate desire for unity with, or even absorption ecstatically into, the Divine Essence above. These consequently maintain their heavenly communion by words, spontaneously welling up from the depth of their being, or merely by rapt devotional feelings, incapable of being bodied forth by distinct verbal utterance. Churches in all ages contain both these types; but as they progress, and develop, and organise, the former predominates, while in times of religious excitement and deep earnestness, the latter becomes the more numerous and prominent. The Church in Scotland, at the Reformation, rejoicing in her new found liberty from all ancient and prescribed forms, naturally felt less regard than before for her old Rituals, or even for Forms of Church Service at all, but the spirit of conservatism and a due regard to decency and religious fitness were not entirely lost. To this was added the want of properly qualified persons to lead the public devotions, which fact necessitated the use of some recognised and approved forms of devotions. When the Catholic Church with her Latin services gave place to the Reformed Church with her new services "understanded by the common people," there was a good deal of uncertainty for a time as to what Service Books, if any, should be adopted. From the paucity of native men of learning capable of drawing up such books in the vernacular, Scotland was long dependent on other countries. Before the Reformation was formally established, and in the absence of any controlling authority, the new reformed congregations, as they were formed, seem to have been left to their own choice. From the necessity of the case, the Second Book of Common Prayer of Edward VI., published in 1552, appears to have been the one very generally used, but it never received the formal sanction of the Church of Scotland. Besides, the close intercourse maintained between Scotland and the Continent, especially with Germany and Switzerland, led to the introduction of foreign forms of devotion, particularly of the Prayer Book drawn up for the use, in the first instance, of the English-speaking exiles at Frankfort. The refugees in that city, being in a state of hot contention among themselves regarding, among other points, an Order of Service, a committee, including Knox, who was then a minister there, drew up, in 1554, a new Order of Service, which, however, failed in its object of promoting peace and preventing schism. Eventually Knox and his adherents were driven away from Frankfort. They found an asylum at Geneva, and formed an English congregation there under Knox's ministry. This new formed body used in their services the Frankfort draft after it had received the imprimatur of Calvin. This Service Book was printed at Geneva, in 1556, and was often called the Geneva Prayer Book, and afterwards, John Knox's Liturgy. Principal Lee, however, says that John Knox had probably nothing to do with the original composition of the book. We are quite of the same opinion; the terse, grave, dignified style in which it is composed being very unlike the quaint, exaggerated, and violent terms in which Knox expressed himself in his acknowledged works. It is generally believed that the book was chiefly the production of Whittingham, who, after leaving Frankfort, was ordained a minister at Geneva, and subsequently became Dean of Durham. Knox, as we have already remarked, finally returned to Scotland, in 1559, and about that time, or even earlier, the Book of Geneva began to be used by the reformed congregations there. We find from the First Book of Discipline, adopted by the Church in 1560, that the book, under the designation of "The Book of our Common Order," was already in general use. Dr. Sprott, in his Introduction to a reprint of the book, states that "in 1562, the General Assembly enjoined its uniform use in 'the administration of the Sacraments and solemnisation of marriages and burial of the dead,' and it was reprinted in Edinburgh in that year with some additions. Between 1562 and 1564, it was modified and enlarged in this country by Knox and others. New prayers were added, chiefly from Continental sources, others, which had been used in Scotland previously, were incorporated with it, and the Psalter (to which it formed an Introduction) was completed. In this form it was printed in Edinburgh, in 1564, and the Assembly of that year 'ordained that every Minister, Exhorter, and Reader, shall have one of the Psalm-books lately printed in Edinburgh, and use the Order contained therein in Prayers, Marriages, and Ministration of the Sacraments'. The Book of Geneva thus remodelled is known as Knox's Liturgy, or Book of Common Order, and it embodied the law of the Church as to worship from 1564 till 1645." As the book is well known and quite accessible, we need not stop to notice its contents or character. It is a question, however, how far these injunctions of the Church regarding its use were carried out. It seems probable that the Order was used by all the readers and by such of the ministers as were of a ritualistic tendency, while we know that by others, who were of a more enthusiastic or self-contained disposition, it was either entirely repudiated, or slightingly esteemed. The rubric of the Prayer-Book itself gave wide license as to its use, merely enjoining the use of the various prayers, *or such like*, and, as among the more ardent Presbyterians, extemporaneous prayer gradually became more prized, it is likely that this rubrical license was so largely taken advantage of, that in some parts of the country prescribed forms of religious services became almost unknown.

As James and Charles proceeded in what was deemed by many their Episcopal innovations, there was felt an increasing necessity for providing suitable books of ritual, and even, if possible, of bringing the Scottish and English Churches into uniformity by the introduction into use in Scotland of the English Book of Common Prayer. Various steps in that direction were taken. In particular, the Assembly, which met at Aberdeen in 1616, acting under orders from King James appointed a Committee to revise the Book of Common Prayer contained in the Psalm Book. The Committee appears to have set about its labours, and to have drawn up a new Form of Service to be strictly followed at all times of public worship both by ministers and readers. But various causes prevented the publication of this work. The MS. was discovered in the British Museum by Rev. Alexander Irwin, and partially printed under his direction in the *British Magazine* for 1845-6. An edition of it with an instructive Introduction has been published by Dr. Sprott, in his *Scottish Liturgies of the reign of James Sixth*, Edinburgh, 1871. Charles I., in 1629, revived the question of a new Liturgy for Scotland, and on coming to Edinburgh, in 1633, for his coronation, being advised by the Scottish bishops not to attempt to introduce into Scotland the English Prayer Book, a commission was given to provide a suitable Service Book for his northern kingdom. This work was taken up chiefly by Maxwell, Bishop of Ross, and Wedderburne, Bishop of Dunblane, and the result was, after revision by Archbishop Laud, and Bishop Wren of Norwich, the noblest and most beautiful of all post-Reformation Liturgies. This book, which has hitherto had such a disastrous career, was entitled, *The Booke of Common Prayer for the use of the Church of Scotland*, and which, when read for the first time, in St. Giles', Edinburgh, on Sunday, July 23rd, 1637, led to such momentous consequences to Church and State. This book as a whole, has hardly ever been used in public service, though its liturgical portion, strictly so called, is virtually the Communion Service of the Scottish Episcopal Church of to-day. Its first edition, printed at Edinburgh by Young, 1637, is now scarce and dear, and so likewise is the reprint by Watson: Edinburgh, 1712. It has been included in Pickering's splendid series of Reprints of English Prayer Books. An inferior reproduction is included in Hall's Reliquiæ Liturgicæ. An edition, from which much may be expected, is announced to be published soon, with a copious Historical Introduction, by Bishop Dowden of Edinburgh.

Singing has always formed an integral part of the worship of God, and this part of Divine Service received a fresh impetus and new direction at the Reformation. Instead of the old Latin hymns of the Roman Breviary and Missal and other Service books, which were chanted or sung only by priests and trained choirs, translations of the Davidic Psalter, as well as hymns of modern composition—many of the noblest of which were composed by Luther and the other Reformers—were sung in the vernacular in all reformed congregations, and in this part of the devotions the commons were encouraged to join heartily. The first compositions of this kind that we find in Scotland were translations by Wedderburne, Vicar of Dundee, and used at the dawn of the Reformation. Subsequently, on the introduction of King Edward's Prayer Book, the 44 psalms translated by Sternhold and Hopkins, it is believed, were used in public worship. The Genevan Prayer Book, first published, as mentioned above, in 1556, at Geneva, contained 51 psalms, viz., the 44 of Sternhold and Hopkins, somewhat modified, and 7 additional by Whittingham. The same Psalter, printed again at Geneva in 1561, was enlarged to

87 psalms, and these would doubtless be introduced into Scotland with the copies of the augmented book, which we know was imported into this country. In 1562, the translation of the whole psalms was completed in England for the use of the Church there. In addition to the original 44 of Sternhold and Hopkins, 20 of those which had been added by the exiles were retained. In 1564, the Scottish Psalter was completed. It retained the Genevan collection of 87, selected 42 from the English edition of 1562, and completed the number with 21 new renderings by Pont and "J. C.," probably John Craig.

We have already adverted to the desire of James I. for uniformity in the Churches of England and Scotland, and this desire induced him to attempt the introduction not only of a Common Prayer Book, but of a common Psalter into both kingdoms. Aided by his courtier, Sir William Alexander, he composed a poetical version of the psalms, which was printed in 1631, by order of his son and successor, Charles I. The reception of this version was, like the other royal innovations, bitterly opposed by the Scots, but, in 1634, Charles gave orders to the Scottish Privy Council that no other version than this one was to be printed or imported; and with a view to its use in Scotland, a new version, a good deal altered from the previous edition of 1631, was published in 1636. This edition was bound up with the new Service Book of 1637, being intended for immediate use; but both shared a similar fate. The old Scottish Psalter kept its hold till 1650, when it gave place to the new, drawn up originally by Rouse, and revised by a Committee of the Church of Scotland, which revision, we may notice, is the version presently used by that Church.

While on this point, we may add that the Psalter, as printed in 1564, contained only psalms. Bassandyne's edition of 1575 has 5 spiritual songs, that of 1587 and several others have 10, while some of the later editions have 14 hymns or spiritual songs.

Of these 2 are peculiar to the Scottish Psalter, the others are taken from those copies of the English Prayer Book, that contain Sternhold and Hopkin's version of the psalms.

In this connection, we may also remark, that the early Presbyterian Church of Scotland rejected the use of instrumental music in her public services, a course easily entered upon and maintained, as, from the poverty of the country, few organs were in use at the Reformation. The introduction of Episcopacy and an increase of wealth led again to their gradual use—but this, as another unscriptural innovation, was bitterly opposed by the extreme Presbyterians. Dr. Sprott. Baird's Chapter on Liturgies. Livingstone's Scottish Metrical Psalter. Laing's Introduction to his Edition of the "Gude and Godlie Ballates".

The doctrine professed by the early Reformed Church in Scotland was authoritatively contained in the Scottish Confession of Faith of 1560. This document, drawn up by a Commission consisting of five of the leading reforming ministers, in four days, was sanctioned by the Parliament, on 17th August, 1560. This Confession had, however, a predecessor, which may have largely influenced public opinion for some years previously. The Geneva Book, as mentioned above, began to be known in Scotland from about 1556, and it contained a Confession of Faith, which "was received and approved by the Church of Scotland in the beginning of the Reformation". This short and admirable Confession is divided into four parts, which are a paraphrase of the Creed, on the Persons of the Trinity, and on the Church. It is reprinted in the Book of Common Order edited by Dr Sprott [Rankin].

The Scottish Confession of 1560 consists of twenty-five chapters, and continued to be the authorised standard of doctrine from the date of its sanction by the Scottish Parliament till 1647. The greatest battles the Church ever waged, were fought under it as a standard. It has received the highest encomiums from men

f

of such diverse ecclesiastical principles as Tytler, the historian, Principal Lee, and Edward Irving. To these and to the Church Histories of Grub and Cunningham, we refer the reader for an account and appreciation of this venerable document. The last named writer thus characterises it: "A clear and logical summary of Christian doctrine, much more concise than the Westminster Confession, but agreeing with it in every essential respect".

The Ecclesiastical Polity of the Church of Scotland during the period of our review, is so large a subject, and has been the ground of so much contention and difference of opinion, that we almost shrink from entering upon it at all. We can here attempt only a few general observations. Of course, the Polity varied with the varying fortunes of Presbyterianism and Episcopacy; and the legality of the establishment of these has been, and still is, the subject of the hottest contention. There can, however, be little doubt that the chief object of Knox and the other early Reformers was to overturn the Roman System and introduce the knowledge of Evangelical Religion, as laid down and sanctioned by the practice and writings of Calvin. For a time, the outward organisation of the Church was a secondary matter; but this, on the overthrow of Catholicism and the establishment of Protestantism, became of paramount importance. Knox and his coadjutors inclined strongly to what has been called Presbyterianism, but this system of Church government, as we now understand it, was not formally set up for several years after the Reformation, the materials for doing so being still wanting. Of the four Judicatories of the Presbyterian Church, the Kirk Session, the Presbytery, the Provincial Synod and the General Assembly, only the first and the fourth were set up during the first twenty years of the existence of the Reformed Church of Scotland. The fundamental idea of what constitutes the Church, defines and settles ecclesiastical organisation and practice. So important, did the Reformers consider a right comprehension of what the Church is, that they embodied a definition of it, not in their books of Polity, but in their Confession of Faith. It will help us to understand the model of Church government which the Reformers contended for, if we glance at the deliverances in their Confession of 1560 under the heads : Of the Church, Of the Notes by which the true Church is discerned from the false, &c., Of the Authority of the Scriptures, and of General Councils, &c. From these we find a definition of the true Church, viz. : That the Church in the widest sense denotes (1) all the faithful, who under the old dispensation, as well as the new, have been chosen of God to be his peculiar people, and (2) the Church militant composed of various bodies of professing believers, as the Church of Corinth, the Church of Geneva, the Church of Scotland, &c. Again, we are told negatively that the Notes of the true Church do not consist in antiquity, title usurped, lineal descent, place appointed, or numbers approving ; and positively, that they do consist in conformity with the Revealed Word in doctrine, a due administration of the Sacraments, and the enforcement of true morality in conduct. The paramount authority to decide differences on these points was declared to be the Word of God, which was also to determine its own interpretation. Consequently, since this Word cannot be self-contradictory, the determination of any doctor, Church, or Council, if repugnant to the plain Words of God written in the Scriptures, cannot be the meaning of the Divine Will, even though councils, realms and nations may have approved and received the same. Another fundamental idea, springing from the above, and though not formally expressed, shaping the policy of the Scottish Reformers, was the entire ignoring of any priestly caste—any fundamental distinction between the clergy and the laity. They consequently included full association of the people in all their conceptions of the powers and duties of the Church. The minister was indeed regarded as an indispensable official of the Christian community for the performance of all the necessary parts of the Divine Service, and for the instruction and exhortation of the people, but as possessing no authority over the other members of the Church in doctrine, unless supported by the written Word. In the matters of rule and discipline, he merely represented the Church or mass of believers generally. With such notions, they recognised no invariable, necessary rite of clerical institution, no law of perpetual succession, in short, no principle which could constitute the clergy an order or caste. The first Reformers, as the Duke of Argyll observes, rejected ordination. "The miraculous outpouring of the Holy Spirit, which had followed the imposition of Apostles' hands, they believed had ceased, and therefore they judged the form 'not necessary'." These principles and the contemplated way of realising them in practice were embodied in the two Books of Discipline. These Books, however, the Scottish Parliament, from various motives, refused to sanction, so that the actual establishment of the Reformers' ideal ecclesiastical polity by the State remained only a devout imagination. The Church, too, gradually divided into two antagonistic parties, the one preserving some, and reviving others, of ancient Church principles, and receiving increasing support from the Court, developed into regular episcopacy; the other, under the guidance of Andrew Melville and his teaching, not only brooked no interference from the civil power, but under the name of spiritual independence sought to set up an order of things having much in common with the ecclesiasticism instituted by Hildebrand. The contentions between these parties, and their various turns of success form the external history of the Church during the whole period under review.

As we have already indicated, the Reformed Church, during the first twenty years of her existence, had neither Synods nor Presbyteries. The germ of the Synod was in the Council, first of the superintendent and latterly of the bishop, and the germ of the Presbytery in what was called "The Exercise". "It was thought expedient, in every town where there were schools and any resort of learned men, there should be a weekly exercise for the trial and improvement of those who were employed in the service of the Church. The ministers and other learned persons, in rotation, were to interpret some place of Scripture. One was to give his opinion succinctly and soberly, without wandering from his text or introducing exhortations, admonitions, or reproofs. Another was to add what the first seemed to have omitted, or to confirm what he had said by apt illustrations, or gently correct any of his mistakes." The first presbytery erected was that of Edinburgh, in 1581. Others gradually followed, and were agreed to by the King, in 1586, and these erections were, in 1592, ratified by Parliament. This more exact sub-division of the Church into Presbyteries was the work of Melville and his party. In the Assembly of October, 1576, it was enacted that all ministers within eight miles should resort to the place of exercise each day of exercise; and, in the Assembly of 1579, it was proposed that a general order may be taken for erecting Presbyteries in places where public exercises were used, till the policy of the Kirk might be established by law [Rankin].

For the designations, duties, and modes of appointment of the various office-bearers of the early Reformed Scottish Church, we refer to the Books of Discipline. How these were afterwards abolished, modified, or merged into others, is fully set forth in the various Church Histories treating of the period. In addition to writers already named, we have consulted the Histories of Knox, Keith, Row, Calderwood, Spottiswoode, Cook, Tytler, Hill-Burton, Froude, Gardiner, Grub, and Cunningham; and the Lectures of Lee, Stanley; and "Presbytery Examined" by the Duke of Argyll.

II.

To render the accounts of the Lives contained in the following *Collections* more continuous and complete, we have thought it not altogether unnecessary to throw together a few notes, drawn chiefly from sources unknown or inaccessible to Wodrow.

JOHN CRAIG.

John Craig belonged to the family of the Craigs of Craigfintray, now Craigston, in the County of Aberdeen. His father, of whom we have been unable to trace anything further than that he was nearly related to the father of Sir Thomas Craig, the famous lawyer, appears to have been a gentleman of Mid Lothian, or according to other accounts, a citizen of Edinburgh, and was killed at the battle of Flodden. Craig's mother may have been left in rather straitened circumstances by the untimely death of her husband, but managed to send her son to the University of St. Andrews. Besides this, Craig's relatives and friends seem to have done little more for him, as he was left afterwards entirely to his own exertions for means of subsistence. His entrance into Lord Dacre's family, as tutor, shows the beginning of friendly terms of intercommunion between Scotland and her old enemy England; which ties were not, however, yet very strong, as shown by Craig's having soon to leave his situation, as his presence in Lord Dacre's household was incompatible with his Lordship's position as one of the Wardens of the Scottish Marches. Craig, thus thrown out of a home, entered, when about twenty years of age, the clerical order, as the most available means for his support. Reformed tenets were then beginning to gain currency in Scotland; and the ecclesiastical atmosphere being in a very perturbed state, Craig found himself an object of clerical suspicion. For greater security he left home for France, in 1536 or 1537;

and is reported to have acted as tutor to some young Englishman there for a time. However, before the end of 1538, Craig, we find, had reached Rome, where by some means he came under the notice of a most distinguished Englishman, Cardinal Pole, and managed to secure and maintain his patronage and regard. By Pole's influence, he was admitted to a Dominican convent at Bologna, where, through his talents and industry, he rose to a station of dignity and trust. During Craig's residence at Bologna, the famous Council of Trent was sitting there for some time, but the deliberations of the famous Catholic theologians seem to have had little influence on Craig. What was the turning point in his religious history was his finding in the convent's library, a copy of Calvin's Institutes, published nearly twenty years before. A perusal of this severely logical treatise ended with Craig's conversion to Calvinistic Christianity, a belief which he henceforth held with unswerving fidelity and consistency to the end of his life. This change in Craig's religious convictions becoming known, he found himself immured in the dungeons of the Inquisition. Row adds some additional particulars regarding this imprisonment, such as his being confined in a deep and gloomy vault, where the prisoners had to stand twice a day up to their waists in water by the admission of the tide. These and other additions to Craig's imprisonment and escape, may be safely dismissed as mythical accretions, as we know there are no tides in the Mediterranean, and consequently none at Rome. We need not repeat his providential deliverance, escape, and journey to Vienna, and his reception by the Imperial House there—with all the startling attending circumstances—events which read more like a chapter of a thrilling romance than a plain and sober narrative of an actual life. Craig came to England, in the spring of 1560, and next year returned to Scotland, where his arrival was hailed as a providential occurrence by the now dominant Protestant party. Like Douglas, Winram, and Willock, he passed at once into the Reformed Church as an acting minister. His efforts were, however, for sometime checked by his want of readiness in the use of his native language, through long desuetude. For a time he was obliged to preach in Latin to a learned audience in Magdalene Chapel. Recovering fluency in his mother tongue, he was given the ministerial charge of the Abbey church of Holyrood, which served as a church for the Canongate district, as well as for the Palace. The arrival of Queen Mary, on 19th August, 1561, stopped the Protestant Services in that Chapel, and Craig was transferred to St. Giles' Church as colleague to John Knox. The General Assembly of 1562 confirmed this change, but Craig's formal appointment was delayed about a year, apparently for want of funds to implement the arrangement. Craig was now fairly launched on his career of public duty, and we find him taking a part, second only to Knox, in all the prominent questions of the time. His biography, now henceforward, is contained in the history of the time, and for which we refer to Wodrow's text and the historians generally. We may, however, notice a quieter, though perhaps not less useful, work in which Craig took an active part. We refer to his share in moulding the Church Forms for public worship. We have already noticed the introduction of the Geneva Book into Scotland, with its subsequent use and modifications, when it became known generally as John Knox's Liturgy. Dr. Story informs us that "the book owed its final form to labours of Knox, Pont, and Craig. To its Psalter, Pont contributed six, and Craig at least fifteen versions of the Psalms. Of these fifteen the 102nd, 136th, 143rd, and 145th, were, with some slight changes, adopted into the version of Rouse's, which, after the days of the Westminster Assembly, supplanted the National Collection. The versions of the 102nd and 145th Psalms, that stand second in our Psalm-books, are virtually

Craig's; and their sonorous rhythm does credit to his poetical capacity." The learned Professor adds that, "in those days each psalm had its proper tune printed along with it, and with the harmonic parts; that the doxology, in corresponding metre, was appended to each; and that larger portions were sung than is now common; the whole of the 103rd, for example, being appointed for singing at the Communion, and the whole of the 51st on a Fast-day ".

Craig, living in stirring times, when the pulpit, as in its palmy days of Chrysostom, exercised the function of the public press of modern times, and boldly criticised public men and public measures, was often brought into direct collision with the constituted authorities for his fearless utterances. On two occasions especially, when Knox found it expedient to be absent from Edinburgh, he had to bear the brunt of public obloquy and official interference. The former occurred, in 1565, on the occasion of Darnley's arrival, when the Court became a scene of gaiety and dissipation, if not of something worse, which scandalised public opinion in the Metropolis and the country generally. Craig felt bound to lift up his testimony in the pulpit against the abounding extravagance and wild license and revelry, with the effect of drawing upon himself such bitter enmity from the courtiers, that his assassination was attempted. The other emergency arose from his official duties in regard to the proclamation of the Queen's marriage to Bothwell. The wretched Darnley had been murdered, on February 9th, and, on the 7th May following, Bothwell completed his divorce from his wife, and immediately made application to Craig for being proclaimed with Mary. As the wildest reports of all kinds were freely circulating, Craig felt in a difficulty as to what he should do under the circumstances. After consultation with his Session, and being shown the Queen's desire in her own handwriting for her banns of marriage with Bothwell being published, Craig gave way, as it was in fact the only legal course for him to take. He made the first proclamation on Friday, 9th May, which was what was called a *preaching day*, and accompanied it with the announcement that he had objections to the intended marriage, which he was to lay before the Privy Council. Wodrow has recorded Craig's own account at length of his conduct in the matter, which we need not notice here further than to note, that the proclamation of the ill-fated marriage was repeated on Sunday, 11th, and concluded on Wednesday, 14th May, with the former protests. The following day, the marriage ceremony was performed by Adam Bothwell, Bishop of Orkney, who, casting in his lot with the Reformers, had contrived to retain his title, and some at least of his episcopal emoluments.

During the civil war which followed the assassination of the Regent Moray, Craig found himself in a trying position as one of the Ministers of St. Giles'. The Castle was held in the Queen's interest by Kirkaldy, and Knox interfered in the civil contest with more than his usual acerbity of language. On a Sunday forenoon, after the city had been alarmed by a sally from the Castle, Knox broke out in a severe invective against Kirkaldy, his mistress the Queen, and all the doings of that party. In the afternoon, when Craig had entered the pulpit, a paper was handed to him to read, purporting to be written by Kirkaldy, to the effect that Knox had that forenoon openly called him (Kirkaldy) a murderer and throat-cutter, and denying the charge. "Craig must have felt in an awkward dilemma, between the guns of the Castle and the wrath of Knox, but he evaded the difficulty by referring the complainant to the judicatories of the Church, which alone could deal with Knox's ministerial conduct; and the quarrel was patched up for the time." The feud however between the preachers and the Queen's champions in the Castle broke out soon again with renewed fierceness, and in the interest of public tranquillity, and for his own personal safety,

Knox withdrew to St. Andrews, leaving Craig sole Minister of St. Giles' in his absence. Craig, less aggressive in speech, though not less honest than Knox, was able to continue his ministry without fear. His conciliatory disposition and attempts to reconcile the belligerents drew upon him the censures of even his own party, and this led him to resign his charge at Edinburgh, before the return of Knox from St. Andrews. Craig was translated, in 1571, to Montrose, where he continued about two years, living there much in the society of his friend, Erskine of Dun, the Superintendent of Angus, and then his services were transferred to Aberdeen as successor to the aged Herriot, the first reformed minister there. In the accounts of Craig's Life given by Dr. Story, Mr. Law, and Sheriff Mackay, the year 1574 is given as the date of Craig's coming to Aberdeen, but this is a mistake, for in the *Chronicle of Aberdeen*, written by Walter Cullen, younger, who was appointed Reader of Aberdeen, in the year 1570, we find this notice: "The sext day of Aguist, the yeir of God 1573 yeirs, Maister Johne Craig, minister, coyme to Aberdein, quho was appointtit be the gennaral kyrk minister of the said burgth, quhome God moitt continew in the trew prechin of his word to the pepill thairof".—*Miscellany of the Spalding Club*, vol. II. p. 40. Craig continued at Aberdeen, about six years, labouring with incessant activity for the modest stipend, according to Dr. Story, of £16 13s. 4d. *per annum*. He discharged the functions of the ministry, as well as acted as Visitor of the churches of Mar, Buchan, and Banff, besides taking an active part in the ecclesiastical business of the country generally, having been chosen Moderator of the General Assembly for the second time, October, 1576. The most prominent acts of his public life, while in Aberdeen, were his sitting in judgment on the Bishop of Moray, his procuring the deposition of Anderson, the last Catholic, and his induction of Arbuthnot the first Protestant, Principal of the University. In proof of the confusion in which the ecclesiastical government then was, we find from Cullen's *Chronicle*, already cited, that when Cunningham was admitted Bishop of Aberdeen, 1577, Craig was one of the collators. Having received the appointment of being one of the King's Chaplains, Craig returned to Edinburgh, 1579. Cullen in his *Chronicle* thus records the event." The xiiij day of September, the yeir of God 1579 yeris, Maister Johne Craig, sumtyme minister of Aberdeen, departtit, with his wyfe and barnis and haill hoissell, owit of the said burght, and left his floik onprowyditt of ane minister, to be preschour to the Kingis grace, as he allegit."

Craig's authorship of the King's Confession and the circumstances which gave rise to its composition, are so fully recorded by Wodrow, that we need not refer to the subject except to point out an error into which Sheriff Mackay has fallen in his Article on Craig, in the Dictionary of National Biography. He there states that on Craig's return to Edinburgh, in 1579, he took part in the composition . . . of "The National Covenant" of 1580, and adds that "in 1581, to meet a panic of a revival of papacy . . . he wrote" "Ane Shorte and General Confession of the true Christian Fayth and Religion," &c. "This Confession," he goes on to say, "was signed by the King and his household, from which circumstance it received the name of the King's Confession." As a matter of fact, the National Covenant and the "Short and General Confession" were one and the same document, which has received various other designations, and which was signed by James and his household, on 28th January, 1580-1.

Craig's life onwards is fully described in the text. In all the deepening contentions which were now constantly arising between the King and his Presbyterian subjects, Craig, as usual, was ever ready to act as mediator, but often with qualified success, and had his motives and his efforts often misunderstood and blamed by both sides. He, however, amid declining years, held on his way with moderation, and latterly in peace. Various attempts were made to provide him with an assistant, but without success; and he may be said to have died in harness, on the 12th December, 1600, at the age of eighty-eight. Of Craig's personal history we have few or no details. No portrait of him is known to exist. "He was married and had a family of whom we have mention of only one, a very able and gracious boy who lived to be Professor of Divinity at Saumur, and returning thence to Edinburgh died, in 1616. His wife, whose name was Marion Smail, survived him for some years, well known in Edinburgh, says Rowe, as Dame Craig, and fond of telling the story of her husband and the dog with the purse of gold."

Craig has been included with Knox by Tytler in a very unjust charge of being accessory to Darnley's murder, or at least being privy beforehand to the conspirators' designs. In urging this against these Reformers, Tytler has allowed the bigotry of the churchman to overmaster the impartiality of the historian; and his allegations were shown to be groundless in a solid and satisfactory manner by the younger M'Crie. The letters of this correspondence are reprinted in M'Crie's *Sketches of Church History*. We should not have noticed these charges had it not been that they are referred to by both Mr. Law and Sheriff Mackay in their respective notices of Craig, without any mention being made of M'Crie's refutation.

For an ampler account of Craig's life and an estimate of his Confession and Catechisms, see an admirable Lecture (unpublished) entitled "Dr. John Craig," by Dr. Story; Introduction to "A Shorte Summe of the Whole Catechism, by John Craig," by Mr. T. G. Law of the Signet Library, Edinburgh; Sheriff Mackay's notice of Craig in the "Dictionary of National Biography"; and "The Confessions of Faith, &c., of the Church of Scotland of date anterior to the Westminster Confession," by Rev. Edward Irving, M.A.

David Cunningham.

David Cunningham was a son of William Cunningham of Cunningham-head, and was probably in orders before the Reformation. He first appears as Minister of Lanark, in 1562, and had confirmation of a pension by James VI., 1st March, 1567, of "five chalders of victuals, quheit, beir, meill, made with consent of Mr. James Thorntoun, Dene thereof (Lanark), for life, as gif he were providit thereto in the Court of Rome with bulls and executorialls". He was translated to Lesmahago, in 1570, whence two years later he was transferred to Cadder, part of the Sub-deanery of Glasgow. In 1574, he received the additional charge of Monkland and Lenzie, with a stipend of £133 6s. 8d. He was appointed, in 1576, joint-Visitor for Clydesdale, Renfrew, and Lennox, and by the same authority one of the delegates who were entrusted with drawing up the Second Book of Policy. These, we are told, met in Cunningham's house, which was a little to the south and opposite the church on the burn Molendinar, the host being then esteemed "a learned man and of very good account". Though he and another of the delegates seemed hearty in the cause against Episcopacy, yet they were both regarded with suspicion by their colleagues, especially by Andrew Melville. These suspicions were justified by Cunningham and his friend's accepting bishoprics before twelve months had elapsed. During his incumbency of Cadder, Cunningham had acted as chaplain, with a pension of £300, to James, Earl of Morton, then Regent. His appointment to the See of Aberdeen was confirmed by the King, 5th Oct., 1577. In Cullen's *Chronicle*, already mentioned, we read, "On Monenday the XI. day of Nowember, the yeir of God 1577 yers, Maister Dauid Cunyngayme, sone to the lard of Cunyngaymeheid, was consicratt biscoip of Abirden, in the said Kyrk, be Maister Patrik Constance [otherwise Adamson], biscoip of Sanctandrowse, quha maid the sermond, Maister Johne Craig, Minister of Aberden, Maister Andro Strayquhen, Minister of (   ), collatraris, and that in presence of the haill congregatioune of Aberden, with oderis of the cuntre present for the tyme". Along with his bishopric he conjoined the office of one of the ministers of the town, which office, it appears from Cullen, he entered upon a little before his consecration. When the parish of St. Nicholas was sub-divided, 14th Sept., 1596, the Old or West-Kirk, with the "Grene and Crukit quarteris," fell to his share by lot. He was also appointed by the Assembly, Commissioner for Aberdeen and Banff, but, as noticed by Wodrow, was brought into no small trouble by a charge of scandal brought against him. This matter came before several of the ecclesiastical courts. The bishop, however, failed to clear himself to the satisfaction of the judges. The King, then came to his aid by summarily stopping the process and taking the matter into his own hands. Cunningham showed his gratitude by advancing the royal policy so far as he could, and seems to have maintained the King's favour, as he was chosen to baptise Prince Frederick, 30th August, 1594. He died, 30th August, 1600. From the dilapidation of the revenues of the See by Gordon, the last Catholic Bishop, Cunningham's elevation to the bishopric gave him no increase above his stipend as one of the Ministers of St. Nicholas. He married Katharine Wallace, who survived him, but he had no issue. Keith's Catalogue. Scott's Fasti, with the various authorities therein cited. Miscellany of the Spalding Club, vol. II.

PETER BLACKBURN.

Of the early history of Blackburn, Wodrow seems to have been entirely ignorant. We learn from Keith (Catalogue) that he was "born at Glasgow, where some years he had regented, teaching philosophy in the College there, and afterwards was chosen minister of Aberdeen". According to Cullen's *Chronicle:*

"Maister Peter Blacburne, minister, coyme to Aberdeen the XXI. day of Nowember, the yeir of God 1582 yeris, and prechitt the XXII. day Nowember, in the paroche Kyrk tharof, and resceuit and admittet minister to the said towne and congregatione thairof". He was appointed one of the Visitors of the College of Aberdeen by the Assemblies, 1582 and 1593, and admitted by the Assembly, 1586, Visitor of Aberdeen, but was "compellit to desist be divers charges of the King's letters purchased by the Bishop of Aberdeen," in 1587. His appointment as Visitor was renewed by the Assembly, in 1588, and changed for Moray, in 1602. In 1595, he was appointed one of the Commissioners for inquiring into the dilapidation of benefices, and on the ecclesiastical division of the town, in 1596 he had the New or East Kirk assigned to him, with the "Evin and Futtie" quarters. On the death of Cunningham, he was promoted to the vacant See, 2nd Sept., 1600; and after holding the titular office for some time he was regularly consecrated at Brechin in 1611, and was thus the first real Protestant Bishop of Aberdeen. After his appointment to the bishopric, he was almost uniformly a member of Assembly, and was by it, in 1606, nominated Constant Moderator of the Presbytery, which was charged by the Privy Council to receive him as such, under pain of rebellion. He was likewise a member of the Courts of High Commission, in 1610 and 1615, but his chief desire seems to have been to discharge with efficiency and quietness his proper ecclesiastical duties at home. His moderation would appear to have kept him under suspicion by Episcopalians as well as Presbyterians. His episcopate brought no addition to his ministerial stipend as one of the city ministers. He wrote a Treatise against James Gordon, the Jesuit. His death took place, on 14th June, 1616. Keith's Catalogue. Scott's Fasti, with authorities. Miscellany of the Spalding Club, vol. II.

Patrick Forbes.

Wodrow's Collections on the life of this venerable prelate are so ample, and put together generally in so fair a spirit that little remains to be said in addition to Wodrow's text. Forbes was born, in 1564, the eldest son of William Forbes of Corse and Kincardine O'Neil, and Elizabeth Strachan, a daughter of the House of Thornton in Kincardineshire. His father spared no expense on his education, sending him to the famous Grammar School of Stirling, then under the charge of Thomas Buchanan, a nephew of the Latin historian and poet, George Buchanan. From Stirling, he was removed to the University of Glasgow to pursue his studies under the care of his relative, the celebrated Andrew Melville. When Melville was transferred to St. Andrews to fill the Chair of Divinity there, he was accompanied by his young kinsman, Forbes. When Melville had to seek a temporary refuge in England, in 1584, for his opposition to the King's ecclesiastical policy, Forbes, in full accord with his relative and teacher's sentiments, went with him; but, returning after a brief stay in England to St. Andrews, he pursued his theological studies with such ardour and success that he was offered a Divinity Chair. This offer he declined in deference to his father's wishes, who wished him to marry and settle on the family property. In 1589, he married Lucretia, daughter of David Spens of Wormiston in Fifeshire, a family which has still representatives in that county as well as in Shetland. On his marriage, he lived in the neighbourhood of Montrose till his father's death, in 1598, when he took up his residence at Corse. His manner of life and studies, while there, are fully detailed by Wodrow, and is a beautiful and interesting record. His desire to benefit his neighbours led him to engage in evangelistic work in his own parish and neighbourhood. There was much need for these services, as several of the surrounding parishes were destitute of regular ministerial oversight, owing to the persecution which the King then was pursuing against all who refused to acknowledge his spiritual supremacy, and support his Episcopal innovations. Among those who felt the full force of the King's displeasure was Forbes's own brother, John, Minister of Alford, who, for holding the Assembly of Aberdeen, in 1605, had been imprisoned, and finally banished for life. Forbes's public evangelistic services were, however, stopped in deference to a command from the King and Archbishop Gladstanes. Notwithstanding this, his reputation for ministerial usefulness and personal piety continued so high, that he was induced to undertake a regular ministerial charge; and was under very peculiar circumstances (recounted at full length by Wodrow and others), ordained and admitted minister of Keith, in 1612. This charge, he held till his promotion to the See of Aberdeen to which he was regularly consecrated, on 17th May, 1618, with universal satisfaction. That was the year in which the well known *Five Articles of Perth* were introduced, amidst much opposition, into the Scottish Church. Forbes wished the Church had not been troubled with these innovations, but as he esteemed them indifferent, he made no difficulty in carrying out the King's wishes, a course which has laid him open to the censure of extreme Presbyterians. Forbes's efforts to promote the well-being of his diocese, in all possible respects, were unwearied and uninterrupted till his last fatal illness. These efforts were highly beneficial, leaving results of which the whole country are to this day reaping the advantages. In particular, to the Aberdeen Colleges he was a generous benefactor, and may indeed be reckoned their second founder. By his exertions and munificence he gathered around him in the Colleges, as well as in the Diocese, a body of clergy and men of learning, who were ornaments to their Church and country, and many of whom—especially the famous Aberdeen Doctors—showed by their fidelity in the day of trial and suffering, the consistency and stability of their principles. After suffering from paralysis for some time, he died, on the 28th March, 1635, and was buried amidst general sorrow in his Cathedral church. He left three sons and two daughters. John, his second son, succeeded him in the property of Corse, and occupied for a time the Chair of Divinity in King's College with the highest reputation for learning and probity. He was extruded by the Covenanters, and after a sojourn in Holland, died at the family seat of Corse. The family of Corse is now represented by Lord Sempill, who holds the lands of Fintray, Craigievar, and others, and who is descended from William, brother of the Bishop. Bishop Forbes's literary remains comprise: "*An learned" Commentarie vpon the Revelation of St. John*, London, 1613, 4to. *A Treatise on the Validity of the Vocation of the Clergy in the Reformed Churches*, Middleburgh, 1614, 4to. *Defence of the Lawful Calling of the Ministers of the Reformed Church against the Cavillations of the Romanists*, 1614, 4to. *A Letter to a Romish Recusant. Eubulus, or a Dialogue, wherein Catholic Questions to the Protestants are confuted*, Aberdeen, 1627, 4to. Also several public letters. The likeness of the Bishop in this volume has been reproduced from an excellent portrait by an unknown artist (probably Dutch), belonging to the University of Aberdeen. Scott's Fasti. Funerals of Bishop Forbes, Spottiswood Society Edition. Dictionary of National Biography.

Adam Bannantyne.

Bannantyne, or as the name is usually spelled, Bellenden, was second son of Sir John Bellenden of Auchinoule, Lord Justice Clerk, and brother to the famous lawyer, Sir Lewis Bellenden, also Lord Justice Clerk. He entered the University of Edinburgh, and in due time graduated M.A., 1st August, 1590, continuing his residence there, however, for sometime after. He was on "the Exercise," and got a "testimonial," on 12th June, 1593, having been presented to the church and parish of Falkirk by James Bellenden of Brochtoun, with advice and consent of Dame Margaret Levingstone, Lady Auchinoule, his tutrix. He was ordained, 19th July following. He was a member of the General Assembly, in 1602, and was one of the brethren "who met at Linlithgow, 10th January, 1606, in conference with the 'imprisoned members,' previous to their trial for declining the authority of the sovereign in causes spiritual". At a later convention, in the same place, on the following 10th December, he proposed a protestation that it should not be held as a General Assembly. He also attended the Convention at Falkland, in 1609, and was suspended, 16th November, 1614, till his relaxation from the horn. He was released and the sentence taken off, 18th January following, but enjoined, on the 22nd of next month, to wait more diligently on his flock in preparing them for the Communion. He demitted his parochial charge, in July, 1616, and was promoted to the Bishopric of Dunblane, the same year, notwithstanding that he had hitherto been a violent opponent of Episcopacy, and even was one of the forty-two Presbyterian ministers who signed a protest to Parliament (1st July, 1606) against its introduction. No wonder that he was censured and denounced by the Presbyterians for accepting this preferment. It seems he was admitted bishop, 14th April, 1617, having received Episcopal consecration some time before. He received from the University of St. Andrews the degree of D.D., 29th July, that same year. He was nominated a member of the Court of High Commission, was a member of the Assembly of 1618, and of the Parliament, 1621, which ratified the Articles of the Assembly at Perth. As the See of Dunblane was one of the poorest in the kingdom, the

Priory of Monymusk and the Deanery of the Chapel Royal of Stirling were annexed to the Bishopric, which procedure was ratified by Parliament, 4th August, 1621. We find that, while Bishop of Dunblane, he contributed two hundred marks to aid in erecting buildings for the University of Glasgow. As Dean of the Chapel Royal, it devolved on Bannantyne to carry out the King's instructions in regard to proper ritualistic services and clerical vestments, and though anxious to meet his Majesty's wishes, he had but indifferent success. It seems he was represented to the King as wanting in zeal, as well as prudence, in introducing the Episcopal innovations, but having cleared himself by the most abject compliance with Laud's behests, he was readmitted into royal favour. After being passed over in the election of a bishop for Edinburgh, he was transferred to the See of Aberdeen in 1635. In the letters—published by Woodrow—which passed between him and Archbishop Laud, he evinces his inferiority to his revered predecessor in the See of Aberdeen—Bishop Patrick Forbes. Bannantyne, being deposed and excommunicated by the famous Glasgow Assembly of 1638, left Aberdeen, 27th March, 1639, and found an asylum in England. It is said that he afterwards received a pension of £100 from the King, and under the name of another person was instituted to the parochial charge of Portlock, Somersetshire, in 1642, and died there, in 1647, aged about 78. He married, 17th February, 1595, Jean Abercrombie, probably daughter of Henry Abercrombie of Kersie, in the parish of St. Ninians, and had six sons—James, Robert, William, Alexander, David, Minister of Kincardine O'Neil, John, who accompanied his father to England, and three daughters. Scott's Fasti, and Dictionary of National Biography, with the authorities cited in these two works.

JOHN DURIE.

This distinguished minister and Presbyterian confessor was

born, in the year 1537, at Mauchline, in Ayrshire. Of his parents we know nothing except that they were in humble circumstances, but were highly respected. They managed to send their son for a time to the Grammar School of Ayr, where Durie showed himself an apt scholar. It does not appear that he ever enjoyed a university training. Through the influence of his cousin, George, Abbot of Dunfermline, young Durie became a conventual brother in that Abbey, but falling under a suspicion of heresy, he was condemned to be shut up till death. However, the Reformation gaining ground, he managed to escape through the influence of the Earl of Arran, and became Exhorter at Restalrig, from 1563 to 1567, subsequently becoming Minister at Leith or Restalrig and Pennycuick. He was translated to Edinburgh, about 1574, where he at once rendered himself conspicuous in the conflicts between the King and the Church, and consequently was often a sufferer for his outspokenness. He was an ardent supporter of Andrew Melville and the other Presbyterian leaders in their contests against the Prelatic tendencies of the King. For inveighing against the Court in a sermon, 23rd May, 1582, he was called before the Privy Council, on the 30th, and ordered to remove from the city and abstain from his ministry. Popular opinion was, however, so strongly in his favour that he was permitted to return to his charge, and made a triumphant return, described at length by Wodrow, on 14th September following. Continuing his attacks against the Court policy, he was again, in November, banished the town, and confined to Montrose, the Town Council declaring, 21st February, 1583, that "the King will nocht that Mr. John return againe to serve or mak ony residence heir, for causes moving His Majesty". While in Edinburgh, he attended the greater part of the Assemblies of the time, and continued enrolled as in the city in the "Book of Assignations," for 1585. While at Montrose, he was a member of the Assembly, 1586, and, with several others, entered his dissent against the removal of the sentence of excommunication pronounced on Archbishop Adamson. The King, though grateful for his absence from Edinburgh, seems to have cherished no bitter feelings against his too faithful ministerial subject, for, on 7th August, 1590, he granted him a pension of £140, in respect of "the greit chargis and expenses maid by him mony zeirs in avancing the publict effayres of the Kirk, and the greit houshold and famelie of barnis quhairwith he is burdynit". James Melville, his son-in-law, says of him, that, though he had not much learning, he was a man of singular force of character, mighty in word and deed, being "a man zealous and mightie in spreit, who conceived matters well, and could utter them fairly, fully and powerfully, with undaunted spreit, voice and action, though perhaps too credulous and apt to be imposed upon". " He delighted," Dr. Scott says, "in having good men around him; was given to hospitality, helpful to the destitute, compassionate to the distressed, and did not disdain occasionally to share, for relaxation and amusement, in the sports of the field, 'for the gown was no sooner of, and the byble out of hand, when on ged the corslet and fangit (snatched up) was the hagbot, and to the fields'." He died, on the last night of February, 1600, with great calmness. Andrew Melville celebrated his courage in several epitaphs, which are printed, with translations, in Wodrow's text. Scott's Fasti, with authorities. Dictionary of National Biography.

DAVID LINDSAY.

David Lindsay was a son of the laird of Edzell, and graduated at the University of St. Andrews, in 1593. He became master of the Montrose Grammar School, whence he was removed, in 1597, to Dundee, to hold a similar appointment. While holding this office, he seems to have also served the cure of the parish of Guthrie from 1599 till, on the removal of Howie, in 1605, he was inducted Minister of Dundee in his stead. On this new appointment, Lindsay did not resign his schoolmaster's place, but within a year he felt himself obliged to do so. "Mr. David Lindsay, minister, and master of the Grammar School, declared that he wes nocht able to dischairge with ane gude conscience baith the offices; and, therefore, upon hope and expectation that the Council sall tak consideration of his estate, and that he may have ane sufficient moyan quhairupon he may lieve as ane honest man in his service in the ministry, demittit in their hands the office of mastership of the school to the effect they may provide ane sufficient qualifeit person to the place." As "moyan," or means, for the new minister, "there were three chalders of victual assignit to him as a pairt of his stipend, furth of the fruits and rents of the Abbeys of Lindores and Scone," which had been assigned for behoof of the ministry of Dundee. But the Abbacy of Lindores having this year been erected into a barony in favour of Lord Lindores, and the teinds, fruits and rents thereof having also been granted to him, these were found, after much contention, to be irrecoverably lost to the Church. The Town Council of Dundee, on 2nd December, 1613, "taking consideration of the gude, true and faithful service done in this commonwealth be Mr. David Lindesay, ane of their ordinary pastors, thir sixteen years, as weill in the education and information of the youth thereof in letters and gude manners as in the dischairge of his office and calling of the ministry; also, of the grite pains taken be him in the recovery of a pairt of the stipend assignit to him be the lords of the plat, furth of the lordship of Lindores—quhilk hes been awing to him thir diverse years bygane; and having regard to the present burden quhilk he bears in the sustentation of his wyiff, bairns and family—they, therefore, bound themselves to pay him the soum of five hundred merks"; not immediately, because of their present burdens, but "at Whitsunday, 1617, without longer delay; and also ane hundred merks for the profit". Lindsay was, in 1619, promoted to the Bishopric of Brechin, and consecrated at St. Andrews, 23rd November of that year. He did not, however, resign at that time his cure in the burgh, but continued to hold it conjointly with the higher dignity, which gave him the oversight of the churches in Dundee, as they were part of his diocese. At the coronation of Charles I. within Holyrood Abbey, 18th June, 1633, Lindsay had the honour of placing the crown on His Majesty's head. The year following, he was translated to the See of Edinburgh and was installed there, on 29th July. The part Lindsay took in the introduction of the new "Booke of Common Prayer," and the defeat of the attempt by a riot in the High Church of Edinburgh, in 1637, are matters of common history and fully related by Wodrow. Along with five other bishops he was deposed and excommunicated, on December 6th, 1638, by the General Assembly sitting at Glasgow. He retired to England, and died there, in 1641. Lindsay was an able man, and along with Wedderburn, Bishop of Dunblane, and the Bishops Forbes, Patrick, and William, shed lustre on the Scottish Episcopate for talent and learning. He married Katherine, daughter of Gilbert Ramsay of Bamff, who survived him, and had a son, John, who succeeded to his estate of Dunkeny. He published *The Reasons of a Pastor's Resolution, touching the reverend receiving of the Holy Communion.* London, 1619, 12mo. This production led to his promotion to the See of Brechin. *True Narration of the Proceedings in the General Assembly, holden at Perth, 25th August 1618: together with a just defence of the Articles therein concluded against a seditious pamphlet.* London, 1621, 4to. The pamphlet referred to was written by Calderwood, the historian. Maxwell's History of Old Dundee: from this the Extracts from the Council's Records are taken. Scott's Fasti, with authorities.

i

Alexander Arbuthnet.

Alexander Arbuthnet, or Arbuthnot, was born in the year 1538, being a cadet of an ancient family, afterwards ennobled. His father was Andrew Arbuthnet of Futhes (Pitcarles according to others), the fourth son of Sir Robert Arbuthnet of that ilk, in Kincardineshire. The place of his early education is uncertain; some say that he studied at King's College, Aberdeen, others, that he finished his philosophical course at St. Andrews, and taught there some time. He visited France, in 1561, and for the period of five years prosecuted the study of the civil law under the famous Cujas, who was then a professor in the University of Bourges. Having taken the degree of Licentiate of Laws, Arbuthnet returned home with the intention of following the profession of an advocate, but relinquishing the study of law for that of divinity, he took orders and was presented, on 15th July, 1568, with the living of Logie-Buchan, to which was conjoined Forvie, whither he removed his residence. On 3rd July, 1569, Arbuthnet was elected Principal of King's College, Aberdeen, in place of Alexander Anderson, who had been ejected with several of the regents for refusal to adopt the Reformed faith. The new Principal was almost immediately after this presented with the living of Arbuthnot. All these clerical appointments he continued to hold while discharging his academic duties. The advent of Arbuthnet brought prosperity to the University, as, according to Spottiswoode, "by his diligent teaching and dexterous government, he not only revived the study of good letters, but gained many from the superstitions whereunto they were given". The Principal was engaged in most of the ecclesiastical transactions of the time, being employed especially in the guidance of matters of delicacy and difficulty, and he enjoyed the esteem and confidence of the Presbyterian leaders. The course he pursued led to his being regarded with but little satisfaction at Court, so that when, in 1583, he had been chosen Minister of St. Andrews by the Assembly, the King ordered him under pain of horning to continue with his duties at Aberdeen. (The statement of Wodrow and others that he incurred the King's displeasure by his editing Buchanan's History, seems to be an error arising from the identity of Arbuthnet's name with that of the printer of Buchanan's History.) To the Assembly's remonstrance the King replied that he and his Council had good reason for the action they had taken. This severity is said to have hastened Arbuthnet's death. He fell into a decline and died, 10th Oct., 1583. It is said he published at Edinburgh, in 1572, a work entitled *Orationes de Origine et Dignitate Juris*, 4to, of which not a single copy is now known to exist. He employed his leisure in writing poems in English, some of which are extant. Three of the pieces, *On Luve*, *The Praises of Women*, and the *Miseries of a Pure Scholar*, are printed in Pinkerton's *Ancient Scottish Poems*. His other pieces, a religious poem of six pages, beginning *Religion now is rakinit ane fabiel*, said to be very dull, another *Cese Hairt*, and a third of even less value, commencing, *Gif it be true that stories dois rehers*, have never been printed. The Bards of Bon-Accord by Walker. Irving's History of Scotish Poetry. Scott's Fasti. Dictionary of National Biography.

James Lawson.

To Wodrow's Collections on Lawson's Life, there is little to add. His birth, in 1538, his parentage, and his early struggles to obtain education, are fully noticed in the text. When the University of Aberdeen was purged of every taint of Catholicism by the expulsion of Principal Anderson and his Catholic colleagues, Lawson, who had been teaching Hebrew for some time at St. Andrews, was presented with the Sub-principalship under his friend Arbuthnet, and entered upon that office, in

1569, holding at the same time the parochial charge of Old Machar, with a stipend of one hundred pounds Scots, equal to £8 6s. 8d. sterling. These offices he had held three years, when he was selected from all his brethren by Knox, to whom "he owed even his own self besides," as the individual best qualified for succeeding him in the charge of the Church of Edinburgh. His conduct in that important station, and during the most difficult times, showed that the reformer had made a sagacious choice. Lawson was admitted to his new charge by his venerable colleague, on the 9th Nov., 1572. Next year, when the Superintendent demitted his office, Lawson and some others were appointed by the Assembly to apply to the Regent Morton for his sanction and authority to their proceedings, and to grace the sittings of the Assembly with his presence. He was appointed one of six for examining such works as were proposed to be published, and was one of the delegates for drawing up the Second Book of Discipline. Taking the side of Melville and the Presbyterians, he incurred the bitterest enmity of the King and his courtiers. Foreseeing that the Church would lose her spiritual independence, and otherwise suffer greatly from the Black Acts of 1584, Lawson boldly inveighed from the pulpit against such legislation and its promoters. A warrant was issued for his apprehension, on the 26th May, 1584, but receiving timely notice, he and his colleague, Balcanquhal, escaped, and travelling all night reached Berwick, early on the morning of 27th May. These proceedings, and the conduct of some of his flock arising out of them, made a deeper impression on the delicate spirit of Lawson, than the case demanded. Besides this, the air of England disagreed with his constitution. To relieve the depression which these circumstances brought upon Lawson, his friends recommended a visit to the Universities, but without beneficial effect. He was seized by dysentery and died at London, on the 12th of October, 1584, in the 46th year of his age. His character has been described in the most favourable terms by all who have treated of his life. Notices of Lawson are to be found in all the historical works treating of his period. He seems to have left behind him a considerable number of MSS., bearing on the events of his stirring times. These it is to be feared are irrecoverably lost. M'Crie's Life of Melville. Lee's Lectures on Church History. Scott's Fasti.

Robert Howie.

From a list of the Burgesses of Guild (*New Spalding Club Miscellany*, Vol. I., p. 90) it appears that Howie was a son of Thomas Howie, burgess of Aberdeen. He was born in that city, but the year of his birth is uncertain. After completing his course at King's College there, he proceeded, in company with his fellow townsman and probably also class-fellow, John Johnston, to the Continent and spent a number of years in foreign universities. In particular, he studied under two distinguished divines, Caspar Olevian at Herborn, and John James Grynæus at Basle; and, during his residence at the latter of these places, published, in 1591, the work mentioned by Wodrow. Various *Theses* are mentioned by Sir Robert Sibbald as having also been published by Howie, at the same place, 1588-1591. On his return home, in 1591, he was appointed one of the Ministers of Aberdeen, and, on the erection of Marischal College, he was chosen, in 1594, its first Principal, an office which he held along with his ministerial charge till his translation, in 1598, to Dundee. Shortly after his removal to that place (26th September, 1598), the Town Council " remembering that Mr. Robert had diligentlie dischargit himself in the ministrie, and has receivit na remembrance nor reward of the town for his sevin yeris service, saiff onlie his bair stipend, and understanding that he may be profitabill to this burgh in Dundy, quhair he now duellis [probably by recommending students to the new college], theirfor thocht meet and expedient that said Mr. Robert be rememberit in sum reasonabil measure, with ane sylver caiss weyand tuelff unces, quhairin the townes armes sal be ingrauit, quhilk is to be made to him". In his new sphere he had not a time of peace, for his predilections appear to have been militant. He showed himself an ardent reformer in burghal matters, and encouraged *the trades* to oppose the Constable and Provost who had long dominated over the town. By this course, Howie incurred the bitterest enmity of these influential persons, who brought such complaints against him that he was deposed from his office. They represented to the Privy Council that "the flourishing state of Dundee has been fosterit be godlie pastors, quha were nocht onlie preachers of quietness, but by their awn modest behaviour to the magistrates gave example of obedience to the common people"; but that "within this few years bygane, some restless and ambitious persons within the burgh perceiving Mr. Robert Howie to be of a hot and vehement humour, and of a contentious disposition, they travellit with him to assist them, and sa far prevailed that he hes tane the defence of their sedition upon him"; and although "the Lords of Council had already been moved for the peace of the town to charge him not to repair within the space of six miles of the same, he notwithstanding came to Dundee without licence"; and when they afterwards "removit him toward within the city of St. Andrews, he likeways hes again disobeyit, and returned back to Dundee to hald the commons upon their course of disobedience". In answer to this complaint, the Privy Council, on 23rd July, 1605, found "that Mr. Robert Howie hes behavit himself very factiously against the Provost, Bailies, and Council, and that his remaining," in the burgh, "hes been an occasion of disorder and confusion, and an impediment to the reconciling of the inhabitants in that Godlie and Christian love quhilk of auld wes amangst them "; and they therefore declared " him naways to be capable of ony public office, function, or chairge within the town heirefter" [Maxwell's *Old Dundee*]. Clearly Howie was a reformer before his time, with the usual results. Dr. Scott in his Fasti states that after his extrusion from Dundee he held a ministerial charge in the Presbytery of Strathbogie. If that was the case, it could have been but for a short time. On the deposition of Andrew Melville from the Principalship of St. Mary's College, St. Andrews, Howie was, in 1607, appointed to occupy that office, and he appears to have shown in his new sphere the same bold and independent spirit which had hitherto marked his conduct. About the time of his appointment to St. Andrews, he seems to have been in harmony with the Court's Episcopal proclivities, and was one of those who appeared on the side of the bishops in the Conferences at Hampton Court. His zeal, however, for the Episcopal cause afterwards cooled, for he not only favoured those who refused to adopt the English innovations, but was in danger of being ejected as a Nonconformist. Howie seems to have maintained the respect of those opposed to him in ecclesiastical politics, for throughout the confidential correspondence between Melville and his nephew, James, he is always mentioned with respect, and there is not an invidious hint thrown out against him. Dr. M'Crie remarks that though Howie's literary and theological acquirements were respectable, yet he did not possess the genius, the elegant taste, or the skill in the ancient languages by which his predecessor was distinguished. Continuing during the establishment of Episcopacy, he remained at the head of the Theological College of St. Andrews, for some time after the restoration of Presbyterianism. The year of his death is not known. M'Crie's Life of Melville. Maxwell's History of Old Dundee. Scott's Fasti.

WILLIAM FORBES.

In none of his *Collections* does Wodrow appear to less advantage than in the present treating of Bishop Forbes. The subject not being congenial to the writer's own doctrinal and ecclesiastical predilections, he seems to have used little exertion to find out the ascertainable facts relative even to Forbes's outward life. Besides, from his natural disposition and clerical training, Wodrow was incapable of estimating aright, or even comprehending, the principles that actuated Forbes as minister and bishop. Not that Wodrow was consciously unfair; he concludes his notice with an extract of a sermon highly laudatory of Forbes as a scholar and a Christian; but the bishop's recondite learning, drawn chiefly from patristic sources, and his leaning after what he conceived to be primitive truth and order, were matters entirely transcending Wodrow's grasp and appreciation. What was merely an episode in Forbes's life—his short ministerial service in one of the Edinburgh churches, with its unhappy concomitants—is dwelt on by Wodrow, almost to the entire exclusion of any estimate of Forbes's life as a whole; and no account is taken of the learning and saintly and consistent life, for which his subject was so distinguished. However, without stopping to controvert Wodrow's statements or indicate his shortcomings, we propose here, as in the other notices in this Introduction, simply to give a succinct account of Forbes, drawn chiefly from Scott's Fasti, Irving's Lives of Scotish Writers, and a notice of Forbes in the Dictionary of National Biography.

William Forbes was born at Aberdeen, in the year 1585. His father was Thomas Forbes, a highly respectable burgess of the city, of the House of Corsindae, which was founded by the second son of the same Lord Forbes, from whom Forbes of Corse was descended. His mother was Janet, sister of Dr,

James Cargill, an eminent physician of Aberdeen, famous for his scientific—especially botanical, acquirements. He was early sent to the Grammar School of his native city, where he made uncommon progress, and at the age of twelve, entered the lately founded Marischal College. After a regular course there, Forbes graduated at the age of sixteen. Gilbert Gray, the Principal, was so pleased with his learning and modesty, that he procured the young graduate's nomination to the Professorship of Logic. This appointment led him to teach the logic of Aristotle, whom he very strenuously defended against the attacks of Ramus. After four years'. service, he resigned his office with a view of prosecuting theological studies abroad. After landing at Dantzic, he travelled through a great part of Prussia and Poland. He studied at several of the continental Universities, particularly those of Helmstadt and Heidelberg, and during this foreign tour he became acquainted with Scaliger, Grotius, Vossius, and several other distinguished scholars. The young student, by diligently resorting to the public libraries, became familiar with the writings of the fathers and schoolmen, and in the Hebrew language he became so proficient, that he was said to have equalled the skill of any Jew. After spending four years in Germany, he visited the University of Leyden in Holland, where his relative, Dr. Jack, was then a professor. Though anxious to prosecute his travels and studies still farther abroad, in France and Italy, he was compelled by the delicate state of his health to sail for England. He visited Oxford, where his learning was so highly esteemed, that he was offered the Chair of Hebrew in that University; but his countryman, Dr. Craig, the King's physician, advised him to consult his health by returning to his native air. After an absence of five years, he returned to Aberdeen, being then about twenty-five years of age. The Corporation immediately conferred upon him the freedom of the city, and when his health was somewhat

k

restored, he was ordained Minister of Alford, about the year 1614, whence he was translated to Monymusk, 27th October, 1615. From this charge he was transferred by the General Assembly to Aberdeen, and was admitted one of the city ministers, in November, 1616. During the King's visit to St. Andrews, in 1617, Forbes was created D.D. The Perth General Assembly, in 1618, he attended, and was selected to defend one of the Articles then enacted, viz., that one regarding kneeling at the Communion. When Aidie, the Principal of Marischal College was forced to resign his office, in 1620, the Town Council who, along with the Earl Marischal, were patrons of the College, thought "it meit and expedient," that Forbes "sal be earnestlie delt with to accept vpoun him to be Primar (principal) of the said College. With this alwayis conditioun that he continew in his ministrie in teacheing twa sermonis everie weik as he dois presentlie." In this situation Forbes discharged his duties with learning and zeal. He not only read lectures in divinity, but also taught the Hebrew language. His labours were too soon lost to the college, for, in the end of the year 1621, he was induced to accept a pastoral charge in Edinburgh, where, however, he soon discovered that his character and doctrines were held in much less estimation than in his native city. As Dr. Irving observes, Aberdeen was then the stronghold of Episcopacy, and its clergy were among the most learned and respectable of the Episcopalians; but in Edinburgh, the Presbyterians were the dominant party, consequently Forbes found himself in a situation far from agreeable. So circumstanced, he gladly availed himself of an opportunity of returning to Aberdeen and resuming his former charge, which he did, to the great joy of the whole community, in 1626. When King Charles visited Edinburgh to be crowned, in 1633, Forbes was one of them who preached before him, and the King was so captivated with his eloquence and doctrine, that he declared the preacher worthy of having a bishopric created for him. Accordingly, when the See of Edinburgh was erected, Forbes received the nomination to it, and was, in February, 1634, consecrated. In Edinburgh he found himself confronted with difficulties arising from his firm adherence to doctrines and discipline highly distasteful in that part of the country. He was not, however, long permitted to enjoy his new dignity, for he died, on the 12th April, before he had completed the third month of his Episcopate, and when he had only attained the forty-ninth year of his age. He was interred in the Cathedral church of St. Giles; his monument was afterwards destroyed, but a copy of the inscription is contained in Maitland's *History of Edinburgh*. A painting of him—an indifferent piece of art, said to have been executed by Jamesone, is preserved in the hall of Marischal College, Aberdeen—this portrait has been reproduced for the present volume. Forbes was married and left a family. One of his younger sons, Arthur, or according to others, Andrew, became Professor of Humanity at St. Jean d'Angel, near the town of La Rochelle.

Forbes's leaning to Rome in doctrinal, and to episcopacy in ecclesiastical matters, led to his learning and piety being ignored by his Presbyterian opponents. Bishop Burnet has left this record of him : "He was a grave and eminent divine ; my father that . . . knew him well has often told me that he never saw him, but he thought his heart was in heaven, and was never alone with him, but he felt within himself a commentary on those words of the apostle, 'Did not our hearts burn within us while He talked with us, and opened to us the Scriptures?' He preached with a zeal and vehemence that made him forget all the measures of time ; two or three hours was no extraordinary thing for him ; these sermons wasted his strength so fast, and his ascetical course of life was such, and he supplied it so scantily that he dyed within a year after his promotion ; so he only appeared taught by Ferme under the principalship of Rollock. There is no notice of any student having ever attended Fraserburgh College. The arrangement by which the Ministers of Crimond, Rathen, and Tyrie, were to act as regents under Ferme appears from the notices of the lives of the incumbents then holding these livings never to have been carried out. There is no account or trace of any endowments for the College having been provided by Sir Alexander Fraser beyond his making it a condition of appointment that the Ministers of Philorth (Fraserburgh), Tyrie, Crimond, and Rathen, should, besides serving their parochial cures, act as regents in the Fraserburgh College. In short, there is no contemporary notice, direct or indirect, that the College was in actual operation with students in attendance under either Ferme or the other designate regents. There seems, however, to have been considerable progress made in erecting the College buildings; but as there is no account of these ever having been put to any use, and from their having been soon used as a quarry for materials for the construction of other buildings, the probability is that they were never completed. The Rev. A. Gruer Forbes of Fraserburgh, in a letter to the late Dr. Lindsay Alexander, printed in the Doctor's notice of Ferme's Life, prefixed to the Wodrow edition of Ferme's *Logical Analysis*, shows that a building which passed for part of the ancient College was of comparatively recent date, and adds that there never was a completion of the College buildings, or an appointment of professors. The old Statistical Account (Sir J. Sinclair's) of Fraserburgh noticing the building of a new school-house there states that there was built into it "a good carving of Moses and the ten commandments on free stone found in the College of Fraserburgh, and said to have been intended for the altar-piece of its chapel". After mentioning the Deed for founding the College, the writer adds, "but it appears nothing further was done". The Rev. John Cumming,

Minister of Fraserburgh, in his Account of his parish in the New Statistical Account of Scotland, says in regard to the projected College, "Owing to some cause which has not been sufficiently explained, most probably to the want of funds, the matter here stopped, for nothing further was done in it". The recent founding of Marischal College at Aberdeen, the remote situation of Fraserburgh, the want of sufficient endowments, and, doubtless, most of all, the troubles of the time, prevented the realisation of Sir Alexander Fraser's generous and enlightened design.

JOHN JOHNSTON.

This eminent scholar, divine and Latin poet, was born about the year 1568. Though he styles himself *Aberdonensis*, yet that does not necessarily imply that he was a native of Aberdeen; but from the fact that several of his near relatives appear among the burgesses and magistrates of that city, it is probable that he was born there. He was of the family of Johnston of Crimond, a branch of the "clerkly" House of Caskieben. He attended a regular course of study at King's College, under the regency of Robert Merser, Parson of Banchory Devenick, whom he in his last will calls, "my auld kynd maister," and to whom he bequeathes, "in taiken of my thankful dewtie, my quhyit cope w^t the silver fit". In prosecution of his studies, Johnston went abroad for eight years, and attended several of the Continental universities, gaining thereby the friendship of the chief literati in France and Germany, With these, we find, he afterwards maintained a close correspondence. In 1587, he was at the University of Helmstadt, whence he sent a MS. copy of Buchanan's *Sphæra* to Pincier, who published a second edition of that poem, with two Epigrams by Johnston. In 1588, he was in the University of Rostock, whither Lipsius wrote to him in very flattering terms, acknowledging the receipt of a letter and poem from him; and, in 1591, we find he was studying at Geneva. Returning home, after spending some time by the way in England, Johnston, about 1593, became colleague to Andrew Melville, in St. Mary's College, St. Andrew's, as Second Master or Professor of the New Testament. He died at St. Andrews, of a lingering and incurable disorder, on 20th Oct., 1611. By his latter will and testament, dated 29th July, 1611, he bequeaths *inter alia* one thousand merks for the maintenance of a student of divinity in the College of Aberdeen [Marischall College] or St. Andrews, and names as his executors "Robert Johnston, of Crimond, Mr. Robert Merser, minister at Ellon, Mr. John Kynneir, minister at Lewcharis, and Mr. William Erskin, minister at Dyninow". In a letter, which Andrew Melville, while an exile in France, received from his nephew, James, dated 25th Nov., 1611, there occurs this passage regarding Johnston: "Your colleague, John Jonston, closed his life last month. He sent for the members of the University and Presbytery, before whom he made a confession of his faith, and professed his sincere attachment to the doctrine and discipline of our Church, in which he desired to die. He did not conceal his dislike of the lately-erected tyranny, and his detestation of the pride, temerity, fraud, and whole conduct of the bishops. He pronounced a grave and ample eulogium on your instructions, admonitions, and example; craving pardon of God and you, for having offended you in any instance, and for not having borne more meekly with your wholesome and friendly anger. As a memorial he has left you a gilt velvet cap [thus described in the Will, "ane fyne new Duche cap of fyne blak velvet, lynit w^t fyne martrik skinnes"], a gold coin, and one of his best books. His death would have been a most mournful event to the Church, University, and all good men, had it not been that he had for several years laboured under an incurable disease, and that the ruin of the Church has swallowed up all lesser sorrows, and exhausted our tears." Dr. M'Crie thus characterises Johnston's literary efforts: "John Jonston confined himself chiefly to the writing of epitaphs and short pieces, which he has executed with much neatness and elegant simplicity, although he falls short, even in this species of composition, of his kinsman, Arthur Jonston, in terseness and in classic point". M'Crie's Life of Melville. Miscellany of the Maitland Club, quoted in Records of Marischal College and University, vol. I. Anderson's Scottish Nation.

ROBERT WODROW.

We feel it due to the memory of the honest and industrious Collector of the Biographical Collections—selections from which form the text of this volume—that some notice, however brief, should be taken of his life and labours. Robert Wodrow, second son of James Wodrow, Professor of Divinity in the University of Glasgow, was born in that city, in the year 1679. His mother's name was Margaret Hair, daughter of William Hair, a small landed proprietor in the parish of Kilbarchan. Report says that she was a woman of considerable strength of mind, great discretion and eminent piety. The year of young Wodrow's birth was a most eventful one in the annals of the Covenanting Presbyterians, as the violence of persecution then raged with more than usual fierceness, and the elder Wodrow nearly fell a victim to its violence. Shortly after the birth of his son, he had to escape from the house in disguise, as soldiers closely beset the premises to effect his capture, and to make sure of their victim, thrust their swords into the very bed on which his wife was lying, who, assured of her husband's recent escape, pleasantly desired them to desist, "for the bird," said she, "is now flown". Wodrow was admitted into the University of Glasgow, in 1691, and went through the usual academical course. He then entered upon the study of Theology under his father's tuition, discharging at the same time the duties of Librarian to the University, an office which may in no small degree have contributed to foster in him those industrious habits of literary composition for which he was afterwards so remarkable. During his theological course, he paid much attention to Natural History, and also developed a talent for historical and bibliographical inquiries. These qualities, and his general acquirements, recommended him to Sir John Maxwell, of Nether Pollock, one of the Senators of the College of Justice. While resident in Sir John Maxwell's family, Wodrow was licensed as a preacher of the Gospel, in March, 1703, by the Presbytery of Paisley. In the summer following, Eastwood, where Lord Pollock resided, became vacant by the death of the Minister, Matthew Crawford, the author of a History of the Church of Scotland, as yet unpublished, and occasionally quoted by Wodrow. Wodrow was chosen for the vacant charge by the heritors and elders, with consent of the congregation, and was ordained, on 28th October, 1703. Here he spent his whole future life in the discharge of his pastoral duties and prosecution of his favourite studies of Church history and antiquities. In 1712, he had an encouraging invitation from Glasgow, and in 1717, and again in 1726, he was solicited by the people of Stirling to become their Minister, invitations which he declined, preferring to remain at Eastwood. Wodrow was one of the most popular preachers of his time, great crowds resorting to Eastwood, especially on sacramental occasions, to hear him. He enjoyed the entire confidence of his ministerial brethren, and was often consulted and employed by them in matters of delicacy and importance. His interest in all public affairs was keen and unremitting, and he was most regular in his attendance on all Church Courts. As Dr. Cunningham says: " Every May he mounted his horse and hied him to Edinburgh, whether he was commissioned by his

Presbytery or not; and in his letters to his wife, written with all the more care that they were to be seen by the aged Lord Pollock, one of the confessors of the Church in persecuting times, and now no longer able to sit in her courts, he gives an account of what was said and done, which, though utterly destitute of graphic power, and without even vivacity, has yet the freshness and the trueness to life which arise from his describing what he himself had heard and seen". His chief work, *The History of the Church of Scotland from the Restoration to the Revolution*, was published in 1721-22, in two volumes, folio. On this important and valuable production he had been employed for many years. On its appearance, it was well received, being approved of, and recommended by, the General Assembly. It was dedicated to George I., and copies of it were, through the author's friend and correspondent, Dr. Fraser, the generous benefactor of King's College, Aberdeen, presented to the King and various members of the royal family. By his Majesty's orders the industrious writer was rewarded by a grant of one hundred guineas. This work, though utterly destitute of the graces of composition and of methodical arrangement, is very valuable from its containing a collection of facts, fortified by documents, the veracity of which has never been effectually controverted. As might have been expected, it was violently attacked by extreme Cameronians and extreme Episcopalians, but few of its statements have been shown to be erroneous. The chief attack made on it was by Alexander Bruce, advocate, first in an anonymous tract entitled *The Scottish Behemoth Dissected, in a letter to Mr. Robert Wodrow*, &c., Edinburgh, 1722; and next, in his preface to a *Life of Archbishop Sharp*, 1723. Fox, however, in his *History of the Early Part of the Reign of James II.* passes a high eulogium on Wodrow's fidelity and impartiality. Bishop Burnet also, in his *History of His Own Times*, confirms Wodrow's statements in every essential particular. The *History* has been republished at Glasgow, in 1830, in 4 volumes, 8vo, with a Memoir of the Author by Dr. Robert Burns.

Wodrow, continuing his historical researches, completed ten small folio volumes, with four quarto volumes of appendices, of biographical memoirs of the more eminent ministers and others of the Church of Scotland. These MSS. with several duplicates are preserved in the library of the University of Glasgow, and a complete list of them is subjoined to the present volume as an Appendix. In 1834-45, selections from these were made and printed for the members of the Maitland Club in two volumes quarto. By the kindness of the senate of Glasgow University, the present volume of Selections from the same collection has been made for the members of the New Spalding Club. Besides these Biographical Collections, Wodrow left behind him six small closely-written volumes, entitled *Analecta*, being a sort of note-book, in which are entered much curious gossip concerning literary and ecclesiastical matters, as well as the more ordinary events of the period. This interesting record of twenty-seven years, from 1705 to 1732, is preserved in manuscript in the Advocates' Library, Edinburgh, and through the munificence of the Earl of Glasgow was printed in 1842 and 1843, in four quarto volumes, and presented to the Maitland Club members. The Advocates' Library also contains twenty-four manuscript volumes of Wodrow's correspondence, from which a selection, in three volumes, 8vo, has been printed for the Wodrow Society. Others of his letters have been printed by Maidment; and his Life of Bruce has been prefixed to the edition of that divine's sermons edited by Cunningham for the Wodrow Society. Besides these, a portion of Wodrow's manuscripts, relating chiefly to ecclesiastical history, was, in May, 1742, purchased by order of the General Assembly, and now remains the property of the Church. Principal Cunningham, in closing his notice of Wodrow, says that: "It is impossible to read his correspondence without pronouncing him to be a good and worthy man. He had not the vigour of mind to shake off the narrow notions which still lingered in the Church and to rise superior to his age; he was imbued with the feelings, the prejudices and superstitions of his day; he believed in witches, reprobated prelacy, hankered after the Solemn League and Covenant; but these things did not seriously sully his piety or virtue."

Wodrow died of a gradual decline, arising from a swelling on his breast, on 21st March, 1734, in the fifty-fifth year of his age, and was buried in the churchyard of Eastwood.

He was married, in the end of 1708, to Margaret, the widow of Rev. Ebenezer Veitch, Minister of Ayr. She was a daughter of Patrick Warner, Minister of Irvine, and grand-daughter of William Guthrie, Minister of Fenwick, author of the *Trial of a Saving Interest in Christ*. Of this marriage there were born sixteen children, of whom four sons and five daughters, with their mother, survived Wodrow. Anderson's Scottish Nation. Dr. Burns' Memoir of Wodrow, prefixed to his edition of The History of the Sufferings. Notice of Wodrow's Life, by the younger M'Crie, in the first vol. of Wodrow's correspondence, printed for the Wodrow Society. Cunningham's Church History.

R. L.

BIOGRAPHICAL COLLECTIONS.

COLLECTIONS AS TO THE LIFE OF Mr. JOHN CRAIG, MINISTER AT EDINBURGH, ABERDEEN, AND TO THE KING'S FAMILY.

This learned and pious person ought not want a room in this work I am now engaged. His recovery from Popery, his escaping the hands of crowel Papists, and strange preservation deserve to be recorded, and more knowen than it is. His seasonable arrival, in the morning of the Reformation in Scotland, wher ther was need of such instruments to cary it on, ought to be remembered. He was extremely usefull for 24 years ther after, and if in his old, aged, declining years, by the weight of a Court wher he was minister, he unwarrily made some complyances not agreable to his former zeal, he is in this rather to be pityed than severely censured, considering his temptations, age, and great usefulnes. Therfor I shall essay to give as distinct account of the most remarkable parts of his life as I can, and besides the hints published already by Bishop Spotswood, the Records of our Assemblys, Mr. Calderwood's Large History, and Mr. Row's MS. History[1] afford severall passages of his life that are very little knowen.

Mr. John Craig was born of honest and substantiall parents, in the year 1512,[2] under the very hight of Popish darknes in Scotland, about which time Mr. Knox, and many other of our great lights, wer sent into the worlde, like so many Moses's, born under Israel's bondage in spirituell Egypt, and wonderfully preserved, as Mr. Craig was, for instruments of the Churche's bringing out from Popery. His father was killed with King James the 4th at the unhappy Floudon Field, when he was but young, which reduced him to some straits. His inclination to letters was very great, and so he found means to get to the University of Saint Andrews, and studied ther his philosophy, and received his degree of Master of Arts with applause. When got through his

[1] Note 1.   [2] Note 2.

University learning, interest was made with my Lord Dacres, and he went to England and waited as præceptor to his sons for two years. Wars arising betwixt Scotland and England, Mr. Craig left my Lord Dacres' family and returned to Scotland, wher he entered into the Dominican Order. He was not long with them till he began to be suspected of heresy, that is, of favouring the Reformation. Whither he had got any knowledge of the truth while in England, wher at this time it was breaking out, I know not. If he was at London with his pupils, this is very probable, or at the Universitys in England; but my Lord Dacres' family was, I think, long Popish, and it was a good while before the Reformation gained much ground in the northern country. A man of his knowledge and learning, when he grew up, could not but discover some of the errors of Popery. But at this time, in Scotland, if a man plyed his books and dipped any way into learning, if he did not run to the excesses of the bigotted clergy, and was any way sober in his life, a charge of heresy was very soon laid against him. However it was, on suspicion of heresy he was cast in prison, but he soon purged himself and got out.

Being cleared of that imputation, and heartily weary of his native country, about the year 1536 he went to England, hoping by my Lord Dacres' interest to have got into a Fellowship in Cambridge. But that some way misgave, and Mr. Craig went over with some pupils first to France, and then to Italy. At Rome he fell into acquaintance with Cardinall Pool [Pole], and, by his learning and good behaviour, got into his favour so far that he recommended him as a youth of great expectations to the Dominicans at Bononia [Bologna].

The monks there received him, and at first he was imployed to instruct the novices of the cloyster. His learning and diligence was soon perceived, and the Dominicans finding him very dexterous in every bussines he plyed himself to, Mr. Craig was generally imployed in all their affairs throughout Italy, and sent in commission to the island of Chios, with power to redres all disorders among the Dominicans there.

Mr. Craig discharged this important trust so much to the satisfaction of the monks, that upon his return he was admitted Rector of their school at Bononia. This gave him acces to their librarys, wher he improved himself very much in all branches of valuable learning, which prepared him for after great services, and a present receiving the truth, when Providence bro't the light of it to him; which, as he used to narrat it himself, was thus: One day in the library of the Inquisition he hapned to find Calvin's Institutions. The stile of it charmed him, and the matter of it much more; [as] he read it, the more he liked the plain, clear spirituall doctrine in it, and could no longer withstand the force of truth there. One day conferring with a reverend old man in the monastery, he began to hint at some of the doctrines that book had opened up to him. The old monk confirmed him in his opinions, and told him he had embraced them inwardly for a long time, but cautioned him, by no means, to open his mind as to those matters, because the times wer perrilous. Had he followed the old father's advice, he had been free of much trouble and danger. But now he had received the truth in the love of it, and the words of our Lord wer much in his mind, *He that confesseth Me before men, him will I confess before My Father; and him that denyeth Me before men, will I deny before My Father and His angels;* and so, in his conversation, Mr. Craig discovered his opinions a little to freely for Italy. He was soon suspected of heresy, wherupon he was taken up by some of the bigotts of the monastery, and after some tryall, wherin he openly mentained the truth, he was sent to Rome to the Holy, or rather hellish, Inquisition, as I take it, in the year 1558. After he was examined ther, he was cast into closs prison, wher he indured great miserys for 9 months, at the end of which he was bro't before the judge of the Inquisition, wher in judgment he gave an open confession of his faith, upon which he was instantly condemned to be burnt as a heretick the next day, August 19.

But the Lord had more work for him, and knew how to deliver him in this great choak [strait]. That same night Pope Paul the 4th departed this life. The people of Rome, who did not love him, upon the accounts of his death, gathered tumultuously together, and came to the place wher the late Pope's statue was curiously erected in marble, pulled it down, and after they had ludicrously dragged it up and down the streets of the city for some time, at last cast it into the river Tyber. One of the first things they did was to go to the prisons, the dores of which they broke open, and set all the prisoners free. Two remarkable things hapened to Mr. Craig when set at liberty. He found it not safe to continou there, and so went to the suburbs. As he was passing these, he mett with a company of robbers, called *banditti* by the

Italians, who in this time of confusion attacked every body they mett with. When fallen into their hands, one of their number knew him, and, taking him aside, asked him if ever he had been at Bononia. Mr. Craig said he had. "Do you remember," then said the other, "that one day, when walking in the field, ther came to you a poor maimed soldier, asking some relief?" Mr. Craig answered he did not well remember. "Well," said the other, "but I do, and I am the man to whom yo showed kindnes at that time. Be not affrayed of us; ye shall incurr no danger," and so conveying him throu the suburbs, and showing him which was the safest way to take, he gave him as much money as would carry him to Bononia, for he intended to go thither, hoping to receive some kindnes from his acquaintances there. But, finding them look very strange, and fearing to be taken up again, he slipped secretly out of town, and went to Millan. Thus Bishop Spotswood relates his singular preservation.

Mr. Row, in his MS. History, relates the same thing, but with different circumstances; and since Mr. Row might have it from Mr. Craig himself, being ordeaned a little after his death, and ther being a great intimacy betwixt his father and Mr. Craig, he might have circumstances Bishop Spotswood has ommitted; and there is no inconsistency between the two accounts save in circumstantialls. So the curious reader will not grudge to have Mr. Row's account, both of this and the yet stranger providence that followes. His words are: "Mr. Craig, being a pedagogue and instructor to the children of a great man in Italy, upon a certain day he sees a man naked and wounded, who had hardly escaped the hands of his enimies [or] robbers with his life, him Mr. Craig refreshed with meat and drink, and provided with cloaths and money. Somtime after, Mr. Craig is taken up for an heretick (so they called all Protestants), and incarcerat in Rome with others. At lenth they wer condemned to be burnt next day. That night they spent in prayer and praises; when they are thus exercised, one cometh and opened the prison dores, telling them they wer set free. The prisoners admired and took it at first for some snare. But the matter was this: the Pope dyed that night, and it's the custom of Rome that, at the death of that High Priest, all under restraint are inlarged. If for heresy, they are once liberat but quickly recalled or bro't back by force. Mr. Craig and his fellows being liberat, got a little out of the town to a house. Commission was soon given to recall the hereticks, and an armed company came to the place wher they wer refreshing themselves. The souldiers asked what they wer, and wer answered with silence, wherupon one cryed, 'Kill the hereticks'. The captain, eying Mr. Craig, restrained his men, took him aside, and asked him if ever he saw a naked wounded man at such a time and place. Mr. Craig said 'Yea'. 'Well,' answered the other, 'I am the man; and to your kindnes and humanity to me then, I think I am called to requite you now. I will hazard my life for you, you shall have my best horse, I will convey you part of the way, and take here some money for your charges. If I be strictly questioned about it, I know I could die for it, but I will run the hazard; your supply was so timeous and full. As for your followers and brethren, I must take them back to Rome, but for your sake, I will shew them all the courtesy I can.' Thus, by a rare providence, he escaped this imminent danger."

But to go on to the other thing Mr. Craig met with after his escape, which is yet more wonderfull. Bishop Spotswood adds, wher I left him: "By the way another accident befell him, which I should scarce relate, so incredible it seemeth, if Mr. Craig himself had not often reported it to many of good place, a singular testimony of God's care of him, and this it was: when he had travailed some days, declining the high wayes out of fear, he came to a forrest, a wild and desart place, and being sore wearied, lay down among some bushes, on the side of a little brook, to refresh himself. Lying there pensive and full of thoughts (for neither knew he in what part he was, nor had he any means to bear him out of the way), a dog cometh fauning, with a purse in his tooth, and layes it down before him. He, stricken with fear, riseth up, and construing the same to proceed from God's favourable providence towards him, followed his way till he came to a little village, wher he met with some that wer travailing to Vienna in Austria, and, changing his intended course, went in their company thither."

Mr. Rowe's account of this extraordinary passage is followes: "Mr. Craig's money being spent, and he in a forraigne nation, and not daring to dissemble his religion, so as to travell as a pilgrim, or to beg at Popish cloysters, he lyeth down at a wood side, in the heat of the day, to rest him, and to seek God in this strait. Behold, a dog comes out of the wood with a purse in his mouth. He, apprehending that some robbers lurking in the wood had sent out the dog to him with a purse, that pursuing him they might make it a ground of challenge, did once and again drive away the dog with stones, not accepting the purse, which the doge came in a fauning way and still offered him. At last the dog, still returning to him with the purse in his tooth, Mr. Craig took it from him, and found a good summ of gold in it, and that the Lord, Who by a raven provided Elijah in a strait, had sent that dog to him with furniture for his journey. The dog travelled some dayes with him, and then left him. The money furnished him spending till he came to London."

When Mr. Craig came to Vienna, he professed himself of the Dominican Order, and began soon to be notticed for his learning and abilitys. He was imployed to preach before the Emperour Maximilian the 2d, who, liking the man and his manner of teaching, designed to retean him for one of his preachers. By this time he came to be knowen at Vienna by some Italians come from Rome, and Pope Pius the 2d was acquainted of his being there, who wrote to the Emperour acquainting him he was condemned by the Inquisition for heresy, and required him to be sent back. The Emperour was not willing to deliver him again to the Pope, and yet cared not openly to fall out with the Pope upon his accession to the See; and, therfor, gave secret nottice to Mr. Craig to remove, granting him letters of safe conduct. With these he came down through Germany, and arived safe in England in the end of the year 1560, wher, being informed of the Reformation now set up in his native country, he came down to Scotland and offered his service to the Church. We need not doubt but such a man was made welcome, and the Lord's singular providence carefully observed, in sending one from Rome to build His house in Scotland.

At first, by reason of his long disuse of the Scots language, Mr. Craig could not be so usefull in preaching, having been about 24 years abroad. Now and then he preached at the beginning to the learned in Latine, at Magdalen's Chappell in Edinburgh.[1] But in a litle time he overcame his disuetude in his native language, and Bishop Spotswood, from whom I have taken most of this account, sayes, in the year 1561 he was appointed Minister of Holyrood House, and next year he was taken to Edinburgh to serve as collegue to Mr. Knox. I suppose when

[1] Note 3.

the Queen came home, 1561, Mr. Craig would not be acceptable to her, and she had her preists with her and her Frenchmen, and so she rid herself of one who knew the abominations of Popery too well: and to give the Bishop's account of him, wholly in this place: "When Mr. Craig had been collegue to Mr. Knox nine years, by ordinance of the Assembly he was translated to Monross [Montrose] (the reason for which I will give in its place). There he continoued two years, and upon the death of Adam Herriott he was removed, having the inspection of the churches of Marr and Buchan committed to his care.[1] In the year 1579 he was called to be the King's minister, and continoued in that charge till, born down with the weight of years, he was forced to retire himself, after which time, forbearing all public exercises, he lived privatly at home, comforting himself with the remembrance of the mercys of God that he had tasted in his life past." Those last 40 years of his life, which the Bishop passeth over in a few lines, and when he was very usefull, and no favourer of Prelacy, I come now to give some larger accounts of.

What I give is mostly from Mr. Calderwood's History, wher I find him Minister of Edinburgh, February, 1564. The state of things at this time is to be found in our historians. In January, the Earle of Lennox was restored to his estate and honours, in a publick Convention, and the designe of the Queen's marriage with his son, the Lord Darnley, was now beginning. In February, the Queen and Council at Hollyrood House wer very joviall, and mutuall banquets betwixt the Queen and lords, and much folly and profanity abounded. The ministers wer mocked, and that which should have supported them was imployed in the kitchin, and banquets, revells, dancing, and masks. The ministers of Edinburgh were not, indeed, personally straitened for their stipends as their bretheren elswher were, and used all the freedom in reproving the prevailing luxury and vice. We have heard of Mr. Knoxe's freedom on his life, and Mr. Craig, with no less zeal, discharged his duty at this time. Inveying against the corruptions of the time, he said, as Mr. Knox in his History tells us: "Hypocrites wer sometimes knowen by their disguised habit, and we had men to be monks and woomen to be nunnes, but now all things are so changed that we cannot discour the earle from the abbot, nor the nunne from the noblewoman. But," added he, "seing ye

[1] Note 4.

are not ashamed of that unjust profession, would God ye had therwith [the] coul, the vail, and the rest belonging therto, that ye might appear in your own collours." This freedom against their masks and revellings provocked Lethington so that he gave himself to the devil, "if after that day he should regard what came of the ministers, let them bark and blou as loud as they list". The courtiers loudly compleaned they wer uncharitably dealt with, and said vice might be reproved in generall, and particular persons not so plainly described, as all saw whom the preacher meant. To this the answer was plain. Let men be ashamed to offend publickly, and then preachers should abstean from particular descriptions. Indeed the ministers, especially Mr. Craig and Knox, had a hard pull and a double battell at this juncture. Their friends had left them, and they had idolatry and other abominations mentained by the Queen to graple with, and on the other hand the ingratitude and frowns of some, who once would have been reputed the cheif pillars of the Kirk.

This same year Mr. Craig distinguished himself in the knowen Conference betwixt ministers sent from the Assembly and Lethingtoun, Mortoun, and other courtiers, of which the reader hath a large account in Mr. Knoxe's life. In short, Mr. Craig very much silenced the Secretary and such as resoned on that side, by laying before them a conclusion set forth and agreed to 1553, when he was at Bononia, and showed with how much greater force that instance struck upon us, as being under a Monarchy and not a Commonwealth. He gave his opinion with the outmost plaines "that princes are not only bound to keep lawes and contracts with their subjects, but if they fail they may lawfully and justly be deposed, since the band betwixt prince and people is reciprocall".

After the Queen's marriage next year with Henry, Lord Darnly, and Mr. Knoxe's trouble for his sermon in Saint Geils' Church before him, Bishop Spotswood says, "when Mr. Knoxe was silenced, his collegue (Mr. Craig), because of Mr. Knox prohibition, refused to do any service in Edinburgh, which put the people in a stirr; yet, upon better advice, he was moved to continue in his charge". I imagine this story is not favourably told. It's probable enough Mr. Craig would complean of the harsh treatment of his collegue, and threaten to leave of preaching if he might not have liberty in reproving vice; but such a man as Mr. Craig would not in a pett throw up his ministry, and leave Edinburgh desolate. Besides, ther was no need of extremitys. Mr. Knox lay aside but a few Sabbaths, tho' the Bishop groundlessly enlargeth them to months.

In the Assembly which conveened June, 1566, the registers bear that " Mr. John Craig, Minister of Edinburgh, desired that John Cairns, who had read prayers and exhorted four years and more in Edinburgh, and had well profited, so that he was near able to be admitted to the ministry, might be joyned with him in the Kirk of Edinburgh as collegue, in regard he was alone. The Assembly ordeaned the Kirk of Edinburgh, with the assistance of the Superintendant of Lothian, to consider whither he wer fitt and sufficient for that place or some other." I do not here enter upon the offices of reader and exhorter, which for some years after the Reformation, like the superintendants, were allowed in the Church till it was better furnished with ministers, and then all the three wer laid aside. Most part of the readers that caryed [behaved] well, and profited in knowledge, wer advanced to the office of exhorters; and not a few of those upon tryall, and after they had come to a good understanding in the Scriptures—especially when knowen to be grave and pious—wer admitted into the ministry. This paragraph looks as if Mr. Knox wer not at present in Edinburgh; and I do not find him mentioned in the Acts of this Assembly, so that I conclude he was not present in it. Whither he was sick, or at some other work at distance, I cannot say; only it's plain enough he returned to his work in a few weeks after his discharge upon the account of the sermon before the King. Whither he and Mr. Craig had two separat kirks by this time, and Mr. Knox a collegue, and Mr. Craig none, and in a few years after this there seem to have been four ministers in Edinburgh, I do not know. This Cairns—as far as I see—was never admitted Minister of Edinburgh. We shall find him a reader at the Queen's marriage with Bothwel, which brings me to Mr. Craig's share in the marriage of the Queen with the Earle of Bothwell next year. Our printed historians give pretty large accounts of the King's murder, Bothwell's cleansing by a sort of assize, and his mariage with the Queen—all which the ingenious and diligent Mr. James Anderson[1] will, I hope, very soon set in a fairer light than yet we have seen them. Mr. Craig's

---

[1] Note 5.

proceedings as to this matter are what only now lye before me. Mr. Calderwood gives the following account of this: "The Reader of the Kirk, John Cairnss, obstinately refused to proclaim the bands of marriage between the Queen and Earle of Bothwell. The elders and deacons, not daring to make any obstacle, lay the burden upon the preacher, Mr. Craig. He granted to proclaim the bands, but withall professed he would declare that he knew some lawfull impediment to stay the marriage. Seing that was the end whereunto proclamations of bands were appointed, the Queen and Bothwell could by no means drive him from his alledgeance, neither yet would they referr the matter to disput or tryall." Accordingly, May 12, 1567, they wer married by Adam, Bishop [of] Orkney, when nobody else would do it, for which he was afterwards conjured by the Generall Assembly. At the marriage, the said Bishop made a declaration of the Earle's repentance for his former offensive life, and that he had left Popery, joyned hemself to the Kirk, and embraced the Reformation; but [it] was all juggle, for it was believed they wer married that morning at mass by a Popish priest.

But the best view we can have of Mr. Craige's part in this matter will be from himself. When the Assembly met in December that year, Mr. Craige was required to give in, in write, his proceedings in proclaiming the banns betwixt the Queen and the Earle of Bothwell. This he did, and I transcribe them here from the Assemblie's registers: "To the end that all that fear God may understand my proceedings in this matter, I shall shortly declare what I did, and what moved me to defend the same, leaving the final judgment of all to the Kirk. First, being moved by Mr. Thomas Hepburn, in the Queen's name, to proclaim her with my Lord Bothwell, I plainly refused, because he had not her handwrite, and also the constant bruit that my Lord Bothwell had both ravished her and keeped her in captivity. Upon Wensday next the Lord Justice Clerk brought me a writing, subscribed with her hand, bearing, in effect, that she was neither ravished nor deteaned in captivity, and therefor charged me to proclaim. My answer was, I durst proclaim no bannes, especially such, without consent and command of the Kirk. Upon Thursday next the Kirk, after long reasoning with the Justice Clerk and amongst the brethren, concluded that the Queen's mind must be published to her subjects the next three preaching dayes. But because the Generall Assembly had enhibited all such mariages, we protested that we would neither solemnize nor yet approve that marriage, but only would declare the Prince's will, leaving all doubts and dangers to the counsellors, approvers, and contrivers of that marriage. And so, upon Friday next, I declared the whole mind and progres of the Kirk: desiring every man, before God, to discharge his conscience before the Secret Council; and, to give boldines to others, I desired of the Lords then present time and place to speak any judgment before the parties, protesting, if I wer not heard and satisfyed, I would either desist from proclaiming or also declare my mind publickly before the Kirk. Therefor, being admitted, after noon, before my Lord in the Council, I laid to his charge the law of adultery; the ordinance of the Kirk; the law of ravishing; the suspicion of collusion between him and his wife; the suddain divorcement and proclaiming within the space of four days; and, last, the suspicion of [the] King's death, which his marriage would confirm. But he answered nothing to my satisfaction, wherefor, after many exhortations, I protested that I could not but declare my mind publickly to the Kirk. Therefor, on Sunday I declared what they had done, and how they would proceed whether we would or not. I took heaven and earth to witnes that I abhorred and detested that marriage, because it was odious and slanderous to the wordle; and, seing the best part of the Realme did approve it—either by flattery or their silence—I desired the faithfull to pray earnestly that God would turn to the comfort of this Realme that thing then intended against reason and good conscience. And, because I heard some persons grudge against me, I used this reasons for my defences: first, I had broken no law by proclaiming this persons at their request; 2ly, if the marriage was slanderous, I did well in forwarning all men of it in time; 3ly, as of all duty I had declared to them the Prince's will, so did I faithfully teach them by word and example what God craved of them. But upon Tuesday next I was called before the Council, and accused that I had passed the bounds of my commission, calling the Prince's marriage odious and slanderous before the wordle. I answered, the bounds of my commission—which was the Word of God, good lawss, and naturall reason—wer able to prove whatsoever I spoke; yea, that their own conscience could not but bear witness that such marriage would be odious and slanderous to all that should hear of it, if all the circumstances of it wer rightly considered. But when I was coming to probation my Lord (Bothwell) put me to silence, and sent me away; and so upon Wensday, I first repeted and ratifyed all things before spoken, and after exorted the bretheren not to accuse me if that marriage proceeded, but rather themselves, who would not, for fear, oppone themselves, but rather sharped their tongues against me because I admonished them of their duty and suffered not the cankered conscience of hypocrites to sleep at rest, protesting at all times to them that it was not my proclaiming but rather their silence that gave any lawfulnes to that marriage,—for as the proclaming did take away all excuse from them, so my publick and privat impugnation did save my conscience sufficiently; and this far I proceeded in that marriage, as the Kirk of Edinburgh, lords, earles, and barrons that heard will bear me witnes. Now, seeing I have been shamefully slandered, both in England and Scotland, by wrong information and false report of them that hated my ministry, I desired first the judgment of the Kirk, and then that the same be published, that all men may understand whether I be worthy of such a brunt or not." Accordingly, I find the General Assembly allow Mr. Craig's defences; but whether they were published I find not. It's probable ther was no need. Bishop Spotswood gives us an abreviat of this, and adds that Mr. Craig, when before the Council, most gravely admonished the Earle of Bothwell to surcease and leave that course, as he would esteem the wrath and indignation of Almighty God; and desired the Lords present to advertish the Queen of the infamy and dishonnour that would fall upon her by that match, and to use their best endeavours to divert her from it.

In the Records of the Assembly, Dec., 1566, I find Mr. Craig, David Lindsay, George Buchanan, Principall of Saint Leonards Colledge, Saint Andrews, and Mr. George Hay,[1] or any two of them, appointed to direct their edicts to all ministers, elders, and deacons of Kirks, under the Superintendant of Fife, his charge, to compear at Coupar, the 22 day of January, with their complaints against the Superintendant, and to try them and report to the next General Assembly. The Assemblys wer much troubled now with complaints against such as wer taken in from the Popish clergy to offices in the Church. Mr. John Winram, who, as I suppose, had been sub-Prior in

[1] Note 6.

Saint Andrews under Popery, and was Superintendant of Fife, Alexander and Adam, Bishops of Galloway and Orkney, with severall others I could name,[1] who came off from Popery, fill the Assembly Registers for some years after the Reformation with grievances tabled against them. But it is of more importance to observe that here the General Assembly subjects the Superintendant to be tryed by two ministers, which is no favourable appointment for such as would have superintendants to have had a prelatick powr.

Mr. Craig continoued a very usefull minister in Edinburgh till the year 1571, when, during the civil war betwixt the Regents and the Lords, who stood for the King's authority, and those who appeared for the late Queen, his silence was not so pleasing to the zealous Protestants in Edinburgh, when Grange held out the castle against the Regent, and Mr. Knox had been oblidged to leave the town in May, as may be seen in his life. Mr. Craig continoued to preach in Edinburgh particularly, May 13, the Sabbath after Mr. Knoxe's departure. What he said was disliked by many. He taught that day upon the 130 Psalm. In his sermon he compared the estate of the Kirk of God within Edinburgh to that of the Maccabees, who wer oppressed sometimes by the Assyrians, and sometimes by the Egyptians. The Maccabees wer, he said, figures of the Kirk; afterwards, he added, that, when wicked men and wicked partys strive and contend for their pride, ambition, and honnour, the Kirk is alwise in trouble. What offended many in those speeches was that he made the case of both partys now contending alike. He further lamented that ther was no neutrall man to make agreement betwixt the parties, seeing whatever party be overthrown, the Country, he said, would be brought to ruin. Such who blamed him aledged that country, wher murderous traitors and bloodthirsty men are punished, is happiest, and this way fred from trouble. It is very easy censuring persons conduct in such a juncture as this was, when the town was fortifyed against the Regent, and ane Parliament held in the Cannongate for the King, and another for his mother, in the town now under the power of the Castle. Mr. Craig behoved to be cautious in what he spoke, and level equally at what he reconed wrong on both hands, and his peacefull temper, in wishing the breach wer made up, ought not to be blamed.

[1] Note 7.

The Commissioners of the Assembly at Leith wer of Craig's sentiments here, and sent up some of their number to the town and castle of Edinburgh to travell for an agreement betwixt the contending parties, and for preventing the effusion of Christian blood. Mr. Winram Superintendant of Fife; Mr. Craig, and some other ministers accordingly went to the castle and had a long conference with the Duke, Secretary Lethington, Sir James Balfour, and others, now opposing the Regent. Mr. Calderwood inserts an account of it, formed by the ministers, and, as Mr. Craig had the greatest share in the debates, so I recon he drew up a great part of the account, and, therefor, and because it conteans the present state of things betwixt the partys, and has not been published, that I know of, I insert it here:

"At our entry in the Castle we passed into the great hall on the south side, wher, soon after, Mr. James Balfour came to us, and, in continuent thereafter, my Lord Duke, and at last the Captain of the Castle, who desired the Duke and us to enter into the chamber beside the hall, wher my Lord Secretary was sitting in a chair. After we wer set, the Superintendant of Fife began the proposition, thus:—'My Lords, because some Commissioners of the Kirk are conveened presently at Leith, who, perceiving the intestine troubles, thought it became them of duty to offer their labours and travells to the end, if it should please God, that therby the same might be quenched; for the which we are come here to offer our travells and labors as said is.' After this proposition was made, silence was keeped a certain space till Mr. John continoued the purpose again in this manner—' My Lords, I think our Commission extendeth this far, that, seing your Lordships are willing we should travell, as ye have declared by your writing to our brother here, Mr. Craig, and we are very willing also to bestow our labours, then it resteth to know and hear your Lordships what heads and articles ye will offer unto us as a ground wherupon we may travell.' To this the Lord Secretary answered—' Ye are overwise, Mr. John, we will make no offers to those who are in the Canongate, for the principalls of the nobility of Scotland are here. They that are in the Canongate are far inferior in that rank; therfor, to them we mind not to make offers, but it becometh them rather to make offers to them that are here, and, if they would come to the point, to consider how far they have gone astray, and desire the noblemen that are here to travell for them, that such things as they have done heretofore, might be remitted to them, and security be had for their lives, lands, goods, and heretages, for them, their friends, and posterity: and I understand that thir noblemen will, to that effect, concur with them, that all security may be provided for them, so that concord may be had among them all; and, otherwise, bid them not look for any offers from us.' 'Then,' said Mr. Winrame, 'it appeareth we have the less to do, seing no ground is offered to us wherupon we may travell.' 'Then,' said Mr. Craig, 'we have somewhat more to say, as it appeareth to me that, seing there is a lawfull authority established in the person of the King and his Regent throughout this Realme, which ought to be obeyed by all the subjects thirof, therfor our duty is, as Commissioners and members of the Kirk, to admonish every one of your Lordships to obey the same.' 'Then,' said the Secretary, 'I will show you the discourse of the proceedings herof from the beginning. When we enterprized the taking of the Queen on Carberry Hill, ther was then two cheef occasions that moved us. The one was to punish the King's murder chiefly in my Lord Bothwell; the other, that the unhappy marriage betwixt the Queen and him might be dissolved; and to this end to sequestrat her body from him. She was put in Lochlevin, and that thir wer the cheif causes the proclamations made at that time, and the writings sent to other countrys do plainly declare, so that we meaned nothing then of the King's authority, or to put the Queen out of her own room, as I myself,' said he, 'the same night the Queen was brought to Edinburgh, made the offer to Her Grace—If she would abandon the Lord Bothwell, she should have as thankfull obedience as ever she had since she came to Scotland, but nowise would she leave Lord Bothwell, and so she was put in Lochlevin; at which, we hoped that all men should have assisted to revenge the King's murder; but never one moe came to us nor we wer at Carberry hill. But be the contrair, the Lord Huntley and many others rose up against us, so that they wer the greater party than we—so that we, finding no other way to preserve us from inconveinences, devised to make the cloak of some new authority. Even as [if] we wer passing over at Kinghorn, and the boat took fire ye would leap in the sea to fly the fire; and, finding yourself ready to drown, ye would press again to the boat; even so the setting up of the King's authority was but a fetch or a shift to save us from greater inconveniencies; not that ever we meaned that the same should stand and continou, as ever therafter I show my Lord Regent, willing him to compone and agree the matter, and, for my own part, I plainly confesse that I did very evil and ungodly in setting up the King's authority, for he can never be justly King so long as his mother liveth, and that which I speak, the whole noblemen within this town, and others here present, I am sure, will affirm the same.' Here the Duke, Sir James Balfour, and the Captain confessed, with mutuall consents, nodding with their heads and high speaking, the promises to be truth. 'Then,' said the Secretary to Sir James Balfour, 'my Lord President, ye can tell thir things as well as any man.' Sir James answered—'Indeed, my Lord, I was privy to thir things, and know them well, and understand the ground of thir proceeding to have been as your Lordship tells.' 'Then,' said I to the Secretary, 'I cannot tell what fetches or shifts your Lordship hath used in thir proceedings, but therinto let your own conscience accuse you before your God, *conscientiam vestram oneramus;* but one thing well I wott, honest men of simple conscience, and upright dealing, meaned nothing of thir shifts and fetches, but proceeded upon an honest and constant ground, having the glory of God befor their eyes, and the punishment of horrible crimes. Neither,' said I, 'my Lord, have godly men of upright dealing used such shifts and fetches as thir of yours, namely, in such notable and weighty matters. But one thing, my Lord, I perceive that methinks God hath beguiled you, that howbeit he hath used you and your shifts as an instrument of the King's authority, yet, it appears, he will not set it down again at your pleasure.' 'Then,' said the Secretary, 'how know ye that are ye of God's counsell? *Quis fuit ejus consiliarius?* Ye shall see the contrary within a few dayes, and then we will see what obedience ye will give.' 'Then,' said I, 'unto that time, my Lord, our argument is good, and ye and others ought to give the King obedience.' The Superintendant added—'Our argument, my Lord, appeareth very good. That the authority once established by order, with the consent of the three Estates of the Realme, ought and should be obeyed; ay, and while the same be set down again by the like power and order.' 'Then,' said my Lord Secretary, 'I marvail that ye will say so, for, I remember I heard Mr. Willocks, Mr. John Row, and the rest of you preach concerning Papistry, that albiet the same wer established by long continuance and authority of princes, yet should the same be rejected without order, and as it came in over the dyke, so should it be shott over the dyke, and not tarry while the like order be used in setting down of it, as was used in establishing of it, even so,' I say of the King's authority, 'that we need not to tarry while the same be set down be the self-same order it was erected, for that, perchance, might be too long.' 'Then,' said I, 'in this, your argument, I perceive a paralogisme, and that, by reason ther is great difference and dissimilitude betwixt religion and matters of policy; for, as concerning the religion, howsoever, a wicked religion entereth in so soon as the same is knowen to be wicked, how long continouance, or whatsoever authority be once established, I presume, it wer by violence or tyranny'—Here the Secretary interrupted me and said—'Mr. John, I am glad to hear that confession out of your mouth.' 'My Lord,' said I, 'givand and grantand that so were alwise, I understand, a lawfull ground in the King's authority, and the authority once established to be obeyed. Neither is it against conscience so to do, but standeth well with a good conscience, as Paul testifieth, writing to the Romans, commanding them to obey the Emperor's authority then established among them; and that for conscience cause,' said I; 'yet if ye shall consider the ground how the Emperors of Rome entered to their authority, I think the ground therof was rather violence and tyranny than any lawfull establishment by the lawes of reason; yet, notwithstanding the Apostle commandeth the samine to be obeyed, which he would never have done concerning the obedience to a wicked religion, and if the argument be good that we shall obey the established authority, howbeit it have entered in by violence and tyranny, then much more ought we to obey the authority established, the ground wherof is lawfull, reasonable, and godly; and, if we should enter into discourse, I cannot tell how many authoritys are established upon a lawfull ground.'

"Here, I understand, we keeped silence a certain space, and therafter Sir James Balfour said to me, 'I marvell to you that in your Kirk you have made an Act decerning the King's authority to be lawfull, and so to be obeyed.' 'My Lord,' said I, 'have you read that Act?' 'No,' said he. 'Indeed, so it appears,' answered I, 'for we have made no such Act decerning any authority lawfull; but we have concluded that the King's authority established should be obeyed, and all the subjects admonished to this obedience, and he to be prayed for in all publick sermons, and what fault find ye, my Lord, in this?' 'I pray you tell me,' said the other, 'how know ye that the King's authority is established?' 'I know, my Lord,' said I, 'by two arguments. The first, because it is established by the three Estates in Parliament; secondly, because it hath received universall obedience within this Realme, without erecting any other face of authority in the contrair.' 'But,' said he, 'how know ye that it's established?' 'Truly, my Lord,' said I, 'I can well answer to this, for I was present in Parliament, when I both heard and saw the samine concluded, if it be true that ye are there standing, or that yon litle dog is lying in the Secretary's lap (for a litle messan[1] was lying on his knee), even so true its that I have said.' Sir James Balfour answered 'that Parliament was no lawfull Parliament, yea it's null in itself'. 'My Lord,' said I, 'is the proces of nullity deduced and concluded by any such order as the Parliament was holden?' 'That needeth not,' said he, 'for it's null in itself.' 'Thirdly, my Lord,' said I, 'I have learned a rule in the law, *sententia facit jus inter partes donec retractetur*.' 'Then,' said the Secretary, 'that Parliament is null upon many causes, and cannot be judged a lawfull Parliament.' 'Then,' said I, 'my Lord, if any Parliament was holden in Scotland these 700^d years, I doubt not but that was a lawfull Parliament, both in substance and ceremonies, and what nullity ye can alledge, I doubt not but may be alledged against any Parliament in Scotland those 700^d years. Men may know what the nullity of this Parliament tends to, seing our religion was therin established'; and herin we wer appearing to fall out in some other termes dividing from the purpose, and therfor the Secretary took up the matter again, and said to us—'See ye not what thir men which are in the Cannongate pretend, nothing else I warrant you, but to rug and reave other men's livings, and to enrich themselves with other men's gear, for how many of them have other men's benefices and livings, and yet cannot be satisfyed.' 'Then,' said Mr. Craig, 'let such things be spoken of them that be yonder, meikle worse is spoken of them that are here.' 'And what is that, Mr. Craig?' said the other. 'My Lord,' said he, 'It's plainly spoken that those that are here traivell only in their proceedings to cloak cruel murderers, and that the consciences of some of you are so pinched with the same, that ye will not suffer the nobility to agree.' 'Yet,' answered the Secretary, 'so

---

[1] A mongrel cur, "a tinkler-gipsy's messan."—Burns.

long as I was with them, Mr. Craig, they never accused me of the King's murder; and the last year they gave me all their hand writs purging me of it, yea, to be short with you, so long as I was a pillar to mentain their unjust authority, they would never putt at me as they do. In the treaty that is begun in England, that is ane of the cheife articles, that the King and Regent's murthers shall be punished to the rigour, in all persons who shall be found guilty therof; and our Queen hath oblidged herself to the Queen of England, under pain of tinsell of her rights that she pretends to the crown of England, that those murtherers shall be punished in all, to the rigour, who shall be found guilty therof.' 'Then,' said Mr. Craig, 'how can thir two stand, that the Queen being set up in authority, who is guilty of the murder of the King, shall punish the murther in any others.' 'My Lord,' said I, 'I heard your Lordship tell a tale, that ther was an appointment upon a time between the Kings of England and Spain, and when matters wer concluded, a merryman said to the King of England: "Sir, who shall be caution for the King of Spain?" even so I say, "My Lord, who shall be caution for our Queen in that behalf?"' 'Mr. John,' sayes he, 'the Queen of Scotland will not tine her right which she pretends to the crown of England for any favour she beareth to any man in Scotland.' 'But it's a marvelous thing,' said Mr. Craig, 'that albiet, my Lord Duke here and some others acknowledgeth not the King's authority, yet ye, ye and ye,' pointing to the Secretary, Sir James Balfour, and the Captain, 'will not deny the King's authority, seing ye have pressed the same and wer the cheif instruments in erecting the same.' 'Then,' said the Secretary, 'the King's authority was set up in respect of the Queen's dimission, to the which I think I was also privie, and travelled as meikle as any in the Cannongate, as they can bear me record themselves; yea, further, without me they had not the knowledge, wisdom, nor union to perform the same, and think ye of your conscience that that dimission was made willingly, seing the Queen was holden in captivity? Howbeit, my Lords Lindsay and Ruthven so deponed publickly, and for verification therof, my Lord Lindsay being desired by my Lord Regent therafter earnestly to pass into England with him, he refused altogether, whither for lack of expenses or otherwise, I cannot tell. But at lenth, when my Lord Regent pressed him so earnestly, being in a house of Leith before an honourable company, that he behoved to go to England. Then my

Lord Lindsay swore a great oath, and said: 'My Lord, if you cause me to go to England with you, I will spill the whole matter, for if they accuse me of my conscience I cannot but confess the truth.' 'Then,' said I, 'trulie, my Lord, this appeareth to me one of your own fetches, that my Lord Lindsay used at that time, for seing he had no will of the journey, he would have used some colloured means, and in this fetch, my Lord, he may appear to be one of your disciples, howbeit he means not so indeed.'

"Here we began to move, and as it wer everyone to laugh upon another, and so to rise. Then Mr. Andrew Hay passed to the Captain and spake to him apart, and therafter I spake to the Captain. When we wer ready to come our way, the Secretary cryeth on me. 'Mr. John, think ye that my Lord Lennox, being an Englishman sworn, can be a lawfull Regent to this Realme?' 'My Lord,' said I, 'whither he be an Englishman sworn or not I know not, for that standeth *in facto*, but I understand that he is a native born Scotsman.' 'But I can tell,' said the Secretary, 'he is an Englishman sworn.' 'But, pre-supposing that,' said I, 'that so wer, what impediment is it whither he be Englishman, Frenchman, Spaniard, or Italian, if he be lawfull tutor of the heir and hath right therunto, why may he not be lawfull Regent in the time of the tutory, for was not the Duke of Albanie a Frenchman born, yet because he was lawfull tutor to our King, he bore the regiment during his minority, and how could he justly by any letts be secluded therfrom?' 'Mr. John,' sayes the Secretary, 'ther is a difference betwixt the two.' 'And what is that?' said I. 'We are joyned in league and amity with France, but England hath been our old enemies.' 'My Lord,' said I, 'that argument now appeareth nothing, for we have peace and amity with England presently, as we have with France;' and thus we took our leave and came our way." This conference showes fully how firm Mr. Craig stood as to the King's authority, and that there was no ground to jealous him for his sermon. However, he blamed both sides.

Yet, after the truce agreed to, and the town of Edinburgh was from under the vassalage of the Castle, many in the town, as we have seen in Mr. Knoxe's life, took a dislike at him for his alledged complyances with those in the Castle, and upon this Bishop Spotswood tells us, he was transported to Monross, and from that to Aberdeen. In those two places he continoued till the [year] 1579 or 1580, when he was called to the King's house. I have very litle of him till he returned to Edinburgh, save a few hints from the Assembly Registers. By some papers before me, he seems to have been Principall at Aberdeen, and I doubt not but Mr. Craig was singularly usefull in the north during the 8 years he was there, both in the pulpit and University.[1]

In the year 1575, I find him Minister of Aberdeen, and he is one of the three appointed by that Assembly to reason upon the question upon the lawfulness of bishops in the Assembly, and after reasoning, the next Assembly, 1576, wher Mr. Craig is Moderator, agreed to the unlawfulness of prelatick bishops, which was the side he reasoned on. The opinion brought in by Mr. Craig and other ministers upon this question, whether bishops, as they are now in Scotland, have their function out of the Word of God, which the whole Assembly, for the most part, after reasoning and long disputation upon every article of the said bretheren's advice and opinion, absolutely affirmed and approved, stands thus in the Assembly's Registers:

"1. The name of a bishop is common to all them that have a particular flock, over the which he hath a particular charge, as well to preach the Word as to minister the sacraments, and to execute the ecclesiasticall discipline, with consent of the elders, and this is his cheif function off the Word of God.

"2. Out of this number may be chosen, some to have power to oversee and visit such reasonable bounds, besides his own flock, as the Generall Assembly shall appoint, and in those bounds to appoint ministers, with the consent of the ministers of that province, and the consent of the flock, whom to they shall be appointed, as well as to appoint elders and deacons to every particular congregation, wher there is none, with the consent of the people therof, and to suspend ministers for reasonable causes, with the consent of the ministers forsaid"; and at the same time the Assembly ordeans the bishops, who have not yet accepted the charge of a particular congregation, to condescend on the morn what particular flocks they will take the care of. More of this matter is to be seen on Mr. Duries', Mr. And. Melvil, and other ministers' lives in this period. By steps the Assembly went on in this matter, as the times and the Earl of Mortoun's eagernes for the Tulchan Bishops[2]

[1] Note 8.   [2] Note 9.

would permitt, and at lenth declared directly against Prelacy, and fred the Church of this first heavy burden of Tulchan Bishops, in which Mr. Craig was very active and usefull.

Bishop Spotswood sayes Mr. Craig was brought from Aberdeen to Holyroodhous, to be Minister of the King's house—1579. Mr. Row, in his history, tells us that at the Assembly (July, 1580), "the King, by his letter, nominat Mr. John Craig to be his minister, for the which choice the Assembly blessed God, and praised the King for his zeal". By the registers of that Assembly, I find Mr. Craig presenting the King's letter to the Assembly conteaning commission to the Prior of Pittenweem and the Laird of Lundy to be his Commissioners in that Assembly, and assist them in his name; so that it's probable Mr. Craig was settled King's minister some time before this Assembly.

Mr. Craig was not long in the King's house, till he was imployed to pen what we now call the Nationall Covenant, or the King's Confession of Faith, and by some, the Negative Confession. This Confession of Faith has been again and again printed, and lately in the collection of our Confessions (vol. 2, 1722), with the Latine version by Mr. Craig himself, who was an exact master of the Latine tongue; yet, being formed by this great man, and what will not take up very much room, it stands in the Appendix.[1] (Copy Colect., Confess. 103.)

Before I enter upon the occasion of its being penned, and some remarks I am to make upon it, let me observe that Mr. Calderwood upon this year gives us a Confession of Faith drawn up by the Popish bishops, to counter the King's Confession. Its title is: "A Short and Generall Confession of the true Christian Faith set forth by us, Archbishops and Bishops, the supreme and chief heads in the ecclesiasticall state of Scotland, to be presented to our inferiors, and be our most lawfull authority, concluded as *grounded upon the express written Word of God, at Edinburgh, the 12 of Aprile,* 1581. *Signed, P. Saint Andrews, I. Glasgow, D. Aberdeen.*" Mr. Calderwood has this remark on it: "I have found this Confession in sundry manuscripts, but do not understand where it should have been subscribed, nor any other circumstance belonging to the same; therefor, I leave it to the reader's judgment". Wer I to make any conjectures at this distance, I would guess this Confession was drawen up by the Popish priests very bussy at this

---

[1] Note 10.

time, to their own followers to signe, and thereby to have it to say that they had signed the Confession of Faith, tho' this was but juggle and equivocation; yet those are their ordinary shifts. Whatever be in this, I have preserved this Confession such as it is.[1] App. N. (Copy Cald. v. 3, p. 23-25). And that the reader may have what relates to this matter of Confessions altogether, I have also subjoyned that Confession which the prelates formed about the [year] 1616 to stand in room of the King's Confession, and to which, instead of the former—which I am ready to think they did not like, tho' they had all subscribed, because of the clauses relative to the hierarchy and discipline, which was undoubtedly Presbyterian—when it was framed, they required subscriptions unto from Papists. It's generally called the New Confession; and I wonder how Bishop Spotswood comes to ommitt it in his History. Perhaps the doctrine was too far distant from the Pelagian and Popish tenets his friend and patron, Archbishop Laud, was bringing into England, and many of his brethren, the Scots Bishops, wer greedily swallowing, about the time he wrote his History. Whatever be in this, the New Confession stands,[2] App. N. (Copy Cald., v. 6, p. 372-8).

To return to the occasion of Mr. Craig's forming his excellent Confession, Bishop Spotswood seems very much to restrain it to some Popish dispensations brought into Scotland, "whereby the Catholicks wer permitted to promise, swear, subscribe, and do what else should be required of them, so as in mind they continoued firm, and did use their diligence to advance in secret the Roman Faith". These dispensations being showen, adds he, to the King, he caused his minister, Mr. John Craig, form a short Confession of Faith, wherein all the corruptions of Rome—in doctrine, as well as outward rites—wer particularly abjured, and a clause inserted because of those dispensations, by which the subscribers did call God to witnes that in their minds and hearts they did fully agree to their said Confession, and did not feigne or dissemble in any sort. I have no doubt but those Popish dispensations wer one occasion of the framing of this excellent Confession. Mr. Petry, in his History, gives the very same account with Spotswood, and observes that complaints wer made of many Papists, come in lately to the country, to the last Assembly, and particularly of Nicol Burn, formerly a Professor of Philosophy in Saint Andrews, but now an apostat to Popery. He

---

[1] Note 11.   [2] Note 12.

nottices that "our former Confession was wholly positive (and so that formed afterwards under Prelacy generally is); but in this ther is one abjuration of all the corruptions of Rome,—in doctrine, superstitions, rites, and the whole hierarchy, together with a promise to continou in the obedience of the doctrine and discipline of this Church, and defend the same according to our vocation all the dayes of our life". Upon this account this Confession justly gets the name of a *Covenant*; and, indeed, the very words of it are levelled against those Popish dispensations, as anybody who reads it must see. But, then, everyone, who considers the state of things at that time, will perceive other occasions of forming this Confession and Covenant, which seem not to have been so much observed as they deserve. Spotswood himself hints the King's concern to bring in his cusin, the Earle of Lennox, to the management of affairs at this time, and *tells how carefully the King was to have the Church satisfyed and the rumors of the Court's defection from religion repressed.*

The reader, then, will bear with me if I consider the occasions of forming this Covenant as to the King, though perhaps they will not be found so fair and laudable as wer to be wished, and, then, as to the ministry and Church, who wer at this time under great apprehensions of Popery. The motion of drawing up this Confession came from the complaints made by the Assembly of the growth of Popery and unaccountable numbers of Papists, and their being connived at this year, 1580. The King went into it when made to him upon severall views. His tender age—about fourteen years—and his good education—tho', alace! much worn off by bad company—will scarce permitt us to question that he was as yet firm to the religion he was educat in. But for his Managers at this time I cannot say so much; and what I am to observe of the Court, I understand of the courtiers rather than the young King. The Court then had for some time overlooked the incoming of Papists and encrease of Popery. Those, who wer now meditating the ruine of the Earle of Mortoun, after he had laid down his regency, wer favourers of Popery, and expected support from Papists abroad, and that the Papists from the north and south would joyn them. And, therfor, when somwhat behoved to be done to satisfy the ministers' complaints, and gull the eyes of the vulgar, who perceived the sensible decline of everything that was good in the Court since the Earle of Mortoun's dimission, they allow the King to give in to the proposall of a new Confession and Covenant. They know that oaths, bonds, and subscriptions would not do much present hurt to their friends, and hoped that many others like themselves under a small temptation would get over them; and yet, at present, the giving in to this Covenant would exceedingly recomend them to the generality of the nation, and they would have a good cover to their real designes—the bringing the Earle of Lennox, who lately had renounced Popery, to have the management of the King, and to get rid of the Earle of Mortoun, a firm Protestant; and thus, indeed, matters turned about. In a very little time Mortoun was challenged by Captain Stewart, afterward Earl of Arran, and imprisoned under pretext of concealing the murder of the King's father, and in a few moneths he was publickly execut, upon which the King fell into the hands of the French faction, Lennox and Arran, and the land was brought to the outmost hazard of Popery. The young King, I believe, was let into litle of the secret, till it ripned and gradually broke out. But except for some moneths after the Road of Ruthven, for four years' time the Civil and Reformation rights of Scotland came to be in the outmost hazard; and matters wer brought very near the admission of the King's mother to a share in the management, had not the wise ministry in England prevented this. Thus wicked men make covers of the best and most sacred and usefull things to promott their black projects. As our excellent Nationall Covenant was thus miserably perverted to serve vile purposes—which does not in the lest derogat from its excellency, since the Holy Scriptures and Religion itself have been so used,—so our Nationall Contract and Solemn League and Covenant with England (1643) was, by the cunning of politick and designing men, perverted to ends perfectly different from the first end and designe; and reformation, according to the example of the best reformed Churches, was made a handle for things not at first dreamed of. However, those base treatments of the most solemn and sacred oaths to God and one another do not in the least lessen the obligation of them, and the just value the very matter of them calls for at our hand.

Upon the other hand, the views of the Church and the ministers who proposed this Confession—the Bishop Spotswood makes it to come intire from the King and Mr. Craig, who drew—wer just, sincere, and great. The former Confession of Faith[1] had no obligatory claused joyned

[1] Note 13.

to it: it was, indeed, a most excellent composure, but not directly levelled at Popery and the other corruptions come, or coming, since it was formed. Ther was now a very sensible declining from the Reformation, and Popery and Papists wer increasing. Our Reformation upon the matter began with a solem Covenant with God and one another in the Lord, as is to be seen in Mr. Knoxe's life; and the Assembly did not know a better way to preserve the Reformation atteaned, and put a stop to declinings, than the making and renewing the Church engagements to the Lord, and the regulating every thing according to His Word. And, no doubt, however this was miserably prostitute by the courtiers, yet it was of very great use. This Confession, being translated and published in Latine as well as English, was highly esteemed by the rest of the Reformed Churches, and the King was much praised by all Protestants for it. Multitudes came under the bond of it, with much sincerity and advantage to themselves: it was of great use to confirm ministers and others, when brought to sufferings three years after this, for adhering to the Reformation right of this Church; and, no doubt, it was accepted graciously by God, through Christ, as a testimony against Popery and a great step of nationall reformation; and great was the pains ministers were at in instructing their people, and explaining it to them before they swore and subscribed to it, which very much improved the country in point of knowledge. I need not add a multitude of other good effects that might be named.

Upon the 28 of January, $158\frac{0}{7}$, this Confession of Faith was solemly sworn and subscribed by the King and his house and severall others. The list Mr. Calderwood gives of the first subscribers deserves a room here. They wer James Rex., Lennox, Argyle, Bothwell, Ruthven, Seaton, James Lord Ogilvy, Allan Lord Cathcart, William Shaw, James Stewart, Alexander Seaton, R. Dumfernline, The Master of Gray, J. Cheestlie, James Hallyburton, James Colvil of Easter Weemes, James Elphingstoun, George Douglas, Alexr. Durhame, Robert Areskine, Walter Stewart, Prior of Blantyre, William Ruthven of Bellenden, John Scrimgeour, younger, of Glasgow, William Murray, David Murray, James Frazer, Richard Herriot, Mr. Thomas Hamiltoun, Walter Kerr, Mr. John Craig, John Duncanson, ministers, Peter Young. The King and Councill's charge, in March following, to subjects of all ranks to sign this Confession, and the Acts of Assembly, approving the Confession, and requiring all ministers to see to subscribing it in their parishes, are printed in the Collection of our Confessions, and I shall not swell this work with them.

Mr. Calderwood's remarks, after he has insert this Confession in his MS. History, deserve a room here. "In this Confession of Faith, under the name of Wicked Hierarchie, is condemned Episcopall Government, for between those words *the Roman Antichrist and Wordly Monarchy* and the words *Wicked Hierarchie* are interjected many other condemned errors, as Prayers for the Dead, Dedicating of Churches, Altars, Dayes, &c., where the Hierarchie is called *his*, as Prayer for the Dead, Holy Dayes, Dedicating of Churches, are called *his* because they are invented and menteaned by him (anti-Christ), and would have vanished if he had not enterteaned them. So the Hierarchie is called *his*, because its menteaned by his lawes, authorized by him with such lordly powr and preheminence, and framed according to his Decretalls and Councils. Did not the Council of Trent thunder an ANATHEMA upon those who would not acknowledge that ther is in the Catholick Kirk an hierarchy, institute by Divine ordinance, consisting of bishops, presbiters, and deacons? Sess. 23 Can. 6. Our Confession damned, not their hierarchy, otherwise than the Tridentine Fathers defined it. Again, when it's said, 'We detest and abhorr all particular heads as they are now damned and confuted by the *Word of God and Kirk of Scotland*,' we profess to abhorr and detest Episcopall Government, for not only in the pulpits the doctrine sounded against it, but also it was, after great deliberation and advisement, condemned by the Generall Assembly, before the Confession of Faith was subscribed. Yea, since the beginning of the year 1556, those who wer called bishops wer not bishops indeed, but commissioners and visitors of the bounds prescribed unto them, together with the Synod, or bretheren deput by the Synod or bretheren of the exercise; and this power, delegat unto them by commission, was alterable at the pleasure of the General Assembly, so that, albiet, they wer vulgarly called bishops, in respect of the benefice, yet had they not the extensive or intensive power belonging to the office of a bishop. Simple ministers had the same office of commission that they had, yea, since the year 1573, their power was declared to be no greater than the superintendants. The discipline, then, wherof mention is made in the Confession of Faith, is not

Episcopall Government, but the jurisdiction of Kirk Sessions, Presbitrys, Synodall Assemblys and Generall, agreed on before, when the Book of Policy[1] was approved, that is, since the first Assembly, 1578, some few heads excepted, which make nothing against the forme of discipline."

To confirm what Mr. Calderwood gives here, but in short hints, having distinctly narrated every particular in the former part of his History, I shall only observe that the 2d Book of Discipline, wherin, by the way, Mr. Craig had a considerable hand, and severall heads of it wer penned by him, was not only agreed upon unanimously by the Assembly, after long examination of it, and was agreed to also by the Commissioners from the State, save in a few minute articles, which do not concern the subject in hand, so that *the Discipline of this Church*, [which] the subscribers of this Confession bound themselves to mentain and defend, can be no other but Presbiteriall Government. But in the last Generall Assembly, July, 1580, Prelacy and bishops, as now commonly taken, wer torn out of the Registers by Bishop Adamson, which would have set this matter in a full light, but by a particular providence, one of the principall Acts of that Assembly this year escaped his wicked hands, and it's as follows:

"For as meikle as the office of a bishop (as it is now used and commonly taken within this Realme) has no sure warrand, authority, or good ground out of the Scriptures of God, but is brought in by the folly and corruption of men's inventions, to the great overthrow of the Kirk of God. The whole Assembly of this Nationall Kirk, in one voice, after liberty given to all men to reason in the matter, not anyone opposing himself in defence of the said pretended office, finds and declares the said pretended office used, and termed as is abovesaid, unlawfull in itself, as having neither fundamental ground nor warrand in the Word of God, and ordeans that all such persons as bruiks, or shall bruik, hereafter the said office, shall be charged *simpliciter* to demitt and leave off the samyne, as an office wherunto they are not called by God, and such like to demitt and cease from all preaching, ministration of the sacraments, or using any way the office of pastors while they *de novo* receive admission from the General Assembly, and that, under the pain of excommunication to be used against them; wherein, if they be

---

[1] Note 14.

found disobedient, or contraveen this Act in any point, the sentence of excommunication, after due admonition, to be used against them." By the same Act, all the present bishops are ordeaned to be cited before the Synodall Assemblys, in August next, and if not subject to it, the proces of excommunication is to go on against them. Let me only further nottice that the erection of the particular presbiterys, with the King's consent, in cohsequence of the 2d Book of Discipline, was now very near compleated. Upon the whole, nobody who understands Grammar and the History of this period can, as far as I see, take the hierarchy in the sense of the Councill of Trent, including bishops or prelates, as standing here for anything else but Prelacy; and the discipline engaged to in the Confession must necessarily be taken for Presbiteriall Government since the Reformation, and at this time the only discipline approven by this Church. I shall conclude Mr. Calderwood's remarks on this Confession with an observation in his printed History, which is not in his MS. " That this Confession is an appendix to the first Confession (1560), and comprehendeth it in the Generall Clause (he might have said expressly names and takes it in) at the beginning, so that he who subscribeth the one subscribeth the other, and therfor our Confession of Faith is not wholly negative, but partly negative and partly affirmative."

I shall conclude this subject I have enlarged further upon than at first I designed, with the reflection Mr. John Row hath in his MS. History, after he has insert the Confession, both in English and Latine. He lived, and might be in the ministry at the time it was made, or a very little after; and I chuse rather to give the reader what may afford light to this Confession in the words of those old fathers than in my own. "This Confession" (sayes Mr. Row) "was, for its exactnes and worthines, much esteemed in all other Christian Churches professing sincerely, and is translated into many different languages"; and, after signifying the King's subscribing it, and giving charge to ministers to see it subscribed, he sayes, " ministers' diligence in this did much good: they laboured severall years to get the oaths and subscriptions of all that would be informed rightly by them to stand to the said Confession unto their lives' end. It was printed and openly set out to all, being made *juris publicis* at the command of the King and his Council, when this Kirk of Scotland was rightly reformed, all corruptions put to the door, and religion and reformation gloriously flourishing—both in doctrine, worship, and discipline. This was the toutchstone to discern Papists from Protestants, and, according to the laudable example of Reformers mentioned in the Scripture, this Confession, called also THE COVENANT, in dayes of espyed defection, was renewed, the Kirk acknowledging that to be the principall mean, by the blessing of God, for the preventing of and reclaiming from apostacy and backsliding; wherefor, at the Generall Assembly, holden at Edinburgh, March 24, 159$\frac{5}{6}$, the beginning of defection being then espyed, this Covenant was renewed. Also, now of late (Anno 1638), it was solemly renewed, with such necessary additions as those times called for; an usurping Prelacy, with an overawing High Commission, being so far set up, and corruption having so far prevailed that Archbishop Spotswood, stiled Primat of Scotland, was also High Chancelour of Scotland. Many ceremonies, Anti-christian or Popish, wer brought in, and, without warrand or order, obtruded upon the Kirk of Christ a book of ecclesiasticall canons framed by the prelates, a book of ordination, a service book or book of common prayer or lyturgie framed much more Popish and Anti-christian, nor was the English service book, whilk yet was very little other than the Mass in English.[1] But, above all, they had taken away the Generall Assembly (the great bulwark, under God, of this Kirk), knowing that the first thing to be done in an Assembly then was to take order with prelates as a crew of perjured men who had transgressed all their limites and caveats; wherfor, after six null General Assemblys—holden 1606, 1608, 1610, 1616, 1617, 1618, for the space of 20 years, till the [year] 1638—there was no Assembly in the Kirk of Scotland."[2]

But to return to Mr. Craig. He was chosen Moderator to the General Assembly, which conveened Oct., 1581. They sat long, and went through a great deal of business, and compleated the erection of presbitrys begun last Assembly; and began proces with the bishops—particularly, Mr. Robert Montgomery[3]—and gave a commission to about 20 ministers to attend the Estates of Parliament, and present the Churches' grievances and crave ansurs.

In the next Assembly (1582) Mr. Craig is appointed to form an order for collecting the Acts of the Kirk betwixt [that] and the next Assembly; and that I may give what I meet with as to this altogether, next year

[1] Note 15.   [2] Note 16.   [3] Note 17.

(1583) the register runs thus: "Anent the labours taken by Mr. Craig in collecting of the Acts of Assembly, seing the great travel taken by him for the weal of the same, not without singular fruit and profit of the whole bretheren, to the effect the same may be absolved and brought to perfection, it's thought good that Mr. James Lawson, Mr. David Lindsay, Mr. Robert Pont, Mr. Walter Balcanquell, Mr. Nicol Dalglish, Mr. John Davidson, Mr. John Duncanson, Commissioners from Edinburgh,[1] travell in perusing the whole work, albeit of the difficultys that occurr; consider and weigh what things are requisite to the full compleating thereof; and put the same *in mundo* betwixt [this] and the next General Assembly, that the judgment of the whole Assembly may be had thereupon." At the next Assembly, that same year, the report is as followes: "Anent the travels of Mr. Craig as to the Acts of the Kirk, the Commissioners appointed for reviewing therof report that they had considered therof, and that in his labours God was to be praised; yet some things they had nottticed wheranent they desired further conference, and would proceed". I have not observed any more in the Registers upon this work of Mr. Craig's. The troubles which fell in by the King's leaving the Lords concerned in Ruthven Road, and falling in with the Earle of Arran and the French faction, and the dark cloud which came upon the Church for two years when the records fell into Bishop Adamson's hands,[2] I imagine stopped this designe, which, as I take it, was to class and put under proper heads all the Acts of Assemblys since the Reformation, and to publish what was of common and standing use, as well as to point out things proper for the compleating the standing rules of the Church, which would have been a singularly usefull work; and Mr. Craig, because of his laborious diligence, acquaintance with the forms and proceedings of the Church since the Reformation, and his intimat acquaintance with the Canon and Civil Law, was pitched upon for it.

Mr. Calderwood takes nottice of a remarkable sermon Mr. Craig had before the King, Sept. 19, 1582, after the Lords at Ruthven had for a season delivered the King and Country from the bondage they wer under to the Duke and Earle Arran. His words are: "Upon Wensday, the 19, Mr. Craig made a nottable sermon before the King, on Psal. 2, 10, the like wherof was never made before in his presence for free rebuke.

[1] Note 18.   [2] Note 19.

He reproved the King for subscribing the slanderous Proclamation at Perth, July 12 last, against the ministry and liberty of their meeting upon the affairs of the Church. The King weeped, and said he might have told him privatly. It was answered that it had been often told him, but to litle effect; and publick vice required public reproof."

Mr. Craig was almost still imployed now in all the messages sent from the ministers to the King, who had now many things grievous enough to grapple with in His Majesty's conduct. He was under a great byass to French councils, and two French Ambassadors wer come to him to propose his assuming his mother into the Government with him; and, however at present he was separat from Aubignie, Duke of Lennox, yet Colonell Stewart, Earle of Arran, was with him, and plaid the same gaim. The French Ambassadors had preists with them, and openly performed their superstitions, which gave great offence; and the Papists gathered about them, and caryed on their treasonable designes pretty openly. Upon the first of March Mr. Bonos [Bowes], the English Ambassador, got some nottice of an English Jesuit, Brewton [Brereton] *alias* Holt, and found means to seize him at Leith as going to a ship. Upon him, among many other letters, one was found declaring a stated designe to seize the King and cary him to France. No wonder those ministers wer allarmed when matters wer at such a pass; and Bishop Spotswood might have spared his mean *punus* upon them, for preaching and acting against Papists, at such a juncture. In a few days the King sent to the English Ambassador and required Holt, the Jesuit, and committed him to Colonell Stewart. In some time he was let slip through their hands. Upon the 19 of March the Presbitry sent Mr. Craig and Durie to the King, to urge the Jesuit's tryall in termes of law. They got fair words, but nothing was done. On the 27, Mr. Craig and Mr. Davidson[1] wer sent again to complean of the French Ambassadour's preist, who was constantly trafficking; and to urge the tryall of Holt. To the first the King said, he was to dismiss the Ambassadour, who nevertheless stayed some time, pretending he had some more bussines with the King; and as to Holt, his tryall was delayed with the English Ambassador's consent, till the removall of the French Ambassador. The Synod of Lothian in the beginning of Aprile laid the same things before the King, and the General Assembly, who conveened April 14, sent Mr. Craig,

[1] Note 20.

Durie, and Hume[1] to the King, desiring that, since his Ambassadours wer going to England, he would instruct them to negotiat a league with the Queen and other Protestant Princes, for the defence of the Word of God and professors of it, against the persecution of Papists and their confederats, joyned and unite together by the bloody League of Trent; and that the Queen of England would disburden their bretheren of England of the yoak of ceremonies imposed upon them against the liberty of the Word. The King's answer was: as to the first, it was reasonable, and in hand before their coming; and, as to the other, that he should instruct his Ambassadors to treat the samine as opportunity served best for advancing the cause. The Assembly also sent Mr. Craig and other ministers to represent the hurt done by the French Ambassador and his preist, and to require Holt, the Jesuit, to be tryed, and, if guilty, punished; but nothing was effectually done. The King's heart was with the French faction, and Colonell Stewart managed him as he pleased, and in a little prevailed with him to cast of the Lords now about him and take a quite other course, which brought both Church and State very low for two years, as our historians nottice.

This brings me to the darkest and most melancholy part of Mr. Craig's life, his complyances with the King and Court, in some things, next year and the following. This was evidently from a weight upon him, for at first he made very brisk and zealous appearances; but things growing still more and more cloudy, and he wanting the advice of many of his bretheren now banished, and being still under the importunitys of the Court, at lenth he yielded, which I only relate to show what need the best of men have to pray, "lead us not into temptation". I shall bring in here the treatment of the ministry who remained in Scotland, while many wer banished by the King, under the management of Mr. P. Adamson, now Bishop of Saint Andrews, from Calderwood's MSS., this part of the sufferings of the Church of Scotland not being much knowen.

I need not deduce the melancholy state of affairs, the end of this year, 1583, and the two next. The King had rid himself of the lords who stood for Reformation and opposed French counsells, declared the Road of Ruthven little less than treason, forced the Earle of Angus, and near 100^d of the best affected nobility and gentry, to leave the country

[1] Note 21.

and fly to England and elswher, declared many of them rebells, and obledged Mr. Andrew Melvin, Messrs. Lowson, Davidson, James Melvil, John Carmichael, and severall others, ministers, to retire, and take a voluntary banishment upon themselves, and their wives and familys wer very hardly used in their absence.[1] When the Court was rid of the most zealous noblemen, gentlemen, and ministers, Bishop Adamson and Colonell Stewart ruled all. A Parliament was called, such as it was, the lords and gentlemen wer forfaulted, and most unaccountable acts framed by Bishop Adamson hastily passed against the jurisdiction and liberty of the Church, overturning almost all that was done since the Reformation, and hard was the part which the few remaining ministers had to act, and no wonder under so sharp a tryall some wrong steps wer made.

One of the Acts of this Parliament required all Ministers, Masters of Colledges, and Readers, within 46 dayes, to subscribe the Act of Parliament now made, asserting the King's unlimited powr over all Estates, both spirituall and temporall, and subject themselves to Bishops, under pain of losing their stipends. Upon the 24 of August, 1584, the King went over to Falkland, and left Arran, Huntlie, Crawford, the Secretary, and other counselours, to examine ministers for their bold speaches against this Parliament, and cause them subscribe the Acts of it. Messrs. Craig, Andrew Blackhall, John Brand, and John Herries[2] wer called before the Council, and asked how they durst be so bold as to control the late Acts of Parliament? Mr. Craig answered, they would find fault with anything repugnant to God's Word and holy oracles. Arran started to his feet, and said they wer too pert, and he would shave their head, pair their nails, and cut their toes, and make them examples to all that rebelled against the King and Council, and immediately charged them to compeer before the King at Falkland, September 4, to answer to what the Council had to lay to their charge. Next Sabbath their was not sermon in Edinburgh, Arran having charged all hearers to interupt ministers, and delate them to the Council if they spoke against the last Parliament, and that by open proclamation.

Upon Tuesday, Sept. 4, Mr. Craig and the rest appeared before the King and Council at Falkland. They wer accused for counteracting

[1] Note 22.   [2] Note 23.

the Acts of Parliament, and especially for not obeying and subjecting to their Ordinary, the Bishop of Saint Andrews. To that they answered, they could not obey him. Ther was pretty warm reasoning betwixt Mr. Craig and Bishop Adamson before the King. But Arran spoke to Mr. Craig most outragiously. Mr. Craig answered him, very meekly, yet he said:—"Ther has been as great men as your Lordship, and set up higher, that have been brought low." Arran, in his foolish jesting way, bowing his knee, said:—"I shall of a false freir make thee a true prophet," and sitting down on his knee said, "now I am humbled." "Nay," sayes Mr. Craig, "mock the servants of God as you will, God will not be mocked, but shall make you to find it in earnest, when you shall be humbled and cast down from the high horse of your pride." This came to pass in a few years, when James Douglas, of Parkhead, run him off his horse with a spear and slew him. His carcas was cast in an open church near by, and was eaten with the doggs and swine before it could be got buried. Others say that Mr. Craig's words, at which Arran scoffed, wer those, *as the Lord is just He will humble the.* The Council discharged Mr. Craig, and I suppose the rest, to preach, and cited them to appear again Nov. 16.

Thus, Edinburgh had no sermon for some time, and the Bishop of Saint Andrews was sent over with a charge from the King to the Magistrates of Edinburgh, to accept of him as their ordinary pastor, which they did, but few, save indifferent men and courtiers, heard him. Great was the scattering of faithfull ministers this summer. Before the Parliament, Mr. Andrew Hay, Parson of Renfrew, Mr. Andrew Polwart, sub-Dean of Glasgow, Mr. Patrick Galloway, and Mr. James Carmichael[1] wer cited for corresponding with the fugitive lords in England, upon Mr. P. Adamson's information. The first appeared, and litle being proven he was confyned to the north. The rest fled to England. Mr. David Lindsay, Minister at Leith, was sent to the King, in the time of Parliament, to intreat him that no Act might pass in prejudice of the Kirk till the ministers wer heard. Arran seized him before he saw the King, under a pretext of correspondence with England, and sent him to Blacknes, wher he was prisoner 47 weeks. Mr. Lawson and Balcanquell, upon hearing of this, fled. Mr. Robert Pont,[2] Minister of Saint Cuthberts and Senator of the Colledge of Justice,

---

[1] Note 24.   [2] Note 25.

at the proclamation of the Acts of Parliament, took instruments in the hands of a nottar, that the Church dissented from them, and afterwards fled, and was denounced and lost his place in the Session. Mr. John Durie, some weeks before, had been removed from Edinburgh and confined to Monros, and now Mr. Craig was discharged preaching, so that the town of Edinburgh was left quite distitute.

The trouble and hardships Mr. Craig, Mr. Robt. Pont, and severall others, worthy ministers, fell under toward the close of this year, for refusing to own the unlawfull Acts passed in Parliament, May last, establishing the King's unlimited Supremacy and Prelacy, and declaring it treason to decline the King's judgment in point of doctrine, being a part of our history that hitherto we are perfect strangers almost unto, the printed Calderwood having only a very short hint at it, I thought Mr. Craig's life a very proper place to set this matter in a fuller view than hitherto it has appeared in, from Mr. Calderwood's MSS., and tho it be a litle large, I can scarce think it a digression. Upon the 2 of Nov., 1584, all the ministers betwixt Stirling and Berwick, were called by open proclamation, to compear before the Archbishop of Saint Andrews and others, the King's officers, in the Kirk of Edinburgh, the 16 instant, and subscribe the promise and obligation in the late Act of Parliament, with certification if they failzie, their benefices, livings, and stipends shall be decerned and declared to vaik *ipso facto*, as if they wer naturally dead, and a copy was delivered to every minister. At the day appointed the ministers compeared. The Archbishop and Chancelor, Sir John Maitland, spoke to them to this effect:—"The King's Majesty is glad of your temperance, for hereby he hath conceived an assured trust of your obedience and good meaning toward him, and therfor willed me to assure you of his goodwill; and to the end you may be out of doubt therof, he willeth you to come to the Abbey of Hollyrood Hous, at two hours afternoon, and you shall hear the same out of his own mouth". This was a turn of the Archbishop's, who had prevailed with the King to call the ministers before himself and Council, and speak to them himself, expecting this would have greatest weight with them, to comply with the Bishop's desire.

In the afternoon, the ministers attended at the Abbey, and at 4 the King called before him and the Council all beneficed ministers in the first room, the Bishop hoping, they having most to lose would be soonest persuaded to comply when their benefices wer at stake. But he was mistaken, and very litle ground was gained. So, in a short space, the unbeneficed ministers wer also called, and to them all, the King had a speech in thir words, as far as can be minded:—" I have sent for you for two causes, the one is ordinary, the other is accidentary. The ordinary is because at this time of the year ye are accustomed to have your stipends appointed, as also to have your Assemblies, and I, being minded that ye shall be as well provided for as before, and better, I have sent for you. The other cause why I sent for you was, because it is come to my ears that you speak against my lawes, and say that I mind to subvert Religion. I thought good to advertise you of the contrary, and will desire you to take no such suspicion of me. Besides this, there are severall whisperings and mutinies among my subjects, raised by such as have attempted against my authority; therfor, I will desire you to persuade all my subjects to obedience, and that ye yourselves will obey my lawes for good examples sake." To this it was answered that they would obey him and his lawes *so far as they agreed with the Law of God.* At this the King was angry, his face swelled, and he said:—" It's true I have made no lawes but they agree with God's lawes, and, therfor, if any of you find fault, tell me now," at the which they keeped all silence, only one said they wer not privy to the making of those lawes; to which the King said he did not think them worthy, and with this, after many high and severe words wer spoken, they wer sent to the chappell. In a litle the Archbishop called out to them, and desired them to attend at the Exchecquer Hous to-morrow, and receive their assignations. So, about 6 at night, they wer dismissed. Many of them wer dissatisfyed with themselves, that they had not entered into particulars, and told the King the lawes wer against God's Word; and they resolved to-morrow to give in their minds in write, but a lost season for a duty is not soon recovered, and matters took another turn ere the morrow.

That night, after they wer dismissed, the Council, at the Archbishop's motion, agreed to require the whole ministers to subscribe the following declaration, bond, and obligation:—

"We, the Beneficed Men, Ministers, Readers, and Masters of Colledges, testify and promise by thir our hand writes, our humble and dutifull submission and fidelity to our Soveraign Lord, the King's

Majesty, and to obey with all humility his Highnes' Acts of his late Parliament, holden at Edinburgh, the 22 of May, Anno 1584 years, and that, according to the same, we shall show our obedience to our Ordinary, the Bishop or Commissioner appointed, or to be appointed, by his Majesty to have exercise of the spiritual jurisdiction in our Diocie, and in case of our inobedience in the promises, our beneficers, livings, and stipends to vaik *ipso facto*, and qualifyed and obedient persons to be provided in our rooms, as if we wer naturally dead."

Next day, November 17, the ministers wer called, and this bond read to them, in order to subscription. A great number hearing of it compeared not. Those who compeared refused peremptorily to subscribe it, save those whose names follow: Mr. George Hepburn, Parson of Hawick; Mr. Alexr. Hume, Parson of Dumbar, a relation of Bishop Adamson's; Mr. Patrick Gait, Parson of Dunce; Mr. G   Ramsay, Dean of Restalrig; Mr. Walter Hay, Provost of Baithans; Mr. James Hamilton, Minister of Ratho; Alexander Forrester, Minister of Tranent; Alexander Lauder, Minister of Lauther; Michael Boukle, Minister of Tranent; Mr. Cuthbert Boukle, Minister of Spot; Thomas Daill, Minister of Stentoun; with diverse readers, who wer old preists before.

Nov. 23, a proclamation was published, bearing "that, whereas His Majesty had called in the ministry in the Dioces of Saint Andrews to subscribe his obedience, and Acts of Parliament—specially those made in the last Parliament, at Edinburgh, May 22, 1584—the which the most part had refused, howbeit certain of the most learned and wise had obeyed (Mr. Calderwood observes this was not fact, and they wer both unlearned and hirelings): therefor, His Majesty discharges the payment of any of their stipends who refused, and requires the Collector-Generall to intromitt with and take them all up for his use". In this proclamation Messrs. Robert Pont, Adam Johnstoun, Niccol Dalgleish, William Pourie, Andrew Simson, Patrick Simson (his son), John Clappertoun, John Craig, and Patrick Kinlowrie[1] were summoned to compear befor the King and Council, and give in their reasons why they would not subscribe.

The Bishop's designe was particularly to reach Messrs. Pont, Johnstoun, Dalgleish, and Clappertoun, whom he reconed most constant in this course, though there wer many others so as well as they. They

[1] Note 26.

all compeared. Mr. Pont, Johnstoun, and Dalgleish wer warded before. Upon Munday, when they compeared, the King, in great wrath and with many harsh words, enquired why they would not subscribe his statutes? They answered they had reasons for this, otherwise they would not have disobeyed, and humbly desired they might be superceded two or 3 days, that they might collect their reasons together, and with one consent give them in, subscribed with all their hands. The Bishop refused to grant this, and consequently the King would not hear of it, and everyone wer required presently to give them in; so many of them as had them in write gave them in. The King told them they should have a full resolution in all their doubts upon Thursday. The Archbishop prepared an answer in write, and upon Thursday ther wer only present the Minister of Linlithgow, his schoolmaster, Mr. Andrew Simson, and his son. The Bishop began to read his answers, to every head of which the ministers offered to reply, but the King would not allow, and caused read them over. When read, they craved a copy, that they might answer distinctly. This was refused, the Bishop being unwilling that his answers should come abroad. The King told them he would allow no more reasoning in that matter; and, seing he had used all lenity and gentlenes, and was not the better of it, he now assured them who would not subscribe the paper that they should not only lose their livings, but also be banished the country.

When they wer thus dismissed, all the nyne ministers resolved to cast their reasons into one papere as softly as they could, and send it by some of their number to the King, if possible to soften him in this matter. What reception it met with I know not. But Mr. Calderwood has preserved the paper itself, and it deserves a room here, being probably formed by Mr Craig:

"To our Soveraigne, the King's Majesty, and his well-advised Counsel, Messrs. John Craig, Robert Pont, Andrew Simson, Patrick Kinloghy, Nicol Dalgleish, Adam Johnstoun, John Clappertoun, William Pury, and Patrick Simson, ministers of the Evangel of Jesus Christ, and your Highnes' subjects.[1]

"The Lord our God, for His mercy's sake, grant that we may discharge our consciences faithfully, and that your Majesty may hear us

[1] Note 27.

with clemency and patience, and follow the rule of equity according to the Word in all your Highnes' proceedings, to the glory of His name, satisfying the hearts of the godly, and advancement of the Kingdom of His Son, Jesus Christ, our only Lord and Saviour. Amen.

"We render thanks unto our God alwise in our prayers, that it hath pleased him to move your Highnes' heart with clemency to hear us, our reasons and alledgeances, wherby we are moved to make scruple and doubt to subscribe a certain letter and obligation offered to some of our bretheren to subscribe, concerning obedience to be given to Patrick, Archbishop of Saint Andrews, their alledged Ordinar, and obedience to your Highnes' lawes, as at more lenth is conteaned in that writing. For we are persuaded by this, your Majesty's gentle dealing, your Highnes' mind to be alwise to give way to the truth, and to have respect unto the equity of our cause, and not to the persons among whom this controversy is moved,—in which mind, we pray the Lord to continou your Majesty to the end. But we marvail not a litle, and cannot pass it over in silence, that we and our bretheren (who mean trulie) are traduced and blazoned in publick places and at market crosses as seditious persons, restles spirits, troublers of your Highnes' Commonwealth, and disobeyers of your Majesty's lawes. Far be it from us to committ any such thing, wherby we may be so justly accused. But, seing your Majesty's good mind towards us in the same, willing us to put our mind in write, and wishing us to be resolved of all scrouple in this weighty matter of our consciences, we will suppose those ill-favoured and slanderous termes to come rather from the penner of the letter, or some sinistrous information given to him by such as love us not, nor the glory of our God (whose name we profess, and whose servants, though unworthy, we avow ourselves to be), than of your Majesty and well-advised Counsell. We will leave that matter to the Righteous Judge, Who knoweth the secrets of all our hearts; and, as concerning our dutifull obedience to your Highnes, we trust that ther is none of us but, after our small powr, have given proof and declaration therof to the wordle at all times, and purpose to continou.

"Now to the matter wherfor we are called. First, we protest in so far as we, only a few number of the ministry, are charged to make answer in this weighty matter, that whatsoever we shall answer therin be not prejudiciall to our bretheren, and we will desire your Majesty most earnestly, in the fear of our God, to give license to all the whole Assembly of the Kirk within your Highnes' Realme, that be the commone consent, this cause concerning the whole policy and order of the Kirk may be entreated and reasoned; and that liberty may be granted to all those of the ministry, who are not here now, to reason in this matter, and cannot otherwise be justly accused, but in so far as they resist the new brought in tyranny of the bishops, and labour for the maintenance of the true discipline of the Kirk, that they may be present at such a day as your Majesty pleaseth to appoint for that effect. But if we always shall be constrained instantly to answer for our parts, although we be most willing to satisfy your Majesty, so far as beeth in us, yet we think it very strange that we should be charged with subscriptions of the lawes and Acts of Parliament, seing it was never required before of no subject within this Realme; and we being leidges unto your Majesty, if we offend against the lawes, we may be punished according to the lawes. And many lawes there be and statutes of Parliament that never pass in practise, because they are not thought expedient for the common weal, and are revocable at the will of the Prince and Estate, and, therfor, to urge us with this new form of subscription, we suppose it not to be your Majesty's will, being well advised.

"Secondly, if so be your Majesty will urge us to subscribe your cause, we offer with obedience also most humbly in that part, by a generall obligation, adding alwise this one clause, *agreable to God's Word*, which obedience was offered to your Majesty when the ministers were called last before your Highnes by some, in the name of the rest, and your Majesty promised to seek no further from us.

"Thirdly, as touching the intitulat Archbishop of Saint Andrews, called in the letter our Ordinary, we answer we cannot, in good conscience, obey him in such an office, as he pretends for thir causes following:

"First, neither the titles of archbishop or ordinary can be found agreable to the Word of God; for that word archbishop, by the interpretation therof, imports a name of superiority and lordship among the servants of God, which the Scriptures deny to be given to any man in the spirituall regiment of the Kirk, as though they should usurp ambition and superiority over their bretheren's faith and consciences, who are ministers with them of the true Word of God, seing that office appertaineth to Christ alone. And concerning the apellation and name of ordinar, we cannot find it in the Scriptures nor in any godlie writers, but only in the Pope's decrees and Canon Law; which Papisticall constitutions and jurisdictions are utterly abrogat furth of this Realme be the Acts of Parliament holden as well in your Majesty's mother's, as in the first year of your Highnes' own reign. And because those monstrous titles of superiority in the Kirk of God, engendered the Popedoms, and is like to engender a new litle Popedome in your Highnes' Realme; being once reformed according to the Word of God and sincerity therof, we cannot, in good conscience, yield or give place to such ambitious titles, pretended be men that seek their own ambition and greedy gains.

"But to leave the names and come to the substance of the matter itself, we say and affirm, holding us upon the ground of God's Word and eternall truth, that it's against the Scripture for a man to claim superiority above his brether, who are yoak-fellowes with him in the ministry and office of teaching; for this name ἐπίσκοπος, which we call bishop, is interpreted an overseer of the flock of God; and this office is all one with the office of ministers, who are all overseers of the flock of God likewise. This is proven by the admonition of St. Paul to the elders of the Kirk of Ephesus, whom he called all ἐπισκόπους in the 20th of the Acts; and in the salutation of the Epistle to the Philippians, he salutes the bishops, all the pastors of that Kirk; and unto Titus he writes that he should constitute elders throughout the cities of Crete, whom immediatly therafter he calleth bishops. Swa that it's plain be the Scriptures, elders and bishops are *synonyma*, and the office all one. So that if the said bishops, that now would move your Majesty to alter the order of the Kirk, of before already established within your Highnes' Realme, and increasing with great fruit of good discipline, would contend with us, and make the Word of God judge (as it should be in matters of religion), we doubt not but our cause should be easily won. But because they leave the Scriptures and fly to consuetude, alledging it to be an old custome that bishops have been superiors to the rest of those who are called *presbiteri* we deny not but this hath been an old error; but we deny that therfor it should be reteaned now in the Kirk of God; for an evil consuetude the elder it be it is the worse; and, seing it is not agreable to the Scripture, it ought to be abrogated, as is plain by the authorities cited in the 8 Distinction of Gratian. And wheras those men would have your Majesty to follow the custome of other countrys in that behalf, in placing bishops above the rest of the ministry, although the argument and example seem plausible at the first face, yet if the matter be rightly considered, they labour to derogate a great part of your Highnes' honour in that point, and to stain that nottable fame which your Majesty and your Realme embraced and received with more purity and sincerity in Scotland than many other realmes. And, seing the order of discipline which was put in practise with so great fruit those years by past, was most agreable to God's Word, and the Kirk therby reteaned in quietnes and good order without any schisme, those men who ambitiously and seditiously would bring in a new order, or rather misorder, not being agreable nor avowable according to God's Word, ought not to be heard; neither claiming to such preheminency above their bretheren, to be received nor admitted. For is it not a great honour and prerogative to your Highnes that other countrys should receive from your Realme, and the practise therof, the pattern and example of good government and well-reformed order in the Kirk? And, by the contrair, is it not a great misliking to all godly hearts, to hear tell that your Majesty, being so brought up in the fear of God, even from your infancy, should now decline to the corruptions of other countries, and from the better to the worse; altering that good order of discipline and ecclesiasticall government which has been received and used of before according to God's Word, and bring in place therof, at the appetite of some ambitious and greedy men, a new form of ecclesiasticall government taken from the pudle of men's traditions and corruptions of other countries? For all that these men can say for mentainance of this kind of tyranny over the Kirk of God, is, that that sort hath been observed in many countries for a long time; that bishops have had the government of the Kirk in such sort as they would have them to be, and produce certain old writers for proving the same, as Epiphanius and others. To the which we answer, that the authority of men cannot be of so great weight as to diminish the truth of the Word of God; and the reasons Epiphanius brings in (although we reverence him otherwise, as any other ancient doctor of the Kirk) are of so little weight in that point that very babes may easily refute the same. And wheras they alledge out of Jerome that to take away schisme and confusions out of the Kirk, those kind of bishops wer brought in to have superiority in the same; giving it was so, we deny they wer such kind of bishops as those men desire to be, that in Jerom's day, as wer placed in the Kirk. For it's manifest by ancient writers that the bishops which then wer, used no office in the Kirk themselves alone, but did all things be advice of their presbytries, as Cyprian testifyes of himself in his Epistles; and it was for cause of order only, as he speaks, that one was constitut out of the presbyterie to gather votes and moderate the whole action and course of ecclesiastical discipline and government: which thing hitherto hath been observed in our Assembly. And if, for removing of schismes, such bishops wer first constitute, as they affirm, for the same cause now they ought to be discharged; for ther wer no schismes or divisions in minds in the Kirk reformed within this Country, till those by claiming to themselves the chief places and superiority above others, had brought it in. And yet, if it will please your Majesty to suffer the former order and policy which was in our Kirk, agreable to The Word and practise of the primitive Kirk, to stand, all schisme and division among us would be easily taken away. And, further, we have to say in special against the person of Patrick, called Bishop or Archbishop of Saint Andrews, that though it wer lawfull for us to render obedience to such bishops, we cannot submit ourselves to him nor to his injunctions; for he is for just causes lawfully suspended from all office and functions in the Kirk, by decreet of the General Assembly, which then, by the lawes of the Realme, had place, the which decreet he hath never sought to be retreated.[1] And as to your Majesty's other Commissioners to be deput in ecclesiasticall causes, we can say nothing to them till we know what they are to be deputed be your Majesty; for if it be concerning temporall affairs and rents of the Kirk, we regard not much who be deput therin; but if it be concerning matters of conscience, and those things that properly pertain to the Kirk, [et] *ad spiritualem jurisdictionem ecclesiae*, we cannot be the Word acknowledge other judges, but such as have the spirituall sword, the Word of God committed to them by the same Word, who are ministers therof, and constitut in ecclesiasticall function: for the keyes of the Kingdom of Heaven, with power to bind and to lose in matters of conscience, are not given by our Master, Jesus

[1] Note 28.

Christ, to civil magistrates or their deputes, but to the Apostles and their lawfull successors, as is manifest be the Scriptures.

"Sir, it will please your Majesty to consider and take in good part those our few reasons, which, for the shortnes of time, we offer most humbly, with this our writing, leaving to amplify the same further at this time lest we should fash your Grace and Councill; hoping alwise that after the diligent weighing of our cause, your Grace and all good hearts shall be satisfyed. For ther is nothing to us so dear under that obedience which we owe to our God (Who, of necessity, must have the first place) than next to render all obedience to your Majesty and your Highnes' good lawes; and we will presume in your Highnes' clemency to find the like favour as the Christians found of Constantius, father of Constantine the Great, who, being but half a Christian, and who never publickly by the law received true religion, set forth an edict commanding all Christians that bore any publick office under him to refuse or renounce their religion, or else to give over their honnours, offices, and stipends perteaning therunto. But, finally, he reteaned them in office who would rather yeild the temperall commodity willingly, rather than give over their religion, and deposed the other sort, saying this nottable sentence: *That they who wer not true to God would never be true to man.* Sir, your Majesty knowes what we mean. The Lord, for His mercy's sake, direct your Highnes' heart unto the best, as we hope assuredly He will, to Whom be all praise and glory for ever. Amen."

Though those worthy persons stood firm, some of them made complyances, as we shall see; and a great number of the ministry discovered much weaknes in this time of tentation, yet many of the ministry stood by their principles. Mr. James Melvil at this time was at Berwick with the Earles of Angus and Marr and other forfaulted lords and gentlemen, and having accounts of what passed at this time, and the defection of so many, he wrot and sent copys of "A letter to the bretheren of the ministry of Scotland who have lately subscribed to the Popish supremacy of the King and ambitious tyranny of the bishops over their bretheren".[1] At the same time he sent a letter in Latine, with the controversy gathered up in some few conclusions, confirmed with manifold reasons and Scriptures, to Mr. Alex. Hume, Minister at Dunbar, provocking him to answer it if he could; and, if not, to

[1] Note 29.

desire the Archbishop, his Ordinary, to answer it himself. Those going abroad in written copyes did much to confirm the bretheren, and helped to convince some that wer fallen. Mr. James Robertson, now a student, and afterward minister at Dundee, and Mr. John Caldclough, for transcribing them, wer forced to fly, and wer enterteaned kindly at Berwick, as also William Aird, a very singular person, of whom, if I can find materialls, I shall give some hints by himself.[1]

Ther wer likewise at this time spread some *Short reasons for not consenting to the generall charge of obeying the ordinary, with some doubts arising from the Acts of Parliament;* and, since those will give us the fuller view of the grounds of ministers' sufferings at this time, I shall also here insert them, being very breif.

The reasons wer as follow: "Under this generall, *obey your ordinary*, may be conteaned many specials contrary to good conscience, as it shall please men to command for the time: therfor, the specials would be expressed and proven by the Word of God, that men may know what they approve. Befor that any innovation be made in the policy of the Kirk, already concluded on by common consent, the General Assembly of ministers would be gathered, wher things in controversy may be openly and freely debated, and decerned to be received or refused in time coming. To begin at particular men (before the Generall Assembly of ministers would be charged) with such a weighty matter, is ready to hurt the consciences of the ignorant, and give occasion of schisme in the Kirk—open a door to hypocrites, and close the mouths of the godly. Those men who crave obedience of us in ecclesiasticall matters have no spirituall jurisdiction in the Kirk at this present, nor ever had in our time such obedience as is now craved. The Confession of our Faith, which we have ratifyed, and the Confession of Helvetia[2] damned this estate, to the which we and many other Kirks in Europe have subscribed, for the manifold corruptions found in that estate. The name archbishop and bishop, given to them only, agreeth not with the Word of God. Their whole estate was devised by man, taken from the profane idolators, and was the fundation of the Roman Primacy. They claim authority and jurisdiction over ministers, and use wordly and ambitious titles, and confound the two jurisdictions, without the

[1] Note 30.   [2] Note 31.

warrand of the Word of God. They are pastors without a flock, and exeemed from the discipline of the Kirk. In the primitive time one town had many bishops, but now ambition and greedines hath given one to the whole province, and many to the archbishop. For what cause? Sure, not for the comfort of the Kirk, but to make those men great, ritch, and honnourable in the wordle. They would apparently usurp to themselves the election, examination, institution, and deposition of ministers, which things appertean only to the eldership of the Kirk, and not to one of them or any others made by man's device. How can those men excuse themselves in God's presence, who with us subscribed the Form of Discipline and promised obedience to the Kirk, and now they will break their promise, and impose over the Kirk before they discharge themselves of the same? It's not reasonable that we follow their defection without the knowledge of the Kirk, and discharge of our promise made to the same; otherwise, who shall credit us in time coming, or belive our preachings, seing we damne our 20 years' preachings made before. In what estate shall we be also, if this policy shall be changed afterward? Shall we not change then again with men? We are falsely bruited that we will have a popular confusion, and grant no care of religion to the Prince, and take his authority, raise sedition in the country to help his rebels, and live as without law. We protest before God and man we never meaned such things, and shall be ready at all times to purge ourselves of such calumnies. But if our purgations cannot be heard, then we remitt our cause to the Eternall God, Whose judgment cannot err."

The doubts rising from the Acts of Parliament wer those: "As to the first Act, we cannot understand for what cause the correct ecclesiasticall with the whole proces of excommunication is taken from the whole Presbitry. As to the 2d Act—that the King of Scotland shall have heretable right to judge and pronounce of the contraversys of faith, religion, and interpretation of Scripture, with their Council—was never heard of in the Kirk of God before. Next of this, it shall follow that no subject may, of conscience, refuse to receive the religion that his Prince doth approve, under the pain of perjury, seing the Prince craveth his own heretable right in this part. As to the 4th Act, the Kirk hath liberty to conveen for all the lawfull affairs of the same, and that of God, without any injury of the Prince,—as may be proven by the examples of the Prophets, Christ, and His Apostles. The same we speak of ecclesiasticall judgment, which God has committed to His ministers, without any condition of the goodwill of any inferiors; for the vassall cannot discharge the command of his superior, and if he do it, his discharge is null. How much less can mortall men discharge God's command to be execute! As to the 5th Act, it is repugnant to the Word of God that any sort of men professing God's true religion shall be exeemed from the common discipline of the Kirk. As to the 20 Act, seing that princes have not the spirituall jurisdiction given them by God, we see not how they can give it to others. They may communicat their civil jurisdiction to whom they please, but not to them that have spirituall jurisdictions, least the jurisdictions be confounded in one person."

Those and the like papers, being now in many hands, keeped not a few from complying with the King and Bishop's designs. The King and Court saw that unless they could break the ministry among themselves, and bring over some persons of reputation to signe this paper now imposed—even tho some allowances wer made of a kind of explication—they could not cary through their designes. Mr. Craige was principally in their eye, to carry him off to their side, if possible. He was a person of an excellent temper; if he had any exces, it was that he was too easy. They took hold upon an expression in the reasons above set down, seeming to purport they wer willing to subscribe with this restriction, *according to the Word of God*, and offered to allow him to add this to his subscription. His bretheren—Mr. Pont, Simson, &c.—wer backward; at lenth, by importunity and the great weight of the King and Court, and by many specious pretences, Mr. John Craig and Duncanson, the King's Ministers, and John Brand, Minister of Hollyrood house, wer prevailed with to signe the above-mentioned bond, adding only this clause, *according to the Word of God*; and when Mr. Craig was thus engaged, he was made use of by the King as a tool to bring other ministers to subscribe; and toward the end of December, 1584, he wrote the following letter, to persuade others to follow his example, which was carefully spread by the Bishop of Saint Andrews among the ministry to corrupt them, with the King's postscript:

"Bretheren, after my hearty commendation, I doubt not but you have either heard, or will hear shortly, how John Duncanson and I have subscribed the obligation of obedience to the King's Majesty and Commissioners, according to the Act of Parliament; wherof, because sinister reports may pass, both of the King's Majesty's commanding and us obeying, I thought good to make you privy to the samine. It pleased his Majesty to grant John Duncanson and me to conferr with him privily, and therafter with my Lords Arran and Secretary, his Majesty being present in the Cabinet, wherafter reasons heard and proponed on every side, two heads wer agreed upon, that by our subscription was not here sought to be allowance either of Acts of Parliament or Estate of Bishops, but to be a testimony of our obedience to his Majesty. Next, it was not craved, but *according to the Word of God*, and, therfor, our obedience conteans nothing but our obedience to the King's Majesty, his lawes, and Commissioners according to the Word of God: which heads are so reasonable that no man can refuse the samine who loves God or the quietnes of the Kirk or Commonwealth. Therfor, I pray you to show this to the bretheren, whom ye may advertish, either by word or write, that they, being informed of the good meaning of his Majesty, may be conformable to the samine, to the end that the Evangell having free passage with powr and quietnes, evil effected persons, who of the schisme of the Kirk or Commonwealth make their advantage, may be frustrat of their expectation."

Rex.

P.S.—"We declare, by thir presents, that this letter within conteaned, was written with our knowledge and directed at our command, to certify all men of our good meaning, that none should have occasion to doubt of the same."

Thus, Mr. Craig was made a coy-duke to draw others in. Too many wer content of any collour to bind the eyes of the people, others went in, as no doubt Mr. Craig did, in the simplicity of their heart, not observing the sophistry of the clause. It might easily have been seen that the added clause was repugnant to the matter and argument of the bond, and *protestatio contraria facto*. They might as well have promised to obey the Pope and his prelates according to God's Word, yet severall wer prevailed with to subscribe with this explication. Mr. Calderwood, in his printed History, has Mr. Archibald Simson's form in which he subscribed, which was acepted, the court being earnest to have in ministers of reputation, at any rate almost, yet many refused and wer warded.

Innovations, impositions, and corruptions in their very nature grow, especially when they are yielded to in any measure. In January, 1585, a new charge was given to ministers to subscribe, and new injunctions from the King and Council, but really from the Archbishop, wer laid before his Diocesan Synod at Edinburgh, in February, conteaning new hardships. These, not being published by any of our historians, I shall insert here from Calderwood's MS., and they are as followes :—

"Articles to be observed by all preachers of the Word and office-bearers in the Kirk within this Realme.

"All the preachers and office-bearers within the Kirk, as well as for conscience sake as for their duty, shall, with all humility, yield their obedience to the King's Majesty, and observe and obey all his commandments and lawes, made and to be made, not directly repugnant to the Word of God.

"They, nor none of them, shall pretend to immunity or privilege in their alledgeance, nor appeal from his Majesty to any other judge or jurisdiction, for the tryall, censure, or punishment of whatsoever things in whatsoever place they speak or do, that may concern his Majesty in honour or surety.

"And, therfor, they nor none of them shall medle with matters of state or civil besides their calling, but alwise contean themselves, both in life and in doctrine, within the bounds of their charge and function.

"And so they, nor none of them, shall publickly rebuke nor in any wise revile his Majesty, nor declaim against his Majesty's person, estate, Council, or lawes, but shall signify greives by his Majesty himself in privat, and crave most humbly remeed therof, by the ordinary and lawfull means.

"They, and every ane of them, in publick doctrine and privat speeches shall speak reverendly of his Majesty's person, Counsell, and lawes, and to their outmost travell to contean the whole subjects in their due obedience to his Highnes, preach the same at all occasions, and what in them lyeth, to observe the publick peace, and abstean from all things, as well in doctrine as example, that may publickly or privatly, directly or indirectly, withdraw the hearts of the people from the due obedience, love, and reverence they owe to his Majesty, or that anywise may disturb the common quietnes.

"They shall abstean from all faction, monopoly, privy preaching by the commone order, in publick or privy places, or any quiet conventicles, thereby to make any of the subjects conceive that any persecution is intended or used against them, to a misliking of any of the King's proceedings.

"They, nor none of them, shall alledge the inspirations of the Holy Spirit (except so far as it agrees with the express Scripture), either when they are accused upon any of their facts and speeches, or when they will do, or refuse to do, such things as want express warrandize of the Word, so to do or so to refuse. But be the contrair, when they offend, and are taxed therof, not to be ashamed truly to grant their offences as men, and humbly crave pardon as subjects; nor fence themselves with the collour of conscience to do or refuse such things, that they want good reason for so to do or to refuse."

Severall things here no good man would have refused, but then many things are throwen in destructive to the freedome of doctrine and preaching the Gospell, and nobody ought to inferr that ministers, now or formerly, wer guilty of thir gross things insinuat, and cunningly enough supposed in those injunctions. Indeed, such groundles reports wer spread by Bishop Adamson and others as to ministers' freedom in their sermons and speeches, and from those malicious reports, and not from facts, came those injunctions, which some say wer formed by the Secretary. And did they suppose facts would be a real lyebel upon the ministry who, generally speaking, wer prudent, wise, and legall, and farr from such things as are insinuat here. Whither Mr. Craig, and the other former subscribers, swallowed those, I cannot tell. I hope not, for one wrong step is enough, though declinings and complyances, especially in ministers, with corruptions, are not oft single. By letters from Mr. David Hume to Mr. James Carmichael, from Berwick, Aprile this year, I find that all betwixt Berwick and Stirling, who had not subscribed the bond he speaks of with the injunctions, wer:—
" Mr. R. Pont, Nichol Dalgleish, Adam Johnstoun, Patrick Simson, John Hall, Thomas Makgie, John Cairns, Thomson at Leith, James Lamb. In the Merse—John Clappertoun, John Hume, Robert French, William

Carroll, Andrew Winchester. In Teviotdale—John Knox, Michael Cranstoun, Robert Ker, George Johnstoun, and William Balfour. In Fyfe—David Ferguson, John Dykes, Mr. Thomas Buchanan. The north was brought in by the Laird of Dun to subscribe, as is reported. Some said John Dury had complyed and Mr. David Lindsay, but of that ther is no certainty.[1] Mr. John Brand is touched with sorrow for his subscribing, and the rather that Mr. Craig's and his example brought in others. The Presbitry of Air subscribed with a protestation, in the hands of a publick nottar, that they dissented from some of the Acts of Parliament, which they call devilish, and are to be prosecut, as they had not subscribed." Those are what hints I meet with in those letters relative to this matter. In a list of ministers warded because of their suspected correspondence with the Lords in England, I find Mr. John Cowpar, Mr. Andrew Hunter, Mr. Thomas Storie, James Gibson in Pencaitland, David Hume of Coldingham, Mr. James Robertson, Mr. John Condon, Mr. James Balcanquell, Mr. Archibald Moncreif, Mr. Robert Durie, Mr. James Hamiltoun, Mr. John Howeson, Mr. Andrew Hay, named as non-subscribers, and Mr. Robert Boyd, perhaps, of Trochrodge.[2]

Thus, I have enlarged a litle upon this first set of suffering ministers since the Reformation, because very litle is knowen as to the hardships put upon them and the grounds of their suffering, which pretty much agree with what befell far greater numbers afterwards, after the King had forced in Prelacy upon us by degrees. This was but a short cloud, and gradually scattered next year, 1585, when the King was delivered by the Earles of Angus and Marr and the rest of the forfeited lords, from Arran's servitude, and an end put to thir impositions for a time, and the banished ministers and others came home. In December a Parliament was holden, and some former wrong steps rectifyed. A great many ministers convened while it sat, but got litle done. Mr. Craig had a sermon befor the King and Parliament, wherin he used some bitter expressions against the ministers that refused to subscribe the bond, as qualifyed in his letter, which, he said, he was led to in self-defence by a sermon Mr. J. Gybson had in Edinburgh about that time condemning the subscribers, wherof Mr. Craig was the cheife. This was like to have ill consequents among the

[1] Note 32. [2] Note 33.

ministers at the next Assembly, had not calm and healing measures been fallen upon for overlooking what had passed in times of trouble, temptation, and confusion, to which the King's declaration upon and explication of his meaning in the Acts of Parliament against the jurisdiction of the Kirk, set down at lenth in our printed historians, contributed very much, and I find Mr. Craig, when matters wer cooled, becam sensible of his oversight and acknowledged so much, as did severall other good men, who fainted in this dark hour, and he and they concurred heartily in the common work of the Church, and a vail of charity and love was cast over all former slips, and indeed for 10 years after this the Church of Scotland had a most bright and glorious day following on this dark night.

The next thing as to Mr. Craig that offers is that short and usefull Catechisme he formed at the appointment of the Assembly. It's printed in the 2d volume of our Confessions and the Acts of Assembly relative to it, from the MS. Register, which I shall resume in short. The Assembly, 1590, find it necessary that ane uniform order be keeped in the examination of people, and appoint a short form to be set down by Mr. John Craig, Mr. R. Pont, T. Buchanan, and Andrew Melvil. Next year, July, 1591, Mr. Craig presents it, and the Assembly order Mr. Craig to print it, after he has contracted it; and May, 1592, after it's printed it's allowed by the whole voice of the Assembly, and ministers are ordered to deal with their people to buy it and read it, and it's appointed to be read and learned in schools, in room of the litle Catechisme, that is, *The manner to examine children*, at the end of Calvin's Catechisme, formerly approved by this Church.[1] Let me only take nottice here further of a glaring mistake of the Honourable Mr. Archibald Campbell, in his preface to his extraordinary book of the Midle State, Fol. 1721. [At] p. 9, he pretends to do justice to the Scots Presbyterians in haling them into his out of the way notions of the Holy Eucharist, and to support his complement to us he cites two editions of Mr. Craig's Catechisme in his hands, printed Edinburgh, 1581, that is nyne or ten year befor the Assembly or Mr. Craig thought upon forming this Catechisme. The words he cites, I assure him and others, are not in Walgrave's edition, 1591 or 2, and I suspect mightily Mr. Campbelles has mistaken Mr. Craig's Catechism for some old Popish

[1] Note 34.

Catechisme printed long before Mr. Craige's.[1] Whatever be in this, if he consider Mr. Calvin's Catechisme and the Palatine Catechisme, both approven by our Assemblys, the Catechismes of Scots Presbiterians,[2] as well as Mr. Craig's, he'l find there what he calls the doctrine of mere remembrance, though the term, in my opinion, is unwarry and unguarded, and what the Church of Scotland, as far as I mind, has not used.

Very litle offers further about this great and good man. He was now about 80 years of age, and his holy zeal against what apeared sinfull was not abated. In December, 1591, the King very narrowly escaped an attempt made upon him by the Earle of Bothwell, as our printed historians observe. Next day, December 28, the King came up to the great Church of Edinburgh to give publick thanks for his deliverance. After Mr. Galloway's sermon, the King had a discourse to the people, showing Bothwell's ingratitude in seeking his life by poison, witchcraft, and now by great violence, after all favours he had heaped on him, and thanked the town of Edinburgh for their help, when he was attacked. Next day Mr. Craig, justly thinking this a proper season for setting home guilt on the King and courteours' consciences, when God had so mercifully delivered them from Bothwell, in his sermon before the King, upon the two brazen mountains in Zechariah, took nottice that his Majesty, and those about him, had not duly punished the sin of murder, and too lightly regarded the bloody shirts presented to him by his subjects (pointing at what had been done in Edinburgh, as our printed historians narrat, after the barbarous murder of the Earle of Murray and others, not long since comitted, which the King neglected to enquire into), and so God, in His providence had brought a noise of crying and fore-hammers to his own dores, which was at Bothwell's attempt upon Hollyroodhous. After [the] pronouncing [of] the blessing, the King rose up and desired the people to stay that he might purge himself, which he endeavoured to do, and added, if he had thought his feed servant (meaning Mr. Craig) would have dealt after that manner with him, he would not have suffered him so long in his house. Old Mr. Craig, for the noise and people, did not hear what the King said, and went his way, and ther was no more of it. Age and infirmity, in a few years, laid Mr. Craig aside from publick work. In the Assembly,

[1] Note 35.   [2] Note 36.

1593, the King desires the Assembly to give him a list of 5 or six of the discreetest of the ministry, that he may choice two to serve in his house, in respect of Mr. Craig's decripped age, which the Assembly agreed to, and order the Commissioners appointed to wait on his Majesty to do so. It seems this was delayed yet for two years, for in the Assembly, July, 1595, one of the King's articles is "in respect Mr. Craig is waiting what hour it shall please God to call him, and is altogether unable to serve any longer, and his Majesty mindeth to place John Duncanson with the Prince, and so hath no ministers but Mr. P. Galloway,[1] therfor, his Highnes desires an order to be made granting him any two ministers he shall chuse." This they grant, and leave to the Commissioners named by them. Bishop Spotswood tells us Mr. Craig died Dec. 12, 1600, without any pain and in peace, at Edinburgh, in the 88 year of his age, and Mr. Row, upon the year 1601, "in respect of Mr. Craig his death, and Mr. Jo Duncanson's great age, at his Majesty's desires, the Kirk named as ministers for the King, Queen, and Prince's house, Mr. Henry Blyth, John Fairfoul, Peter Ewart, Andrew Lamb, James Nicholson, James Law, and John Spotswood,'' persons generally of another character than the former ministers there.[2]

Bishop Spotswood gives this character of Mr. Craig, and that very justly. "That while he lived he was held in great esteem. He was a great divine, an excellent preacher, of a grave behaviour, sincere, inclining to no faction, and which increased his reputation, living honestly, without ostentation or desire of outward glory." Mr. Charters,[3] in his short hints, sayes he had been once a Dominican, but turned Protestant, and became Minister of Halyroodhouse. He wrot a form of examination before the communion, Edinburgh, 8vo, 1581, wher he was in Mr. A. Campbell's mistake. I shall conclude with Mr. Livingstoun's account of him in his MS. remarks:[4]—"Mr. John Craig, Minister at Edinburgh, he it was that penned the short Confession of Faith, or the Nationall Covenant, of the Church of Scotland. I have heard my Lord Waristoun report an history of such rare dangers and deliverys he met with when coming out of Italy, and how a dog brought him a purse with some gold, but I have forgot the particular relation."

[1] Note 37.   [2] Note 38.   [3] Note 39.   [4] Note 40.

This is all I can gather about Mr. Craig.

Mr. John Craig was married. What other children he had I know [not] but he had a very worthy and excellent person to his son, Mr. William Craig, of whom I shall drope a word here. He was educat under Mr. Rollock,[1] I suppose at Saint Andrews for his first 3 years, and when he came to Edinburgh, as Mr. T. Crawford[2] nottices, he was laureat by him, 1593. That year teaching began in the Colledge of Edinburgh. In October, 1597, upon Mr. Sands going to travail, Mr. William Craig, at Mr. Rollock's recommendation, was chosen in his room. Mr. Crawford termes him a very able and graciouse young man. He taught Philosophy with much approbation till 1601, when, in December, he demitted, and went over to France, and was elected Professor of Philosophy in the Protestant Accadamy of Saumure. Upon Boyd of Trockoroge, his life, ther are severall hints concerning Mr. Craige. He was Professor of Theology at Saumure, as well as Philosophy. Ther was a great intimacy between Trochredge and him. I suppose it began under Mr. Rollock at Edinburgh, before they went to France. By his close study he fell into a decay, and came over to Scotland, 1616, as his native air, but it did not recover him. He dyed in his oun house in the Blackfreir Wynd, in November. Trocherege calls him his friend, beloved brother, old condisciple, and colleague, Professor of Theology at Saumure. He sayes, he was grave, learned, retired, moderat, without reproach. Mr. Charters sayes he wrote *Theses Theologicae, item orationes et poemata.*

[1] Note 41.   [2] Note 42.

COLLECTIONS ON THE LIFE OF Mr. DAVID CUNNINGHAM, MINISTER AT LANARK, MONKLAND, SUB-DEAN OF GLASGOW, AND MINISTER AND BISHOP OF ABERDEEN.

I am unwilling to pass any of such as wer advanced to be bishops in this Church, since the Reformation, in this Collection, that my readers may have some view of their character, who fell in with this office, which, in the good times, especially those which followed after the Reformation from Popery, was so much disliked by the generality of ministers, and the best affected of our nobility, gentry, and common people. This Bishop was a person of learning and considerable abilitys, imployed in forraigne negociations, and reconed a person of wisdome and prudence, but seems much to have failed or been blasted in his abilitys, after his departure from what he once vigorously appeared for as truth, and in the midst of his appearance deserted openly, from what motive, it's only to guess. I shall put together what I meet with about him in Mr. Calderwood's MS., Mr. James Melvil's Life, and some other papers come to my hand.

His parentage and education I find nothing about, if he was Minister at Lanark, 1562. He has been educat under Popery, to be sure. He seems to have been born in Clydsdale or Renfrewshire, and in that case would be educat at Glasgow. But the state of that seminary of learning was quite neglected under the last Popish archbishops, and it's at the next dore to a totall ruin at the Reformation, and till Mr. And. Melvill reeneued it, 1574. It's not improbable Mr. Cunningham was in orders before the Reformation, and, it may be, abroad in his travails, wher he got the knowledge of the truth, and when he returned to his native country, he struck in heartily with it, and that leads me to add—

That, in the Roll of the General Assembly, June, 1562, which

Mr. Calderwood has preserved, I find one, whom I take to be the same with the Bishop, David Cunninghame, Minister at Lanark, member of that Assembly. He is not named among those whom our first Assembly, December, 1561, declare fitt to be ministers and teachers; and the Superintendants, I recon, had as yet received few or none to the ministry; and all others I find ministers, I guess, wer in orders under Popery, or had received them in England. Mr. Cunningham did not long continue Minister at Lanark, probably for want of encouragement; for, in the 1567, I find another Minister there, who likewise wanted encouragement, and Mr. David Weems is ordered by the Assembly to allow him to remove, if he cannot prevail for his suitable maintenance; as is to be seen in Mr. Weems' Life.[1]

Probably he came from Lanark to the parish of Munkland, a few miles from Glasgow, and there I find him, 1573, in the General Assembly, which mett in Agust. I find him with some others appointed to visit the books of bishops and commissioners; and Mr. Pont, Mr. Row, Mr. Garden, and Mr. David Cunninghame, Minister at Monkland, are appointed to form the instructions to be given to the ministers appointed to conferr with the Regent, anent the distribution of ministers, providing stipends and other things not yet ended between His Grace and the Kirk. After this, I find him much imployed in our Assemblys.

Mr. Cunningham went on with Mr. Andrew Melvil and others, at this time, with a great deal of vigour in opposing the Tulchan Bishops, and endeavour to help that scrape which was fallen into by the Earle of Mortoun's influence at the Convention at Leith, before Mr. Melvil came to Scotland, and when Mr. Knox was much confyned to his room.[2] And as soon as Mr. Melvil came west to Glasgow, Mr. Cunningham fell intirely in with him, and was very active in framing the 2nd Book of Discipline. In the Assembly, Aprile, 1576, an Act was made, ordeaning the Tulchan Bishops, and all others who had the title of bishops, to take themselves to the charge of some one congregation, and appointing a good number of commissioners and visitors to the particular bounds, wher the bishops before had the inspection and the superintendance, as also for those parts, wher ther wer neither superintendants or nominal bishops. And this every

[1] Note 43.   [2] Note 44.

Assembly continowes to do till the 1602. At this Assembly they agree upon pretty large instructions to visitors, which stans in the printed Calderwood, and Mr. Andrew Hay and Mr. David Cunninghame are appointed Visitors of Air, Clydale, and Lennox. He is still continoued in this work for severall years.

This year, or probably some time before, Mr. David Cunningham was brought in from Monkland, to be sub-Dean of Glasgow, and I reacon Minister of that town joyntly with Mr. Weems. But of that I am not certain, the Registers of the Sessions at Glasgow, going no further back than the 1583. However, it's plain he had his house and lived in that town by what followes.

Ther had been many reasonings about the jurisdiction of the Kirk, and forming the 2nd Book of Discipline. But this Assembly, Aprile, 1576, brought that mattter to a greater bearing, as I have given larger accounts of, upon the Laird of Dun, Mr. Robert Pont, Mr. And. Melvill, and others, their Lives. Ministers in each quarter wer ordered to meet, and put their opinions on our discipline in write. For the west county, Mr. And. Melvil, Mr. Da. Cunninghame, Mr. Andrew Hay, and Mr. James Greg wer nominat. These met, together with the bretheren of the east and north, and the result was our 2nd Book of Discipline. Mr. James Melvil, in his own Life, who was present with his uncle, says :—" That this summer, 1576, the 4 bretheren for the west conveened at Glasgow, in Mr. David Cunningham's house, then sub-Dean of Glasgow, and then Dean of the Facultyes, a man of good account at that time ; none was so frank in the cause as he. He moderat the reasonings, gathered up the conclusions, and put all in write and in order, to be reported to the Assembly. Meanwhile, such was the sagacity of my uncle, Mr. Andrew, that he suspected neither he nor Mr. Patrick Adamson would prove frinds to the cause in the end ; they were so courtly ; and so it proved, indeed."

Next year, 1577, as far as I can guess, Mr. David Cunninghame left Glasgow, and became Minister to the Regent's family for a little, and next year, 1578, he was Minister of Aberdeen, Parson of Nicholas, as the writter of the Appendix to Bishop Spotswood's History termes it, and next year was made Bishop of Aberdeen, that is, had the rents of that Bishoprick conferred upon him in the title, but enjoyed a small part of them. Mr. Adamson, who had for some time deserted his ministeriall charge at Paisley, and was Minister to the Regent's family, and Mr. Cunningham wer great intimates, and when this year, 1577, Mr. Patrick accepted of the Bishoprick of Saint Andrews, it's probable he recommended his freind, Mr. Cunningham, to be his successor in the Regent's family; and soon after he came to be nominat Tulchán Bishop of Aberdeen. So much I gather from another passage in Mr. James Melvil's Life. On the year 1577, after he had given account of Mr. P. Adamson's acceptance of the Bishoprick of Saint Andrewes, he [says]: " Mr. Patrick betaking him to the Bishoprick ateans [at once], the suffragan room is filled be Mr. David Cunninghame, who leaves Glasgow and the good cause, and becomes the Regent's Minister; but with a curse accompanying him, for he had never that wealth nor estimation whilk he had before; howbeit, within a year, thereafter advanced to the Bishoprick of Aberdeen; and not only so, but after the Earle of Mortoun's execution, he became one of the miserablest wretches in all the west country, lyand, debocht, and out of all credit, in a cot house, himself at the ane syde of the fire, and his cow at the other. Thus God cursed that Bishoprick of his. As for Mr. Patrick, we will have mair adoe with him hereafter."

In the Assembly, 1577, which met in October, when, as I take it, Mr. Cunningham was brought to be Minister to the Regent's house, he is named by the Assembly in a lite of six, out of which the Regent was to chuse 3 to goo from the Church of Scotland, to assist at a Council, to be holden at Magdeburg, for establishing the Agustan Confession,[1] as is hinted on the Lives of severall of the ministers named, Mr. A. Melivil's, Mr. Adamson's, and others. However, I observe that neither he nor Mr. Adamson wer fixed on by the Regent, but Mr. A. Melvil, Mr. G. Hay, and Mr. Arbuthnet. It's probable the Earl of Mortoun had work at home for those two. All this project came to nothing by the King's taking the administration in his hand, and the Earle of Mortoun's fall next year.

Before this turn, probably, at least sometime next year, I recon Mr. Cunningham was named by the Regent to be Minister at Aberdeen, and Titular Bishop of that place. This is strenthened, though it's but my conjecture, and the writer of Bishop Spotswood's Appendix makes his

[1] Note 45.

admission 1579, but what I meet with in the Assembly Registers, which conveened June, 1578, appoint him Visitor of Aberdeen and Bamf before this time. He had still been Visitor of Clidsdale and Lennox. I recon on some pretext or other he got to be Minister of Aberdeen, and the Assembly name him Visitor: for they owned not the Tulchan Bishops so far as to give them the stile of bishops.

Those Tulchan Bishops, however, took their titles to themselves, and I have befor me a letter of the Bishop's, Jan. 24, 1580, to Robert Barton, Comptroller to the King. I have a copy of it from the Cotton Library, Caligula, B. 1. It is quotted on the back: " Bishop of Aberdeen to Robert Bartoun, Comptroller. Disliking the Queen's wilfull courses and fearing that inconveniencys will ensue thereupon." The letter runs thus: " My Lord Comptroller, I recommend me unto you right heartily, and have received your writing this Tuesday. Mister Ogilvy hath showed me, as touching these Articles, sent by my Lords here to the Queen's Grace, for the universall well of the Realme. She hath made no answer therunto, nor satisfyed with the same, the which I trust shall redound to a great inconveniency hereafter. Ye would in your said writing that I should have come into Edinburgh, and keeped my promise, that I made unto the Queen. Had I been heal and in good health, I had been there long ere this time. But seing it is so, that the Queen's Grace will follow no counsell, nor will look to the weall of the King's Highnes her son, his realme, and commonweal, I am right glad that God sent me sicknes that stoped me, for I see much appearance of much evil to come, and I had rather hear of evil than see it. I would not be in the company, wher good council is not heard, but will all [good] utterly to have domination. There's nothing may make this Realme in peace, but the unity of the Lords, and that is all utterly refused, as appears. Therefor I have marvail of you, that desires me to be there, where evill hath dominatioun, and reason oppressed, and I to incurr sclander by being in that company. I would ye ever well, and quitt of all inconvenience, and let me shift the best that I may; for I belive, within few dayes ye will hear of neuse that ye have not yet heard yet. I will follow nobody but the King's Grace and the Commonweal. God keep you. At Saint Andrews, the 24 of January.

" Your own Bushop of
" ABURDYNE."

The state of things at this time was in great confusion. D'Aubigney was come over from France. The Earle of Mortoun was this moneth accused of accession to the murder of the King's father. The Queen of England was interposing against D'Aubigney with no success, and came to that height of displeasure, as to refuse to allow a hearing to the person sent up from our King. In such circumstances, it was no wonder the Bishop, now it seems at Saint Andrews with Mr. P. Adamson, refused to come into Edinburgh, and joyn in the violent courses now carrying on against his patron, the late Regent. I guess, upon the Earle's prosecution and execution, both the Bishops of Saint Andrews and Aberdeen fell under a cloud, having been both of them Ministers to the Regent and much upon his councils, yet when they came to be better knowen to those, who had the King under their management, and after the Earle was execute, they came both into favour again, and wer made use of to manage Church affairs. However, as Mr. Melvil nottices, Bishop Cunningham, after the Earle of Mortoun's execution, was oblidged to abscond for some time in the west country, in very mean circumstances.

I meet with the Bishop again before the Assembly, which met Aprile, 1583. In the 10 Session I meet with this Act " Anent Bishops and Commissions given in the last Assembly, concerning the order to be taken with them, in respect that an oversight is found, in execution of the said Commission, on sundry occasions. Yet least that estate, so long slanderouse to the Kirk, be not overpast, as it hath been negligently, the whole Assembly hath continoued the Commission given to the bretheren concerning the Bishop of the Isles and Dunkeld. As concerning the Bishop of Aberdeen, in respect some process hath been before the Presbitry of Edinburgh against him, wher his answer hath been given in negative, and no probation led against him, the Assembly ordeaned the officer of the Assembly to warn him to compeere before the bretheren—Mr. James Lawson, Andrew Melvil, Walter Balcanquell, John Dury, John Craige, David Ferguson, Jo. Davidson, Jo. Brand—to hear witness received against him, the morn at six hours, to whom the Assembly gives power to examine, to try the saids witnesses everyone of them, upon the points denyed by the said Mr. David, and to report the probation again to the Assembly." Ther is no report made this Assembly that I observe; ther are many places about this time razed by Mr. P. Adamson. The confusions of this time wer so many, and turns so suddain, that I doubt nothing was done concerning him. During the next two years, when Mr. Adamson, his freind, managed the King, no doubt he was much in favour in Court.

At the first Assembly, after the King was taken out of the Bishop and Colonell Stewart's hands, I find him processed for a sclander of adultry. Assembly 1586, Sess. 6, "ordeans a citation to be directed forth, to summond Mr. David Cunningham, Bishop of Aberdeen, to compear before the Presbitrys of Glasgow and Stirling, the 21 day of June next to come, in the town of Stirling, wher they shall be assembled for the time, to be tryed if he be guilty of the sclander of adultry committed with Elizabeth Sutherland, or any other person, and if he shall be found by good appearance to be guilty or criminal, after the said tryall, to suspend him from the function of the ministry till the next General Assembly, and to summon him to compear before them to hear the determination of the whole bretheren theranent. And that the summonds to be directed against him be executed personally, if he can be apprehended, and failing thereof, at the Kirks of New and Old Aberdeen, and at his own dwelling-places by the Ministers of New and Old Aberdeen."

That tryall by some methods was postponned, and altogether neglected, and so in the Assembly, which meets June, 1587, Sess. 5, I make this out :—"Touching the Commission given to their bretheren of the Presbitrys of Glasgow and Stirling, to summond Mr. David Cunningham before them, to be tryed for the slander of adultry, &c., is at more lenth conteaned in' the said Commissions, wherof the execution being craved of the saids Commissioners, and certain excuses pretended by them for the non-execution therof, which the bretheren esteemed of small importance, the Assembly of new giveth and comitteth power of new to the same Presbitrys, to direct out summonds to such a short and convenient day, as is possible to him, to compear before them in Stirling, to be tryed for the said slander, either with the said Elizabeth or with any other person, and if they find him by any good appearance criminall and guilty after the said tryall, to suspend him from the function of the ministry untill the next General Assembly, wherunto they shall summond him to hear the determination of the whole bretheren theranent, and what shall be done therin to report therunto; ordeaning if the said

Mr. David's resort be in Aberdeen, to cause the summonds be direct to him for the execution therof, as they will answer to the Kirk ".

It seems upon the Assembly's rigourouse prosecutions of this slander, the King was applyed to by Mr. David or his freinds, and among the King's Articles given in to the Assembly, Session 17, he requires them "if any contraversy fall in about Mr. P. Adamson's, that it be reasoned in His Majesty's name, and that the Bishop of Aberdeen be not interested (perhaps it should be molested) in his living and jurisdiction, but the same to be exercised by himself, because the alledged slander, wherby he is damnifyed of before, is sufficiently tryed and removed ". The rest of the Articles are against Mr. John Coupar and Mr. James Gybson, as may be seen in their Lives; and in favour of the Laird of Fintry, a Papist, and execute afterwards.[1] It [was] not very favourable for the Bishop to have application made for him in such company. The Assembly's answer as to the two Bishops, by the Commissioner sent to the King's, is:—" The Assembly's judgment be followed and notified to His Majesty ". Mr. Calderwood nottices that the Assembly, in "their 16 Session, have agreed that, as to Mr. David Cunningham, ther was a notoriouse slander in his person, and the brethren could not see nor know any clear purgation as yet ". It's not for the Bishop's reputation to have the enquiry thus interupted. However, I find no more about him, and, till the slander be fixed on him, we are to consider him innocent.

He continoued enjoying his Bishoprick and serving the King for his favour done to him. Upon his successor, Mr. Peter Blaickburn, his Life, I have notticed his influence upon the Synod of Aberdeen, Oct., 1596, to traffick the Earle of Huntly, after a prohibition of the Commissioners of the Kirk, and his favourable reception by the King and Councill for so doing, with the disapprobation of the Commissioners, in December that year; and I observe no more about the Bishop.

I'll conclude my account of him with the character given him by the writter of the Appendix to Spotswood's History. His words are: "The Bishoprick of Aberdeen suffered much by Mr. William Gordon,[2] the last Popish Bishop, for he alienated the profits therof, and in a short time brought the revenues of that See almost to nothing; indeed, this benefice at his death was scarce worth the accepting. About the year

[1] Note 46.   [2] Note 47.

1579, Mr. David Cunningham, Parson of St. Nicholas, was preferred to the See. This Bishop was a grave, wise, and learned man, and imployed by King James the 6th in an embassy to the King of Denmark and the Princes of Germany, wherin the Bishop did faithfully discharge his trust to his great commendation. He dyed about the 1603. His successor, Mr. Blaickburn, was made Bishop by the King, 1600;" so that one would think Bishop Cunningham was either dead or had compounded the matter with Mr. Blaickburn.

COLLECTIONS ON THE LIFE OF Mr. PETER BLACKBURN, MINISTER OF ST. NICHOLAS CHURCH, AND BISHOP OF ABERDEEN.

This person bore a very considerable share in our Assemblys from the 1580 and downwards, till the introduction of Praelacy. Whether he succeeded Mr. Heeriot, the Minister at Aberdeen after the Reformation, I know not,[1] but I find him for severall years pretty closely associat with Mr. Andrew Melvin, Mr. Smeton, Lawson, and the rest of our most learned and zealouse of our ministers, till the fatall turn of things in the 1597,[2] when misunderstandings wer of designe betwixt the ministers of the north and south, and insinuation suggested by the courteours, in order first to rend, and then to ruin the ministry, as if the ministers of the south, and particularly in Edinburgh, had too great a share in the guiding of the affairs of the Church, to the excluding of the equally deserving ministry of the north. This poor, pitifull pretext was used, and a game played with too much success to bring in ministers' vote in Parliament and Praelacy. But for a good many years before, Mr. Arbuthnet, and after him Mr. ———, seem to have had the great weight of affairs, which came from the north, in our Assemblys. Mr. Blaikburn was a man of great sufficiency, learning, and for a while of much zeal for the constitution of this Church. It is another instance of defection from former professed principles, when he embraced a bishoprick. I have but few materialls for his Life—only a few hints in Calderwood's MS., and some letters of his in the Advocats' Library.

Nothing has offered to me concerning his parentage. His education probably was at Aberdeen; and I think I have somewhere read he was a Regent in Philosophy ther, not very long after the Reformation.[3]

Neither know I if he was minister anywher else, or first ordeaned

[1] Note. 48.   [2] Note 49.   [3] See Introductory Notice.

to the holy ministry at Aberdeen. The first time I meet with him is in the Assembly, Aprile, 1583, when Mr. Thomas Smeton was Moderator. He names him to be one of his assessors, with Mr. A. Melvil, Lawson, Smeton, Arbuthnet, and other very zealouse ministers. It's probable he was ordeaned severall years before this, and may have been overlooked by me in former Assemblys, as severall others of whom I am collecting those short hints.

In the next Assembly, which met in October, 1583, I find him named with some of the firmest and gravest members, to meet with the Moderator on the affairs of the Assembly, twice every day. The Assembly Records runs, after the choice of Mr. Robt. Pont, Moderator: "For the riper resolution of matters, which are to be treated in this Assembly, the Assembly ordeans their bretheren, Mr. Ja. Lawson, A. Melvin, Thomas Smeton, John Craige, Walter Balcanquell, Peter Blaikburne, and Polwart, John Davidson, Nicol Dalgleish, with 3 or 4 gentlemen, to concurr and daily meet with the Moderator, at 7 hours in the morning on the preaching day, and at 8 hours on other dayes, and in the afternoon at two hours, in Mr. Lawson's gallery, and consult with him on such things as they shall think meet to be propouned, to the end of the Assembly". This seems to have been usuall in most of our Assemblys since the Reformation. At first they wer called Assessors to the Moderator, and named by him and approven by the Assembly. Most of the perplexed cases wer remitted to them to ripen for the Assembly, and they prepared matters and set them in their best light. They wer generally persons of the greatest experience and abilitys, as I have observed on some other Lives.

The Assembly in this period took a particular care of visiting the Universitys, and upon doubts arisen upon the late erection of the College of Aberdeen,[1] and the hazard of the scholars skailing to Saint Andrews, they appoint Mr. Blaikburn to cite the Masters to compear befor the Assembly's Visitors. The Record runs thus: "Forasmuch as the Commission given in the last Assembly to certain bretheren, to try and examine the qualitys of the Members of the College of Aberdeen, if they be correspondent to order and provision of the new erection, as their Commission at lenth bears, hath been negligently overseen, and left unexecute by the bretheren having direction therof, and partly by the

[1] Note 50.

fault of the Members and Regents not resorting to the place appointed: therfor, the whole Assembly of new have given their full power and commission to their bretheren—the Rector, Mr. Andrew Melvil, Mr. Thomas Buchanan, Mr. Robert Wilky, Mr. James Martine—to examine and try the qualitys of the saids Members, as said is, and the said examination to begin and proceed in Saint Andrews in this manner, at thir speciall diets following, viz.: the sub-Principall and one of the Regents the 6th day of March next to come, and the other two Regents the last day of Aprile next therafter; and to the effect they pretend no ignorance of the conclusions of the Kirk herein, the Assembly hath ordeaned their bretheren, Mr. Peter Blaikburn, Minister of Aberdeen, to warn the saids Members and Regents to compear in Saint Andrews, at the times and in the manner above specifyed, to be tryed and examined, as said is, by the said Commissioners, under pain of disobedience to the Kirk, and what herin be as proceeded, to return to the next Assembly the report thereof". We had none Assemblys for some time, and the heavy change, by the King's falling under unlucky hands soon after this,[1] I suppose, prevented any enquiry to be made at the time appointed. Neither does Mr. Calderwood in his MS., whence I take this, give the doubts and grounds of this visitation as I could wish to see them.

In the year 1584, upon Mr. Lawson's death, as has been noticed, that unhappy man Bishop Adamson penned some letters in his name, full of bitter satyre and groundles calumnies upon some of the most eminent ministers of this Church. Mr. Blaikburn was one of such reputation as could not escape Adamson's virulent pen. To show what malice Mr. Adamson and the corrupt party, that followed him, had at him, little knowing he would afterwards be a Prelate, I'le here give his letter to Mr. Blaikburn, Mr. Craig, and Mr. Duncanson, as I have done the rest of them, and they are to be understood be the rule of contrarys, and only taken as commendations for their present zeal and adherence to what the Bishop had so much spite against. It runs: "Bretheren, the worthynes of the places, which ye three occupy, require a correspondent worthines in your persons, wherfor I thought expedient to admonish you, in the name of God, to reform some general and particular corruptions in yourselves, wherby your ministry may be more profitable to the honourable places wher you serve: first, ye are all

[1] Note 51.

three of an avaricious, greedy nature, which ye know the Apostle affirmeth to be the root of all sin; ye are malicious and envyfull, which proceeds from an evil spirit and the instigation of Satan; ye are feigned and double in all your proceedings, although ye know that single and upright dealing is the cheife ornament of the ministry; and ye, Brother Mr. Craige, are vehemently bruited to be a quiet usurer, albiet ye read in the Scriptures that usurers shal not inherit the Lord's Tabernacle; and ye, John Duncanson, are much addicted to your ease and belly, and has procured plurality of benefices, wherof you are neither able nor willing to discharge the cure; and, as I understand by the common complaint of the ministry of the north, our Brother Mr. Craig has conveyed to himself the whole fruits of the Diocy of Aberdeen to his particular stipend, wherby the whole ministry is redacted to miserable poverty; and ye, Brother Mr. Blackburn, are bruited to be of a proud and ambitiouse mind and inclination, and to have learned the lessons of sedition and rebellion against the Prince for troubling the State, by the novations of Mr. Andrew Melvin, a man whom I wish to be of a more quiet disposition. Ye are bruited to exerce your discipline with such austerity and severity, that you are like to eject moe men from the Kirk, than ye by your doctrine are like to adjoin therto, albiet ye know that this over-great severity, used by the fathers in ancient times, gave occasion to the rising of schismes and heresies, wherby the unity of the Kirk was miserably confounded—wherfor I extend you all to amend thir forsaid corruptions, wherby your honourable audience may be instructed by your doctrine, and taught by the better example of your behaviour and conversation." These wanton, freakish letters are not worth preserving, save as token of the reputed honesty and usfulness of the persons to whom they are directed, which gratted the writter. Mr. Craige's Life, with the testimonys more to his character, will fully vindicat him. Mr. Duncanson was the reverse of what he charges him with. Mr. Blaikburn—he has very litle to say against him. And for the generall charges he gives against them in common, they are poor, unsupported, common-places of scandall he casts upon all the objects of his satyre, and amount to a real commendation of them to all impartiall readers.

At the next Assembly which we had, May, 1586, Mr. Peter Blaikburn was put on the lite for Moderator, and probably designed by the gravest of the Assembly to be chosen. But the Lord Privy Seal and other courteours signified it was the King's pleasure that the Assembly should delay their choice of a Moderator to the afternoon, and adjourn to the Palace of Hallyrood House, wher the King would be present himself. The Assembly found that this was but a little alteration of the circumstance of time and place, and agreed to obey the King's desire for this time, upon condition that it should not prejudge the liberty of Assemblys in time coming. The courteours declared they understood no prejudice meaned therby. In the afternoon, they conveened in the Chappell at Holyrood House, the King being present with them. After complemeants from Mr. Pont, former Moderator, that the King, so good a Christian Prince, decored their meeting with his presence, the Moderator named Mr. Blaikburn, Mr. David Lindsay, Mr. Dalgleish, and James Balfour on the lite. The King voted first for Mr. Lindsay, and the plurality of voices went for him. Mr. Calderwood nottices that this was the first Assembly, since the Reformation, at which Court influence was felt. Mr. Blaikburn is named among the assessors, and upon the committy for fixing the bounds of presbitrys; and he is named by the Assembly to visit the bounds of Aberdeen till next Assembly.

The General Assembly conveened upon an alarme of the Spanish Armada, Feb., 1588; their chief designe was to doe what lay in their power for defeating the Popish designs. Mr. Andrew Melvil was chosen Moderator, this being a kinde of extraordinary Assembly, and he particularly fitt to be in the chair upon this emergency. Mr. Blaikburn is one of his assessors. They appoint visitors in their 14 Session, as was ordinary at every Assembly, and name Mr. Pont, Mr. Blackburn, and Mr. Nicol Dalgleish, as their Visitors for the north parts till next Assembly.

In the year 1596, when the dangers from the excommunicat Earles,[1] who wer Papish, wer very great, and it was thought we wer in as much in hazard of the return of Popery as we had been in since the Reformation, the Commissioners of the Assembly conveened Oct. 20, and amongst other remedys, for the present dangers of Religion, appointed "an ordinary number of Commissioners from all quarters, viz., one from every quarter shall have their ordinary residence at Edinburgh, to conveen every day, with a number of the Presbitry of Edinburgh, to communicat such advertishment as shall come from diverse parts of the country, and consult on the best expedients in

[1] Note 52.

every case. For this end they appoint Mr. Alex. Douglass, Peter Blaikburn, George Gladstanes, and James Nicholson for the north quarter. For the mid quarter—Mr. James Melvil, Thomas Buchanan, Alexander Lindsay, and Will. Stirling. For the south quarter—Mr. John Clappertoun, John Knox, George Ramsay, and James Carmichael. For the west quarter—Mr. John Howeson, Andrew Knox, John Porterfield, and Robert Wilky.[1] They did nominat, for the first moneth, Mr. James Nicholson, Melvil, Carmichael, and Andrew Knox, and their charges to be born by their quarters, and their kirks to be supplyed by their presbitrys in their absence."

This is the *Council of the Kirk*, which Bishop Spotswood and the Prelatick writters make such pother about, as hath been notticed on some other of their Lives. The Church had been in use to appoint such meetings since the Reformation; they had been of great use to the King and Government in imminent hazard from Popery, and allowed by the King. They wer nothing else but a current meeting of the Commissioners of the Generall Assembly in a time of great perill. The King and courteours took the very same method in their Generall Commission next and following years, when they got the management of the Church affairs in their hand: with this difference, that they turned the generall affairs in the Church into a few hands to pave the way for Prelacy, for ordinary, and when ther was no publick hazard; and the Church formerly had only used this extraordinary remedy for extraordinary hazards, leaving the ordinary affairs in the hands of the stated judicatorys of the Church, Presbitrys, Synods, and Assemblys. I shall only further observe that almost one-half of the 16 persons named to meet monthly for a quarter of a year turned afterwards bishops, and severall others of them fell in with that change, though at present they appeared zealouse upon the other side. But the vigorouse stand they made in Mr. David Black's case,[2] which stands in his Life, at their first meeting in November following, displeased the Prelatick writters: but the prosecution of Mr. Black at this time proceeded from such who favoured the Popish Earles, and was ane under part of their plott. In short, the Torry writters, in bespattering this step now taken, fling dirt on the faces of the half of their own first bishops.

[1] Note 53.   [2] Note 54.

To return to Mr. Blaickburn, I see he, in particular, came up, according to appointment, to Edinburgh, and was present the 2nd moneth, Decr., 1596. And in the north ther had been pains taken with the Earle of Huntly, which was approven by the King and Council, who, however matters appeared [at present, seemed to approve of the ministers' conduct].[1] Thus, Dec. 11, as the Minutes of their proceedings before me bear: " Mr. Peter Blaikburn, Minister of Aberdeen, declared to the Commissioners, that while he and Mr. David Cunningham, called Bishop, wer called before the King, and enquired if ther was conference between certain barrons, in name of the Earle of Huntly, and certain bretheren of the Synod; he answered that ther was conference; but they had referred the conclusion to His Majesty and the General Assembly. That, therafter, being called before the Council, they declared the same, the which doing His Majesty and Council approved, and gave liberty to deal further with the said Earle. The which being heard, the bretheren found fault with thir doings of the said bretheren of the Synod of Aberdeen, in so far as they had written over to them, forbidding them to do anything in that matter. 1. That they had promised conference upon the King's license, without mentioning the Kirk. 2. In that they had promised to report the said conference between them and the Earle's freinds. Therfor, the Commissioners ordeaned them to desist from any further dealing with the said Earle's freinds, untill the time, the advice, and license of the whole Kirk, in Generall Assembly, wer craved and obteaned." These Minutes are but short hints. Mr. Calderwood's History in print hath a pretty full account of this matter. In short, things stood thus. The Earl of Huntly and the rest had been excommunicat by the Assembly, and the King had promised they should not be permitted to return till they applyed to and satisfyed the Church as to their turning from Popery, notwithstanding they wer permitted to return, and were in the country, raising forces, and in a fair way of getting the King into their hands and management, by severall persons about him suspected to be Popishly affected. The King was particularly favourable to his cusin Huntley, and it was belived ther was, notwithstanding his promises to the contrary, a correspondence betwixt His Majesty

[1] Passage in brackets deleted in Wodrow.

and Huntly; and, instead of preventing their return, he favoured it. Huntly, in the north, by his freinds, made proposalls to the ministers there, and they, living in his country, wher ther wer many Papists, and he had very great interest and influence, it was not proper that he should be dealt with by the ministers there, but by the Generall Assembly, who had excommunicated, or approven the excommunication of the Synod of Fife pronounced on the Popish Lords. The King liked to have the ministers in the north to be agents in this affair, because he knew they wer easilyer dealt with than the Assembly. The Commissioners of the Assembly saw the hazard of separat courses in treating with thir Popish Earles. Many unhappy advices wer at present given the young King; and at this very time letters wer writ, calling a General Assembly in February next, for considering the limites of the civil and ecclesiasticall power, and the discipline and government of the Church, that is, to embroile and overturn the Church Constitution; and by a rent bring in the Popish Earles into the management of the King. The Commissioners of the Assembly wer awarr of all this, and laboured to prevent it, and so disliked the separat courses taken by the ministers in the north, and discharged them. The tumult,[1] which hapned, Dec. 17, brought things to a crisis, and helped on the courteours' designe, which was yet very much accomplished nixt year, by the divisions cast in among the ministry. Whither Mr. Blaikburn was at this gained over to the Court I cannot say, but I suppose this was the pretext Sir Patrick Murray and the courteours had for compleaning of the Popes at Edinburgh, and the zealouse ministry there and in the south, and their imposing upon the northern ministers.

Mr. Blaickburn, I see, comes up to the meeting of ministers at Perth, wher the King inclined to have the constitution of the Church and standing discipline therof disputed, but matters wer not fully gote ripened at the first meeting, though I see the ministers now appointed to confer on the King's Articles are mostly from the north, and the greater part of them such as afterwards wer made bishops. Mr. Blackburn is one. Things wer remitted to the nixt Assembly, and gradually after this, things wer got caryed in our Assemblys much to the King's

[1] Note 55.

good liking. I doubt Mr. Blaikburn had now thoroughly changed sides, and very few got what he was aiming at.

Accordingly, he was named votter in Parliament and Bishop of Aberdeen by the King, with consent of the Commissioners of Assembly, after they had got rid of Mr. Ja. Melvil, Mr. William Scot,[1] and Mr. Ja. Carmichael, whom they sent out upon an Aprile errand. Perhaps this has been notticed upon some other of their Lives, but I'll here transcribe the whole paragraph from Mr. Ja. Melvil's Life: "Upon the 14 of October, 1600, the Commissioners from Synods met in the Palace of Hallyrood House. The King was earnest to have the Kirk of Edinburgh planted with other ministers than Mr. Bruce, Balcanquell, Balfour, and Watson. The bretheren answered that could not be done, unless they wer deposed by the Kirk, or cut off by some civill form of judicature: the King assured them he was determined they should never come in Edinburgh again. The present disgust at them was their refusal to give thanks for Gowrie's conspiracy, but the true cause was their firmness to the government and discipline. It was thought proper rather than that kirk should vaik, that the Ministers of Edinburgh themselves should be asked if they were content, of their own accord, to yield to transportation. Therfor, Mr. Ja. Melvil, Mr. William Scot, and Mr. Jo. Carmichael wer directed by the King and ministers conveened to aske at them, and report their answer. After they were sent out, the King with his Commissioners and the ministers their conveened, nominat and chused three bishops: Mr. David Lindsay, Bishop of Ross; Mr. Patrick Blaikburn, Bishop of Aberdeen; Mr. George Gladstanes, Bishop of Caithnes; and appointed them to vote at the nixt Parliament in the name of the Kirk, without any regard had to the caveats and conclusions made. The bretheren sent out to deal with the bretheren of Edinburgh knew nothing of the matter till the Convention was dissolved." The votters in Parliament under the name of bishops wer, by the last corrupt Assembly, yeilded to under proper restrictions and caveats. Votters in Parliament are meaned here under the appellation of bishops, for they had till the 1606 and 1610 no further power granted them. Mr. Calderwood and Mr. Melvil add: "Mark the craft of the King and his Commissioners of the General Assembly; they name those three who wer esteemed the wisest of those, who stood for the

[1] Note 56.

libertys of our Kirk in another action (Mr. David Black's case), that they might the more easily circumveen the rest who wer present. This Convention had no power of a General Assembly, but any collour was sufficient for thir proceedings, having authority on their side. As to the Ministers of Edinburgh, the King took Mr. J. Hall in his own hand, and indeed he was very stedable to him, and advanced to King and the Commissioners' cause, more secretly and underground than any of the rest did. He was reponed to his own place, but none of the rest." Thus, our first bishops wer brought in by a few, under pretext of votting in Parliament. But those nominat did not take the state of bishops for severall years, but caryed on their work and purposes under the name of Commissioners of the Generall Assembly, as stands fully enough in our printed historians. Mr. David Cunningham, Tulchan Bishop of Aberdeen, was yet alive for a year or two. How that matter was compromised between those bishops of one See I cannot tell.

I have not very much more about him after he was bishop; he seems to have not been so keen and zealouse as the rest of the bishops; and in the letter subscribed by the Commissioners and bishops till the 1609, I scarce ever observe him with the rest. We shall see this was represented to the King, and he writes an apology from his age and infirmitys. He seems to have taken joynt counsels against Popery and Papists in the Synod with the rest of the ministers. Two or three of his letters I meet with in the ecclesiasticall collections in the Lawyers Library.

In February, 1605, he sends up a very warm letter and address from himself and the Synod against the practises of Huntly and the Papists in that country, which I shall give here from the originall :—
"Sir, it may please your most excellent Majesty, we your Majesty's most humble subjects, the province of Aberdeen, lamentably offers to your Majesty the greives of the Kirk and all good men in our bounds, whilk except your Majesty provide speedy remeed, both Kirk and Commonweal are likely to fall into miserable confusion in the north part of your Majesty's Realme. First, that Mr. John Hamiltoun, Mr. James Smeaton, Luke Gordon, and others, uncouth preists under them, and Jesuits, are resett and are heard saying mass in Caithnes, Sutherland, and this province, by great men and others under them, abusing the Sacrament of Baptisme to their infants; sparfling (spreading) Hamiltoun's

blasphemous new book¹ amongst them, seducing them everyway that are simple. 2ly, That the Lairds of Gicht and Newton, excommunicat Papists, cheif menteaners of those things, are suffered, and no order taken with them. 3ly, That, when the ministry of the Synods of Aberdeen and Murray labours by the censures of the Kirk to reduce the Lord Marquise of Huntley and Earle of Errol, to the acknowledgement of the truth, and leaving of Papistry, they are continoually discharged by your Majesty's letters of horning. 4ly, That an great number of kirks in this country are left altogether desolat, by the long continouing in ward of their pastors (Mr. Forbes, Mr. Welsh, Mr. Firm, &c.)², seing the most part of other kirks are unplanted. 5ly, By this occasion, the most part of the ministry are contemned and railed upon, their doctrine not heard, and their discipline mocked, and Jesuits enters in the kirks in parochies wanting pastors. The greives in Commonweal are many deadly feuds arisen, amongst Forbeses, Irvings, Lesleys, and Leythis, and are likelie by their parties to draw on the whole country to bloody factions.³ 6ly, That every man that pleases wears guns, pistols, rides with jacks, speirs, knapsknays [headpieces], without controlment. Beseiking therefor your Majesty, in all humility and reverence, to cause and command the saids enormitys to be stayed, that your Majesty's good subjects of thir parts may live in the fear and service of their God, and your Majesty's obedience; and so the glory of God and His truth being reverenced, your Majesty may procure the continouance of His blessing, and prosperouse reigne to yourself, and peace to your good subjects, and so praying most earnestly for the samine, we take our leave from our Synod at Aberdeen, the 20 day of February, 1606 years.

"Your Majesty's humble Servitors and Daily Orators,
"MR. JOHN STRATHAUCHINE, Mod.⁴
"P. BLAICKBURN.

"Mr. Robert Reid, Scribe to the Assembly."

This letter would not be acceptable at Court, wher ther wer not a few that did not love to be enterteaned with complaints of the disorders from Papists, and to be sure, that Article compleaning of the desolation of so many parishes by the imprisonment of the ministers at Blacknes would yet be less acceptable. Upon Mr. John Forbes of Alford, his Life,

¹ Note 57.   ² Note 58.   ³ Note 59.   ⁴ Note 60.

I have given a pretty zealouse letter of the Synod of Aberdeen, subscribed by the Bishop, recomending Mr. Forbes, when he went up last year (1605) to deal with the King for some more effectual course to be taken against the growth of Popery.[1]

I have another letter of the Bishop's without [date], which I shall bring in here; it must have been [written], probably after the Parliament, 1606, or the following Parliament. It's probable his fellow bishops informed the King against him, as not so active as they in, what was called, the King's cause; that is, bringing the Church of Scotland to conform to that of England. In answer to those, he pleads infirmity, and present service, and resolutions in time to come. His letter runs thus:

"Most Graciouse Soveraigne,—It may please your most excellent Majesty upon the hard information your Majesty received anent my carriage in the affairs of the Church and your Majesty's service; it pleased your Majesty to direct your Counsell to call me to my count, which I, with very good will in all humility, gave to the Lord Chancelour and President, with the greatest number of the bishops here assembled, to whom I hope I have given such satisfaction as will liberat me from any wilfull offence; and if I have given not, being now of good age and infirm, such uttered forwardness as the present service requires, I mind by the grace of God to be mindfull to please your Majesty and serve in this calling, with as good heart and affection as any of my equalls, and at this present Parliament I have not been deficient in any good service; swa, your Majesty may expect of me, that in all services competent to my place, I will refuse no burden that my mean hability [permits]. Thus the God everlasting bless your Majesty in person, estate, and government.

"For ever I shall remain,
"Your Majesty's most humble Servant and affectionat Orator,
"PETER, BISHOP OF ABERDEEN."

If this letter was write after the Parliament, 1606, it will be proper here to add what Mr. Calderwood observes in his account of the bishops riding the first day of that Parliament in their robes. He tells us: "They all road in state save Mr. Peter Blackburn, Bishop of Aberdeen, who thought it not becoming the simplicity of a minister to ride that way in pomp, therfor he went on foot to the Parliament House.

[1] Note 61.

Because he would not ride as the rest did, the rest of the bishops caused the Chancelour to remove him out of the Parliament House." This was a hard censure for a little modesty; better founded, one would think, than the practise of his bretheren, the bishops, on the last day of this Parliament, when all the members save them rode. But they, humble prelates! went to the Parliament House quietly on their foot, because they got not the place which they alledged belonged to them, viz., before all the earles, and next to the marquises. Had the Chancellour served them as they would have their brother of Aberdeen, they had been turned out that day. This, Mr. Calderwood sayes, made the nobles take up their presuming humors, and mislike them as soon as they had set them up, fearing they wer set up to cast them down.

Bishop Blaickburn seems to have been as much in earnest against Popery, profanity, and for bearing down of Papists, as any of his bretheren; the zeal of the most part of them running in another channel. Thus I find him writing to the King a very earnest letter upon the growth of Popery, and the Bishop of Murray, whose bounds were infected, joyns with him. Their letter is worth preserving: "Please your sacred Majesty, upon our humble suit made to your Highness, before your Majesty's removing from the Kingdom of Scotland, anent the open profanity of the Sabbath dayes with the salmond fishings in our Diocess, withdrawing therby many persons from the publick worshiping of God, it pleased your Highness to set down an Act of Council, inhibiting all persons to profane the Sabbath dayes under a penalty; commanding all shiriffs to exact the penalty of all contraveeners. Nevertheless, the shiriffs have overseen this care of the profanation of the Sabbath dayes, wherby many continoues in their publick sin and offence, and albeit diverse men of the Religion, especially in Aberdeen, would gladly desist, yet, truth it is, that sundry Papists, having dispensation from the Paipe, are still refractory, respecting their own gain more than God's worship, and all because ther is no execution of your Majesty's lawes. And, howbeit, we ourselves have been urged by diverse well-affected professors and ministers to have cited them before us to have censured them ecclesiastically, yet we would do nothing therin still, without your Majesty's knowen will and contentment; wherfor we most humbly intreat your Highnes to direct your Majesty's missives to the shirriffs of Aberdeen, Elgin, Forres, and Inverness, commanding them to put your Highnes' Acts of Councill against the profanation of the Sabbath to due execution, as they will answer to your Highnes; as likewise, in case the sherriffs be negligent, yet, as of before, that we have your Highnes' missive direct to us, willing us, if need bees, to proceed against the contraveeners ecclesiastically; and because the Earle of Enzie, who should be shirriff of ane part of that bounds, presently may do good therin, it's meet your Majesty signify your Highnes' mind to him, by your Highnes' own word, willing him to see that the said act receive its own execution. So shall your Highnes greatly honour God, and give full contentment to all religiouse harts within this your Majesty's Kingdom, whose continouall prayers and ours are, and shall still be, offered up for the continouall increase of all good blessings of this life to be multiplied upon your Majesty and your Highnes' Royal posterity, and for that eternall blessing in the life to come.

"Your Majesty's most humble and obedient Servants and Subjects,
"PATRICK, BISHOP OF ABERDEEN.
"AL., BISHOP OF MORAY.
"Edinr., the 15th December, 1609."

No more offers as to this Bishop, till his death, July, 1616, according to Mr. Calderwood, whose words are: "Mr. Peter Blackburn, Bishop of Aberdeen, departed this life, about the beginning of July, after he had lyen a long time, little better than benummed. He was said to be ever more mindful of a purse and 500 marks in it, which he keeped in his bosome, than any thing else." It seems he was reconed covetouse; how well grounded this common charge was, I know not by any thing of his come to my hand. He seems to have minded his proper busines, and appeared more heartily against Popery and profaness, and his letters savour more of a seriouse, earnest concern about what was his proper work than most of the bishops in this period. The author of the Appendix to Bishop Spotswood's History places his death 1615, and sayes he sat in that See 12 years, but recons, it seems, from the death of his predecessor, Cunningham, 1603; but it's certain he was named Bishop 1600. He was burryed in Saint Nicholas Church, and was succeeded by Alexander Forbes, Bishop of Caithnes.[1]

[1] Note 62.

COLLECTIONS UPON THE LIFE OF PATRICK FORBES, BARRON OF ONEIL AND LAIRD OF CORSE, MINISTER OF KEITH AND BISHOP OF ABERDEEN.

This learned gentleman is taken nottice of by forraigners through his learned son,[1] whose Life may come afterward in its own place, [and] is yet more famouse by his many and justly valued writings. The father's Life has never been yet given by itself. It's but Collections concerning him, and the rest of the piouse and remarkable persons in this period, that I am essaying. Indeed, I have more helps as to the Bishop than in most persons at this time. There was published, 1635, the year he dyed, Funerals of a Right Reverend Father in God Patrick Forbes of Corse, Bishop of Aberdeen.[2] It's a collection of sermons and funnerall discourses upon his death, letters to him and concerning him, and poems upon his death. It's very probable that his son, Mr. John Forbes, then at Aberdeen, had the oversight of those things published at that time concerning his father. That book is but in the hands of few, and I shall make the best use, I can, of the collection of papers therein. More lately, 1703, Doctor George Garden[3] published his son's works in two vols, in folio, at Amsterdam, and in his son's Life, gives an abstract of the Bishop's. In both those ther are high encomiums of the Bishop; and indeed, I am ready to think, he deserved them much more than most of Scots prelates after the Reformation. Mr. Calderwood, in his MS. history, gives us severall things concerning this gentleman, which we are not to expect from the other two. The truth is best to be gathered by comparing writters upon every side. From those and some other papers, I'le endeavour to give as regular an account of his life as I can.

This gentleman was born at his father's seat, August 24, 1564. His family and parentage are well known in the North of Scotland.

[1] Note 63. [2] Note 64. [3] Note 65.

He was son of William Forbes, son to David, son to Sir Patrick Forbes, knight, Barron of Oneil and Corse. This Sir Patrick was the 3d son of the Lord Forbes, ane ancient and honourable house in the north, from whom [came] a very numerouse company of gentlemen of this surname in the shire of Aberdeen, some of them of considerable fortunes; and the name is spread to the shires of Murray and Invernes likewise. This Sir Patrick was a courtier and familiar of our King James the 3d. That king had a particular liking to this gentleman, and bestowed a large tract of lands in the east [west?] part of the shire of Aberdeen upon him, lying between the waters of Dee and Don. The charter yet extant, and dated Edinburgh, Dec. 17, 1476, runs: "Jacobus Dei gratia dedit, et ad feudifirmam dimisit, dilecto, familiari, armigero suo, Patricio Forbes fratri germano consanguinei sui Gulielmi Domini Forbes, pro suo fideli servitio illi impenso; omnes et singulas terras, Barronei de Oneil, viz., terras de Coule, Kincraige, et Corse, cum tenentibus et in feudifirmam et hereditatem perpetuam, tenendas," &c. To this Sir Patrick succeeds, and his son; to David succeeded his eldest son and heir, William, who was among the first gentlemen in the north who embraced the Reformation. It's pity we have not larger accounts to give of those gentlemen who early fell in with the truth, and shook of Popery. His eldest son was William likewise, who had the character of a wise and gallant man. He had a numerouse posterity, of whom Doctor Garden gives those hints. Seven sons were born to him, and severall of them deserve to be notticed. His first son was the Bishop, his 2d son, William, acquired the lands of Craigivar and Fintray in Aberdeenshire, with others in the hands of his posterity to this day. The 3d was the excellent and worthy person, Mr. John Forbes, Minister at Alnes [Alford?] and Moderator of the Assembly at Aberdeen. Doctor Garden gives him the character of a pious and learned man, famouse by his writings abroad and at home, but adds, he was still fond of Presbiterian government; and for holding the Assembly at Aberdeen, 1605, against the King's command, he was first imprisoned and [then] bannished, and dyed Minister of Delf, in Holland. His son, Mr. Patrick, was, after the Restoration, by King Charles the 2d advanced to the Bishoprick of Caithnes, in which he dyed in very advanced years, after the 1676. His 4th son, Arthur, betook himself to a military life; and after he had been advanced to a collonell's post in forraigne service he bought some lands in Ireland, and King James created him a knight barronet. His son, Arthur Forbes, was made Earle of Grenard in Ireland by King Charles the 2d, wher many years he went through the most considerable offices, civil and military, in that kingdome with much reputations. His posterity enjoy the honnour and estate.

It's time now to the Bishop. This gentleman [was] eldest son and heir. His father, observing his excellent genius, took great care of his education. He sent him to Stirling School as soon as was proper, and ther he was taught the Latine Tongue by Mr. Thomas Buchanan, whose Life stands in this Collections, and whom Doctor Garden calls nephew to the celebrated Mr. George Buchanan. From Stirling he went to Glasgow, to his kinsman Mr. Andrew Melvil, the Principall of the University of Glasgow, whom the Doctor termes a learned man and a celebrated poet, whose name is famouse among Scots historians. At that time, adds he, the New Colledge of Saint Andrews, before cheifly destinate to Philosophy, was turned to a Divinity seminary, the other two of Saint Leonards and Saint Salvators being allotted to Philosophy and Mathematicks, and is the most illustriouse this way of any in Brittain, yea, the only one the Doctor knowes of destinat to the education of candidates for the holy ministery; in which there are two Divinity Professors, and a third of the Orientall Tongues, with good sellarys, and the students in food and lodgings provided within the Colledge walls. There they are under the immediat inspection of the Masters, and subjected to their authority, lawes, and exercises, as students wer in Scotland of old, and the scholars of the Jesuits in their seminarys. When Mr. Melvil, as we see in his Life, was transported from Glasgow to be principall Professor of Divinity in the New Colledge of Saint Andrews, his relation, Mr. Forbes went with him, and under him studyed Theology and the Hebrew Tongue. In this he made such progress during some years, that the Curators of the New Colledge, considering his advances, prudence, gravity, and strict life, solicited him to take upon him the office of Professor of Divinity there. But his father, now growing old, thought proper to call him home to himself, that he might marry and build his family. The Doctor goes on to his marriage.

He either did not know, or was not willing to tell us, that in the year 1584, when Mr. Andrew Melvil was forced to fly in[to] England, Mr. Forbes either went with him, or soon followed him, and stayed some weeks with him at Berwick, which place they left, and went southward to London, June this year, as Mr. Calderwood nottices. As far as I can perceive, Mr. Patrick, Aparand of Corse (as Mr. Calderwood terms him), continued in England till the banished noblemen and ministers returned to Berwick, October, 1585. Mr. Forbes stayed behind them some days in Berwick, and wrote there to his relation, Mr. James Melvil. I know not but I may have notticed his letter in Mr. James Melvil's Life. However, it should properly stand here ; and I give it as preserved by Mr. Calderwood. [*Vide* C. IV. p. 383.]

As far as I can perceive, Mr. Forbes returned to the New Colledge, when it was next year filled again with Mr. Andrew and James Melvils, and, when Mr. James Melvil entered upon the care of a congregation, I guess the offer of his teaching the youth joyntly with Mr. Andrew Melvil was made, which, Dr. Garden says, his father stopped by calling him home to himself. He obeyed his father, and during his life was married to Lucretia Spence, daughter to a good gentleman, David Spence of Wermistoun.[1] By Mr. James Melvil's Life, I see he was maryed by him in summer, 1589; and that he had some share in making up that marriage. Mr. Melvil's words are : " This winter, 1588, I passed over to Dalkeith, and obteaned the gift of the stipend of Anstruther Wester, wher God, by some help of me, an unworthy instrument, called Mr. James Nicholson from the Court to the ministry ; and in returning, of mere providence, I was the occasion of the marriage of Patrick Forbes of Corse with Lucretia Spence, sister to the Laird of Wilmerstoun. They wer maryed in Anstruther the summer following."

I have litle more about Mr. Forbes for severall years, till he came to be Minister of Keith. Dr. Garden tells us that during his father's life, he and his wife lived in a litle country seat near the town of Monross. Ther, adds he, because of his remarkable learning, prudence, and piety, in a litle time he came to be so famouse that his house was continoually filled with the neighbouring gentry and ministers, fond of his learned and usefull conversation.

Upon his father's death he came and dwelt in the House of Corse; and ther he gave himself to better and improve his lands and estate; but continoued a closs student, improving his mind with his books and learning. While he dwelt there, every Lord's day, as the Minister of

[1] Note 66.

his own family, he expounded the Holy Scriptures and the principles of the Christian religion to those that wer in his house. For many years after he left Mr. Andrew Melvil, he had no temptation to leave the principles and doctrine taught by him, and warmly espoused and professed by Mr. Forbes. When the alterations and innovations wer gradually brought, after the 1597, by some hints in Calderwood I find he did not fall in with them, and probably from this he chused to live privately upon his own estate, and did not, though very weel qualified, incline to enter upon publick teaching for some time, though educat in those studyes. He seems to have lived in the neighbourhood of his brother, Mr. Jo. Forbes, and we have seen how staunch he was to our Presbyterian constitution, and it's probable the Bishop continoued so likewise, for some time after his sufferings.

Doctor Garden adds that, in the year 1605, when his brother was imprisoned for holding Aberdeen Assembly with severall other ministers in his neighbourhood, the congregations about him wer severall of them destitute of preaching. In this state of things, the Presbitery and some other Presbitrys of the Synod of Aberdeen, earnestly pressed him to turn his privat ministeriall teaching of his own family to more publick usefulnes, and instruct the people of his neighbourhood. At their desire, Mr. Forbes of Corse preached in the church nearest his own house every Lord's Day, to the great edification of the people.

Mr. Patrick Blackburn, then Bishop of Aberdeen, as the Doctor continoues his account, with his Diocesan Synod again and again importuned Mr. Forbes of Corse to take ordination, and the pastorall charge of any parish he pleased in his neighbourhood. But he would not comply from the deep sense of the weight of the pastorall charge, and the difficultys of the times. I recon this was after bishops wer set up by the Parliament, 1606; before which they pretended litle superiority in Synods. However, with the approbation of the Synod, he continoued to preach in that church as before, till they should be supplyed with a pastor. I give it only as my guess, that hitherto this gentleman had not got over his difficultys from his principles as to Presbiterian goverment. This was so represented to Mr. Gladstanes, Archbishop of St. Andrews, that he sent his orders to the Laird of Corse to give over his preaching, till he should enter into orders. Those, the Doctor says, the Laird of Corse religiously obeyed, and returned to his former way of instructing his own family, waiting on the publick worship in the nearest church in the forenoon, and in the afternoon he explained a peice of Scripture to his own family. This way (continoues the Doctor) he continoued for seven years, and closly attended publick worship in the church, so far was he from being any wise schismaticall; and in that period the neighbouring ministers, and many other good people, very closly attended his house instructions. During that time he explained the Epistles to the Romans and the Hebrews, and the Book of the Revelations. His son afterwards published an Abbreviat of his Discourses on the Revelation, turned into Latine by him. In all this the gentleman discovered his great abilitys, and a singular desire to advance piety and religion, with his deep and feeling sense of the importance and weight of the ministeriall work, and yet his own concern to exercise his talent, with all due regard to the peace of the Church, and his care against schism.

At that time a most deplorable case fell out. A piouse and diligent minister in the parish of Keith, a village in the Diocese of Murray, under the power of melancholy and by a violent temptation of Satan, cut his own throat, and under the deepest remorse sent for the Laird of Corse, by whose dealing with him in this extraordinary case he was brought, before his death, to give evident signs of repentance and faith; and he came to dye with so much comfort and hope, as very much removed the horrible offence given by this dreadful attempt on himself. Those general hints, with some very just reflexions upon some paliations of self-murder advanced by some modern deists and freethinkers, in the case, as I take it, of Mr. Cretch and some others, is all the account the Doctor gives of this extraordinary incident.

I'll therfor give a larger and very circumstantial account of this tremendouse self-murder, which Mr. Calderwood hath preserved to us, with Mr. Chalmers' own confession. I sett down Mr. Calderwood's narrative, which agrees with another old copy of an information as to this very singular fact I have by me. [*Vide* C. VII. p. 160.]

I suppose Mr. Calderwood hath taken this relation of his from a letter (wherof I have an old copy) from Mr. William Gordon, a minister, who was with him during much of his illnes and at his death, to my Lord Saltoun, which, being somewhat fuller than what is above, and the case being so very extraordinary, I have put it into the Appendix N (copy MS., fol. v., 42, n. 84).[1] I have brought in this account of Mr. Chalmers on the Laird of Corse his life, because Doctor Garden takes nottice of his singular usefulnes to him in this extraordinory case, which I doubt nothing of; but by the above account Mr. Chalmers appears to have had comfort and setlement before Mr. Forbes came to him. We see by Mr. Gordon's letter that Mr. Chalmers recomended Mr. Lesley to be his successor. Whether he afterwards altered his mind, and besought the Laird of Corse to take the charge of his flock, I know no further about but what the Doctor adds, which brings me again to the Bishop's life.

Doctor Garden tells us that nothing more nearly touched poor Mr. Chalmer than that Satan had got an opportunity to wound religion through his sides; and therfor, in the most earnest manner, and in the bowells of Christ, he obtained the Laird of Corse to take the pastorall care of the people of Keith upon his decease: that way, he reconed, the wound given by him might be healed, and hoped that his piety and prudence would go far to put a stop to the scandall, and prevent the evils he had opened a dore to. The people and neighbouring ministers joyned Mr. Chalmers, in the warmest manner, with the gentleman. Hitherto he had waved entering in [to] orders, though his heart lay still to the holy ministry. But now the ardent obtestations of the dying man, in such remarkable circumstances, struck him so strongly, and he thought ther was so much of the call and interposition of Providence in it, that he could no longer stand out, and, in a little time after, he was ordeaned Minister to the congregation of Keith, wher for severall years he was a burning and shining light both to that people and the pastors about. The Doctor hath no more about him till he be raised to the Episcopall dignity, six or seven years after this.

I'll add a hint or two from Mr. Calderwood. When the General Assembly met at Aberdeen, August 13, 1616, there was a fast appointed by the King's proclamation, and indyted by sound of trumpet. Mr. Forbes was imployed to preach in the morning. The Bishop of Saint Andrews succeeded him in the fornoon, and Mr. William Forbes in the afternoon. Now that he had come over the difficultys he once had against Episcopall government, and joyning

[1] This Appendix has been apparently lost.

with it, the bishops made a great deal of him; and they had reason, for he was among the most considerable a man as they had brought over to their side. At this Assembly, as we have seen in Mr. Will. Scot and Galloway's Life, Mr. Forbes is at the head of the nomination made of persons to review our old Discipline and Canons, and form a new Body of Discipline.

Next year, 1617, when, as we shall see at greater lenth, Mr. Calderwood was prosecute and deprived by the High Commission for his share in the protestation,[1] Mr. Walter Whiteford came from the bishops with a message to Mr. David to say that if he would do anything, they would procure him his liberty. Mr. Forbes of Corse came with Mr. Whitford, but whether he was sent by the bishops or not, Calderwood knowes not. He asked Mr. Whiteford what the bishops would have him to do to procure his liberty. To admit their sentence, saith the other. Mr. Calderwood said he would rather be banished his native country than do that. The Laird of Corse interposed here, and said: "Ye may obey any unjust sentence, though you acknowledge it not". "How can that be?" answered Mr. Calderwood. "Can I be silent, seeing their sentence is null?" To this it was replyed that they caryed about their power as bishops wherever they went. Mr. Calderwood thought otherwise, and said, at that way of arguing, they might cary about their power as members of the High Commission, and bring it into Synods.

In December, 1617, Mr. Alexander Forbes, formerly Bishop of Caithnes, and now Bishop of Aberdeen, dyed at Leath, the 14 of the moneth. He would fain have spoken with Bishop Spotswood, but he was so keen at the cards that he could not leave his game, and so did not see his brother bishop. The preachers of the Bishop's death, and Dr. Garden nottice that the offer of this Bishoprick came to him without the least motion for it. Mr. Calderwood, who seems to be displeased with his intermedling in his trouble, observes that he never consented to enter into the holy ministry till bishopricks wer a-dealing.

Let me give an account of his being made a bishop from originall papers, without dipping into the springs of things, and I shall place severall in the Appendix that relate to his advancement to this office,

[1] Note 67.

though they might be ommitted, wer it but to preserve the formes used at this time, about the Bishop. No doubt, Mr. Forbes of Corse, upon the death of the former Bishop, was named to the King by the bishops in Scotland, at least by the Primat, who had the cheife management of the disposall of vacant bishopricks. Accordingly, a letter came down in the beginning of February to the bishops, nominating him to that vacancy, as follows: [*Vide* Funerals p. 193].

Both the King, who generally had the form of such letters from Edinburgh, and the bishops, take nottice of the application made by the ministry and gentlemen of Aberdeenshire to have the Laird of Corse made bishop, on Mr. Patrick Blaickburn's death, 1614. Bishop Spotswood, in his letter to Mr. Mitchell to be notticed just now, sayes he was then for Mr. Forbes being preferred to Aberdeen. Bishop Blackburn was earnest to bring over this gentleman to be ordeaned at Keith, 1612, and Mr. Calderwood seems to hint at promises made to him of succeeding to the Bishoprick. How farr those influence him, now that he had new light to joyn with Episcopacy, none ought to judge. The bishops in their letter free him from having any share in seeking after this preferment now.

Very soon after the receipt of the two former letters, Mr. Forbes returned an answer to the Archbishop of Saint Andrews. This is pretty long, and is not published in his Funeralls by the editors of that collection. Mr. Calderwood has preserved it; and I think it ought to stand in his Life. It runs thus: [*Vide* C. VII. p. 291].

Mr. Calderwood suspects the Bishop's sincerity in this letter, and sayes he conveyeth his answer so craftily that the bishops might easily perceive that he would accept the Bishoprick, *nolens volens*, as it was said of old. He thinks that a presumptouse spirit appears in this letter, and that the Bishop insinuats that his accepting of the Bishoprick might grace the office; and upon the Bishop's declaring that he is unwilling to urge the ceremonies upon others, yet Mr. Calderwood observes that he was keen enough for them in the Assembly at Perth, and in the Parliament holden afterward for the approving of them, and in his Diocesan Synod at Aberdeen, 1627. Although the King at that time was not urging the ceremonies, he threatened the ministers of the Diocess in those words: " Ye think there will be no more din of conformity. Beguile not yourselves; I shall make the best of you conform." And Mr. Calderwood adds: "It's well enough knowen that Mr. Forbes of Corse did not enter upon the ministry till bishopricks wer a-dealing, and that he could find no better means to repair his broken lairdship. He pretends in this letter, that he would not accept of the Bishoprick but upon such and such conditions, yet he entered by the election of a Chapter, which was condemned before in our Kirk, and without swearing to the caveats prescribed to the Commissioners voting in Parliament; and yielded to be consecrat, howbeit consecration to such ane office, was not so much as dreamed of at the Assembly holden at Glasgow." We shall find the writters upon the other side have a quite different opinion of him. Indeed, we shall find the Bishop much altered in his way of speaking in this letter, after he is in the office of bishop. Lordships, they say, changes manners, and probably upon this view the Primat and the rest of the bishops wer very keen to have such as had once been zealouse for the Reformation Establishment brought over to bishopricks, as Mr. James Nicholson, Mr. William Coupar, Mr. Adam Ballantine, and others; yea, bishopricks were offered by the courtiers even to the humblest Presbiterians, as Mr. James Melvil, Mr. Calderwood, and others.

I imagine there is a mistake in Calderwood's date of this letter of the Bishop's, and that he received the King's letter on the 12, and made his return on the 13, at least. By the Archbishop's letter of the 16 of February, just now to be insert, it appears that the return made by the Laird of Corse was come to him. That same day the Primat writes to Mr. Thomas Mitchell, Minister of Udney, one of the Proctors of the Chapter of Aberdeen, and tells him that the bishops had obteaned his Majesty's consent to place the Laird of Corse at Aberdeen, which, adds he, you and I much desired in the last vacancy. He trusts nothing will prove more favourable to God's Church, and no man will be better able than he to bear down enimies in those parts. He tells him that he is daily expecting the King's Warrand to the Chapter to proceed in that election; and when it comes he promises to send particular directions anent the proceedings.

At the same time, the Archbishop writes to the Laird of Corse the following letter, upon his receipt of what hath been just now inserted. It's directed *To my very loving brother the Laird of Corse*, and runs: [*Vide* F. p. 204.]

There seemes to have been a particular intimacy between the Laird of Corse and the above-named Mr. Thomas Mitchell, and that same day, Feb. 13, on which he received the King's letter nominating him bishop, he writes to him that he had just now received the King's letter, very plainly and peremptorily nominating him to be bishop. He adds, it's so free and peremptory as it hath casten him into great anxiety of mind, and so he stood much in need of his counsell and prayers to God for direction. He wishes the Lord may be his Counsellor, and referrs all to Him. Again, on the 12 of March, the Laird of Corse writes another letter to him, which, not being long, I have inserted it. [*Vide* F. p. 206.]

Upon the 24 of March, the Chapter of the Bishoprick of Aberdeen met there, and choiced Mr. Forbes to be their Bishop. Whether it was common at this time in elections, I cannot tell, but, in this case, the whole Presbitrys in the Diocess met with the Chapter, by their Commissioner, and gave their consent, which they signifyed to the Bishop by their Moderator in the following letter, which was directed thus: [*Vide* F. p. 206.]

I incline to preserve the Formes of Procedure in thir matters; and the curiouse reader, I believe, will not grudge my transcribing this direct Form of the Chapter's electing bishops, which, bating some small circumstances peculiar to the Laird of Corse, was an common form of electing bishops, now used, and so the certificat of his election runs thus: [*Vide* F. p. 207.]

At that same time, the Chapter gave their Procuratory to Mr. John Strathauchin, Rector of Kincardin; Mr. George Hay, Rector of Turriff; Mr. John Reid, Rector of Logie; and Mr. Thomas Mitchel, Pastor of Udney, a Procuratory and Commission to signify their election to the Bishop, and intimat the same to the King, and to ask his confirmation and doing what other things were necessary to the final expeding of it. This I have cast into the Appendix N (copy Fun. pain, 4to, 196, p. 189). The subscriptions need not be repeted. [*Vide* F. p. 209.]

As soon as the election was notifyed, there came down from Court the King's patent to the Laird of Corse to be Bishop of Aberdeen, dated the 8 of Aprile, which I shall also subjoyn, as what may be of use to some readers, and such who have no tast that way can soon overlook it. Its title is *Diploma Regium, De provisione Patricii Forbesii, Episcopi Aberdonensis.* [*Vide* F. p. 211.]

Those letters for constituting the Bishop, with a mandat for his consecration, came to the Primat on the 26th of Aprile, as he acquaints Mr. Thomas Mitchel by a letter that date, of which he sayes the one must pass the Great Seal and the other the Privy Seal. He adds that the 17 of May is the fittest time, and he advertised the bishops to meet that day. He will have the Laird of Corse to dine with him on the day of Consecration; he bid Mr. Mitchel take care the Bishop be accompanyed with some grave ministers besides his own freinds, which would attend him. He tells His Majesty is exceedingly well pleased with their procedure at Aberdeen, and expecteth good service from it both to God and him. What he would further have done, when the papers are passed the Seals, on the Primate's part, he desires to be advertised, and he will do and prepare it.

Accordingly, he was admitted and enthronized Bishop at Saint Andrews, upon the 27 day of May, as an instrument taken by the Bishop of Aberdeen, under the hand of nottars publick, makes plain; and I have set it in the Appendix N that the reader may have all the papers relating to the entry of this gentleman on his Episcopall office (copy Fun., 4to, pain, 196, pp. 196, 197). [*Vide* F. p. 215.]

Having thus brought this gentleman to the bishoprick, I have litle more about him till his death, about 17 years after, save his appearances for the Act of Assembly at Perth, and in the Parliament held for the ratifying the Acts of Assembly.

I meet with an abstract of the Bishop's sermon, at the opening of Perth Assembly, in an original letter from my Lord Binning to the King, dated Saint Johnstoun, 27th of Agust, 1618, which I transcribe from the Advocats' Library, as much of it as relates to Bishop Forbes:—
" Most Sacred Soveraigne,—At our coming to this town, finding the most precise and wilfull Puritans wer chosen Commisioners by many of the Presbitrys, especially of Lothian and Fife, I was extremely doubtfull of the success of your Majesty's religiouse and just desires. At the privat meeting of your Majesty's Commissioners and the bishops, My Lord of Saint Andrews deemed not of the apparent difficulty, but declared that being hopefull that the happiness, which alwise accompanys the justice of your royall designes, would not fail in this action, he thought the victory would be more perfect, and the obedience more hearty, when the Puritans should see the Articles concluded in the

presence of their greatest patrons, their opinions being confuted by lively reasons and undenyable truth. The Assembly sermon was made by the Bishop of Aberdeen, who with great dexterity propounded the weight of the purposes to be entreated, and the necessity of consideration that the Body of the Church being assembled by your royall direction for treating of Articles propounded by your Majesty, first to a number of the principall ministers at Saint Andrews, and therafter in the Assembly at Saint Andrews, your Majesty had conceived great offence for the delays then used; and, being persuaded in your excellent wisdome and conscience, that the Articles wer just and godlie, ardently shifted because propounded by your Majesty by such as had gloryed to be opposit to your sacred desires, it was to be feared that, if at this time your Majesty should not receive satisfaction, your wrath might so burn as the Church, losing your wonted fatherly favour, might feel the heavy prejudice of that consequence, and therefore exerted them in humility, zeal, and Christian love to dispose themselves to proceed wisely and with all due respect to your Majesty."

Upon the 29th of March, the Archbishop of Saint Andrews writes up to the King for his assent to the person thus chosen. I shall insert here what of the letter relates to this; the whole of it stands in Bishop Spotswood's Life. "Most Sacred and Graciouse Soveraigne,—I have caused the election of the Bishop of Aberdeen to be orderly done, according to the form sent to me by the Dean of Winchester, in every point. The certification of their proceedings is now to be presented to your Majesty under the subscription of the Chapter and their Common Seal, upon the sight wherof I most humbly entreat your Majesty's royall assent to the person elected, with a Warrand for his Consecration, both which I have made here to be firmed, and have sent herewith. I am in good hope he shall prove worthy of your Majesty's favour, and that his service shall be profitable to this Church. Much I hear of some Puritans' bussynes diswading his acceptation, but the particulars will be better understood afterwards."

Any other things I meet with about him want dates, and, therfor, I shall nottice them on his generall character. Upon Mr. Jo. Carmichael and Mr. William Scot's Lives, the reader will find an account of the conference after Perth Assembly, Nov. 24, 1618, betwixt the bishops and severall ministers who opposed those ceremonies then imposed. The Primat, as we have seen on his Life, pretended the end of this meeting was to take the ministers' advice what methods were best for the present preserving the peace of the Church. The Primat began with the Bishop of Aberdeen, as the person whose authority would go furthest with the ministers, he being reconed to have the warmest side to them. Mr. Calderwood hath preserved to us the substance of Bishop Forbes speech as followes: [*Vide* C. VII. p. 398.]

The Bishop at this conference proposed a lesser meeting, and that the ministers should name their own conferrers, and seemed very tender of them. The event of the conference is to be seen in the Lives referred unto.

The Bishop grew more severe upon the ministers, the longer he continued in his office. His sermon, two years after this, was much taken nottice of. In November, 1621, during the Convention which was called to support the King's son-in-law, the illustrious Elector of Palatine, in the Bohemian warrs, the Bishop [preached] in the Litle Kirk of Edinburgh, Nov. 26. The whole of it was an invective against the ministers who stood out against Perth Articles, Mr. Calderwood tells us. [*Vide* C. VII. p. 453.]

With the same force the Bishop exerted himself in behalf of the Perth Articles in the Parliament which conveened July, 1621, to give them the force of a law. He was one of the Lords of the Articles. There the Acts of the Assembly at Perth passed pretty easily. The Laird of Preston, Commissioner for East Lothian; the Laird of Huttoun for West Lothian; the Laird of Leyes, Burnet, Commissioner for the shire of the Mearns; and Duncan Paterson, Provost of Stirling, wer the only persons upon the Articles who votted against ratifying the Acts of Perth Assembly. The Earle of Mortoune absented, and it was thought of purpose, because not for them; albiet the matter was carryed by a great plurality, yet the Bishop of Aberdeen showed his discontent that the vote was not unanimouse, and broke out in this expression: [*Vide* C. VII. p. 491.]

I shall give the reader a view of the Bishop's management for 17 years as Bishop of Aberdeen from Doctor Garden, who appears to have been a very great admirer of his; and though we must make allowances for an author, who drawes the Life of a man he values very much, and expect to find everything he hath observed to his advantage, yet I am ready to suppose ther wer not many bishops in this period, who deserved better the panagyrick the Doctor bestowes, as to most branches of his management. I'le just give the reader as full an abreviat of what the Doctor hath, as I can, without ommitting anything remarkable he hath as to the Bishop, tho' I change his order in his narrative a litle, and because it comes best in after the accounts we have had from Calderwood. I shall begin with what the Doctor hath as [to] his love to the Churche's peace, and his abhorrence of schism and division.

The Bishop was gravely averse from all schisme. He used bitterly to regrate the intestine divisions of the Church of Scotland, and foretold their hazardous consequences. He declared himself against innovations as to rites and externall formes to this Church, even tho' those should appear usefull to promote piety; being, as he said himself, persuaded they would still be accompanyed with strife and contention, which holy men would certainly cast up, when meanwhile the kingdom of God consists not in meat or drink, but in righteousness, and peace, and joy in the Holy Ghost. Therfor, as long as his health would allow him to attend upon publick meetings, he opposed the bringing in of the Liturgy and Formes of prayer and administration of Sacrament according to the English usage: not that he either reconed them unlawfull, or altogether without their use, but because the generality wer possessed with such prejudices against them as, he was of opinion, their introduction would be the occasion of mobbs and confusions in the nation, and schismes and contentions in the Church. Upon the other hand, he was for a closs observation of what was brought in by the constitutions of the Church and lawes of the land; and did not think [it] the interest either of Church or State to yield meanly to the perversity of some, who stood out against Holy Scripture, Catholick antiquity, and the practise of all Reformed Churches, and set up their own will in their room; pretending, in order to render the rulers in Church and State the more odious, that the usages brought in (Perth Articles) wer sinfull, superstitiouse, idolatrous, and anti-Christian. To vouch this the Doctor cites a passage of Archbishop Spotswood's letter to the Bishop's son after his father's death, April 2, 1635: [*Vide* F. p. 217.]

The Doctor has translated this into Latine for the use of forraigners. How far this fitt of keenes in a man that had once been violent enough against the innovations introduced, his making them hereticks for their dislike of kneeling at the Sacrament, and requiring a publick confession of their error and heresy, in a word, his stopping a freindly application to the King in behalf of tender consciences, how far this will recommend the Bishop to forraigne Protestants, or be any way for his reputation with sober Christians, I must leave to the reader to determine. I wish the Primat hath not magnifyed the Bishop's zeal, because so very agreeable to his own sentiments and violent pushing of conformity.

The Doctor gives the following account of the Bishop's care and diligence in his Diocess. He had frequent visitations of those under his care in the summer season, that he might understand the state of his Diocess, and excite ministers to diligence in their office, and take away differences and variances among neighbours. He visited parochiall churches without any parade, that he might not be burdensome to ministers or others, when discharging his office. Those visitations wer not overly, but very faithfull; his great care was to the pastors feeding the souls of their flock. On the Saturday's evening, he used to come privatly to the neighbourhood of the parish church he had in his eye, and on the Sabbath he was present at public worship. After sermon was over, he used secretly, and with much affection, to admonish the minister of anything he observed in his preaching, or any other branches of his office, or his life and practise, as he found cause. Wher the minister was ignorant, supinely negligent, or untender in his life and practise, and scandalouse, in those cases he made publick visitation with his clergy, and removed such from their office, and provided the parish with better men. In parishes, wher through the covetousness of such as had the teinds in their hand, and the [lands] burdened with ministers' stipends, yet they minded the fleece more than the flock, and two or more parishes had been cast under one pastor, he vigourously set himself against this evil, and generally before his departure obtained a disjunction. In larger parishes, too wide for the people to attend worship, and too numerouse or distant for one man's inspection, he brought about a division into two or more, and allocat stipends, and provided pastors to them; and because the town of Aberdeen was the cheife post of his Diocess, he had a peculiar care to provide learned and piouse ministers there. And such were brought thither by him, sayes the Doctor, who, a litle after his death, wer in great reputation through all Europe. He means the Doctors of Aberdeen, who managed the disput about the Covenant and Episcopacy with Mr. D. Dickson and others after the great turn, 1637.[1]

The Bishop was not only a frequent visitor of his Diocess but a vigilant, assiduous, and prudent preacher. Every Lord's Day he preached the Word of God to the people, reconing that to be a necessary and cheife work of a bishop. The Doctor termes him wonderfull and divinely eloquent. His sermons wer not filled with an idle pomp of words, nor swelled with philosophicall reasonings, and things too abstract for the capacity of the common people; he did not affect the gestures of the stage nor fine words, but being touched himself with the inward seeing of divine things he indeavoured to communicate a sense of them to others. Speaking from the heart to the heart, not in the words of humane wisdom but of the Holy Ghost, and sincerely, copiously, gravely, and with power, he opened the mysterys of God.

He had all his clergy for his bretheren; without their counsell and consent he made no Ecclesiasticall Constitutions. He was far from showing his Episcopall authority in pride, envy, or ostentation. His integrity and constancy was such that dangers did not scarr him, flattery did not move him, nor the solicitations of great men: no, not those of the King never prevailed with him to be wanting to his office, or consent to anything he thought iniquous. It was too ordinary in country parishes for neighbours to fall by ye ears about their seats in the kirk. The designation of rooms in the church for all concerned was by law in the hands of bishops. Upon the rising of a debate of this nature betwixt two persons in a certain parish, one of them ritcher, and who had some more interest among the courtears than the other who, in the Bishop's opinion, had justice on his side, obteaned a letter from the King to the Bishop to decide in his favour. Notwithstanding, he gave sentence wher he thought equity lay, and wrote to the Secretary, "that he had his gown from the King, but his conscience was God's". This was so gratefull to King James, says the Doctor, that he thanked God ther was such a bishop as had the courage to discharge his office under the weight of solicitations.

[1] Note 68.

His prudence and equity wer so conspicuous, that most of the differences among laicks in his Dioces wer referred to his arbitration; and he was so happy in his determinations, that fewer vexatiouse suits wer in the shire of Aberdeen than in most other places in the Kingdom. His great knowledge in divine and human matters, his happy talent in expressing his mind, his diligence in everything he applyed himself to, brought him universall regard and the goodwill of all ranks; and he was much respected even by his enimies and ill-wishers. He was Counsellour to King James and King Charles, and such was his reputation in Civil and Church matters, that generally his opinion was gone into by the Council.

Many wer the good offices he did for the Colleges at Aberdeen, while he was Bishop. He had observed a great neglect as to students of Divinity and candidates for the ministry, one of the greatest sources of the greatest evil to a Church. Socrates, in his *Apology*, laments the supine neglegence of the Athenians as to the education of their youth, and compleans they wer more solicitous about their dogs and horses than their children. To remedy this evil, the Bishop, with the consent and concurrence of his clergy, set up a seminary at Old Aberdeen to students that had their eye to the ministry, and he with his clergy, who wer able, contribute a fund for a Professor of Divinity to take the care of them; and in a short while after, he prevailed to get a fund laid down in the new town of Aberdeen for another Professor of Divinity there, to take the charge of such as had their eyes to the ministry. He lived to see very comfortable consequences of both. He, with the consent of his clergy, laid down rules for the education and management of the students, as to their life and manners, and their examination before they entered the holy ministry.

Indeed he may be reconed the Restorer of the two Colledges of Aberdeen—the 2 Colledges in Old and New Aberdeen, about a mile distant, the one at the mouth of the watter of Dee, the other near the watter of Don. This last, now called the Old Town, is the Bishop's seat, hath the Cathedral church and the College, founded as we have seen by Bishop Elphingstoun, 1494, and named the King's Colledge, having stately buildings, large rents, and good lawes. At the Reformation the Franciscan monastery in the new toun of Aberdeen, chiefly through the activity of the Earle of Marishall, was erected into a

Colledge, and it bears the Earle's name. By the foundation of the King's Colledge the Bishop is its Chancelor, and hath the chief care of the admission of presbyters, management of the rents, and directing the students. Bishop Forbes, at his accession, found all out of order, and with the greatest vigilance and diligence restored that University to its ancient glory, revived the liberall sciences, recovered and bettered the Colledge revenues, repaired the buildings, restored the Professions that wer disused, and brought their excellent old statutes into practise again; quicked the Masters to their work, and reformed the manners of Masters and students by his own excellent example. And because, from the first foundation, that society was designed to be a nursery for the Church, the Bishop took a particular care that it should be so, by reviving their old statute, appointing the Regents and Professors of Philosophy themselves to have their eye to the ministry, and to be still under the direction of the Professor of Divinity, and requiring them, after six years teachings, as the Bishop should see cause, and determine their fitness, to offer themselves to the ministry, and take the pastorall charge of a flock. This useful statute the Bishop, as long as he lived, took care to see put in execution, and was at pains, when parishes became vacant, they should be supplyed by one of the Regents, and then saw their room were filled with another youth of pregnancy and points. Though this, after the Bishop dyed, was too much turned to desuetude, yet the Bishop during his life applyed himself to see it execute, being persuaded this was a great advantage to the Church, a preventive of the Regents' negligence in their studys, and a spurr to their diligence. By this means he filled the Diocess of Aberdeen with pious and learned men; and indeed a remarkable change to the better was this way soon introduced among the ministry of that bounds.

In the Bishop's advanced years he fell tender, and was much afflicted with a paraliticall distemper and other distempers. Those abstracted his mind much from earthly things, being pretty frequent upon him through his life. From this, Doctor Garden makes an observation that his mind was so weaned from the wordle, that, while he was Bishop, he did not better his paternall estate, nor add one furr of land to it.

Doctor Jas. Sibbald,[1] in his sermon after his death, takes nottice

[1] Note 69.

that [the] Bishop was a closs student of holynes throu his life, and had very much of the secret atteanments which follow from a close study of it. Those supported him under the aflictions and crosses he was tristed with, especially in his last period under his palsy. His judgment, prudence, and speech wer graciouslly continued with him; his holyness now shône forth, and tho' his distemper was most heavy, he was much happier under them than others in their health; his care about God's glory and the Church did not abate; he was very usefull by his prayers, sound advice, and wise, frequent, and powerfull letters. Doctor Sibbald cannot pass one instance of his care and self-denyall. A little before the Bishop's death, the town of Aberdeen earnestly sought his son to be one of their pastors, and his father willingly condescended to his transplantation, notwithstanding he was the manager of his estate at that time, and under God the stay of his old age, and solace of his solitarynes and sicknes. The Bishop declared that to have had his son with him in such circumstances, he would willingly have tripled what advantage and sallary he was to have by his transportation. But his father preferred the publick good to all other things.

In his last illness, which ended in his dissolution, he had much comfort and consolation, and discoursed, too, much to his relations and such as come to visit him. In his conflict with his last enimie, it seems that portion of the Scripture was made exceeding sweet to him— Ps. cx. 1—"The Lord said to my Lord, Sit thou at My right hand till I make all Thine enemies Thy footstool". This was the occasion of his son, the learned John Forbes of Corse, soe much knowen in the Christian wordle by his Works, chusing that place to preach on at Old Aberdeen after his father's death. His sermon is not printed in the Funeralls with severalls others, but in stead of that, a Latine discourse (which is reprinted also in Doctor Garden's edition of his Works) upon that text. There, after a criticall explication of the words with some application, he considers of the dutyes arising from that text, and showes how exact his father was in the discharge of them, and there gives a large and handsome panegyrick on the Bishop. From this I shall gather out some passages concerning the Bishop's carriage during his last sicknes, and more immediatly before his death, because I recon this in pious persons is one of the most usefull and affecting part of their life.

When the Bishop was attacked by that fitt of the palsy which portended his death, even then he did not in the least slacken his religiouse exercises, but when he perceived the time approaching, when he was to give account of his stewardship, he stirred up all the powers of his soul and body in a diligent preparation, that, when his Lord came, he might be found so doing. In that last shock of his desease, he was present at some Ecclesiasticall meetings, and caused himself to be carried in the chair, in which he used to be taken in his old age to publick worship, to the church, presided at the meetings, and even sometimes preached with his former eloquence and life, being strengthened evidently by his Master's presence. His son adds that good ministers in the Diocess of Aberdeen remain witnesses of this.

At length, his trouble increasing upon him, he was confined to his chamber. His many visitants can tell, sayes his son, his patience, the vigour of his inward man; and with what meakness, humble boldness, and piety, he bore up under his affliction; how chearfully and willingly he drunk the cup his Father put in his hand, and with thankfulnes he acknowledged God's goodnes in the graduall approaches of death. He gratefully acknowledged a particular kindnes that, when his whole left side was disabled by the palsey, God preserved his tongue, and judgment, and senses. And even when at some seasons his pain turned severe, he was so much subjected to the Divine will that he never uttered one impatient word, yea, under his very pain he was kind and affable to all that came to see him. He received them with chearfullness, and gave them pastorall instruction and fatherly consolations.

He used often to declare that his great desire was to be with Christ, but he neither durst nor would limite the Holy One of Israel, or fix times and seasons, nor in the least offer to set bounds by impatience to God's fatherly providence, or by murmuring. He added, he knew to Whom he had committed himself and believed; and in a very litle He That was to come would come, and would not tarry.

When he found his end drawing near, he showed his earnest desire of partaking of the Eucharist, and accordingly it was given him; and six ministers, wherof his son was one, joyned with him in that ordinance. He participated with the greatest devotion, reverence and comfort. His son asked him whether he had not felt the life-giving sweetnes of the Bread of Life abundantly. He answered that just now he was singing

Simeon's song to God: "Now letest Thou Thy servant depart in peace, for mine eyes have seen Thy salvation". When the Communion was over, his fellow-communicants, children, family, and friends present earnestly desired he might bless them. His palsy had left him one of his hands. That he stretched forth, and laid it on each of their heads, and in a most ardent prayer to God he gave each of them his pastorall and fatherly blessing. All of them kneeled when they received it, and his son sayes it was most comfortable at the time, and matter of sweet reflection to them since that time.

The Bishop had many pleasant conferences with his son upon spirituall subjects during his illness, upon the miserable state of mankind since the Fall, the Divine goodnes, the happines of such as are partakers of the Redemption by Christ, the vanity of this wordle, the shortnes of humane life, and that sweet invitation and promise, Matt. xi. 28: "Come unto Me all ye that labour and are heavy laden, and I'll give rest". He spoke much upon righteousness, peace, and joy in the Holy Gost, the death of the body, the immortality of the soul, the resurrection, and heavenly inheritance, and beatific vision, with the greatest pleasure and delight. A few days before his death, he was seized with very sharp pains, which wer the worse to bear that his body was now very low. His son put him in mind that now was the time confidently to trust in God, and that the afflictions of saints ought not to strangle their faith, since the greatest afflictions that could fall upon a person in Christ justifyed by His blood, and having his Just Judge to be his friend, would never separate him from the love of God in Christ our Lord. The Bishop declared his unshaken faith, repeating in Hebrew the close of the 5th Psalm: "Thou wilt compass the rightiouse with Thy favour as with a shield," which he explained of crowning and fortifying the afflicted as with a sheild, and soon after fell upon a sweet and refreshing rest. His son one day told him of the death of a relation of theirs, and observed a vast difference betwixt his exercise and carriage in the sicknes, which in a day or two carryed him of, and his condition about three year before, when threatened with a deadly distemper. In his first sickness he was under terrible fears and terrors, and could not without sighs and tears think of his death, but in his last sicknes he declared to the relater, that he could now with pleasure look forward to his dissolution, as what would soon bring him to his God, as it fell out very soon. The Bishop made this remark upon what was told him—"That such was the Lord's kindnes to His own people, that He would not bring unwillingly even to the enjoyment of Himself, but even before their death brings them to an intire subjection to Himself, and to be willing to lay down this tabernacle and go to a better state". Augustine observes [1] that a Christian desires to dye, not out of a dislike at life, but that he may live better after death. The Bishop's assertion, adds his son, did not import that he thought every Christian was able to encounter death with the same measure of courage and chearfullnes. He knew that faith and fortitude are bestowed upon God's people according to the measure of the gift of Christ, that is, just as Christ sees proper to measure out, or, as the Apostle elswher expresses, *according to the measure of faith given to every man*, and this measure is exceeding variouse. But still this holds that though in every one there is lawfull desire and love to the body, and a naturall abhorrence at death, that to every one who dyes in the Lord a sufficient and insuperable grace is vouchsafed, and His strength is made perfect in our weaknes, and by this we have the victory ascertained to us. This same gifted grace, by which we at first believe, enables us, when we have finished our course, willingly to dye. The Bishop himself for many years had been trained up to a willingnes to depart, neither from a weariness of life nor from any slavish force from the terrors of death, but from a vehement longing to be with God Himself and his fortaste of the raptures and joyes of the future state ; and when all about him wer wishing and praying that he might be spared some time longer, he answered them in the words of Ambrose [2]: "*Non ita inter vos vixi, ut pudeat me vivere, nec timeo mori, quia Dominum bonum habemus*. He had not lived so among them as to be ashamed to live, neither was he affrayed to dye, since we have a good God to go to." The Bishop, however, added that he had a strong desire to leave the wordle and to be with Christ.

When those who came to visit him began to commend his former life, he used to say : " It becomes one, who has been caryed through by mere mercy, to return all God's free gifts to Himself, however great victory over temptation he has had ; and only to glory in God Who hath mercifully vouchsafed everything to him. He may indeed take pleasure

[1 St. Augustine, *Opera*, tom. vii. p. 376, Benedictine Edition.]
[2 St. Amb., *Opera*, tom. ii. Benedictine Edit.]

in the testimony of a good conscience, that in the simplicity and sincerity of God, not with fleshly wisdome but by the grace of God, he hath had his conversation in the wordle. But," added he, " by this I am not justifyed. May I find mercy through Jesus Christ at that day. This I wish and hope." This brings to his son's mind a passage of Ignatius in his Epistle to [the] Trallians. "It's good," says that primitive saint, " to glory in the Lord, although I have been hitherto strenthened in the things of God; neither do I give any heed to those who would lift me up with commendations, for such who praise me scourge and try me."

A few dayes before his death, directing himself to his son, he said : " John, I perceive now that I am near the end of my course, and death hastens, which I am well assured shall be happy and full of consolation."

That day before he dyed, being Passion Day, Aprile 27, 1635, his son was dwelling in his thoughts upon the life-giving passion of our Saviour upon the Cross, and reflecting upon Christ's prayer to his Father, " Into Thy hands I commend My Spirit," he suggested those words of Christ to his dying father, with this remark, that Christ in that prayer did not only commend to Jehovah His own soul hypostatically united to the Deity, but likewise all the souls of every believing Christian when leaving the body; and therfor, he added, that his soul (his father's) was, by the abiding virtue of that prayer really commended to the Father by Christ, now sitting at His Father's right hand and interceding for us. The Bishop upon hearing of this, lifting up his languishing eyes, said : " Without controversy you have given the treue meaning and just sense of those words, as our Lord designed them, Who prayes the Father for us and is alwise heard of the Father ". Augustine, adds his son, hath a saying which clears this as to Christ's praying to the Father, and being alwise heard by Him. " *Quo modo non Patrem rogat ut homo, qui cum Patre exaudit ut Deus*,"[1] and elswher, " *De Trinitate*, lib. i., cap. 10 : *Ex hoc enim rogat, quo minor est Patre quo vero equalis est exaudit cum patre*.[2] What may not Christ as man ask of God in prayer, since with God He is the Hearer of prayer? He askes who is inferiour to the Father, and as He is His equall he hears."

In the evening before his death, his son put him in mind how near he was that blessed welcome from Christ : " Well done, good and faithful servant, enter into the joy of thy Lord "; that now he was entering

[1 *August.*, tom. viii., p. 707.]   [2 *Item*, tom. viii., p. 763.]

the blessed rest, and was to have a crown of glory that fadeth not away put upon his head. He answered in a word, for he was not able to speak much: "God grant it, John". His son further exhorted him that he might comfort himself, as many a time he had done, with that sweet invitation of our Saviour, our Beloved, to every believing soul, and stablish his heart from it, that ere long his begun journey to his Father's kingdom would be perfected, though it lye through the valley of death, Song ii. 10: "Arise, my love, my fair one, and come away," adding by this most sweet compellation and kind exortation, his Beloved, his Saviour, was now calling him out of the wordle full of sin and affliction, to hasten to heaven, the habitation of His holy[ness] and glory, that this night you may be with Him in Paradise. His father answered: "O blessed journey, none can be compared to it, or equalled with it!"

When, in a little after this, his speech failed him, as long as he was able to hear what was said to him upon the Divine mercy, the blessednes of those that dye in the Lord, the heavenly mansions prepared by Christ for him, in which, in a very litle, he was to be in, with that of the communion with the angels, patriarchs, apostles, martyrs, and other spirits made perfect, of the fulness of joy before God's face, and the rivers of eternall pleasures at His right hand;—when those subjects were insisted upon, he gave signes of his rapturouse delight in them that his soul was carryed out in the earnest desire of them, and fixed in the hope of them, by lifting up his hand, of which he had yet the power, and frequent darting up his looks to heaven. After those discourses to him, his son asked him if he and those who wer present go to prayer in his behalf to his Heavenly Father, that [He] out of His unsearchable and immense mercy, and His unshaken love to His elect in Christ, might grant him a happy passage to the Lord? He raised himself up in the bed, as he was able, lifting up his hand and fixing his eyes heavenward, with all the signes he could give, [showed] how acceptible this would be to him; and we perceived by his hand, eyes, and countenance, that in the outmost ardency he joyned in that prayer.

After prayer, for a litle we perceived that he heard what was spoken to him; but very soon his hearing and all motion failed, and we looking on with tears, and the most ardent inward prayer, mixed with the assured confidence of his happy change, soon perceived him fall asleep in Christ, and breath forth his soul ripe for heaven, into the hands of his Heavenly Father. Then, sayes his son, perceiving him as if I had seen the old patriarch Jacob expiring, I kissed his lifeless mouth, washing his face with tears, and closed his eyes with my hand. Thus he dyed piously and peacefully in the Lord, about 3 in the morning, the day after Pasch, April 28, 1635, in the Bishop's palace adjoyning the Cathedrall church, in the town of Old Aberdeen. This is the best and clearest account I could give of the last stage of the Bishop's life, from his own learned son, who continually waited on him and published this account of him that same year he dyed.

From the formentioned time of his birth, the reader will see he dyed in the 71 year of his age. Upon the 9th of Aprile following, he was buryed in the Cathedrall church of Aberdeen, betwixt two of his predecessors, Gavin Dumbar upon his right hand and Mr. David Cunningham upon his left side.[1] His son took care to affix a marble stone to his grave, with the arms and bearing of his family, and the following inscription cut upon the marble : [*Vide* F. p. 3.]

Doctor Garden observes that the Bishop's death was lamented deeply by all ranks: ministers, orators, poets concurred to celebrat his good qualitys when dead. Their sermons, orations, and funeral verses were collected and printed in a good sizable 4to at Aberdeen, by Edward Raban, 1635.

I have not any of his printed works by me, and can only give the titles of them from Mr. Charters: " Patrick Forbes, Bishop of Aberdeen, a wise and moderat man; he wrote a Commentary on the Revelation Lond., 1613. [Item] Eubulus 4to, Aberdeen, 1627. Item De pastorum evangelicorum vocatione." I have in MS. a paper of some more than two sheets, conteaning remarks upon Bullinger's answers to the questions of two English pastors upon Ministers' Habites. This paper was once in Caldwood's hands, and in his own write he quotes it on the back, *Mr. Forbes upon Habites*. But whether it was writt by the Bishop before he was consecrate, or by Mr. William Forbes, I cannot say. It deserves to be preserved, we having litle of our divines on the subject, and so may stand in the Ap. (Copy MS., fol. 44, n. 17.)[2]

[1] Note 70. [2] This Paper has not been found.

COLLECTIONS UPON THE LIFE OF Mr. ADAM BANNANTYNE, MINISTER AT FALKIRK, AND BISHOP OF DUMBLANE AND ABERDEEN.

Most part of the bishops in King James the Sixth his time, in the beginning of their ministry, set up upon the strictest lay of Presbiterians, and seemed to outrun many of their bretheren in zeal and strictnes in matters which wer then debated. Too much keeness, even on the best side, does not promise much in younger persons, especially when interest and applause happen to be on that side. A real conscientiouse, rooted principle natively leads a person to be modest, cautiouse, and fearfull, least by running to any extremity he should hurt the cause he loves conscientiously, and desires to appear for; whereas one, that acts not from a reall conviction and principle, is swayed only by present interest and reputation, minds not the cause he seems to contend for but himself, and stands not much at extremity and excesses, if he be sure of applause by them. The very same root of self leads him to appear with as much keenes, when he changes sides, as time and tyde alters, and reputation and outward interest attends the other side of the question. I am not at all surprised, then, to find most of Scots praelates run from the one side to the other, and to be very keen, and for hights and extremitys upon each of the sides they appear upon. This fact is very plain in most of the bishops in this Collection; and it holds pretty much upon Mr. Bannantine, of whom I shall give some short account from Mr. Calderwood's MS. History, and several originall letters in the Advocats' Library, and [in] my hands, and what other books and papers I meet with which touch him.

Mr. Bannantine was descended of the Lairds of Kilconquhar, an ancient family.[1] He was either an immediate cadet or a nephew, and on the death of his brother or nephew, when Minister at Falkirk, he

[1] Note 71.

succeeded to that estate. I have not met with the time of his birth, nor anything about his education.

When he was admitted Minister at Falkirk, or if he was anywher else befor he came there, I know not. It's probable he was first setled Rector of Falkirk, since we shall find him about 43 years in the ministry, from the 1595, when I meet with him there.

In the year 1595, by the Registers of our Assemblys, I find him there, and it's probable he was ordeaned some years before. In the General Assembly which met in June that year, ther was an enquiry ordered to be made as to the dilapidations of benefices made by ministers. The Assembly appoint committys to meet at Edinburgh, Stirling, and elswher, to receive from each shire and presbitry complaints of the diminusion of benefices by wrong tacks, and other alienations of the state of benefices, with the help of their respective presbitrys, and lay them before those judges. Mr. Bannantyne is named for the shire of Stirling.

When the imprisoned ministers for keeping the General Assembly at Aberdeen wer processed for their lives at Linlithgow, January, 1606, as we have seen on Mr. John Forbes' Life, the most part of the zealouse ministers within 50 or 60 miles round came to strengthen their hands. Amongst them I find Mr. Bannantine, and indeed he, as well as Mr. Coupar, Abernethy, and others who turned bishops, appeared with much keeness at present for the Reformation principles of this Church. And I do not find Mr. Bannantyne as yet thought by the bishops, and such as wer hunting after bishopricks, to be favourable to their side, and so he is not, that I have observed, nominat upon the generall Commissions who brought in all our innovations, after the 1597.

Mr. Calderwood observes that Mr. Bannantine's zeal continoued at the Convension of Linlithgow, December that same year. The designe of that meeting was to establish constant Moderators, which was the first step to Prelacy, and very necessarily drew it after it. This was a meeting of such ministers as the king pleased to conveen. When a Moderator was chosen, many of the sincerer sort refused to vote, or act in a judicative capacity, since they had no Commissions from presbitrys. They were desired, as privat men conveened by the King, to give their advice, vote, or act, in a judicative capacity. Since they had no commissions from presbitrys they wer desired, as privat men conveened by the King, to give their advice, vote, or act as they pleased. Thus Mr. Ja. Nicholson was chosen Moderator. Severall ministers feared that this would afterwards be palmed on the Church for a Generall Assembly, [and] wer forming a protestation against their acting, partly Mr. Arch. Simson, as we have seen on his Life, and Mr. Bannantyne. As soon as the bishops had nottice of this they prevailed with the King's Commissioner to call those two before the Councill, who were chapterly conveened at Linlithgow, when they compeared, and the [There must be some omission here. There is a line left blank in the MS.] after his brisk appearance. Methods, I have reason to belive, wer used to gain Mr. Bannantyne to be more favourable to the bishops; and he seems soon after this to have been softened, and so, in the year 1609, he is a member of the Conference at Falkland. He was still reconed upon the stricter side, and appointed on that side of the Conference, with Mr. Will. Couper by this time gained to favour the bishops, and Mr. Galloway and Hall, tho' they wer indeed the King's great instruments to bring in the bishops: this cunning in naming reall enimies though professed freinds to conferr on the strick side was of great use in the bishops' cause, and a peice of refined policy.

Mr. Calderwood observes that about this time, and for some years before, Mr. Bannantyne was exceeding negligent as to his parish; that Falkirk was destitute of preaching, the half of the Sabbaths of the year, he being most frequently at Kilconquhar or Edinburgh about civil affaires. And he adds, that it's no wonder he aspired after a bishoprick when he was so negligent of his parish.

When Bishop Gladstanes kept his first Diocesian Synod at Edinburgh, after his consecration, February, 1611, as may be seen in his Life, [he] craved an helper and fellow-labourer to be granted to him upon his own charges, in respect of the far distance between the kirk at Falkirk and the lands of Kilconquhar, now fallen to him by the death of the Laird. He was not much in as yet with any side of the ministry, and the Bishop was unwilling to appear briskly for him at his first Synod, and so the vote went against him; and he was ordeaned either to transport himself conform to the act of last Synod that the kirk may be declared to vaik, or else to demit the said benefice, or to serve in person and residence, and himself teach and minister Sacraments, all substitutes and fellow-labourers being secluded, under pain of deposition; and, the premises failing betwixt and the next Synod, that he be deposed from all function in the Kirk. I suppose this came a litle to be softned, and it seems hard to hinder him, in case of urgent civil avocations, from a helper menteaned on his own charges; and I take Mr. William Annand, Minister afterward in Air, [became] either his helper or his successor in Falkirk when made a bishop.

In the year 1615, he gote into the Bishoprick of Dumblain, wher he continoued till the great turn, 1638, save 2 years or therby, in which he enjoyed the Bishoprick of Aberdeen. Mr. George Gladstanes, Bishop of Saint Andrews his death made a kind of revolution among the bishops in Scotland. Severall translations insued, and upon Mr. Grahame's translation to Orkney from Dumblane, Mr. Bannantine was his successor. Mr. Calderwood tells us that, in October, 1615, " Mr. George (some writters call him Mr. Andrew, as the writter of the Appendix to Spotswood's History) Graham was apointed Mr. Lawe's successor in Orkney, and Mr. Adam Bannantyne, Minister at Falkirk, and somtime a vehement opposit to the bishops was consecrat Bishop of Dumblaine. He had said before, that Mr. Graham, the excrement of bishops, had got the Bishoprick of Dumblaine, the excrement of bishopricks: now, he is not ashamed to lick up his excrement, and accept of that mean Bishoprick to patch up his broken lairdship." It seems Mr. Bannantine was aiming much higher, for Mr. Calderwood adds "He and Mr. William Murray, Person of Dysart, and Mr. John Abernethy, Minister at Jedburgh, made everyone their own meen [suit] at Court for the Archbishoprick of Glasgow. But the King preferred Mr. Law for the good service he had done in the overthrow of the discipline of the Kirk. This man was engaged in debt likewise before he engaged in that course, which was a speciall motive, besides his covetousnes and ambition." Whether Mr. Calderwood means Mr. Abernethy, to whom I have applyed it in his Life, or Mr. Bannantine, in the last clause, I cannot be certain.

While bishop he was zealouse for all innovations, as formerly he had seemed to be against them before the Assembly at Perth, 1618. He was very keen to get members of the right stamp for the Articles brought up. Mr. Calderwood in his remarks upon the nullity of that Assembly, observes that, though by the Act of Assembly, 1597, it was provided that no presbitry should send above 3 members, which had been observed generally even in the corrupt and bribed Assembly at Glasgow, yet, at this Assembly ther wer 6 or 8 admitted out of one presbitry, as, for example, Mr. Andrew Allan and Mr. James Bourden wer chosen for the Presbitry of Auchterarder, yet Mr. A. Bannantyne added 7 or 8 unto them, and their names wer called among the rest, and they voted.

After this Assembly we have few other publick meetings of the bishops. Their Records in their own Presbitrys and Synods are all by this time lost, so that ther remains litle afterward as materialls for their Lives but a few of their letters. Severall of Bishop Bannantyne's are preserved, with Bishop Gladstane's and Spotswood, in the collection of their letters in the Advocate's Library, and I have some original letters to him; and those are the bulk of what I have further on this Bishop's Life, and I still recon those the most instructive and sure materialls. Severall hints concerning his using the English Ceremonys in the Royall Chappell, of which he was Dean, come in upon severall of the Lives of his collegues and contemporarys; and I shall now much confine myself to letters from and to him.

Many of his to the King are lost since. I see he had frequent occasions to write upon the state of the Chappell Royall: the first I meet with is dated May, 1623, and runs thus: "*Most Graciouse Soveraigne*, the estate of your Chappell Royall being well founded for the time, by your Majesty's most worthie predecessors, has received such ruin since the Reformation by most shamefull dilapidations, as has been seen by those, who, at your Majesty's command, has visited the samine; for ther wer founded 16 Prebendarys, besides the Dean, and 9 boyes, whilk had a reasonable provision asigned them, above 3 thousand pounds Scots money by year, whilk now will not be 1200 pounds Scots yearly. Your Majesty has sufficiently provided the Dean for his dutie. What remeed can be had by law to recover any part for the Prebendaries shall be essayed. The best mean to supply the rest is by mortifying of some church rent, whilk is at your Majesty's gift yet undisponned, to the use of the Chappell; for by this course your Majesty's patrimony is not burdened; and in the search of those church livings, that remain unerected, the bearer, Mr. James Law, has made great search, and taken great pains to try out the samine with other overtures for the bettering of the Chappell, whilk I would your Majesty might be pleased to consider, and according as they, or any of them, shall be found meet, to give way unto them. In the mean time, forbidding your Majesty's Commissioners at home in Scotland to pass any new grant of any church living, that is yet free undisposed, and commanding your Majesty's Registers to be open for a more full enquiry and search of things of this kind, it may shortly prove a great benefite to the Chappell, and a full reparation of the samine to your Majesty's perpetuall honour, who is, and has been, God's blessed instrument to restore the Gospell, whilk by dilapidations was almost extinguished. Thus, wishing your Majesty a long and blessed reigne, we rest

"Your Majesty's humble and obedient subjects, the Prebandars of your Chappell, and in their names,

"AD., BISHOP OF DUMBLAN, Dean of the said Chapell.

"Canongate, 17 of May, 1623."

Nixt moneth the Bishop and Dean receives a round summ in those days from the King, and makes a return to the Viscount of Annand, directed "To my very honourable good freind, My Lord Viscount of Annand," which runs thus: "My very good Lord,—My duty remembered, I did write to your Lordship upon the receipt of the 500 pound sterling, whilk his graciouse Majesty was pleased to send unto me. I think such a summ came never in a better time, and the Lord ever bless His Majesty, who had that remembrance of his poor servant. I know not, neither does it beseem me to enquire about that money, but I most hombly crave your Lordship's advice in this particular, and I besech your Lordship to write me an answer. When I was in England, His Majesty did promise to me the making of two Sergeants-at-law, and I travelled with some to that effect, with whom I covenanted that if they wer made Sergeants by my means they should give eleven hundred pound sterling a-peice, and the projector 100d. pound of it for his pains. Now I have received an letter, that those same men are called to be Sergeants and has received His Majesty's writt to that effect, and desires me to write to them anent that indenting. I besech you to know if it is His Majesty's will, that I be payed by that course or not. If it be, it will be to me a good weil and great; if His Majesty will not, far be it from me to offend His Majesty in any matter, having received his favour in a beginning (albeit, alace! it does small to my burdens). I will attend His Majesty's will and pleasure and laizour, in time, and manner, and all; for I will not be taxed with avarice, for all my wants, and importune pressing so graciouse a Sovereigne, of whose bounty I have tasted; albiet, if against Martimass, if I get not some farther again, as ever I may serve your Lordship, try, if by that course of Sergeants I may expect help or not, and if to be had without offence, but not also. Further it, and write to me your Lordship's counsell, that I may send up my son if need bees, for I will not leave my charge. Thus, expecting your Lordship's answer, I rest,

"Your Lordship's, in all duty to my power,

"AD., B. of DUMBLANE.

"Edin., 21st August, 1623."

The Bishop insists in the same petitory strain in his next to the same person, which I meet with next year. It runs: "*My good Lord,*— I have often written to your Lordship, but has never received any answer, for I see no hope that by Sergeants-of-law-making any good can come to me, fifteen being made lately, and I not being remembered. Truely, that whilk I got, saved me from falling, and was the most timouse help ever came. The Lord ever bless His Majesty, who therin did save me from ruin; but seeing it did [not] free me of my burdens, but only payed some annuals and rigorouse comprizings, I am even, and will be against Whitsunday in the like misery, or greater. Praying your Lordship to essay what means may be got to do me good without hurt or offence to His Majesty, for I see nothing here but more poverty; for of all Dundranan I have gotten nothing this two year. That country is so extremly impoverished that I must needs forgive them. Thus I humelie beseech your Lordship to remember the best way as occasion shall offer, and write to me your Lordship's opinion and advice, whilk I shall embrace, and rest,

"Your Lordship's, to my outermost power,

"AD., B. OF DUMBLANE.

"Cannongate, March 5, 1624."

Mr. Row in his History gives us the following account of what passed concerning the Bishop of Dumblane in November, 1629. I shall give it in his own words. "In the moneth of November, fell out a thing not to be ommitted. Mr. Adam Bannantine, returning from Edinburgh from the buriall of a noblman, whose funerall sermon he had preached, lodged in Culros, where Mr. Robert Melvil was a fellow-helper to the actuall minister[1] of that place; but without a free and a lawfull entry he would not submit to be admitted to the calling of the ministry in that place. The Bishop, hearing that Mr. Robert was to preach tomorrow morning, said: 'I will go and hear him, for I hear much good of him for his learning, zeal, and painfulnes'. The Minister of the place, hearing the Bishop was to be present, desired Mr. Robert not to make any particular application of his doctrine to the Bishop, as he had done to some others in time of sermons, both there and elswher. A litle before his going out to preach, ther was suggested to him by the Lord a pertinent application, on which he reasoned thus with himself: 'If I utter this I need never look for favour at this or any other bishop's hand, but how dare I conceal God's undoubted truth?' and thus went to the pulpit begging direction from Heaven as the Lord saw most for His glory, and the edification of His people. His text was Acts viii. 32. 'Now the place of Scripture was, He was led as a lamb to the slaughter,' &c. After severall good observations, he concluded his sermon thus: 'We see the way wherby our Lord went to His glory was by humility and suffering (Phil. ii. 5, 6). His humility and sufferings wer for a short time, His glory is eternall: so must Christ's members do; they must enter into glory by humility and sufferings, and, by the contrary, the way to endles shame is when men take to themselves honours contrary to God's Word—as ye, Sir! and the rest of the brethren who has taken lordship to themselves in God's Kirk. Ye enjoy honnours indeed for a short time, but your shame and pain shall be eternall until ye repent. I speak it in love, and say it again, though I should never speak more from this place—that you and the rest of you who bear down God's servants, and count them fools for their suffering on account of such things as they suffer for—that one day you shall count them wise, and yourselves fools, that for so short a preferment and small profites, has brought yourselves to endless shame and torment in hell-fire, except in time ye repent, which we would be all glad to see, if it wer the Lord's will.' In time of the delivering of the

[1] Note 72.

words the Bishop lifted up his eyes to heaven, as if he had been moved with them, but after he came from sermon, he flyted[1] [scolded] exceeding angry, seing sundry persons there who wer opposit to bishops, and one who had been silenced. And though he discharged him to preach again, yet shortly after he was content to oversee and misken him. 'Albeit,' said he, 'I know that the rest of the bishops will be discontent with me'; and it was, adds Mr. Row, no great marvell that he did so, because sometime the Bishop himself was a great opposit to bishops, and the Minister, who uttered the doctrine, protested that all was in love, nor had he any stipend or ordinary provision for his pains."

I have no more as to the Bishop till the year 1633. When the King came down, he found matters not yet ripe for introduction of the whole of the English usages in worship to Scotland. However, to prepare for this, when the Liturgy should be ready, he ordered the English service to be set up in his Royall Chappell, and wrote the Bishop who was Dean of it, and sent him his directions. I have the King's originall letter he sent with the directions, which it seems Mr. Collier has not seen when he published the directions, History v. 2, p. 760. It's proper they stand both here. Mr. Collier introduces his account of this matter thus: "The King, when in Scotland, had observed the order of the late reigne, for officiating in the English Liturgy at Hallyroodhouse had been discontinued, and being resolved to attempt the bringing this whole island to an uniformity of worship, he conceived the use of the English Common Prayer in the Chappell Royall might prove a serviceable introduction for tryall of this experiment. He ordered Bannantine, Bishop of Dumblan and Dean of the Chappell there, the following instructions." I'le begin with the King's letter to the Bishop, which came with them from the originall, and it runs thus: "*Charles Rex*, Reverend Father in God, and trusty and well beloved Counsellor, we greet you well. We have thought good for the better good ordering of the Divine Service to be performed in our Chappell Royal there, to send down some Articles under our own hand, to be observed therein, which we send you here inclosed. And it's our speciall pleasure that you see everything carefully performed, according as we have directed by those enclosed Articles; and, likewise, that you

---

[1] The word in Row is *kythed*, i.e., seen, to be manifest. Used by Burns and Chaucer. From *cunnan*, to know. —*Skeat*.

certify to the Lords of our Privy Counsell, that, if any of those, appointed by our former letters to them to communicat in our Chappell Royall, shall not accordingly perform the same, to assert such order may be taken by our Counsell therein, as by our saids former letters to them, we did appoint. Wherin expecting your diligence and care, we bid you farewell from our Court at Whitehall, the 8 day of October, 1633."

This letter is quotted on the back: "To the Reverend Father in God, and our right trustie and well beloved Counselour, the Bishop of Dumblane, Dean of our Chappell Royall, in the Kingdom of Scotland"; and above the address is, *The letter and orders for the Chappell Royall.* The orders follow :

Charles Rex.

" 1. Our express will and pleasure is, that the Dean of our Chappell that now is, and his successors, shall be assistant to the Right Reverend Father in God, the Archbishop of Saint Andrews, at the coronation, so often as it shall happen.

" 2. That the book of the form of our coronation, lately used, be put into a little box and laid into a standart, and committed to the care of the Dean of the Chappell successively.

" 3. That there be prayers twice a day with the choirs, as well in our absence as otherwise, according to the English Liturgy, till some other course be taken, for making one that may fit the customes and constitutions of that Church.

" 4. That the Dean of the Chappell look carefully that all, that receive the Blessed Sacrament there, receives it kneeling, and that there be a Communion held there the first Sabbath of every moneth, in our Chappell.

" 5. That the Dean of our Chapter that now is, and so successively, shall come deuly thither to prayers on Sundays, and such holy dayes as the Church observes, in his whites, and preach so, whensoever he preaches there ; and that he be not absent thence, but on necessary occasion of his Diocess, or otherwise according to the course of his preferment.

" 6. That those orders shall be our warrand to the Dean of our Chappell ; that the Lords of our Privy Counsell, the Lords of Session, the Advocat Clerk and Writters to the Signet, and Members of our College of Justice, be commanded to receive the Holy Communion once a year at least, in that our Chappell Royall, and kneeling, for example's sake to the Kingdome; and we likewise command the Dean aforesaid to make report yearly unto us how we are obeyed therein, and by whom, and also if any man shall refuse, in what manner he doth so, and why.

"7. That the copies which are consecrated for the use of our Chappell be delivered unto the Dean, to be keeped upon inventory by him, and in a standart provided for that purpose, and to be used at the celebration of the Sacrament in our Royall Chappell.

"To those orders we shall after add others, if we find others more necessary for the service of God there. Oct. 8, 1633."

Mr. Collier suspects the Bishop, as not fully come of from his old Presbyterian principles, but in my opinion he wrongs him. His words are: "And the King possibly, being apprehensive that Bannantine would be warping towards the Presbyterian persuasion, gave the Archbishop of Canterburry a warrand in write to correspond with this Bishop of Dumblane, and transmit His Majesty's directions to him for the management of the Chappell". I do not doubt of this, and I have some of Bishop Laud's originall letters to the Bishop. In consequence of this warrand, no doubt ther wer more of them, but they are now lost, and the few I have are sadly crazed [creased] and torn, and a good part of the last is past reading. I shall give them as they are.

The first is dated Jan. 14, 1633—in our stile, 1634—and runs: "*Salutem in Christo, my very good Lord,* you are much beholden to my Lord Stirling,[1] and after myself I did you the best service I could. I am glade your troublesome suites are at an end. I hope what the King hath now done will preserve you against your pressing necessitys, through which I pray God send you a good passage. But for Westminster foes, they did you much wrong, whoever they are that made those relations to you. For my former letters I trust to you as to your Lordship's preferment; when that place falls, I can say nothing, but I assure you His Majesty hath a very good opinion both of you and your service, and therfor I do not doubt but he will take you and your condition into consideration. At this time you have given His Majesty good content, and he expects you will contineu in that course, and let him still receive a note of who they be that conforme, and who

[1] Note 73.

not, for I see His Majesty is resolved to go constantly on, and therfor you must not fail. I have considered how much reason you speak concerning the poor singing men, and have received their petition which you sent enclosed. I must needs say their case deserves a great deal of commiseration; and the very first time I got access to His Majesty, after the receipt of your letters, I acquainted him with their necessitys, and he, like a graciouse and good prince, was very much moved with it, and commanded me to deliver their petition to my Lord Stirling, that some course might be taken for them, and this I will do so soon as I can meet with that lord, God willing, which I hope will be this day, and so soon as I can drive it to any good issue, you shall hear from me. So in hast I leave you to the grace of God.

"Your Lordship's very loving Friend and Brother.

"W. Cant.

"Lambeth, Jan. 14, 1633."

This letter is addressed "To the Right Reverend Father in God, my very good Lord and Brother, Lord Bishop of Dumblane, at Edinburrow"; and above the address, all in the same hand, *Anent his encouragement and anent noncommunicants.* The Primate's next letter is in May, that same year, is directed as the former, and above the address stands, *Anent the Liturgy and his sermon.* I know not what to make of those summarys above the address on Bishop Laud's letters, unless they wer like contents in the Primate's Register of letters, for the better perusall of them, and put also on the back of the letters when sent away. That letter runs thus: "*S. in Christo,* my very good Lord, I am right sorry for the death of the Bishop of Edinburrow, the loss being very great, both to the King and the Church. I acquainted His Majesty how needful it was to fill that place with an able successor. When mention was made of diverse men to succeed, I did as you desired, show His Majesty what your desires wer, and what necessitys lay upon you. After much consideration, His Majesty did resolve to give the Bishoprick of Edinburgh to my Lord of Brichen; as for yourself, he commanded me to write expressly to you that he did not take it well that, contrary to his express commands, you had ommitted prayers in the Chappell Royall according to the English Liturgy, with some other ommissions there, which please him not. Besides, His Majesty hath heard that ther have lately been some differences in Edinburgh about the sufferings of Christ, &c., and that your Lordship was some cause of them, or at least such an occasion as might have bred much disturbance, if the late Bishop of Edinburgh his care and temper had not moderated it. And this His Majesty is not well pleased with neither, and this hath been the cause why His Majesty hath, as I conceive, past you over in this remove; and you shall do very well both to apply yourself better to his Majesty's service and the well ordering of that Church, least you give just occasion to pass you by, when any other remove falls. I am sorry that I must write thus to you, but the only way of help lyeth in yourself, and in your own carriage, and, therfor, if you will not be careful, I do not see what any friend can do for you. Therfor, not doubting but you will take those things into your seriouse consideration for your own good, I leave you to the grace of God, and rest,

" Your Lordship's very loving Friend and Brother,

"W. Cant.

" Lambeth, May 6, 1634."

I do not mix in my remarks with those principall papers; it's enough I lay them before my readers, who will make naturall enough reflections on them. This letter is as discreet, and yet quick and handsom a banter upon the Bishop of Dumblan, as weel as a strong threatning of him, if he came not in intirely to the Primate's schemes and measures, as one can read almost. Everybody knows that Laud was sole Minister for Scotland at this time, at least as to Church matters, and did all. And one cannot doubt easily that the reasone of overlooking the Bishop of Dumblane wer suggested to him by the writter of them. Bishop Spotswood, as far as I can guess, would not suggest them, because he was no bigott for Bishop Laud's way, and the old bishops wer none of the known sticklers for Arminianisme. Probably Sydserf, Maxwell, and the rest of Laud's followers, informed him of those things, and he laid them before the King. Bishop Bannantine was zealouse enough for the ceremonies, and, according to Laud's own testimony, did the King good service that way a few moneths before this. No doubt he had given his reasons why the English Liturgy was not used in the Chappell, though they would be very strong ones, which would convince the Primat of England. But the great point was that of doctrine. From the summ on the back of the letter, *Anent his sermon*, I guess the Bishop of Dumblain had a sermon at Edinburgh in the old strain of the doctrine of the Church of Scotland, and probably against the Papisticall and Arminian doctrines, which Laud countenanced in England, and his creatures, Sydserf, Maxwell and Forbes, late Bishop of Edinburgh, used to teach to gratify their patron, Laud. Considering the detail given here, it appears, before Bishop Forbes' death, it may be before January last, when Bishop Bannantine stood very well with the King, otherwise Bishop Forbes could not have by his moderation prevented the ill consequences of it. Probably, indeed, Bishop Laud knew not of Bannantine's sermons till of late, but after he had cooled upon the English Liturgy, and especially when he had opposed the Arminio-Pelagian Popish doctrine, he must stand wher he is and not be advanced. But to return to the Primate's letters.

In July following, when the Bishop of Dumblane had made a return to the former [letter], which it seems drew forth an apology, Bishop Laud writes again to him with the former address, and this above it: *Anent reading the Liturgy and his Sermon at Edinburgh;* and it runs thus from the originall, as they all are :—" S. *in Christo.* My very good Lord,— My hast at this time forces me to write very breifly, and those are to let you know that I wrote nothing in my former letter but as the King's Majesty was informed, and myself by him commanded. I have now read your Lordship's letters to His Majesty, which hath in some part satisfyed him, but not altogether. As to the first, His Majesty saith that, though the gentlemen of the Chappell Royall did absent themselves for fear of arrests, having not to pay, and that might hinder the service in the Chappell in a solemne and formal way of singing by them; yet His Majesty thinks you might have gote a chaiplain of your own to have read the English Liturgy, that so the work for the main part of it might have gone on; and for the payment of those men, I think your Lordship knowes, I have done all the good offices I can, but have it not in my power to mend all the difficultys of the time concerning the disturbance that was in Edinburgh. If any wrong was done your Lordship, it must lye on them who misreported you to the King, whoever they wer; and albiet the King took it not ill that you advised the late Bishop of Edinburgh to appease the disturbances, for that was very worthily and discreetly done in you. But, in as far as I remember, the charge laid upon you to the King was, that in your own sermon, which you preached about that time, you did rather side with one party than either reprove or compose the difference, though I must needs confess to your Lordship that, by reason of the multitude of bussinesses, which lye upon me, I cannot charge my memory with the particular. You have done well to acquaint the Lords of Council and Session with His Majesty's resolution concerning the Communion in the Chappell-Royall, and I doubt not but, if you continou to do what His Majesty looks for, and which is most just and fitt to be done, but that you will easily recover His Majesty's favour, and find the good of it. So in hast I leave you to the grace of God, and rest,

"Your Lordship's very loving Friend and Brother,

"W. Cant.

"Lambeth, July 1, 1634."

The next letter is dated Oct. 4, that same year, but more than the half of it is consumed and torn, so I can give only a paragraph at the beginning and the end. It runs thus:—"*S. in Christo.* My very good Lord,—I have a second time moved His Majesty concerning them that obeyed or disobeyed his commands in receiving the Communion in the Chappell at Hallyroodhouse, and you shall not fail to receive His Majesty's answer by my Lord of Ross, so that I have not need to be further troublesome to you in that particular." (The next paragraph of 5 or 6 lines I can make nothing of; it seems to import that His Majesty was now satisfyed as to the Bishop's carriage with respect to the English Service in the chappell.) Then he adds: "That one of the gentlemen of the Chappell-Royall had been at London and received half of the money, which had been promised them, and he was told that the other was payed also to one of their company whom themselves employed to receive it, who it seems was bankrupt, and either run away with their money, or mispent it, or also served his turn with it. Now what to say to this (adds he) I cannot tell, for the chequer is not in that case that I can think it fitt for, if I do I am sure the Lord Treasurer will not think so, that the King should pay the same summ twice; and yet I must confess it falls very hard upon the poor men to bear the loss, but they should have been wiser in the choice of their agent. Notwithstanding, if ther can be any hope in this case to relieve, I shall do my best, and for the future My Lord promises to me they shall be dulie payed. So I leave you to the grace of God, and rest,

" Your Lordship's loving Freind and Brother,

" W. CANT.

" Croydon Oct. 4, 1634."

The next letter, if I mistake it not, clears what is wanting in the former, and is addressed as the first, and above it is written : *About wear-the whites.* It runs: " *S. in Christo.* My very good Lord,—I am very glade to hear your resolutions for ordering the Chappell Royall, and that you are resolved to wear your whites, notwithstanding of the maliciousness of foolish men. I know His Majesty will take your obedience and care very well, and being fully satisfyed both concerning your sermon and all things else committed to your trust, you may, as opportunity serves, expect from His Majesty all reasonable things ; and I shall not be wanting to give you all the assistances that I can, upon all occasions, of which I heartily pray you not to doubt. My Lord, the Earle of Traquair is now come, and I shall take the first opportunity I can to speak once more to him about the gentlemen of your Chappell, and shall shew him what your Lordship writes concerning one Edward Kelly whom you mention, and what answer soever I can get you shall receive from me. So in hast I leave you to the grace of God, and rest,

" Your Lordship's very loving Freind and Brother,

" W. CANT.

" Lambeth, Jan. 12, 163$\frac{4}{5}$.

" P.S.—I have spoken with my Lord Traquair, and he tells me (if I mistook him not) that payment was made to Kelly with relation to the gentlemen of the Chappell, and that your own hand, as well as others, is to some agreement made about it ; the paper was not then about him, else he had showed it me. Your Lordship then shall do very well to speak with him again about this particular. As to the time to come, he hath assured me they shall be dulie payed."

Next year, it seems Bishop Bannantyne continoued to do all things in the King's Chappell so as to please the King, and, therfor, when the

Bishoprick of Aberdeen fell vacant by the death of Mr. Patrick Forbes, whose Life stands here, the King bestowed a bishoprick on him in May, 1635.

I have before me Bishop Laud's letter upon this. It's directed as before, and above it is written: *Anent their encouragement.* It runs: "S. in Christo. My very good Lord,—The King has been acquaint with your care of the Chappell Royal, and is very well pleased with their conformity which have been there at your last reception of the Blessed Sacrament; and for my part I am heartily glad to see in what a fair way your Church bussinesses now are in those parts. I hope, if your bishops be pleased to continou their good example and their care, all things will setle beyond expectation. The King hath declared his pleasure concerning the bishopricks now void, and hath given you the Bishoprick of Aberdeen, as you will hear more at length by my Lord of Ross. But being an University and a place of consequence, he will have you reside there, and relyes more upon you for your well ordering of that place. I am very glad the King hath been so mindfull of you, and given you so good a testimony upon this occasion of your remove. So I leave you to the grace of God, and rest,

"Your Lordship's very loving Freind and Brother,

"WILL. CANT.

"Lambeth, May 19, 1635."

Very litle offers to me concerning the Bishop after he went to Aberdeen. In Bishop Spotswood's Life, the reader hath a letter from Bishop Laud complaining heavily of the Bishop of Aberdeen's allowing a fast to be keeped in his Diocess, 1637, not appointed by the King or bishops. Matters wer now come the lenth that ministers resumed the native power of their office, and it's probable the Bishop knew the fast would be kept whether he allowed it or not, and so chuse to comply.

In the Assembly, 1638, he was cited, with the rest of the bishops, and did not appear or send any excuse, and it seems stood firmly to his Prelaticall principles. And so he was not only deposed by the Assembly, but for his contumacy and other crimes excommunicat by the Assembly, with the bishops who had given in a declinature. The sentence stands thus: "Sentence of deposition and excommunication," &c. Transcribe it here from Act. Ass., 1638, p. 15.

After this Bannantine fled to England, and soon after, 1639 or 1640, dyes there. The writter of the Appendix to Spotswood—"Though he being outted by the Covenant he retired to England, wher he dyed shortly after. His house in Old Aberdeen, for new things in magnificence like a palace, was plundered by a regiment of the Covenanters, and afterwards quite demolished by the English usurpers."

COLLECTIONS UPON THE LIFE OF Mr. JOHN DURIE, MINISTER AT EDINBURGH AND MONROSS.

The commone Lord of the vineyard gives various gifts unto such as He sends to labour in it: some shine in their wisdome and prudence, others are eminent for their learning and knowledge, others for their diligence, laboriousnes, love to souls, and zeal against sin, and for the glory and interests of their Master. Perhaps it may be a harder question than at first it appears, to determine which of those gifts and graces are most to be wished for. Everyone that considers the present state of things, and the need of all of them in the Church as a society, will rejoice that the dispensations of those is in better hands than those of any creature. The most excellent gifts are to be coveted, and those that render one most usefull for the good of souls and glory of the Redeemer, seem to be most excellent; and the prudence, wisdome, and learning, in eminent degrees, render a person both usefull and conspicuous. Yet diligence, laboriousnes, and zeal for Christ and souls seem to be the more immediat springs of acting and usefulnes. For those Mr. John Durie was very eminent; and although, in point of learning and knowledge, he came, perhaps, not up to the lenth of other shining lights, yet those made him extremely usefull; and he well deserves a room here, both that severall things, worthy of recording, fall in upon the hints of his Life we have, and because he has been unfairly represented; and, therfor, chiefly from the MS. Calderwood, I shall glean up the following hints concerning him.

Mr. Dury was born of mean but honest parents, in the town of Mauchline, in Airshire, in the year 1537, when the Reformation was scarce begun to dawn. He, showing some inclination to learning, was sent to learn his Latine in the town of Air. Whither in his youth he took some liking to the truth, from the glimrings of it remaining here and there among some few in Kyle, since the Lollards wer there, I cannot say; but after he had been some time trained up in letters at Air, his cusine, George Dury, Abbot of Dumfermeline, called him to that monastry, and he remained one of the monks for about 3 years. Mr. Petry remarks that he was a monk of Dumfermline, and nottices that severall of our usefull ministers after the Reformation wer sent us out of those convents, and, excepting the Laird of Dun, none of them wer persons of rank and riches; yet by such weak instruments the Lord made His glory to shine in this land.

Bishop Spotswood tells us that, when in the monastery of Dumfermline, Mr. Durie fell into some suspicion of what was then called heresy; that is, a love to the Reformation. He was delated to the Abbot, and, after a tryall, wherein it seems he was not affrayed to confess the truth in as far as yet he knew it, he was condemned to be immured, that is, shut up secretly betwixt two walls till he dyed. His friend, the Abbot, was the severer upon him, because he had brought him to the convent, and least, in those suspiciouse times, he should be jealoused himself because he was his relation. But the Lord had considerable work to put in his hands, and, therfor, by the intercession of the Earle of Arran, to whom Mr. Dury's friends had applyed, means wer found for his escape. When Mr. Knox came to the country, he was a diligent hearer of his doctrine, and therby came to be further enlightned and confirmed by him in the truth, as it is in Jesus.

Not long after the Reformation, he was ordeaned a minister, and served first in the parish of Hales, some miles from Edinburgh, and was thence brought to the town of Leith, wher he was soon taken nottice of for his serious, fervent, and usefull gift of preaching; and a little after Mr. Knoxe's death, and the civil warrs betwixt those that stood for the King and such as set up for his mother wer over, he was called to Edinburgh. The particular year I can only gather from Spotswood, who sayes he continoued there minister 20 years. We shall see, in the 1584, Mr. Dury was removed from thence for his zeal in reproving vice, and so he was fixed there about the 1574.

Next year, at the Assembly, August 6, 1575, when the tryal of bishops was entered upon in the first session, Mr. John Dury protested that tryall of bishops by the Assembly prejudge not the opinions and reasons, which he and other bretheren of his mind have to oppone, against the office and name of a bishop, which was received, and in the 4th session that matter is resumed. The account of this, as it is in the Registers, follows: "Anent the question propounded by certain bretheren of the Assembly, Whither if the bishops, as they are now in Scotland, have their foundations of the Word of God or not? or if the Chapters appointed for creating them ought to be tollerat in this Reformed Kirk? For better resolution herof, the Assembly appoints their loved bretheren Mr. John Craige, Minister of Aberdeen; Mr. James Lawson, Minister of Edinburgh; Mr. Andrew Melvil, Principall of the Colledge of Glasgow, on the ane part; Mr. George Hay, Commissioner of Caithnes; Mr. John Row, Minister of Perth; and Mr. David Lindsay, Minister of Leith, on the other part, to conveen, reason, and opinion therupon to the Assembly before the dissolution therof, if they be resolved therupon betwixt and then." Accordingly they did report their oppinion in write. They moved an answer to the first question, but declared it their mind, that, if any bishop be chosen, who has not the qualitys God's Word requires, the Assembly try him *de novo*, and depose him. The points, wherein they agree as to the office of a bishop and superintendant, wer that the name is common, and so the office, to all pastors over a flock. The after procedure of this Church on this head will be seen in the Lives of Mr. Craig, Mr. Row, the Laird of Dun, and Mr. Andrew Melvil, wher Bishop Spotswood's account of this matter is considered.

Mr. Calderwood observes that about this time, God glorifyed Himself mightily by the Ministers of Edinburgh. Mr. Dury, Mr. Lawson, and, I think, Mr. Balcanquell came in before the 1580. They wer, he sayes, men of knowledge, uprightnes, and zeal, and they dwelt commodiously together as in a colledge, and sharpened one another, as iron sharpneth iron.

In December, 1580, Mr. Walter Balcanquell preached December 7, and he proved with great freedom the vices of the Court. The King now had taken the reins into his own hand, and was much under the management of D'Aubigny and French influence. Upon the 9 of December, Mr. Durie, in his sermon on the last of Hosea, confirmed all Mr. Balcanquell had said, with severall additions when he came to the application. Mr. Dury, in September, had with freedom discovered the danger the King and country wer in by Frenchmen, and such as were sent here by the bloody King of France. Mr. Balcanquell and Durie wer, soon after their sermon in December, cited before the Council, and required to give in write that part of their sermon, against which exceptions wer taken. This Mr. Durie refused, least it should be a preparative to the King and Council's making themselves judges immediatly of ministers' doctrine, wherupon he was charged to enter ward in the Castle. However, upon consideration, they both agreed to give in their sermons in write for the King's information, and to shew that the reports gone [abroad] of them wer ill-grounded, but still under protestation that His Majesty and Council should not judge them as [to] their doctrine. This was admitted, and the sentence of warding was recalled.

Upon the last day of December, the Earle of Mortoun, while sitting in Council, was accused by Captain James Stewart, 2d brother of the house of Ochiltree, and afterwards Earle of Arran, now a great favourite, of forknowledge and treasonable concealing of the King's father's murder. The account of this great man's tryall and condemnation is given by our printed historians. He was first imprisoned in Dumbartun, and, in May, brought to his tryall at Edinburgh, when the sentence was pronounced, which went on the testimony of witnesses he had excepted against. It was pronounced that he was guilty of concealing the King's death, and was art and part in the same. He repeated the words *art and part*, and knocking on the ground with his staffe said, " God knoweth the contrary ". Spotswood gives us a hint of his confession to the Ministers of Edinburgh, that morning before his execution. But Mr. Calderwood having preserved the whole of the Ministers' conference with him, and a pretty large account of his cariage and religious behaviour at his death, from that, and another copy I have taken from the Bodleyan Library, I will insert it here, Mr. Durie being cheifly concerned in it, and the paper itself not published, and very suited to the designe of this biography, wher I incline to preserve the principall papers of this nature, as they offer. It is as followes:

"The Summ of all the conference which was betwixt the Earle of Mortoun and John Durie and Mr. Walter Balcanquell, and the cheif things they heard of him, so far as they could remember, that day the said Earle suffered, which was the 2d of June, 1581.

"1. Being exhorted that he should not be discouraged in consideration of that estate, wherinto he had once been in this wordle, being in honnour and glory, and of the downcast wherinto now he was brought, but rather, in consideration of the glory to come, he should rejoice and be of good comfort, his answer was: 'As concerning all the glory I had in this wordle, I care not for it, because I am persuaded now that all the honnours, riches, freinds, pleasures, and whatsomever I had in the wordle, is but vanity. And, as concerning the estate wherunto now I am brought, I thank God for it; and now am at this point, that I am content rather to render my life than to live, because I know, that as God hath appointed a time for my death, so He hath also appointed the manner therof; and, therfor, seeing that now is the time, and this is the manner that best pleaseth God to take me, I am content. And as for my life in this wordle, I care not for it a pennie, in respect of that immortall and everlasting joy which I look for, and wherof I am assured.'

"2. Being required what was his part or knowledge in the King's murder, he answered with this attestation: '*As I shall answer to my Lord God, I shall declare trulie all my knowledge in that matter.* The summ wherof is this. First, after my returning out of England, when I was banished for Davie's slaughter, I came out of Wedderburn to Whittinghame, wher the Earle of Bothwell and I met together, and in the yeard of Whittinghame, after long communing, the Earle propounded unto me the purpose of the King's murder, requiring what would be my part therunto, saying it was the Queen's mind that the King should be taine away, because, as he said, she blamed the King more of Davie's slaughter than me. My answer to the Earle of Bothwell at that time was this—that I would not in any wise medle in that matter; and that for this cause, that I am but newly come out of a new trouble, wherof as yet I am not ridded, being discharged to come near the Court be seven miles; and, therfor, I can not enter myself in such a new trouble again. After this answer, Mr. Archibald Douglas entered in conference with me in that purpose, perswading me to aggre to the Earle of Bothwel's desire. Last of all, the Earle of Bothwell, yet being in Whittinghame, earnestly propounded the said matter to me again, persuading me therunto, because it was the Queen's mind, and she would have it done. Unto this my answer was: I desired the Earle of

Bothwell to bring the Queen's hand write unto me in that matter for warrand, and then I should give him an answer; otherwise I would not medle therewith: the whilk warrand he never reported to me.' Then, being enquired what would have been his part in case he had gotten the Queen's warrand in that matter—would he, in respect therof, medled with such a filthy murder as that? he answered: 'If I had got the Queen's write, and so had knowen her mind, I was purposed to have bannished myself again, and turned my back upon Scotland, until I had seen better'. Then following furth the discourse of this matter he said: 'I being in Saint Andrews to visit the Earle of Angus, a little before the murther, Mr. Archibald Douglas came to me there, both with write and credite from the Earle of Bothwell, showing unto me that purpose anent the King's murther was to be done, and near a point; and to require my concurrence and assistance therunto. My answer was to him—that I would give no answer to that purpose, seing I had not gotten the Queen's warrand in write, which was promised to me; and, therfor, seing the Earle of Bothwell never reported any warrand of the Queen, I never medled further in it.' Then, being enquired whether he gave Mr. Archibald any command to be there in his name, he answered: 'I never commanded him'. Being enquired if he gave him any counsell therunto, he answered: 'I never counselled him to it'. Being required if he counselled him in the contrair, he answered: 'I never counselled him in the contrair'. Then it was said unto him, that it was a dangerouse thing for him, that his servant and depender was to pass to such a wicked purpose, and that he, knowing therof, stayed him not, seing it would be accounted his deed. He answered that 'Mr. Archibald was at that time a depender upon the Earle of Bothwell, making court for himself, rather than a depender of mine'. After this, following furth the said discourse [he said] 'The said Mr. Archibald, after the deed was done, showed me that he was at the deed doing, and came back to the Kirk of Feild-yeard with the Earles of Bothwell and Huntley'. Then being enquired if he received in his company the said Mr. Archibald after the murther, answered: 'I did indeed'. Then it was said to him: 'Apparandly, my Lord, ye cannot justly complean of the sentence that is given against you, seing with your own mouth you confess the forknowledge and conccealing of the King's murder, of which two points only ye should not be able to abide the law'. He answered: 'I know that, indeed; but they should have considered the danger that the revealing of it would have brought me to at that time. For at that time I durst not reveal it for fear of my life; and at that time, whom to should I have revealed it? To the Queen? She was the doer of it. I was minded, indeed, to the King's father, but I durst not for my life; I knew him to be such a bairn that ther was nothing told him but he would reveal it to her again; and, therfor, I durst no wise reveal it to him. And, howbeit, they would have damned me of art and part, forknowledge and concealing, of the King's murder, yet, as I shall answer to God, I never had art or part, rid or counsel, in that matter. I forknew, indeed, and concealed it because I durst not reveal it to any creature for my life.' Being required why he should not sensyne [since then] reveal it to the King's Majesty, he answered he durst not for the same fear. Then he said: 'After the Earle of Bothwell was cleaned by an assize, sundry of the nobility and I also subscribed a band with the Earle of Bothwell, that, if any should lay the King's murther to his charge, we would asist him in the contrair; and, therfor, I subscribed to the Queen's marriage with the Earle of Bothwell, as sundry others of the nobility did, being charged therunto by the Queen's writt and command'. Then being required, in the name of the living God, that seing this murther of the King was one of the most filthy acts that ever was done in Scotland, and the secrets therof hath not as yet been declared, neither yet who wer the cheif doers, whither he was wirriet [strangled] or blown up in the air, therfor, to declare if he knew any further secret in that matter, therunto he answered: 'As I shall answer to God, I know no more secret in that matter than I have already told, and heard by the depositions of such as have already suffered for it, which depositions are yet extant'. Being required if he knew any presently to be about the King, who wer the doers of that work, be whose company the King and Commonwealth might be hurt, he answered: 'I know none, and will accuse none'. Last of all, it was said unto him concerning his purpose, that, in respect of his own deposition, his part would be suspected to be more foul than he declared. He speired, 'For what reason'? It was answered: 'Because ye being in authority, howbeit ye punished others for that murther, ye punished not Mr. Archibald Douglas, whom ye knew to be guilty therof'. He answered: 'I punished him not, neither indeed durst, for the causes before showen '.

"3. Being required of the Earle of Athol's poisoning,[1] and if he had any art or part therof, he answered, with a great attestation: 'Let God never be mercifull to me, if ever I knew anything of that matter, or heard of it before I heard the common bruit of the country'. And being enquired if he knew that Mr. John Provand brought home any poison, he answered: 'I know nothing of Mr. John Provand but honestie'; and said: 'Fye! ther is over meikle filthines in Scotland already: God forbid that the vile practice of poisoning should enter among us! I would not for the Earldome of Athole have either ministered poison to him, or caused it to have been ministered to him; yea, if I had been an hundred, and he his alone, I would not have stirred a hair of his head.'

"4. Being enquired if he made any conspiracy against the Earle of Lennox, he answered with the like attestation as oft before: 'I never thought in my heart, or purposed any conspiracy against the Earle of Lennox, nor minded ever to do him hurt in body or otherwise. But I was greived that by the moyen [contrivance] of the Earle of Lennox, who as yet knew not the state of our country, nor perceived the danger of the King's person, but being therunto requested by others, sundry wer brought home that wer the King's enimies, waltherers [subverters] of his kingdome, and enimies to religion, which was an apparent danger to his person and realme, which I hoped by council to have helped when the Earle of Lennox' familiarity and mine should have been greater.'

"5. Being enquired whether he had any traffecking with England for transporting the King or otherwise, or if he had any pension of the Queen of England for that effect, he answered: 'As I shall answer to God, under the pain of condemnation or salvation, I never had trafecking with England that way. Ther was never one in Scotland or England, neither the Queen nor any in her name, that ever meaned such a thing to me, directly nor indirectly, as to transporting or putting the King in England, except it had been for his profite and honnour that he had been crowned King of England. Then would I have ridden with him to have debated his right, according to my power.

[1] Note 74.

And for more clear purgation of myself in this matter, I will say this: If ever I meaned hurt, directly or indirectly, to the King, my master, but meaned alwise his weal, let God never be mercifull to me; and I shall never ask God's mercie for any thought that ever entered into my heart against the King; yea, ther was nothing I required more in this life, than that he should be brought up in virtue and godlines. And I will say more: If I had been as carefull to serve my God and walk in His fear as I was to see the King's weal, I had not been brought to this poynt that I am at this day. And wheras they say I was the Queen of England's pensioner, as I shall answer to God, I never had pension of the Queen of England in my life. And albiet they cause the bruite to goe that I should have furnished the Queen of England's souldiers, when last upon the borders, I never knew or heard of it. And, last of all, wheras they alledge I should have been a trafficker with England, I praise God I never had trafeckking with them but for the well of the King, his country and subjects. Indeed, about a year since, the Queen of England wrote to me a letter, the summ wherof was this: that she was informed that sundry Papists and enimies to the King wer familiar with him, and come in credit, which could not be without his hurt, hurt to religion and the estate of both the Realmes, and, therfor, desired my counsell how it might be remedied. Unto this I sent her an answer, the summ wherof was this: I besought Her Majesty that she would not burden me with such a thing, for I would no wise medle in that matter. She would not be content that any of her subjects would medle with a forraigne prince for the reformation of her affairs. After this answer I received a letter from Mr. Bowes, howbeit not subscribed by the Queen of England, yet, as I understood, sent by her meen and dyted by her secretary, Walsinghame, wherin was declared that by this purpose there was nothing meaned either to my hurt, or the hurt of the King, or the Realme, but for the well of the King, both the Realmes and the subjects therof, and especially of the religion. But I wrote no answer again, nor would medle further in that matter.'

"6. Being demanded what was his part of the enterprize of the Castle of Stirling,[1] he answered: 'As I shall answer to God, I knew nothing of it while it was done; but being in Lothian, I received advertishment out of the Castle of Stirling, and a writing from the

[1] Note 75.

King that I should come there. And wheras they say I minded to keep the King captive there, I never minded to keep him in captivity there, or in any other place. But I understood by the King's own speaking, that he was as free at that time as ever he was before, or desired to be for the present. And if I had understood that his Grace would have gone to any other place, wher greater liberty had been, I would have gone with him.'

" 7. It being laid to his charge that he was a great hinderer of the matters of the Kirk, and authorizer of bishops and other corruptions, wher he might have done meikle good for the furtherance of God's glory and advancement of His Evangell, both in the time of his government and sensyne, his answer was : ' As concerning religion and doctrine, as it's now preached and professed in Scotland, I ever meant alwise well in my heart to it, and acknowledge it to be the very truth of God, in so meikle that rather than any hurt had come to the religion, I would have been content to have wared my life, lands, and goods in the defence of it, like as now I am content to die in the constant profession of it. But, indeed, as concerning some things that wer in question betwixt me and the Kirk, I did therin according to my knowledge, and followed that opinion that I thought to be best at that time, in consideration of the state of all things as they wer. And, therfor, howbeit I will not stand in defence of those things which I then did, yet I will make this protestation, that, as I shall answer to God, I did nothing in these matters either of contempt, malice, or otherwise ; but if ther was anything done amiss, it was of ignorance, and for lack of better knowledge ; and if I had knowen better, would I have done otherwise, and was now purposed, at last, to have helped that so farr as I might.'

" 8. Being desired, in the name of God, not to stand in defence of his own innocencie, but plainly to confess his sins to God's glory, and to think, that, however it might be that man hath done in this matter, yet God hath alwise done justly, and that he was to suffer nothing but that wherof, before God, he was worthy and more, his answer was : ' That however it be that men have done, I remitt them to God and their own conscience ; but I acknowledge, indeed, that God hath alwise done justly unto me, and not only justly, but mercifully also, because I acknowledge myself, of all sinners, to have been one of the greatest—a filthy abuser of my body in the pleasures of the flesh, given over meikle to the wordle and pleasure therof, and such other sins as God might justly lay to my charge; and that I expressed not the fruits of my profession in my life and conversation; and, therfor, I beseek God to be mercifull to me. And, indeed, now I acknowledge the great mercy of God in this, that among all the benefites He hath bestowed upon me, this is one of the chiefest, that, in this my last trouble, He hath given me space and laizour to repent of my sins, and to be at a point with my God. In which trouble also I have found greater comfort than ever I could [have] found before, because therin I concluded with myself, that if God should have spared my life, and have delivered me out of this trouble, that then I should have cast away all the cares of the wordle, the pleasures of the same, and delight of all earthly things, and dedicat myself to serve my God in all kind of queitness and simplicity. And if it should please God to take me in this trouble, I had concluded to be content therwith also, being alwise assured of the mercys of God; and, therfor, I thank God, that now I find me at this point, that I am rather content to dye than live, and that I shall not see the miserys to come; for I assure you that I think this to be the most acceptable time that ever God could have taken me. For I perceive and forsee such miseries and confusions to ensue, that I thank God I shall not see them; and ye, who fear God, and live behind me, when you see thir changes, ye shall wish of God to be where I shall be, that is, with Him.'

"9. Being demanded what he thought of the form of judgment used against him, and what was his judgment therto, whither he thought any wrong was done him or not, and exhorted not to blame man without cause, he answered: 'I would be very loath to find fault, or blame the noble gentlemen that have tane upon their consciences to condemn me; but I remitt them to God and their own consciences. Yet I am moved to speak somewhat freely in this matter, and it is this: I saw so partiall dealing against me, that it had been all alike to me, if I had been as innocent as St. Stephen, as I had been as guilty as Judas; for I perceived plainly that ther was nothing but my life sought, however it had been, which appeared in this, that no exception against any person that was to pass upon mine assize could avail. For I required the Earle of Argyle to purge himself of partiall counsell given to the pursuer, my accuser. He purged himself, indeed;

but I know the contrair, that he gave particular councill to him. Likewise, the Laird of Wauchton, the Lord Seaton, and such others who wer knowen to be my enimies, notwithstanding any lawfull exceptions, wer put upon my assize. In consideration wherof, I cannot but be persuaded of a thing which it behoveth me to communicat with you, and it's this: I perceive it's not my life only that they are seeking, but they, who are the authors of my death, had some other purpose in hand, which they perceived could not goodly be done, except I, and such others who favour the good cause, wer tane out of the way. And, therfor, I cannot but suspect that I have been so handled, and such as I hereafter shall be put at [attacked], that they may have a more patent way to do their turn; and I pray God that ye, that are to live behind me, see not the practise therof. But I fear it sore. And, therfor, in respect of this appearand danger of the common cause, I give my counsell to the King, my master, and wish you, in the name of God, to bear it to him. The summ wherof is this: that they who have been the King's unfreinds—enimies to his crown and common cause—are brought in credit and in court; and they who have been mentainers of his crown, and good freinds, discredited and disliked of. And sicklyke, such as are knowen to be Papists, and suspected to be enimies to religion, are over familiar, and in over great credit with his Majesty; which appearandly cannot be without great hazard to religion, and hurt to his estate. And, therfor, I admonish him, in the name of God, to bewarr with them, and put remeed therunto; and, as he hath been brought up in the fear of God, and company of good men, to continou therin, and not to go back, or else he hath done with it forever. For I tell you what moveth me to speak this: the estate of religion in this country appeared never to be in such a danger; and that for this cause: I hear say that ther is a dealing and present traffecking betwixt France and England, and Monsieur's marriage with the Queen is heavily to be feared. If France and England band together, and that marriage go forward, ye may easily understand, that the one of them will persuade the other to their religion. The Monsieur dare not change his religion, if he ettle [aspire] to the crown of France; and, therfor, ye must be assured he will persuade the other to his religion, and to bring Papistry in England, which is ever easy to be done, the twa parts of England being Papists. If England and France band together, and both be Papists, we are left one alone, we have no league with England. And, therfor, I know what we will do, viz.: we will cleave to the old league with France; and to band with France as France is now, and France and England being one, judge ye, in what case the religion shall be with us. God give to the King and the nobility wisdom to forsee the danger in time!'

"10. Being required to give his counsell to the Earle of Angus, and to show him what was meetest to be done, seing presently he was in great trouble, he answered: 'Truly, I dare give him no counsell. The Lord help him! for truly, I dare give him no counsell; and I will tell you why. To bid him come in presently, I dare not. All men may see in what danger he is, as things go now, if he come in. And to counsell him to abide furth, I dare not, for then he shall lose the King's favour for ever; he shall tyne himself, his herctage, his whole freinds. And, therfor, the best council I can give him is, that he make all moyen possible to purchase the King, my master's favour again, and to see if he may have any assurance of his life, that he may serve his God and the King truly, and submitt himself and all that he hath to his Majesty; for, poor man! he hath done nothing yet, but it may be mended. I say no more; but the Lord give him His Spirit to follow that which is best.'

"11. Being required to declare what was the summ of the admonition that John Knox gave him before he accepted the regiment, when he came to him a little before his departure, he answered: 'I shall tell you so far as I can remember. First of all, he speired if I knew anything of the King's murder? I answered: "Indeed I know nothing of it". Then said he to me: "God hath beautifyed you with many benefits, which he hath not given to every man, as he hath given unto you riches, wisdome, freinds; and now is to preferr you to the government of this Realme; and, therfor, in the name of God, I charge you to use all the benefites aright, and better in time to come than you have done in times bypast—first, to God's glory, to the furtherance of the Evangell, to the maintenance of the Kirk of God and His ministry; next, for the well of the King, his realme, and true subjects. If so ye shall do, God shall bless you, and honour you; but if you do it not, God shall spoil you of thir benefites, and your [end] and shall be ignominy and shame."' Then being required if he had found this true, he answered: 'I have found it, indeed; yet I doubt not but the Lord will be mercifull to me'.

"12. Then being enquired for what cause he held some of the neibours of Edinburgh in ward, he answered: 'Surely I meaned no evil to those men; but it was done upon this respect: we had the matter of the bullion then in hand. I was informed that they wer the hinderers therof. I thought it best, at that time, to put them in ward for a while, till the turn had been done, and if I did them any wrong, I crave them forgiveness, as I forgive all men.'

"13. Being enquired if he knew that he would be accused of the matter before, he answered: 'I was advertized of it, and might have escaped; but I would not, leaning alwise upon mine innocency, and not supposing they would have condemned me upon such a thing'. Then after this, he and we called to God together by earnest prayer; during the which prayer he shewed most evident tokens of the inward motion of the Spirit of God. The prayer being ended, he sayeth to us: 'I thank you heartily for your comfort which you have offered unto me, for now, indeed, is greatest mister [need] of comfort; and, therfor, as ye have begun, I beseech you to continou with me. And now, after I am come to the knowledge of my own sins, there resteth only two things that I will crave of you; that is, first, that ye may shew to me all kind of arguments wherby I may be comforted, and hold me sure upon the mercy of God; and next, seing flesh is but fearfull and weak, that ye will comfort me against the naturall fear of death.' Which desire we travelled to satisfy by long conference, which wer too long to rehearse in every point; yet the summ of it was this. It was said to him that ther wer 3 things chiefly, that might make him assured of the mercy of God in Christ. 1. The innumerable and comfortable promises of God's mercies conteaned in His Word, wherupon it behoved him alwise to lean, wherof there wer some cited unto him. 2. The example of God's mercies towards His own servants, howbeit they had been great sinners, as appeareth in David, Magdalen, Peter, the theif, &c. 3. The oft experience of God's mercies which, from time to time, he had found in his own person, ought to assure him now also of His mercie in the end. Unto this he answered, saying: 'I know all this to be true, for, since I passed to Dumbarton, I have read all the 5 Books of Moses, Joshua, the Judges, and now I am in Samuel; and I'le tell you what I have found there. I see there the mercys of God are wonderfull, and [He] alwise inclined to have pity upon His own people of Israel; for there it appeareth that, howbeit that He punished the people of Israel when they sinned, yet, how soon they turned to Him again, He was mercifull to them, and when they sinned again, yet He punished them; and so oft as they repented, He was mercifull unto them again; and, therfor, I am assured that, howbeit, I have oft offended against the Lord my God, yet He will be mercifull to me also.' Further, it was said to him on this point, that, in case Satan would travell to discourage him, in consideration of the justice of God on the one part, and of his sins on the other part, we exhorted him, by the contrair, to be of good courage, and even, in respect of the justice of God, to be assured that his sins should not be laid to his charge, and that because God was just—for the justice of God will not suffer Him to take twice payment for one thing; that, as we know that in the common dealing of men, he that is a just man will not crave payment of that wherof he hath been already satisfyed. And, therfor, seing that Christ hath already satisfyed for our sins, and payed God for the uttermost farthing He could crave of us, He cannot lay our sins to our charge, being satisfyed in Christ: so that His justice will not suffer Him to take payment twice for one thing. Unto this, he answered: 'Trulie, that is very good'.

"As concerning the naturall fear of death, we exhorted him to be alwise occupyed upon the consideration of the glory of God, the joy and felicity of the life that is to come; and that should be the only way to swallow up the fear of this naturall death. He answered: 'I praise God I do soe'.

"All this being done, having in his hand a pretty treatise of the Meditation of Death, written by Mr. Bradford,[1] which, he said, he had gotten from the Lady Ormestoun before he past in ward; and, therfor, before his passing forth, he gave it to Mr. James Lowson, desiring him to deliver it to the same lady again. Having this book in his hand, he willed Mr. Walter to read to him a peice therof, which he did. In reading wherof, with sundry conferences upon the thing that was read, both he and we got great comfort. In so much that he said, 'I praise God, I hear now with other ears than I heard before.' With this, being

[1] Note 76.

called to his disjoon, he desired us earnestly to take part with him; as we did. He did eat his disjune with great chearfulness, as all the company saw, and as appeared in his speaking. Now saith he: 'I see ther is a great difference betwixt a man that is occupyed with the cares of the wordle, and him that is free therof; and this I have found in the 2 nights' rest going before. For in the night before my accusation, I could get no rest for care, because I knew I was to be accused the morn; and, therfor, being solicite to answer to every point that should be laid to my charge, I could not sleep. But this night, after I was condemned, and knew that I should die, I was at a point with myself, and had no thought of the wordle, nor cares of my life, but cast my only care upon God; and I praise God I never sleeped better in my life time nor I did this night.' And [he] said to William Stewart: 'William, ye can bear me record of this?' who answered: 'It is true, my Lord'. Then Mr. Walter said: 'I will drink to you on a condition'. He answered: 'What condition?' 'Upon this condition, my Lord, that ye and I shall drink together in the Kingdome of Heaven of that immortal drink, which shall never suffer us to thirst again.' He answered: 'Truely, Mr. Walter, I pledge you upon the same condition'. After he had received the cup, he said to Mr. Durie: 'I drink to you on the same condition,' who answered: 'I pledge you, my Lord, and am assured it shall be so'. The disjune being ended, and thanks given to God, he passeth to his chamber again at what time Mr. James Lawson came to him, with whom he conferred the substance of all those things again, after that we wer departed from him.

"In the afternoon we came to him again, with sundry of the bretheren of the ministry, as Mr. James Lowson, Mr. Robert Pont, David Ferguson, Mr. David Lindsay, John Brand, Mr. James Carmichael, and Mr. John Davidson whom he received very lovingly in his armes, and said to him: 'Mr. John, you wrote a little book, indeed, but truely I never meant evil against you in my heart. Forgive you me, and I forgive you.' At this Mr. John was moved with tears. All thir bretheren being present, to their great comfort he repeted again the cheif substance of all those things wherof he spake before, being demanded point by point, as their testification of this matter, subscribed be them at more lenth, will declare.

"Thereafter he was called to his dinner about two in the afternoon. Seing that the bretheren of the ministry wer informed that ther was wrong reports made of his confession to the King, and that he should have confessed much otherwise than he did, wherby the King might have had a worse opinion of him, [they] thought good to send doun some before his suffering to inform his Majesty of the truth of his confession, as, namely, David Ferguson, John Durie, and John Brand, who before his death told the whole simple truth of his confession, as it was, to the King's Majesty. At their returning again from the Abby, his keeper required him that he should come forth to the scaffold. He answered: 'Seing they have troubled me overmuch this day with worldly things, I supposed they should have given me this one night to have advised ripely with my God'. The keeper said: 'All things are now ready, and I think they will not stay'. He answered: 'I am ready also, I praise my God!' And so a comfortable prayer being made, he passed doun to the gate to go directly to the scaffold. But the Earle of Arran stayed him, and brought him back again to the chamber, and required him to tarry till his confession might be put in writte, and subscribed with his own hand and the ministers' that wer present. He answered: 'Nay, my Lord, I pray you trouble me no more with these things, for now I have another thing to advise upon— that is, to prepare me for my God—seing now I am at a point to go to death, I cannot write in the estate that I am now in. All thir honest men can testify what I have spoken in that matter.' With which answer the Earle of Arran being satisfyed, he said to him: 'Now, my Lord, you will be reconciled with me, for I have done nothing upon my particular against you'. He answered: 'It's no time now to remember upon quarrels. I have no quarrell to you or any other. I forgive you and all others, as I will all to forgive me.' And so therafter, with good courage, he went unto the scaffold.

"Being upon the scaffold, he repeted in few words the substance of those things which before he had confessed, except he concealed Mr. Archibald Douglas' name, and eiked [added] some words and exhortations on the scaffold to the people, which he spake not before; as, namely, he said: 'I am sure the King shall lose a good servant this day'. And so he exhorted the people, saying: 'I testify before God, that as I have professed the Evangell, which this day is taught and professed in Scotland, so also now I willingly lay down my life in the profession therof. And though I have not walked according therunto as I ought, yet I am assured God will be mercifull unto me; and I pray all good Christians to pray for me. And I charge you all, in the name of God, that are professors of the Evangel, that you continou in the true profession, and mentain it to your power, as I should have done, God willing, with my life, lands, and all, if I had [had] dayes. Which if ye doe, I assure you God shall be mercifull to you; but if ye do it not, be assured the vengeance of God shall light upon you, both in body and soul.' As concerning all the rest of the things wherof he spoke comfortably on the scaffold, he spoke them in effect, and more amply before, and therfor we think it's [not] needfull here to repet them again.

"Therfor, all his speeches being ended upon the scaffold, a comfortable prayer was made by Mr. James Lawson, during the time of the which prayer the Earle of Mortoun lay on groof upon his face,[1] before the place of execution, his body making great rebounding with sighs and sobs; and he had evident signes of the inward and mighty working of the Spirit, as they who wer present, and knew what it was to be earnestly moved in prayer, might easily perceive. The prayer being ended, after that sundry came to him befor his death to be taken all, that wer about him, by the hand, and bidden farewell in the Lord, he passed constantly, patiently, and humbly to the place of execution, and laid his craig under the axe, his hands being unbanded. And while he was speaking what Mr. Walter was crying in his ear, 'Lord Jesus receive my soul; into Thy hands I committ my spirit! Lord Jesus receive my soul!' the ax fell on his neck. And so, what ever he had been before, he constantly dyed the true servant of God. And however it be that his unfreinds alledge, that as he lived proudly, so he died proudly, the charitable servants of God could perceive nothing in him but all kind of humility in his death, in so much that we are assured that his soul is received in the joy and glory of the heavens; and we pray God, that they that are behind may learn by his example to die in the true fear of the Lord. 2 June, Anno Domini 1581."

This is Mr. Durie and Mr. Balcanquell's account of the last exercises of this great man, and I recon the curious readers will not grudge the lenth of it, since it conteans many valuable and uncommon facts. Mr. Calderwood adds, "the Earle of Mortoun was execute on

---

[1] Lying with the face on the ground.—Ed. of *Calderwood.*

Friday, about 4 of the clock in the afternoon, June 2," and observes that Scotland never enjoyed greater peace or plenty than under his government. Papistry durst not set up its head so long as he ruled. As he was one of the cheife instruments of the Reformation of religion, so he was a defender of the same, and of the King in his minority, for the which, adds he, the Earle was unthankfuly dealt with; wherby we may see how absurd a thing it's to committ the reigns of government to the hands of a child, who cannot govern himself. In the time of his government he set on foot a nottable work, which he had perfected if he had continoued Regent—to witt, the drawing of our lawes in some certain and easy form. It was committed to Sir James Balfour and Mr. John Skeen.[1]

But to return to Mr. Durie. For 3 years after this, while he continoued at Edinburgh, his life was almost one continouall struggle with the King and courtiers, who could not bear the reproofs he and other faithfull ministers at this time wer obligded to give of their corruptions, vices, and open sin. Those who managed the King at this time, being rid of the Earle of Morton and others who wer firm Protestants, wer taking very wide steps towards Popery, and a designe was formed to bring the King to renounce the crown to his mother, and receive again from her with her benediction, and privat mesages tending that way wer sent to France in the end of the year 1581. This coming to the knowledge of the ministers, Mr. Durie's zeal for the Reformation did not permitt him to be silent at such a juncture, and upon Wednesday, January 24, 1582, preaching in the great kirk of Edinburgh, he warned his hearers of the present imminent hazard of religion, signifying that the King was moved by some courtier to consent to send a privat message to the King of France, the Queen Mother, and Duke of Guise, to ask his mother's benediction. Mr. Durie's information was certain, having it from George Douglas of Lochlevin, who was imployed in the message. After sermon, Mr. Lowson, Dury, and Davidson conferred with the Earles of Argyle and Ruthven, in the council-hous, touching these things. Argyle confessed more of that matter than they looked for. In their conversation, mention being made of Rizzio's slaughter, Mr. Davidson, as is notticed on his Life, warned Ruthven of his hazard, if matters went on as they

[1] Note 77.

wer like to do. Mr. Lowson undertook to the Earle of Argyle to prove that G. Douglas' message was downright treason. The Earle acknowledged he had gone too far in that matter, and promised to be warry in time coming, adding, if he saw anything intended in the Court against religion, he would forsake the intenders, and oppone himself to them. The ministers blamed the nobility very much, unworthy of their places, for suffering the young King to lye [lounge] at Dalkeith with a stranger, and the whole Realme going to confusion.

Mr. Durie's boldness before the King and Council, Aprile this year, as to the affair of Mr. Robert Montgommery,[1] fell in upon Mr. Davidson's Life; but here I'le take some more particular nottice of it. When the Church was going on in the proces of Montgommery's excommunication, the Synod of Lothian wer charged, at Mr. Robert Montgommery's instance, to appear before the King and Council, at Stirling, Aprile 12. The ministers met at Stirling among themselves, before they appeared before the Council, and agreed unanimously to declyne the judgment of his Majesty and Council, if they offered to try their process against Montgomery; and yet to declare they wer content the King, or any of his Council should hear the whole of their proceedings against the Bishop extrajudicially. In the afternoon the ministers wer called befor the Council. The King himself opened the matter, and then left the prosecution of it to the Abbot of Dumfernline, secretary, who began to try and enquire into the proceedure of the eldership and ministers, wherupon Mr. Robert Pont, in name of the rest, declined the Council as their judges in this matter, and yet made the declaration, as formerly agreed upon. Mr. Dury added to what Mr. Pont had said, that if ther was not just cause to excommunicat the Bishop, he knew no just cause of excommunication. The King said: "If ye begin after that manner, ther will other things follow upon it than ye look for. I bid you be warr." Arran snapped John Durie in his expressions, and said he broke the rules of logick, and the like. They wer, after some conference, desired to withdraw, and when they did so, the King and [the] Duke went away, and the ministers wer not called again. When they found this, fearing their carriage might be reconed a deserting the cause, and flight, Mr. Dury and Davidson went to John Andrew, the Council Clerk, and desired that, at the least, they might have a copy of

[1] Note 78.

the declinator utered be Mr. Robert Pont befor the Council. He refused this, and seemed to deny that such a thing was done before the Council. The ministers insisted on it, as a thing so openly made, though verbally, that it could not be denied. Mr. Andrew insisted that he could not give them any extract. Mr. Davidson answered: "Then we must declare our part in time and place, wher God hath called us to speak, and how we wer handled". Upon this, the Clerk yeilded to grant their desire, though not for some time, nor till after a conference next day 'twixt the King, Mr. Lawson, Mr. Durie, and some others. Mr. James Lawson desired the King might allow them the copy of their protestation. His Majesty answered, there was all reason for it. Mr. Lawson, after thanking the King for this justice, proceeded to show his Majesty that this manner of proceeding in the Council, declaring the King's and their own power to dispone bishopricks, *pleno jure*, both spiritually and temporally, at their own pleasure, greived the hearts of the godly very much. Mr. Durie wished the King to take heed to this gear [stuff], and earnestly prayed God to keep his throne from such offences, and signifyed that they behoved to proceed to the excommunication of Mr. Robert Montgommery, in case he proceeded any further in that matter. The King answered: "We will not suffer you". The other answered: "Sir, we must obey God rather than men: we pray, will pray, and will desire the people to pray, to deliver your Grace from the evil company that is about you. The welfare of the Kirk is your welfare, and without this you have done with it. The plainer and sharper vice be reproved, it will be the better for you." "The King," sayes Mr. Calderwood, "seemed to be much moved, and not far from tears." What followed is to be seen in our printed historians, and in Mr. Davidson's Life.

In May following, Mr. Durie fell under further trouble for a sermon upon a Fast Day, appointed by the Assembly. Things wer in a most lamentable state. The author of the *Vindiciæ Philadelphi* (Mr. Calderwood), p. 42, gives us very plain accounts that D'Aubigny Lennox was sent from France, and instructed by the Guisians to Scotland, to make a change in religion if possible; and for two years now and more since his arrivall, the plott for bringing us back to France and Popery was going pretty openly on. The Earle of Mortoun was so firm a Protestant, that it was necessary he should not only be removed from the management, but cutt of, and the Earle of Angus, another knowen enimie to Popery, was forced out of the country. D'Aubigny, first Earle and then Duke of Lennox, got the revenues of the Archbishoprick of Glasgow and the Abbacy of Arbroath. Montgomery was to have the name, and was forced in upon Glasgow, and the Moderator and Presbytery of Glasgow abused with terrible violence. All this was knowen, and upon the Fast, we need not be surprized to find the ministers lamenting these open attacks upon the Reformation, and warning people of their hazard. Bishop Spotswood tells us the causes of the Fast wer the abounding of sin, the oppression of the Church, the danger the King stood in by the company of wicked persons, who did seek to corrupt him in religion and manners; the late insolency committed at Glasgow was likewise adjected. We need not wonder that those furnished large matter to the preachers, as the Bishop sayes, and adds, that John Dury exclaimed mightily against the Duke of Lennox, on whom all the blame was laid, and certainly very justly.

Mr. Dury's particular expressions are not preserved by any of our historians; but his trouble was heavy enough which followed, though I doubt not his expressions were safe and cautious, though free and faithfull. I shall give the hints of it from Calderwood's MS. Some things fell in before Mr. Dury's sermon, which heated the violence of D'Aubignie against Mr. Dury. On the 9th of May, after the Assembly was up, he was one who brought the desires of the Assembly to the King, who very kindly received them; but the Duke and Earle of Arran fell out on the ministers in very outragious words. The Duke hardly conteaned himself from giving Mr. David Lindsay and Mr. Robert Pont the lye, and twice over Arran called Mr. Dury a knave, and told him he would find a way to bring him to order. On the 10 of May, Seignior Paul, master of the Duke of Guise's horses, arrived at Leith with a present of 6 horses from the Duke of Guise to the King. He had been eminently active and bloody in the massacre at Paris. Next day, Mr. Dury rode to the King, then at Kinneil, and represented what offence was taken at the person and the gift. He said plainly the gift was odious, in respect of the person who sent it, a cruel murderer of the saints, and the end of it, to allure the King to make defection from religion. On the 16th, Mr. Durie went to the King, then in Dalkeith, and spoke to him again upon the French present, and because ther wer

T

some rumors of a proposall of the King's marriage, Mr. Dury cautioned his Majesty to ponder well before he matched himself. The King answered he would never marry a woman but one who feared God and loved the Evangell. On the 18 of May, a ship arrived from France, with gunpowder, bullets, and other warluk things, which wer laid up in the Castle of Edinburgh. The ministers in their sermons warned the people of the hazard of religion from their present familiarity 'twixt the Court and the King of France and Duke of Guise, two bloody murderers.

But Mr. Dury's sermon, on the 23 of May, was what fretted the courtiers most, and nothing would satisfy the King but his removall from Edinburgh. He had pointed out the Duke and Earle of Arran as persons who abused the King. On the 28 of May, Mr. Dury, Balcanquell, and Lowson wer called befor the Councill at the Abbey. The King and Duke wer not there, but Arran was, and some harsh methods wer designed, had not the downcoming of 3 or 400 of the citicens of Edinburgh, who conveyed their ministers to the Council, stayed them. Upon the 30 of May, Mr. Lowson and Mr. David Lindsay wer cited to appear before the Counsell at Dalkeith. Many wer discontent at Mr. Durie's going thither. Indeed he was in the outmost hazard. The Duke's cooks and servants came out on him with spitts and knives; and, had ther not been 15 of the inhabitants of Edinburgh waiting on their ministers, probably he had not escaped with his life. The Duke and Earl wer cheifly enraged against Mr. Dury, and the Council commanded him to remove out of Edinburgh, during the King's pleasure. Upon the last of May, a charge was sent to the Magistrates of Edinburgh to remove him out of their burgh, under pain of horning. Meanwhile, the Presbitry of Edinburgh had Mr. Durie's case before them, and, after reasoning the matter, whither it was fit to name particular persons in pulpit, justifyed the whole of Mr. Durie's conduct both *in materia et forma*, as Mr. Davidson worded it. However, the Council of Edinburgh and Deacons of Crafts met, June 1, and the plurality, to the greife of many, concluded that Mr. Dury should give place. Mr. Dury, after he had protested that he had given no just cause of offence, obeyed, and next day, Saturnday, departed out of the town.

In the meantime, severall of the ministers about supplied Mr.

Dury's room in preaching, and did not spare to show the sinfulnes of the severitys used in this matter. Mr. Patrick Simson preached, June 6, and compared the ministry of Edinburgh to a chain about the neck, wherof one chain was already broken, so farr as enimies could. The 3 following dayes, Mr. Davidson preached with great plaines, and the people wer extremly moved. He assured them God would dash the devil in his own devices, and that Mr. Dury would be relieved, and, in the meantime, would be a mean to stirr up others, wherever he went. He compared the priests blowing the trumpet to the allarrume by ringing the bell, and told them he was now ringing the common bell, waken who pleased. On the 11, the Presbitry of Edinburgh resolved to call a General Assembly, according to the power lodged in their hand, in case of imminent danger, and the bretheren wer warned to meet, June 27, 1582.

Accordingly, the Assembly conveened in Edinburgh that day. Just before the meeting of the Assembly, Mr. Durie, who had by this time secretly returned to his own house, was charged by a macer to leave the town, and the Magistrates required to put the charge in execution. But Mr. Durie came into the Assembly, and immediately after they wer constitut, he gave them an account of his citation before the King and Counsell, his answers, and the whole proces used against him; and laid before them a charge he had got that very day, to remove off the town, and craved the whole bretheren's advice, whether he should remove from his flock, according to the King's charge, or abide with them, according to his calling; declaring himself alway ready to follow their determination, howsoever they think it expedient to give it. The Assembly sent David Ferguson and Mr. Thomas Buchanan with a letter to John Duncanson, the King's Minister, desiring his concurrence to wait upon the King to understand his meaning, and humbly to crave the performance of the promise made to certain of the bretheren concerning Mr. Durie. On Mr. Davidson's Life, we have seen that he dissented from this message, because he thought, the Assembly had another remedy in their power, and that they ought not to seek Mr. Durie's reposition from him who had no power to displace him, albiet his flock had foolishly and sinfully yielded. When the ministers wer gone out to wait upon the King, the Magistrates, and some of the Town Council of Edinburgh came in, and craved the Assembly's advice as to their obedience to the King's charge of removing Mr. Durie from their burgh. The Moderator asked the Magistrates whether they sought the Assembly's advice, as far as it concerned conscience, or otherwise. They answered they wer fully resolved in point of conscience. Then the Moderator told them they could not medle with it, so far as it was civil. However, after some warm reasoning in the Assembly, they ordeaned Mr. James Lawson, Mr. Thomas Smeton, Mr. Andrew Hay, Mr. Robert Pont, Mr. David Lindsay, and Mr. John Craig, to concurr with such as the Council shall appoint to-morrow, at half-an-hour to seven, and to consult, conferr, and reason upon that matter. Their advice was that the Magistrates should supersede their charge till the return of those sent by the Assembly to the King at Stirling; but the Town Council and Session met and concluded, by a plurality, that Mr. Durie should depart privatly; if not, that the Magistrates should deliver him the charge sent to them by the King. In the 3d session of the Assembly, they came to consider this conclusion, and gave their opinion therupon without dipping upon the King's charge, and made the following Act:

"Anent the information of their brother, Mr. John Durie, that certain bretheren, directed from the Council of the town, moved, as appeared to him, of good affection, have desired him, for avoiding the danger that might fall upon his flock, to absent and withdraw himself a space off the town privily: desiring herin to understand the good judgment of the Assembly, protesting that for his own opinion, that because his removing may be prejudiciall to the common cause, and his privy departing appear an accepting of the vice upon him, wherwith he is unjustly charged that, without their councill, herin his own deliberat mind is to abide, be it with the hazard of his life; and, further, seing that his doctrine, wherof he was accused in Councill, in force and substance, was justifyed at his own Presbitry, and by his own Session of Edinburgh, that the bretheren would give him that testimoniall, that he had travelled faithfully in his vocation, and no fault found with him in his doctrine, nor imput to him in his life: as also, if it please God that he be compelled to remove, that he may have liberty elswher to preach the Gospell, wher God shall give him the occasion of time and place, for discharging his own conscience and calling: the bretheren, after good advice and deliberation, in ane voice, thought it not meet that he should remove off the town privicly, but to abide the charge to be given by the Provost or Bailays to him, and as to his life, or conversation, and doctrine, the whole Assembly acknowledged nothing in him, but true, sound, and wholsom doctrine, and upright and honest life and conversation, giving liberty in case of his removing, as said is, to preach the Gospell faithfully, wher God shall offer the occasion, untill it shall please Him to restore him to the charge of his own flock."

On the 28 of June, because Mr. Durie would not leave his flock privatly, the Magistrates charged him to remove presently out of the town and libertys therof, wheras the King's command specifyed no time, and mentioned only the town, and not its libertys. The Magistrates would not delay till the return of those sent to Stirling, but required him that very night, 'twixt 8 and 9. They alledged it was against their will, and they were forced to this summar procedure. Mr. Durie resolved to obey the charge, especially to prevent a tumult. Accordingly, at 9 of the clock that night, he went, accompanyed with a good many ministers, to the Cross, wher he made protestation, and took instruments in John Johnstoun and George Gibson, publick nottars, their hands, touching his honesty and sincerity in life and doctrine: that the narrative of his charge—to witt, his absolute submission to the King and Council in all things—was false, and that he would obey no man's charge to leave off from the preaching of the Word, wher soever he should have occasion, according as the General Assembly allowed him, and that notwithstanding the King's charge, which peremptorily required him not to preach. Mr. John Davidson, standing closs by, protested also, and took instruments that, as that was the most sorrowfull sight to Edinburgh ever he saw, that they removed their pastor, speaking the truth, for pleasing flesh and blood: so the plague and fearfull judgments of God should light upon the devisers, inventers, and procurers, actors, authors, consenters, and rejoicers at that banishment of Christ in that man's person, unles they repented speedily. Next day, the bretheren returned from Stirling with the King's answer in writing: that as soon as the Duke came to Stirling, who was cheifly interested in what Mr. Durie had said, upon a petition given in, his affair should be considered, and some of the bretheren might wait again on the King, and receive the answer when the Duke came. In the 6 session, the Assembly made the following Act: "Anent the place occupyed by John Durie, one of the ministers of Edinburgh, in the function of the ministry there, presently removed of the town, the Assembly and whole bretheren present, inhibites and discharges the Kirk and Presbyterie of Edinburgh to elect, choice, or admitt in any wise, any minister in his place of the ministry thereof, to displace him; discharging alswa all ministers, or such as aspire to the ministry, to attempt the usurping or taking upon them his charge or place therof; except at the desire of the ministers of Edinburgh to relieve them at all times, while the Generall Assembly be further advised, and in case any shall be chosen, or elected, as said is, the whole Assembly discerns the said election to be void and of no effect." Much freedom was used with the Magistrates for their treatment of Mr. Durie by Mr. John Davidson, Mr. Andrew Melvil, and the ministers of Edinburgh, too long to be here insert. At length, the town sent 3 Commissioners to the King and Duke, to allow Mr. Durie to return. The Duke said if he had knowen their mind sooner, somewhat should have been done.

However, it was som time before Mr. Durie had liberty to return. The King upon the matter was held a captive by the Duke and Arran: he was watched wherever he went, and few or none of the nobility allowed to be with him, which brought some of them to enter into a bond for the preservation of the King's liberty and one another's safty. This obliged the Duke and Arran to some more popular methods; but upon the 23 of Agust, the Earle of Gowrie, and the rest of the Lords came to the King, and obliged the Earle of Arran and Duke keep at distance from Court. Some Commissioners wer sent in Agust to seek Mr. Durie's return, and to assure the Court that if the King came not to Edinburgh, whence he used not to be so long away, they (the town of Edinburgh, whence the Commissioners wer sent) behoved to look on the King as a captive. Upon this, Mr. Durie was called to preach before the King and Court at Stirling, and the King gave him license to return to his flock, the tennor wherof followes:

" REX.

" John Durie, Minister of the Evangell at Edinburgh, we greet you well. It is our will, and we command you, that, in continent after the sight hereof, ye adress you to our said burgh of Edinburgh, and there attend upon your flock according to your function and calling, as you will answer to God, upon the duty of your office. Subscribed with our hand, at Stirling, the 1st day of September, 1582." This license was signed by the King, Glencairn, and Dumfermling.

Mr. Durie's return to Edinburgh was so remarkable, and in the manner of his flock receiving him unconcocted, and discovered so much love to him and gratitude to God, that I shall transcribe it here from Calderwood. "Mr. Durie came to Leith at night, September 3d. Upon Teusday, Sept. 4, as he was coming to Edinburgh, ther mett him at the Gallow Green about 200d of the inhabitants, but before they came to the Nether Bow they wer increased to 400d. They wer no sooner entered but they increased to 6 or 700d, and in a litle the whole street was filled even to St. Giles Kirk. The number was reconed about 2000d. At the Nether Bow, they took up the 124 Psalm, *Now Israel may say*, and sung in such a pleasant tune, in all the 4 parts, those being weel knowen to the people who came up the street bareheaded and singing, till they entered the kirk. This had such a sound and majesty as affected themselves and the hudge multitude of beholders, who looked over the shots and forestairs with admiration and amazement. The Duke himself was a witnes, and tare his beard for anger, being more affrayed at this sight than anything ever he had seen since he came to Scotland. When they entered the kirk, Mr. Lowson made a short exhortation in the reader's place to thankfulnes, and after the singing of a psalm, the people departed with great joy."

The Lords now about the King, since Ruthven Road, wer positive that the Duke should leave the country. Nothing frighted the Duke more than the warm reception he saw the town of Edinburgh give to Mr. Durie, even when their Magistrates and Council wer in some measure his friends. This very much hastned his leaving of Edinburgh upon the message sent him by the Lords Harris and Newbotle from the Lords now about the King, the best account of which is in a letter from Gourie to Mr. Durie at this time, which I insert here. The Magistrates being favourers of the Duke, the noblemen had few others to correspond with save the ministers. The Earle's letter had this direction: "To my right trustie freind and brother, John Durie, Minister of God's Word at Edinburgh," and is as foilowes:

"Brother, after my hearty commendations, this is to advertish you that the Lord Herries is returned to the Duke with our answer, which is: if he will instantly deliver the Castle of Dumbarton, and therafter depart out of the country, betwixt this and the 20 of this instant, and in the meantime to remain either at Dalkeith or Aberdour, accompanyed with 40 persons or within, we will cease from all acts of hostility against him; otherwise, if he agrees not to thir conditions, no assurance. And herof the Lord Herries will return with answer upon Thursday next, and as it shall be, you shall be advertised. Praying you effectuosly in the meantime to be making all the freinds you can, and providing, in case we have the occasion to hold forward to the town, that the ports may be made open to us whither we come by night or day, I pray you make my hearty commendations to Mr. James and Mr. Walter. So I committ you to God. Of Stirling, this 4th of September, 1582.

"Your right assured freind,

"GOWRIE."

Next year, the King rid himself of the Lords who had been with him since the Road of Ruthven, and fell again under the management of such as wer under French influence, and realy of his mother's party. Upon this, the Laird of Fentry, a violent Papist, and severall others had too much conversation with him, and his own person and the interests of religion wer in no small hazard. This made the ministers remonstrat to him his hazard in admitting Papists, and particularly the Laird of Fentrie, a very active, dangerous person, afterwards execut for treason. When the Assembly mett, Fentrie, forseing the Assembly would take nottice of him, practised upon Mr. McKeson, an honest but weak man, to recomend him by letter to Mr. Duncanson, the King's Minister. This letter the King pretended to be a recommendation of Fentrie by the Presbitry of Edinburgh, being signed by their clerk, and gave it to Comissioners of the Assembly as the reason of his admitting the said gentleman to his presence, when they compleaned of this among other greives they laid before the King. This brought the Presbitry to vindicat themselves upon this point, by sending some of their number to wait upon the King, and to give him a true account of that letter. And they found it proper to write a letter to Mr. Duncanson, that he might disabuse the King, and vindicat them before the Commissioners came. Mr. Dury was Moderator, and probably drew the letter, and not being long, I set it down here as signed by him.

"Understanding, beloved brother, by His Majestie's answer to the Generall Assembly, to their greife, twitching [touching] young Fentrie and his receiving into the Court, and admission into familiar communing with His Majesty, that a letter of commendation from our Presbitry, directed be you, in his favours was pretended as sufficient excuse of that fact; as it was most greivous to us that the Kirk of God therby should be anywise frustrat of their expectation, touching the speedy reforming of that abuse, so it was the more grievous to us that our name should be most falsly abused to that fact. For neither was any such thing ever meaned by our whole Presbitry in generall, neither by any person therof in particular, that ever he should come near the Court, being the man he is, much less that ane letter should be writt in his favour either to you, or any other about the King's Majesty. Alwise, after diligent tryall we have found that Mr. George McKeson, our clerk, being craftily circumveened by the said Fentrie and his subtile persuasions, has written to you in our names, to the effect forsaid, which, as he confessed particularly befor the General Assembly, so has he more fully declared all the manner therof, this day before our Presbitry, being urged earnestly therunto in the name of God; and for the same he craved God and us forgiveness, promising that it should be a lesson to him all the dayes of his life hereafter, never so simply to give credit to the fair and feigned speeches of any Papist whatsomever; and what a man Mr. George is in simplicity, as we term it, you know weel enough. Wherfor, brother, albiet the Commissioners of the General Assembly will inform the King's Majesty of his treachery and false dealing, we doubt not yet, but as both we and ye have been abused by a letter in our name, so we thought we could do no less than inform you truely therof by a letter from ourself, subscribed by our Moderator in our name, to the end ye having the more for you, ye may the more freely inform His Majesty what truth may be looked for at this man's hands, and what kind of religion his is of, who beginns so soon with craft and falshood to abuse such a company of the servants of God. What lyes (think ye) will this man be bold to make herafter, who begins so soon, when he promises most truth and plain dealing. But he keeps kind of them he came from, *ex unguibus leonem estima*. From Edinburgh, the 22 of October, 1583.

"JOHN DURIE, Moderator.
"At the command of the Presbitery."

When the King, in the end of October—or rather the violent party about him—wer giving out severe charges against the Protestant noblemen and gentlemen concerned in the Road of Ruthven, Mr. Durie, in his sermon, Nov. 5, 1583, declared with much plaines the iniquity of such proceedings. However, the King and courtiours went on, and prevailed with Mr. David Lindsay and Andrew Hay to go to Berwick, and make fair proposalls to the gentlemen and others retired to Berwick to bring them back, that their persons might be seized under collour of conference. Mr. Durie and Davidson in the Presbitry opposed any ministers medling in that matter, as that would not be very honnourable to such as wer engaged in it. At this time, the ministers wer very plain in their sermons, showing the danger of religion, and vindicating the lords and gentlemen concerned in the Road of Ruthven, knowing them to be hearty freinds to the Protestant religion, according as those fell in their way. Mr. Durie's knowen zeal did not suffer him to be silent at such a juncture, and he was first attacked; though in a litle time, Mr. Andrew Melvil, and the ministry of Edinburgh, and the ministers of any note almost everywher wer attacked, one way or other. At present we are only concerned in Mr. Durie.

His prosecution stood thus: In December, Mr. Calderwood sayes, the King sent a charge to remove Mr. Durie: he does not give the reason. This Mr. Petry narrates thus: Mr. Dury in a sermon said, "As the blind man, whose eyes Christ had opened, when the Pharisyes said, *We know this man to be a sinner*, did reply, *Whither he be a sinner I know not, but one thing I know, that though I was born blind, yet now I see,* so whatsoever sort of men those (concerned in Ruthven Road, and now banished) men be, I know not, but this I know, that the Church was miserably vexed, and almost oppressed, but by their means it was delivered". For those words, probably magnifyed, he was called before the Councill, and, standing in defense of what he had said, was confyned to the town of Monros. Calderwood tells us, upon the 19 of December, the Laird of Colluthie, and Mr. Mark Ker came from the King and Councill to the Session of the Kirk of Edinburgh, to crave that John Durie might be dismissed, and to intimat that it was the King's will he should pass over Tay, and remain at Monross; that he preach in no place till he come thither; and this be obeyed in 9 dayes. They answered they could not put him away unless he wer willing. After some consultation, seing ther was no peacable staying at Edinburgh, he yielded, and took his leave of the Council of the town, Dec. 20, and of the Session, Saturday, Dec. 21, who gave him an ample testimoniall approving his life and doctrine. From this we may gather how litle Bishop Spotswood knew of this matter, when he sayes (p. 329): "John Dury, this winter, had in one of his sermons justifyed the fact of Ruthven, for which, being cited by the Council, he stood to the defence of what he had spoken, yet, upon taking advice of his colleague, Mr. Lawson, he was moved to submitt himself to the King, who continoued the declaration of his pleasure till he had proof of his better behaviour"; and then (p. 333) adds that "in May, 1584, Mr. Dury was removed from Edinburgh to Monross". I only notice this among many other instances of the unexactness of the Bishop in his dates and the facts he sets down.

Mr. Calderwood adds: "That same day, December 21, he took journey to Dumfermline, accompanied with some of the professors of Edinburgh to Queensferry, and by some further. After he had stayed some dayes with his son-in-law, Mr. James Melvil, at Saint Andrews, he went forward to his ward at Monross, Mr. Melvil accompanying him. When they wer coming on their journey to the ford of the watter of Lounan, a sow entered the water before them, and swame through. The watter was in a speat [flood], and, when they wer in the midle of it, Mr. Durie's horse lay down, and he was near caryed away with the stream. But it pleased God that Mr. Melvil caught him by the coat neck, and he got hold of his horse's main [and] gote safe to land." He adds that upon January 22, 1584, Mr. Robert Pont and John Brand from the Presbitry of Edinburgh, John Adamson and Alexander Udward from the Kirk, Mr. Michael Chisholm and Robert Henrieson from the Council, wer sent to the King to suit license for Mr. Durie to return to his charge till the next Generall Assembly, that further order might be taken. The King gave them very hard words, and said he took all for his enemies who spoke in favour of John Durie; that he was unworthy to be in the ministry; that his doctrine was false and erroneous; that he could not abide his lawes; that their request tended to sedition. Mr. Robert Pont answered he had often heard his doctrine, and heard nothing but what he was able to defend. But no other answer could be obteaned. The King rebuked the Provost of Edinburgh severely for suffering any from the Counsell to suit for Mr. Durie.

Mr. Petrie remarks that "soon after Mr. Durie's coming to Monross, the minister of that town dyed, and the Church there made choice of Mr. Durie to suceed. Then the King gave him and his son during their lives 200 pounds out of two abbeys." And Bishop Spotswood sayes he continoued minister 16 years at Monross, till his death, the last of Feb., 1600, in the 63 year of his age. Mr. Crawford takes nottice that Mr. Dury having no acces to return to his charge, and having a joynt call from the people, with the consent of the Presbitry, he accepted the call *pro tempore*, and continoued minister there till his death. The King, when the turn came in the end of the next year, would not allow of his return to Edinburgh, and it's probable, to encourage him to continou in Angus, he gave him the gratuity Petry speaks of. During his ministry at Monross nothing offers to me from any papers come to my hand. I doubt not but he was singularly usefull while there.

After I had writt what is above, I find the following account of Mr. Dury by his son-in-law, Mr. James Melvil, in his own Life, which I give in his own words: "The last night of February, 1599, my father-in-law, John Durie, departed this life, who, as he lived happily, walking with God in prayer day and night, so he dyed glorifying God, with great joy and assurance of everlasting salvation and life. For, after he had called for the Magistrates and Council of the burgh, and exorted them, and admonished them of certain things for their well, both together and severally, sicklike the elders of the session, and severall of the brethren of the ministry, at last, after he had put his house in order, and directed, instructed, and comforted his wife and children present, he took him to privat meditation and prayer. Therafter he enquired what day of the moneth it was. Being answered it was the last of February, and the morrow the first of March: 'O! then,' sayes he, 'this is the last day of my wretched pilgrimage and the morn the first of my rest and glory!' Not long after, delivering his soul into the hands of God through Jesus Christ, leaning his head to his eldest son's breast, who held him in his armes, most quietly and sweetly he gave up the ghost. He was upright, and zealouse, and falon [extremely] familiar with God; so that if anything had been weighty and doubtsom to him, he had no resolution, rest, or releif till he found it in meditation apart with God. And surely, both in his particular turns and publick affairss, when things seemed very hard and dangerouse, however melancholious and fearfull by nature, he somtimes got great assurances, particularly as to our return from England, 1584, and our safety from the Spaniards. He showed me ofttimes that his God assured him night and day therof. Whatever had come came comfortable to him— he went incontinent to prayer and thanksgiving. His whole conference and speaking of the works of God was to the glory of His name; all other things was, as he used the word oft, tyn-time—only vanity and loss of time to him. So that, I may say, the whole course of his time was an unwearyed constant occupation in doctrine, prayer, and praise. The more I think on him, the more I thank God that ever I knew him, praying God, that as I have seen the outgate of his conversation (Heb. xiii. 7), so I may follow the same in faith. He often regrated, and inveghed against the wordly falsines and bussines of the ministry, saying, he feared they should become as vile in the people's eyes as ever the priests wer. As concerning the matter of bishops, my uncle, Mr. Andrew, expressed his mind therin in his epitaph, which, being most pertinent for that which even at his death was in hand, I have here insert (and Mr. Melvil gives his own translation both which I am to add). He, indeed, desired earnestly to have lived to the Assembly hard at hand, that he might have discharged his mind to the King and brethren; but that which alive he could not do, Mr. Andrew supplied faithfully after his death. On the whole Mr. Melvil remarks that it's good to be faithfull in a good cause, for a good cause will honnour such a person both in life and in death.

"*Epitaphium D. Joan. Duraei, pastoris integerrimi et fidissimi Celurcani,
qui diem extremum clausit, Kal. Mart.* 1600.

"Duraeus ore tonans, Edena pastor in urbe,
  Arcuit a stabulis quos dabat aula lupos.
Celurca in coelum migravit nunc, quia (nonquit) nequit
  Arcere a stabulis quos dabat aula lupos.

"In English, by Mr. J. Melvil—

"In Edinburgh the thundering of John Durie weel was heard,
When courtly wolves from Christ His flock he flegged and debarred.
Now in Monross to heaven he flytes, for greife that he can naught
The courtly wolves debar from Kirk which Christ hath dearly bought.

"*Ipse de se, sive J. D. pastoris fidelissimi testamentum et extrema voluntas.*

"Intonui ipse tuba grandi, cum jus fuit et fas,
  Arcere a stabulis quos dabat aula lupos.
Nunc cedo statione lubens, cum non datur ultra
  Arcere a stabulis quos dabat aula lupos.

"*His testament or latter will, he uttering it of himself.*

"I blew a trumpet terrible, when right and freedom served,
To make Christ's flock from courtly wolves be keeped and preserved;
And now I willingly man [must] yield, sen that we may na mair
Keep Christ His flock from courtly wolves, wherof we stand in fear.

"*Aliud de Synodis.*

"Res grata ac jucunda fuit mihi coetibus inter-
  esse sacris, quando sancta corona fuit.
Nunc patribus sanctis, quia successere profani,
Quae mihi cum diris spes ululare lupis?

"*Another of the Assemblys.*

"A gracefull and a pleasant thing to me it was to be
Ay present in Assemblys, where God's servants I might see;
But now, for holy fathers, when profane usurp the place,
To bide and youl with wicked wolves, I cannot have a face!

"*Aliud.*

"Cum fuit Archi-unus mihi Christus Episcopus, uni
    Vivere et in vita hac vita placere fuit.
Nunc postquam Archi-unus non Christus Episcopus, uni
    Ut Christo moriar stat mihi vita mori.

"*Another.*

"When Christ was only Arch-Bishop, I pleasure had to bide,
To Him to live, and Him to please—I liked time and tide.
But now, sen only Christ is not Arch-Bishop, I do chuse
To dye to Him, and ay to live, and all the wordle refuse.

"*Aliud.*

"Celurcae expectabam ultro Regemque fratresque,
    Et sanctum in Lethi limine Concilium,
    Quo multum obtestarer ego Regemque fratresque
    Est qui ovium custos ne siet inde lupus;
    Nunc quia me e terris sublimem ad sydera caeli,
    Dux meus imperio de statione vocat;
    E caelis obtestor ego Regemque fratresque
    Est qui ovium custos ne siet inde lupus.

"*Another.*

"I looked gladly for the King and bretheren at Montrose,
And at the dore of death to see Assembly made of those,
That I might earnestly obtest the King and bretheren all,
That keepers of the sheep should not to wolfish fashions fall;
But sen that now from earth to heaven my Captain does me claim,
According to His right, I do beseek them all for shame,
Furth of the heavens obtesting both the bretheren and the King,
That keeper of the flock of Christ do not as woolves our-reing [reign
    over].

"*Ad Symmistas.*

"Ardua res totumque hominem haec res una requirit,
    Caeleste in terris pascere ovile Dei.
    Huc vocat ille ovium Pastor bonus, ille vocatos
    Et regni atque aliis avocat a studiis,

Hanc unam imponit cum solicitudine curam,
　　Quam feret impensam, praemia magna ferens.
Caetera de manibus vestris non ille requiret:
　　Neglecti ad paenas exiget officii.

" To his fellow-ministers.

" A thing most hard, and which requires the man in whole indeed,
Is here on earth the heavenly flock of Christ to guide and feed.
That Pastor good to this doth call, the Same does separat
The called from all wordly cares, as to Him dedicat;
And this, as only care, He does with great solicitude
Impone, and of rewards for it does promise multitude.
And as for other things, He will none of your hand require.
But faithlese negligence of this, He plagues with burning fire.

" Extrema voluntas et verba ad Regem.

" Compellat Regem divino carmine vates
　　Duraeus, in fati limine dulcis olor.
Inclyte Rex, qui tam mihi Regum a Rege secundus;
　　Quam spe reque omni Rege priore prior;
Pro te vitam ultro objeci vel mille periclis;
　　Pro te vota Polo millia multa tuli;
Pro te quo pugnavi animo, qua mente praecatus,
　　Hac mente, hoc animo, hoc te precor unum abiens.
Ne regnum caeleste geras mortalibus ausis;
　　Neu sacer Antistes Rex tua sceptra gerat:
Mystica pertractent mystae, regalia Reges,
　　Publica jure suo, publicus ordo gerat:
Da divina Deo: cape Rex tua, sint sua plebi:
　　Distinctum imperium sub Jove Caesar habet.

" His latter will and words to the King.

" John Durie with a verse divine doth call upon the King,
As sweetly singing swan, when death his dayes to end did bring.
O noble King! whom I esteem to brook the second place,
Next under Him Who is aboon, and first in every case.

For thee I jeoparded have my life in dangers many a one,
For this my prayer has ardent[1] been, both publick and alone,
And with what mind I prayed for thee, and with what heart I fought,
With that same mind and heart, at death this one thing I have sought:
Let not the heavenly Kirk of Christ be ruled on earthly wise;
Let not the pastors for to twitch thy scepter interprize;
Let ministers, all mystic things, and kingly kings intreat,
Set counselors for civil things and lords into thy seat :
Give things divine to God, take thine; let people have their own,
For under Christ the King impyre destinguished has and knowne."

FINIS.

Consider Burnet's *Life of Bedell*, p. 137.

I know not any further as to his posterity but that he left a son behind him, and his daughter, an excellent woman, was married to Mr. James Melvil, and by her he had a pretty numerous posterity. Whither the famous Mr. John Durie, who spent so much of his life in the designe of uniting Protestants, was a descendant of his I know not.[2] I find also another Mr. John Durie, Minister at Dalmenie after the 1633, whom Mr. Livingstoun terms a man of rare invention and gift of preaching. He might be this Mr. Durie's grandchild, but of that I am not sure. I know no writtings this worthy man has left behind him.

His character is given us by Bishop Spotswood pretty much, as I suppose, with a view to the account he gives of his moderation while at Monross, wherin I am not alone when I say the Bishop has imposed on his readers. In the generall, he tells us, Mr. Durie was a man earnest and zealous in every thing he gave himself to, but too credulous—a fault incident to the best of tempers—and easily abused by them he trusted, which brought him great trouble whilst at Edinburgh. This is the excuse the Bishop makes for Mr. Durie's zealous appearances while at Edinburgh, which all our historians agree in, and they are not easily reconcileable with the Bishop's account of the last part of his life. He adds he was a sound-hearted man, far from all dissimulation, ever professing what he thought, and following the course he thought

---

[1] J. Melvil has *aydant, i.e.,* constant.   [2] Note 79.

most expedient for the Church. To the poor he was exceeding helpfull, compassionat on those that wer in distres, and mercifull even when he seemed most severe. I belive the Bishop is right in all this save as to his credulity, of which I find no evidences. But I cannot say so much for what he mixes in concerning Mr. Durie at Monros. "Though," he sayes, "he lived in great quietnes, making it appear that the many contests and strifes, he had in former times, proceeded not from his own disposition so much as the suggestions of others, for all the 16 years he lived at Monros, no man did cary himself with greater modesty and with more dutifull obedience, and was therfor well beloved and esteemed of the King. He wished earnestly to have lived to the meeting of the Assembly, that he might have declared his mind touching the matters then in hand; but when he perceived his sicknes increasing, and that he should not continou so long, he intreated some bretheren to visit him, and to show the Assembly, as from him, 'that ther was a necessity of restoring the ancient government of the Church, because of the unrulines of young ministers that could not be advised by the elder sort, nor keeped in order. And since both the estate of the Church did require it, and that the King did labour to have it received, he wished them to make no trouble therfor, and to insist only with the King that the best ministers and of greatest experience might be preferred to places.' This, as he directed, was reported to the Assembly, and of the most part well received." I cannot help suspecting that the Bishop has made this message to the Assembly for this good man. It's directly inconsistent with the whole former chain of his life given by the Bishop and our other historians; and this agrees so much with the changes palmed upon some of our most eminent ministers by Prelatick writers, of which many instances offer in this Work. This story, the Bishop gives of the last part of Mr. Durie's life, is what cannot be easily reconciled with his education under Mr. Knox and great veneration for him; nor with his being the first mover of the question anent the lawfullnes of Tulchan Bishops; nor, in a word, with any one passage almost of the former part of his life. Neither is the reason put in his mouth for what Spotswood calls the *ancient government of the Church* of any force. The unrulines of young ministers, Mr. Durie knew by long experience, would be better restrained by presbytrys, and other judicatorys of Christ's appointment, and their subordination, than by a single bishop and Prelacy; which was at best but a temptation to fiery, aspiring, unruly spirits; and far from a bridle and restraint to such an ill temper. In short, it was the only refuge the Bishop and other Prelatick writers had, when the generall stream of innumerable facts, and the knowen inclinations of the whole ministry almost, as well as the Protestants in Scotland, discovered the generall bent for our Reformation Government, and against Prelacy, to coin such little inconsistent storys and innuendos as this. And thus I call this inconsistent, not only with the whole tract of Mr. Durie's former appearances, but with the state of things when Prelacy was forced in upon us. All our remaining accounts of those times make it clear, that it was not some of the younger ministers that opposed Prelacy, but the eldest and most experienced and gravest then in the Church; as does appear in this Work that I am on, and is plain from our printed historians, and in some measure from Bishop Spotswood himself; and it had been much nearer truth, if it had been said that it was a few of the younger corrupt and unruly ministers, such as Bishop Spotswood, Law, and others I could name, who, from the aspiring after honnours and benefices, fell in with the King's designe to force in Prelacy upon us.

I take it, therfor, to be a very just remark my worthy predecessor, Mr. Crawford, has, upon this passage of the Bishop, "As for what Spotswood relateth, that Mr. Dury desired some bretheren to show the ensuing Assembly that ther was a necessity of restoring the ancient Government, &c., it's not to be credited, but to be esteemed like the rest of his lyes and calumnies, wherwith he reproacheth good men". And I shall conclude with giving the opinion of two elder writers, who, both of them, may be supposed to know Mr. Dury as well as Spotswood, and lived very near his time—Mr. Row and Calderwood, in their MS. Historys. Mr. Row brings in Mr. Durie as one of the constant and zealouse opposers of Prelacy, and nottices his moving the question anent the lawfulnes of bishops as brought in by the Earle of Mortoun. Mr. Calderwood nottices all the facts we have had, which are inconsistent enough with the Bishop's account of the close of his life, and I shall end my Collections as to Mr. Durie with Mr. Calderwood's generall character of him. "John Durie was of small literature, but had seen and marked the great works of God in the first Reformation, and, being a doer both with tongue and hand, had been a diligent hearer of Mr. Knox, and an observer of all his wayes. He delivered his doctrine with bold utterance, and a mighty voice and spirit. He was a holy man, and walked with God daily and nightly in meditation and prayer. Ther lodged in his house Mr. Andrew Melvil, Mr. Thomas Smeton, Mr. Alexander Arbuthnet, 3 of the learnedest in Europe, and sundry others."

COLLECTIONS UPON THE LIFE OF Mr. DAVID LINDSAY, MINISTER AT DUNDEE, BISHOP OF BRECHIN, AND THEN OF EDINBURGH.

Having given the Lives of the most of our Scots bishops in this period who wer of any note for learning, and particularly of Bishop Forbes, immediat predecessor to Doctor Lindsay, I'le essay to gather up what I can meet with concerning him. He was, at his first entry to the ministry, pretty well looked on by such as favoured our Reformation Constitution. But in a litle he fell in with the measures of the Court and aspiring bishops. Mr. Lindsay was the only person almost that drew his pen in behalf of Perth Assembly, and was the person imployed by the bishops for supporting the ceremonies; and his writing in vindication of Perth Assembly procured him a bishoprick. It's but a few hints I have to offer about him from Calderwood's MSS., the Collections from 1589-1641, and some originall letters of his in my hands.

His parentage and education—I have nothing about them; nor do I know precisely the time he was setled Minister at Dundee. I guess it might be about the 1600. The first accounts, I have of him, are in Mr. Calderwood and Row's MS. Historys: [he] casts up upon Mr. James Nicholson's death, 1607, as in part I have hinted on that Life. Mr. Row sayes Mr. Lindsay was marrayed to Mr. James Nicholson's wife's sister, and this raised a great familiarity betwixt them, and upon Mr. Nicholson's declaring that none could cure him of the disease he was under save King James, by taking away his mitre and bishoprick given him, Mr. Lindsay made the knowen lines:

Solatur frustra conjunx solantur amici, &c.

The rest stand with an English translation on Mr. Nicholson's Life. Mr. Calderwood sayes: "Mr. David Lindsay, Minister then at Dundee, Mr. Nicholson's familiar friend, privy to his greife as much as any man, set down Mr. Nicholson's speeches in Latine verses; and among the rest his exhortation to himself not to haunt the Court, and to eschew all the King's imployments. But neither Mr. Nicholson's greife, nor his admonition to him, wrought any good effect upon Mr. Lindsay, for afterward he made no scruple to accept the Bishoprick of Brechin, and to defend all the corruptions and innovations it pleased the King to obtrude upon our Kirk."

After this he fell slump in with the course of conformity to Prelacy. In the year 1616, when Bishop Spotswood got the High Commission renewed, I find Mr. Lindsay a member of it, and he is present next year in a meeting of it at Saint Andrews, when Mr. Archibald Simpson, Mr. D. Calderwood, and Mr. Peter Ewart wer harrassed, and deprived for their share in the petition to the Parliament against innovations. On the 11 of July, 1617, the King came from Falkland, and dined with the Archbishop of Saint Andrews at Dairsie on his way to Saint Andrews. In the afternoon, he came to Saint Andrews, and went to the church and heard a flattering sermon by Mr. Gladstane's Archdeacon. Next day, July 12, there was a publick disputation in the kirk of Saint Andrews upon some theses, formed and defended by Mr. David Lindsay, *upon the power of kings and princes.* The King himself, Mr. Calderwood sayes, acted the part of a *preses.* Those theses wer formed by Mr. Lindsay, and a publick dispute susteaned upon them, in quality of a Doctor in Divinity, which degree had been conferred upon him not long before: at least I guess it was thus.

Doctor Lindsay was a member of Perth Assembly, 1618. Upon Thursday, August 27, the bishops violently urged that the King's Articles, as they termed them, should be put to the vote. The ministers who opposed them craved that they might be reasoned upon; and some litle liberty this way was allowed, but with many interruptions. The King of Great Brittain was opposed to Zanchius, and all other learned men whose sentiments wer advanced against the Articles; and the Primat, who was Moderator of the Assembly, asserted him superior to any that wer produced, or could be produced, in learning. He told the Assembly plainly, that neither their reasonings nor numbers should cary their point; that the 5 Articles must be concluded, and should be so, wer there none for them save the 11 bishops and His Majesty's Commissioner. After some reasoning, and such returns as those, it was reasoned by those on the Primate's side, that if His Majesty would have been pleased, or any way put of, they would have reasoned against those Articles and the introducing them to this Kirk. Doctor Lindsay, Minister of Dundee, being posed in conscience by one of the ministers, acknowledged they had neither reason, Scripture, or antiquity for kneeling; but to avert the King's wrath he thought it best to yield.

The papers I am going to insert have no date in either of the two old copyes of them I have before me; but I take them to be writ about this year, 1618, or the following, before the Doctor was made Bishop; and they being not yet published, I take them to be worth preserving. They are writ by some minister or other person on the side of our Reformation Establishment. The first is directed to Doctor Lindsay, the next *to the Bretheren of the Ministry*, the third *to the People*, and the last is *5 Questions to be Studyed*. They are solid reasonings on the debates at this time, and but short, and so I have cast them into the Appendix N. (copy MS., 4to, 84, N. 11), and compare with MS., fol. 43, N. 70. [These papers appear to have been lost, as they are not now to be found.]

I have, I believe, upon Mr. Thomas Hogg's process before the High Commission, next year, 1619, for noncomplyance with Perth Articles, noticed Mr. Hogg's protest. Mr. Calderwood, after he has set it down, adds, when all the bishops wer silent, Doctor Lindsay would shoot his blunt bolt. He told Mr. Hogg a story of two men that had communicat, the one kneeling and the other sitting, but with his head uncovered, and the kneeler defended his kneeling from the other's being uncovered without a positive institution for communicating uncovered. Mr. Hogg easily gave him a reply, that ther was a great difference betwixt the two ceremonies, which I do not resume here. The disput was a litle long.

The Doctor wrote about this time his Resolutions for kneeling, which wer answered by Mr. Calderwood, who sayes it was no hard task to answer them. However, the Doctor had for his reward the Bishoprick of Brechin bestowed on him; and was consecrat Bishop by the Primat at Saint Andrews, Nov. 23, 1619.

Bishop Lindsay began to distinguish himself as a bishop in the Conference which was held at Saint Andrews, Nov. 23, 24, and 25, that same year. I have, on Mr. Scot's and Mr. J. Carmichael's Lives, given some account of the Conference. The ministers had urged a forbearance of them who had real scruples against the ceremonies obtruded, and urged that, as necessary to, and very consistent with, the unity and peace of the Church. The Bishop, in answer to this, said: "It had been reasoned on the other side that unity in religion might well consist with diversity in ceremonies; but he behoved to observe that that assertion might hold in the Catholick Church, but by no means did it hold in a particular Kirk under one regiment. He added that this held especially in point not only of practise, but doctrine; and when one side held things indifferent, and the other necessary, the one must needs be a heresy, and therfore not to be tollerat in the same Kirk." His brother Bishop of Ross differed a little from this pretty odd reasoning, and owned that a diversity of ceremonies wer consistent with unity even in a particular Kirk, unless the diversity run close to the Constitutions of the Church.

I have litle more concerning him while Bishop of Brechin. He went on harmoniously with the rest of the bishops in pressing the ceremonies; and was on that side of them who properly wer Bishop Laud's party, and for pushing a full conformity with England, and even going beyond the Constitutions of the English Church, and falling in with Bishop Laud's reformation or deformation; but that mostly appeared when he came to Edinburgh. He continoued in Brichen about 15 year.

Upon Bishop Forbes' death, the King, at Bishop Laud's desire, who indeed managed all affairs ecclesiastic in the three kingdoms, had Mr. Thomas Sydserf, at this time Dean of Edinburgh, in his view to succeed to that Bishoprick. When the accounts of this came to Edinburgh, the Magistrates, and indeed all ranks in Edinburgh, wer much discontented. The town had some of their Commissioners at Court upon some other affairs, and the Magistrates wrote earnestly to them that they should use their best endeavours to stope Mr. Sidserfe being their bishop, and desired them to inform the King and Archbishop of Canterbury that, if Mr. Sidserf wer thrust in upon them, it would certainly occasion commotions in Edinburgh, which would tend to the prejudice of the bishops and the course of conformity. Upon this, the Archbishop of Canterburry named Mr. David Lindsay, Bishop of Brechin. The writer of the Collections from 1589-1641, from whom I take severall things about the Bishop of Edinburgh, sayes Mr. Lindsay was not only a great scholar and learned man, but a great politician, and both able and willing to advance the estate of bishops, and had spoken and written more than any other in Scotland for conforming [to] that course.

Accordingly, on the 29 of July, 1634, the Bishops of Saint Andrews, Glasgow, Ross, and severall other bishops, met in the Royall Chappell of Hallyroodhouse, and received Mr. Lindsay upon the King's nomination and presentation Bishop of Edinburgh, and Mr. Sydserf was consecrat Bishop of Brichen in his room. Upon the Sabbath before, the English Liturgy was read in the Chappell Royall, and worship was performed and the whole service [conducted] according to the English Rites, all the bishops [being present], and the two to be received for Bishops of Edinburgh and Brichen with them.

In the end of October, Bishop Lindsay was made one of the Lords of Exchecker. The words of the Collections I take this from are: "About the 29 of October, 1634, ther came sure word from Court that His Majesty had changed the whole Lords of Exchecquer, and had removed all the noblmen that wer Lords therof, to wit, the Chancelor, Earle of Marr, Haddingtoun, Winton, Roxburgh, Lauderdale, and Southesk, with some others of inferior degree; and had put in their room the Bishops of Saint Andrews, Glasgow, Ross, and Edinburgh, four Lords of the Session, and four Barrons, with the Threasurer, Deput Advocat, and Register". The Bishops, thrusting themselves in to be Lords of Councill, Exchecquer Chancelors, brought no small odium upon them both here and in England.

I have an originall letter of the Bishop's before me, so spoiled that in some places I can scarce make it out, direct to the Presbitry of Dalkeith, and dated this same moneth. I'le set it down as farr as I can make it out.

"Moderator and Bretheren of the Presbitry of Dalkeith,—
Forasmeikle as we are informed by Sir John . . . of Leswalt, Knight, there are some questions and contraversies moved against him before you by Mr. James Porteous, Minister at Leswalt, and that he is summoned to appear before you for the same, and seing [he] is content to sette all his questions and contraversies be m . . . time we shall appoint. We therfore . . . ye continou all manner of process and citation be direct against the said Sir John in . . . he . . . till some competent day that we shall appoint for hearing and setling of those particulars. This, not doubting, ye

will do, we bid you farewell at . . . Burntisland, the 28 day of October, 1634 years.

"DA. EDINB."

Mr. James Porteous, Minister at Laswade, four miles from Edinburgh, was a zealouse, faithfull minister, severall time prosecuted before the High Commission for his nonconformity to Episcopacy and ceremonies. What was the occasion of this gentlman's prosecution before the Presbitry of Dalkeith I know not, but the Bishop, we see, interposes, and takes the nomination of a day for hearing that matter in his own hand, and sists the Presbitry's procedure in the meantime. Only this I know, that by such interposalls of the bishops, presbitrys wer frequently stopped in processes of scandall and other matters of discipline competent for them, and matters of considerable importance wer delayed and shuffled over, and this engratiat the bishops with some persons, who expected more easy treatment from them than at the hand of presbitrys.

The next originall letter I have of the Bishop of Edinburgh is to the same Presbitry of Dalkeith, and I suppose the like wer sent to all the presbitrys in his Diocese. Whither the ordinary time of the meeting of the Diocesan Synod of Edinburgh used to be the last Teusday of Aprile, and for some reason or other was this year altered by the Bishop, when the pressing of the Service Book upon ministers was in hand; or what the occasion was of this letter to the presbitrys, I do not precisely know, but, on the 28 of Aprile, 1637, the Bishop writes the following letter, which is worth preserving. It's directed on the back;—

> "To his well-beloved Bretheren, the Moderator and remanent Bretheren of the Exercise of Dalkeith, *those well-beloved Bretheren.*

"A great number of the ministers of this Diocess, thinking the day of the meeting of the Synod had been the last Wensday of Aprile, did come to this town, and finding themselves mistaken, presently returned to their own homes, with whom I spake not. Those presents, therfor, are to desire you to keep precisely the time appointed, which is the last Wensday of May, for, at that time, there are sundry things that I have to impart unto you, and in speciall concerning the Service Books that are to be received in our Church, of the which Books it's thought ex-

pedient that at present every minister and congregation buy two on the common charges of the parish, one for the minister, and another for the reader, or him that shall assist the minister in the service. The price of the book, I think, shall be 4 lb. 16 shilling, that is, 9 lb. 12 shilling for the two. The matter is of no great moment, and the imployment very necessary and profitable, as experience shall prove. I hope, therfor, you will not fail to bring in your moneys and receive your books; for it's appointed that the printer be payed and the books taken off his hand by the first of June. In the mean time, I expect you will observe the Commemoration of Christ's Assention upon Thursday, the 18 of May, and on Friday, the 28 of May, therafter called Whitsunday, a Commemoration of the Descending of the Holy Ghost, which have been, and are, solemly observed through all the Christian wordle to the honnour of Him, Who is the God of order, unity, and peace, to Whose grace I leave you, and shall ever remain,
"Your loving Brother,
"DA. EDINB.
"Hallyroodhouse, 28 Aprile, 1637."

According to this letter, the Bishop's Diocesian Synod met at Edinburgh, the last Wensday of May. All the account I can give of this Synod is from the Collections above named. The Synod met in the Colledge Kirk, and had four sessions. The Bishop moderated, and urged the bretheren to receive each of them two copyes of the Lyturgie, and read them in their kirks for daily service. The Liturgy, a good part of it, had been laid before the last meeting of the Synod, and many objections made against it by the ministers, that it conteaned some points of plain Popery and other errors, and the Apocryphicall Books to be read in the same manner as if they had been Canonicall Scripture. At this Synod, the Book being fully printed, severall other parts of it wer read before the Synod, which had not been read before, but severall of the members withdrew and walked without the kirk, while those places wer reading. When, at their next meeting, the Book was again urged to be received, Mr. Andrew Ramsay, Minister at Edinburgh; Mr. William Arthur, Minister at Saint Cuthbert's Kirk; Mr. James Porteouse, Minister at Laswadd; Mr. John Aird, Minister at Newbottle; Mr. Robert Balcanquell, Minister at Tranent; Mr. John Oswald, Minister at Pencaitland; Mr. James Fleeming, Minister at Caithaness, refused to receive the Books, and gave these reasons: 1, That the Lyturgy was not appointed by any Ordinance of any Assembly of this Kirk, without which no change and novation ought to be brought in; 2ly, That in the Lyturgie there wer many gross errours, and passages not agreeing with the Analogy of Faith; 3ly, That the Books of Apocrypha, there prescribed, wer not parts of authentick Scripture, and not to be read publickly in the Kirk; lastly, That there wer many passages of Popery scattered up and down the Book. The Bishop was very crabbit and angry, and upbraided the ministers for severall of their speeches. After the matter was referred to a Conference at length, the Bishop formed an Act of Synod to this purpose, that such of the ministers of the Diocess of Edinburgh as had received the Books, and did not allow of them, should have time given them to advise, and after that, they wer to make their report to the Bishop; and that the rest should begin and read them for the daylie service in their kirks. However, it was expected that the bishops would push their designe, and have the Book soon read through all kirks, whatever respite was granted for a litle. The tumult that fell in, in Agust, upon reading the Lyturgy, and the great turn of affairs afterward, soon put a stope to the bishops' designes.

Before that tumult fell out, I find the Bishop giving another sist to the procedour of presbitrys by a letter of his, the originall wherof is in my hand, and it followes. The address on the back stands thus:—

"To his worthy and well-beloved Bretheren, the Bretheren of the Presbitery of Linlithgow.

"Beloved Bretheren,

"I wrote to you of before in favours of John Bannantyne of Boutoun, and have receivd no answer, but, as I am informed, you are to proceed with all rigour. Wherfor, I require you that you proceed no further in that bussiness untill I meet with your Moderator, and confer with him theranent. Swa, leaving you to the grace of God, and rests,

"DA. EDINB.

"Hallyroodhouse, July 17 or 7, 1637."

We shall, in the Lives in this period, frequently hear of the tumult at Edinburgh, July 23, 1637, because Bishop Lindsay was immediatly concerned, and present in reading the Liturgie that day, and in some hazard in the confusion. I'le here insert the writer of the above-named

Collections his account of that matter, he being in the place at that time; and a carefull observer of what passed, and the rather, because it conteans severall particulars, which I do not observe in the many other narratives we have of that daye's work.

Upon Sunday, the 16 of July, 1637, ther wer a number of litle printed advertishments, ordeaning intimation to be made in all the pulpits of Edinburgh, and the congregations about, that it was resolved by authority that all should be advertished to prepare themselves to receive the Book of Common Prayer and Service, and to put it in practise next Lord's Day. This intimation was made in many of the kirks of Edinburgh, and round about, but not in all. In the Gray Freirs Kirk, wher Mr. Andrew Ramsay preached, he would not read the intimation, and the reader did it very unwillingly. In many places wher the ministers intimat this paper, it appeared they did it unwillingly, and generally the people murmured when it was read, as an uncouth novelty. Next Sunday, July 23, in the Old Kirk, Grayfreirs, and Tolbooth Kirk, after the Common Prayers wer read, the Dean of Edinburgh in the Great Kirk, Mr. James Fairly in the Gray Freirs Kirk, Mr. David Mitchell in the Tolbooth Kirk, went up to their pulpits, having the Service Books with them; the Bishop of Edinburgh being in the Great Kirk to assist the Dean. They all agreed to go in at the same time, between 8 and 9 in the morning. When they opened their books to read the Liturgy, all the people began to murmure, and especially the women of all sorts that wer present. They weeped and cryed out they wer going to say Mass, and uttered many angry speeches and bitter, calling them traitors, belly-gods, and deceivers. They got up upon their feet, crying, and shouting, and casting their stools at them, many men and women going out of the church, so that the said Bishop and Ministers in all the said three kirks wer compelled to leave off the reading of the said Service Book, with the danger of their lives, within half ane hour or therby, some going out of the kirk, and some remaining still. The tumult ceased, and the Bishop in the Great Kirk, Mr. Fairly and Mr. Mitchell in the other two, began their ordinary prayer, read their text, and delivered their sermon, wherin they notticed the disorder that had been, and concluded with the ordinary singing of psalmes; only it's to be notticed that in the Great Kirk, all the time of sermon, the dores wer shutt, and some of the Magistrates and their officers waited at them in case of any tumult. When the people wer dismissed, and the Bishop came out with some persons with him, the tumult began again in the street, especially by the woemen shouting and crying after him, calling him traitor and many other reproachfull words; they cast stones at him, and treas, and rungs, to the great perill of his life, so that with difficulty he got to his chamber. In the afternoon, the people resorted to the kirks, at the ordinary time, to hear sermon. When they came to the Great Kirk ther was no reader, nor any minister to preach; in the rest of the kirks ther was ordinary preaching and prayers. About 3 of the clock afternoon, or therby, the Bishop of Edinburgh came in to the Great Kirk with the Dean and Alexander Thomson. He read the Service Book with litle skill though good will enough; the Bishop made the sermon, and the kirk dismissed about 5 of the clock. When the Bishop came forth, ther arose a great clamour in the streets, and the cry was "Kill the traitour". They cast stones at the Earle of Roxburgh's coach, who had taken him in with him, and followed him down the street to the Nether Bow with shouts and cryes and casting of stones; and in the Canongate the people did the same. Some of the stones hitt the Bishop in the coach, so that with great difficulty he got to his lodgings. In like manner, when Mr. James Fairly had ended his sermon, in the fornoon, in the Gray Freirs Kirk, and was going to his house, the woemen followed him, crying and imprecating curses upon him, he also cursing them. Also, all the bishops, and ther wer 8 or 9 of them in Edinburgh at the time, and all of them in the Auld or Great Kirk that day, wer in great fear, and the Chancelor also. In the afternoon, the Councill met in the Chancelor's lodgings with the bishops in town, to consult what was proper to be done. Upon the Munday therafter, the people mett in the Auld Kirk, as they used to do, waiting for prayers, as wer wont to be, but they had none, either morning or evening. On Teusday and Wensday therafter, ther was neither prayer, preaching, nor exercise. But on Teusday, ther was a proclamation at the Cross, with sound of trumpet and the Lyon with his coat upon him, discharging all persons, under pain of death, to use any outragious speeches against any bishop or minister, or to speak evil of the Service Book or anything conteaned therin, or to injure any person or persons mentainers therof, under pain of death; declaring, also, that if any person should hear any speeches uttered against bishop or minister, or any reproaches on the said Book, and did [not] incontinent reveal the same to some of the Council, should incurr the same pains. It was likewise intimat that the Councill was every day to sit in Hallyroodhouse. Mr. Andrew Ramsay, Minister of the Gray Freirs, was charged to keep his house upon Sunday, July 23. All the week following, ther was no preaching or prayers in any of the kirks of Edinburgh, nor any bell rung for preaching or prayers as usuall, save on Sunday, nor the week after that. Upon the Wensday in the 3d week, and Friday therafter, ther was a sermon in the Great Kirk. This is the plain and circumstantial account this writter of the Collections gives of this tumult, and, [he ?] being in town at the time, I thought it worth transcribing.

I have before me another short hint of this tumult, given by Mr. Thomas Crawford, Professor in the College of Edinburgh, in his account of the Masters of that Colledge, which, coming from a man of learning and piety present on the spot, we may depend upon; and being short, I'le transcribe it: " The public Laureation was this year Munday, July 23, the very nixt day after that fatal check given to the prelates in the Kirk of Edinburgh. They, being set on by Laud, Primat of Canterburry, had framed a new Service Book for the Kirk of Scotland, ingrossing the seeds of the most part of the Popish and Arminian errors; and had procured a Mandat from His Majesty that it should be read and received in all the kirks of Scotland. Beginning at Edinburgh, only Mr. Andrew Ramsay stoutly opposed it, and Mr. Harry Rollock, having first given way, therafter repenting himself, did not read it. Mr. David Lindsay, Bishop of Edinburgh, came himself to the Mid Kirk of Saint Giles (the East Kirk being at the time repairing for the altar and other pendicles of the idolatrouse service), attended by Mr. James Hannay, Dean of Edinburgh, and Mr. Alexander Thomson, Minister. So soon as the Bishop began to such unknowen service, some good people arising to bear testimony against it, which they intended to do in all modesty, ther arose such a tumult of unknowen and as inconsiderable people, that all the bussines was disturbed, and the Bishop, after sermon, forced to run into the nixt lodging for shelter; and, notwithstanding the diligence used by the Magistrates, the like uproar continoued in the afternoon, both in the Great Kirk, West Kirk, and Grey Freirs, where the service was attempted to be read, and on the streets. From this small beginning, wherin the hand of no knowen person could be found to have been, proceeded the overthrow of the Episcopall Jurisdiction in Scotland."

About the end of this year, 1637, Bishop Lindsay, giving a warrand contrary to law to deforce a messenger-of-armes, made a great noise. I give the account of this in the words of the writter of the Collections just now cited: "At this time, December, 1637, ther wer many masses said in Edinburgh, Canongate and diverse other parts, as was constantly reported, swa that ther was no order in the commonweil; but all government both in Kirk and Policy was like to go into great confusion. And especially ther was ane great injury done by the Bishop of Edinburgh (wherby it may appear if the bishops had the government of the country that they would commit great injuries), to wit, ther wer letters of captioun used at the instance of ane great barron and laird in Argyle, the Laird of Auchinbreck, against some men in Leith who had bought some cows from him, and given their obligation for payment of summes of money as the prices therof, for the which they wer denounced His Majesty's rebells, being lawfully charged conform to order; and the messenger using his letters of caption, according to order, the Bishop sent a warrand to discharge the officer from any further using the letters, under pain of taking his blazon from him if he refused. Likeas the messenger refusing to desist, according to the Bishop's warrand, his blazon was taken from him. Upon this, the Laird of Auchinbreack pursued the Bishop before the Council sitting at Dalkeith, and produced the Bishop's warrand ordeaning the messenger to be discharged. The Bishop was excused by severall of the Counselours, and the matter would have been dropt under pretext of the Bishop's simplicity, and that he had been abused by some people who had purchased the warrand, had not the Lord Lorn (afterwards Marquise of Argyle), the pursuer's cheiff, and a Privy Counsellour, who was present, insisted that what was done by the Bishop was a gross injury to justice, and an evil example to others; and yet, all done was, the Councill ordeaned the Bishop to see the party payed the debt. This was observed by all sorts of people to be partiality to the estate of bishops more than other persons."

The great alteration which ensued after this tumult in Edinburgh is pretty weel knowen. The Bishop of Edinburgh seems to have continoued in the country, when most of the rest of the bishops retired to England; at least, I find him at Hallyroodhouse in October next year, when things wer preparing for the meeting of the Generall Assembly at Glasgow. A proces was raised against Mr. David Mitchell, Minister at Edinburgh, before the Presbitry of Edinburgh, as shall be notticed on his Life when I come to it, and the Bishop by his Episcopall power [interposed] to stope their proceedure, as we see he did in severall other cases; but now his letter was not much regarded, he himself being summoned, or very soon to be so, before the approaching Generall Assembly to answer for crimes laid to his charge. However, I shall insert his letter here, from the originall in my hands. It's directed thus on the back:

To my well-beloved Bretheren, the Bretheren of the Exercise of Edinburgh, these:

and runs:

"Right worshippfull and well-beloved Bretheren,

"I am informed that you have summoned Mr. David Mitchell to appear before you and to be censured for certain points of erroneous doctrine delivered by him from the pulpit, as is alledged; and that ye are to proceed against him, after tryall, if he be found guilty, either to suspension or deposition. And, because it's ordeaned by an Act of Generall Assembly, holden at Glasgow, in the moneth of June, 1610, and by an Act of Parliament, holden at Edinburgh, October 23, 1612, it is statuted by an inviolable law in all time coming that the Bishop of the Diocess, associating to himself the ministry of the bounds wher the delinquent serveth, is to take the tryall of the fact, and upon just cause found, to deprive; and the like order to be observed in the suspension of ministers from the exercise of their function. Those are therfor to require you not to proceed to any of the forsaid censures against the said Mr. David, untill that I, associating to myself you, the ministry of the bounds, take tryall of the fact wherupon he is accused, which I, by these presents, offer myself to do, at any convenient time and place to be appointed by us with common consent; otherwise, in my judgment, ye shall do best to continou this process and all others of this kind till the Generall Assembly indyted by His Majesty, that there all things may be handled without prejudice. So hoping you will take this matter to your wise consideration, and direct some of your bretheren to me with your answer, that, after conference with them, both you and I may advise, and do that which shall be found most expedient for the honnour of God, the peace of the Church, and the quietnes of our own conscience at the gloriouse appearance of our Saviour, the Lord Jesus, Who shall render unto every one according to that which he hath done in the body, whither it be good or evil, to Whose grace I do recommend you in Him to rest.

"Your very loving Brother,

"DA. EDINB.

" Hallyroodhouse, 9 of October, 1638."

The Bishop, though he would have Mr. Mitchel's proces referred to the ensuing Generall Assembly, wher things wer to be handled without prejudice, yet when they sat he declined their authority ; and no doubt being one of the most learned of the bishops and their ammanuensis in writting for their cause, he had an active hand in the declinature and reasons therof given in to the Generall Assembly at Glasgow, and, it may be, was one of the cheife formers of the papers upon that side. The printed Acts of that Assembly bear the sentence of deposition and excommunication passed against him and the rest of the bishops.

After this sentence, I have no more concerning him. He was now an old man, and had been near 40 years in the ministry, and it's probable he dyed soon after this. He engaged in the dispute upon Perth Articles; and I know no farther of his works in print save what relate to those. In the year 1619, he wrote *Resolutions for Kneeling*, 8vo, London, 1619. To this Mr. David Calderwood printed a reply, that same year, under the title of *Solution of Doctor* [Lindsay's] *Resolutions*. The Bishop wrote also an *Account of Perth Assembly, with a Defence of it*, 4to, London, 1621. This was an answer to Mr. Calderwood's *Nullity of Perth Assembly*, and Mr. Calderwood defended his *Nullity of Perth Assembly* in his *Altare Damascenum*, and in his *Re-examination of the 5 Articles enacted at Perth*, 1618, 4to, 1636, of which likewise he published an abreviat that same year in 8vo.

COLLECTIONS UPON THE LIFE OF Mr. ALEXANDER ARBUTHNET, FIRST MINISTER AT ARBUTHNET AND LOGY-BUCHAN, AND THEREAFTER PRINCIPAL OF THE KING'S COLLEGE, ABERDEEN.

It's a pity we have so very few materialls remaining for the Life of this very learned, pious, and usefull person, who had few equals for universall literature, extensive knowledge, and prudent zeal, in the period he lived. His Life is lately writt by Dr. McKeinzie, but with a plain byass; and what he gives us is filled up with large extracts from the printed Calderwood and Petry of the procedure of the General Assemblys whereof he was Moderator. With what view he spends so much paper in reprinting what is in every bodie's hands, I do not know, unles it was to make his account of him a litle longer with things he was not much concerned in. I shall take notice of some of the Doctor's mistakes about this good man, and draw together what I have met with relative to him in the MS. Acts of our Assemblys and Calderwood's MS. very shortly, without mixing extraneous things that have been formerly published.

Mr. Arbuthnet was born in the House of Arbuthnet, in the shire of Merns, 1538. He was a son of the Barron of Arbuthnet,[1] a very ancient and noble family, created Viscounts of Arbuthnet by King Charles the I. The mean extract and parentage of the ministry in Scotland after the Reformation is a very poor reflection used against them by some Popish and Prelatick writers; and as it does not at all hold in severalls, as Mr. Knox, Mr. Arbuthnet, Mr. Bruce, and others, so, tho' we had not so many contrary instances, the Lord's wise and kind providence in bringing so many, wer it from the sheep-coats to feed Israel, ought to be wisely observed, and is not at all a subject of mocking and ludibry. I believ our circumstances this way, both after the Reformation and since, are much the same with those of other Christian Churches since

---

[1] See Introduction.

the primitive times. At our reformation from Popery, the Lord very wonderfully stirred up the hearts of many to offer themselves to the holy work of the ministry; some of very noble and honourable familys, as Mr. Patrick Hamiltoun[1] and those just now named, and others descended of the more common rank; and, after the Church was constituted, a mixture of both still continued, tho' I imagine upon a calcul it will be found that the bulk of the ministry in succeeding times have been made up of the posterity of such as wer before them in that holy function. Our sellaries appointed for the sustentation of the ministry are not indeed so great, as to tempt familys of rank to educat their cadets with an eye to large benifices and dignitys, as things stand in the Popish countrys, and wher prelacys and other emoluments are to be had in some Protestant churches; yet we have not wanted some of very good parentage, who have devoted themselves to the service of God and the souls of His people; and the less outward temptations they had from gain, their aims and end will appear to be the more pure and disinterested.

We need not doubt of Mr. Arbuthnet's liberall education. After he had finished his studys in the belles lettres, he was sent to the University of Saint Andrews, wher, he being class-fellow with Mr. Lawson, the friendship began, which continued throu' their lives. When Mr. Arbuthnet had taken his degrees at Saint Andrews, in the year 1561, his parents sent him over to France to follow the study of the civil law, then taught at Paris with much applause by the great Cujacius. We may suppose, both in the shire of the Mernes, wher the Reformation made great advances at the beginning of it, and at Saint Andrews, which was reformed some years before he left it, he had drunk in the scripturall reformed doctrine, in which he was more and more confirmed by the many Protestants there, as well as in seing the bloody and unchristian practises of the bigotted Papists, the Guisians. After he had studyed the lawes 5 years under so good a teacher, he had the degree of Licentiatus Legum conferred upon him, and returned to his native country, 1566.

Thus Bishop Spotswood recons, and upon what grounds Dr. McKeinzie brings him home 3 years sooner, I cannot tell; nor shall I enquire. All along he seems to give broad hints of his having no great

---

[1] Note 80.

respect to the memory of this great man. He makes the Reformation's now being prevalent the motive of his declaring himself for the Reformers. I am persuaded he had far higher and better motives in joyning them. I agree with the Doctor that he was very instrumentall in carying on the Reformation. His parents and he himself designed other work for him than preaching the Gospell, no doubt. The ministers, observing his piety and good qualifications, urged him to apply himself to the study of theology; but man proposes and God disposes, and His kind providence in thir things ought to be observed. The Doctor adds he entered into Orders, but what sort of ordination he got he cannot tell. Ther is no great mystery in that, and the Doctor needed be in no strait, tho' by this innuendo he would glance at the validity of the ordination of our Reformers because not Episcopall. A litle reflection would have discovered how he was ordeaned, very probably by the Laird of Dun and the ministry of that bounds; and the Doctor in a very few lines after tells us he finds him designed Parson of Arbuthnet and Logy-Buchan. What need was ther then to doubt but he was regularly ordeaned to that Charge?

The first Assembly I find him in is 1567, and it's probable he was not in the country before this year, and such was his reputation that he was put upon one of the hardest tasks in the Assembly—the answering of questions—so the Ass. Registers bear, 11, Sess. 3. The Laird of Braid, Elphingstoun, and Whittingham, Mr. Alex. Arbuthnet, and Jo. Brand, minister, wer joyned to the bretheren nominat in the 2 Session appointed to concurr with the Lords of Secret Council and Session for decision of questions after the Assembly.

Mr. Arbuthnet is appointed to revise a book complained of to the Assembly, July, 1568, and we may suppose he was ordeaned sometime before, since he was member of this Assembly. Their Order stands thus in the Registers, Sess. 3: " The Assembly ordean Thomas Bassandon, printer,[1] to call in the books printed by him intituled the Fall of the Roman Kirk, wherin the King is called Supreme Head of the Primitive Kirk, &c., and to keep the rest unsold till he alter the forsaid title. Item, to delet the baudie song, 'Welcome Fortune,' &c., printed in the end of the Psalme Book without license; and that he abstain, in times coming, from printing anything without license of the supreme

[1] Note 81.

Magistrate, or, if it concern religion, be such as shall be appointed by the Assembly to revise. Mr. Alex. Arbuthnet was appointed to revise the fornamed tractat, and report to the next Assembly." I find no report ther.

It would seem Mr. Arbuthnet was Minister at Arbuthnet and Logy-Buchan towards two years. Upon the visitation of the Colledge of Aberdeen and turning out of the Popish Masters, he was, in 1569, admitted Principall of the King's Colledge there, in room of Mr. Alex. Anderson, as is to be seen in the Laird of Dun's Life, who was imployed by the Regent in that matter. Ther he continued 13 years or more, singularly usefull by his laborious teaching, and prudent government, among the youth, and informing many who wer eminently serviceable afterward in the North, wher he may be reconed the first restorer of learning. He recovered multitudes likewise in that country, formerly involved in Popish superstition and idolatry.

In the General Assembly, March, 1572, Mr. Arbuthnet was named with severall others to meet in Mr. Knox' house at Saint Andrews, and sight and revise the Heads and Conclusions drawn at Leith and referred to this Assembly, as has been notticed in the Laird of Dun's Life. Those Heads and Conclusions Doctor McKeinzie calls The New Book of Discipline. Whether he gives them this designation of designe to confound those Conclusions with The 2d Book of Discipline, or by mistake, I know not, but I find them nowhere else get this name. They wer vastly different from our Books of Discipline, and just their reverse.

Next year, 1573, Mr. Arbuthnet is chosen Moderator of the General Assembly in Agust. Doctor McKeinzy spends much of what he gives us of Mr. Arbuthnet's Life in giving the proceedings of that Assembly, where, indeed, litle was done but discussing complaints against the Tulcan Bishops. The following year, the Principall, who was alwise a vigorous opposer of Tulchan Bishops, drew up some animadversions by way of complaint to the General Assembly upon the procedure of the Dean and Chapter of Murray in their election of the Bishop of Murray, as not agreeable to the Act passed in the last Generall Assembly. Mr. Andrew Simson and Mr. John Keith gave in written replys to the said complaint. This affair was before severall Sessions in this Assembly, Agust, 1574. At lenth, it was found that the Bishop was not regularly sisted befor this Assembly, and the matter was delayed till the next. What was the issue I cannot distinctly find.

In the [year] 1577, he is appointed to revise The 2d Book of Discipline, as hath been notticed in Mr. Craige's Life; and there seems some ground to think he had some hand in the first draught of that book, and the rather, because he is chosen again Moderator to the Assembly which mett particularly to consider The Book of Discipline, in April this year.

In this Assembly, Mr. Arbuthnet, being absent from the last Assembly, and so not so ripe as to what regularly was to come in before this, made a very innocent motion which was gone into: for some ministers to be joyned with him to advise as to the method of things coming in before the Assembly. This was continued for a good while without any ill consequences, till at lenth, as some of the best things have been made a handle of by cunning and corrupt persons, it was turned to a very dangerous and unreasonable barr upon the liberty of the Assembly. I the rather nottice this, because Doctor McKeinzie gives this matter a very false turn, and misrepresents Mr. Petry as his voucher, that he may, throw Mr. Arbuthnet's and Petry's side, give a wound to all our after Assemblys, as litle better than the Council of Trent; and to make his reader believe they wer all prelimited. I will, therefor, set this matter in its just light, and therby lay open the Doctor's most unfair representation of this affair of the Privie Conference. The Assembly Registers as to this run thus, as Mr. Calderwood's MS. has shown: "The General Assembly conveened at Edinburgh in the Council-hous, the 1 day of Aprile, 1577. Mr. Alex. Arbuthnet, Principall of Aberdeen, was chosen Moderator. Because he was not forseen of such things as wer appointed in the last Assembly to be determined in this Assembly, in respect of his absence, therfor, at his desire, the Assembly appointed their loved bretheren, the Laird of Dun; Mr. James Lawson, Minister of Edinburgh; Mr. Robert Pont, Provost of the Trinity Colledge; Mr. David Lindsay, Minister at Leith; Mr. Andrew Hay, Commissioner at Cliddisdail; Mr. John Craig, Minister of Aberdeen; and Mr. Andrew Melvil, Principall of Glasgow, to concur with him the morn, at 7 hours, in the Nether Tolbooth, to conferr and advise upon such matters as shall be tho't good to be handled in this Assembly." One would not think ther wer any hazard here, nor prelimitation of the Assembly; and no such thing was designed or endeavoured for many years; only the regular manner of the tabling of what was unfinished by the former Assembly was concerted, but so as every body had liberty to object against anything done by them, in open Assembly.

However, so tender wer ministers of anything that might look like an infringement upon the liberty of Assemblys, that some exceptions wer made against the Moderator's naming persons as above, who wer termed Assessors, in the Assembly, 1580; but the matter being ripely advised, no hazard was seen in them, and they were continoued. I shall likewise give the Minute of this Assembly from Calderwood, that the reader may have all I know in this matter: " The General Assembly was holden at Dundee, and began the 14 day of July, 1580. The bretheren chose Mr. James Lawson, Moderator. He desired certain bretheren, whom he should nominat, to conferr with him, and give their advice in such matters as are to be treated and reasoned during this Convention, to the effect that matters may proceed more formally and with readier expedition. Upon whose desire, because it was meaned [hinted] that certain bretheren wer offended with the order of Assessors, which wer not wont to be joyned to the Moderator to give their advice to him, as tho' some tyranny or usurpation might creep in therby, or liberty might be taken from the bretheren, the question was moved to the whole Assembly: whether the said order was worthy to be allowed and continoued as it hath been before, or to be rejected as prejudiciall to the liberty of the bretheren, to the effect that all occasion of murmure might be taken away; all that would reason in this question being required publickly to reason. At last, the General Assembly concluded the said order to be good and necessary, and to be keept as it was before, without any prejudice or hurt to the liberty of the bretheren, and for conference with the Moderator. As is above said, the Assembly appointed their bretheren following, at his own nomination, to wit, Mr. Robert Pont, Mr. Thomas Smeton, Mr. Andrew Melvil, Mr. George Hay, William Christieson, David Ferguson, Mr. John Young, Mr. Patrick Auchinleck, Mr. Thomas Buchanan, the Laird of Braid, and John Johnstoun, Commissioner from Edinburgh, to conveen at extraordinary hours, 7 in the morning and two in the afternoon, in the Assembly place." Thus this matter stands in Calderwood, and thus matters continoued for a good many years, till, by the influence of the Court, corruptions wer piecemeal bro't in, and this custome among others was unhappily perverted.

But let us see how unfairly Doctor McKeinzie represents this. His words are: " But in the beginning of this Assembly, because Mr. Arbuthnet, the Moderator, was not in the preceding Assembly, therfor they ordered that the Superintendant of Angus and other six ministers should attend him every morning, from 7 of the clock till the sitting doun of the Assembly, for preparing such things as should be bro't before them; and Mr. Petrie observes that in all the following Assemblys those Privy Conferences, as they wer called, wer like to that which in the Councill of Trent was called the Congregation ". By comparing this with what is above, the reader will observe as many mistakes as there are lines. The Doctor sayes the Asessors wer to attend on the Moderator, every morning; the Registers, only to-morrow at 7 of the morning. The Doctor gives them power to prepare matters, and all that should come before the Assembly; the Registers, only to conferr and consider such matters as shall be tho't good to be handled, that is, the order in which they wer to be tabled, without any prelimitation of the Assembly. The Doctor cites Petry for his voucher, and referrs us to Calderwood. This I would have reconed a typographicall error, if what is put in Petry's mouth had not been a gross imposition upon him and the Doctor's reader, and a downright falsification of this authour, who never tho't nor said, that in all the following Assemblys the Privy Conferences wer like to that which in the Council of Trent was called the Congregation. Such grossly false citations are intolerable, and can scarce be attributed to hast and oversight, but designe.

This oblidges me to insert Mr. Petry's own words, and so I shall leave the reader himself judge of the Doctor's candor and integrity in this matter. After he has given an abbreviat of the proceedings of this Assembly, he comes to make some observations upon it, as his use is, and p. 391 says: " Observe that a little thing was begun for a personall use, and therafter the same was contioued and turned to a common evil. Those who wer appointed to informe the Moderator at that time, [and] in the Assemblies following, wer chosen under the name of the *Privy Conference*, and power was given to them to confer with the Moderator upon the purposes to be treated by the Assembly, and to form the Acts before they wer read in the Assembly. This was like to that which in the Council of Trent was called *The Congregation*. Within some years, all matters wer debated and concluded in the Privy Conference, and the body of the Assembly had litle to do, namely, after the year 1597. Such men wer named to be on the Privy Conference, who for the most part wer known to favour the purpose intended; and one or two whom the cheif leaders knew to be contrary-minded wer also named to be there, to the end they might know what the contrary party would object; and when the Acts wer in votting and penning these two or mo could do nothing by their few votes. And when their conclusions wer propounded in the open Assembly, it was called presumption to oppose what was debated and concluded by the Privy Conference, especially after the erection of bishops. The Bishop of Saint Andrews did by his power name the Privy Conference, and so wer things carried both in the Generall and Episcopall or Diocesan Synods." Mr. Petry's remark is certainly very solid and just, but its weight falls not on Mr. Arbuthnet nor the Presbiterians, but upon the Doctor's freinds, the prelates, and their inbringers. Mr. Petry never dreamed that all the following Assemblys wer prelimited, and directly restricts his observation to the times after the [year] 1597, whence the Church of Scotland begins to number the corrupt and pretended General Assemblys. I have insisted the longer on this matter both to put it in its proper light, and that I might give another instance of the Doctor's candor in citations, and vindicat Mr. Arbuthnet and our General Assemblys.

At the next Assembly, Mr. Arbuthnet was nominat as one to go from the King to the Protestant Council at Magdeburgh, as hath been notticed on Mr. And. Melvil's Life, which is a proof in what estimation he was held in this Church for his learning and prudence; and Aprile, 1578, he is one of the persons appointed to present The 2d Book of Discipline, with a supplication, to the King and Council, and conferr with such as they should nominat upon the heads thereof. Doctor McKeinzie contracts this, and would make his readers think that Mr. Arbuthnet and the rest wer only to reason upon the ceremonies of the Church, and how far ministers may medle in civil affairs, and if they may vote in Council and Parliament, but there is but a power cast in at the close of their commission to present and conferr upon The 2d Book of Discipline, and runs in the Assembly Registers: "And that the said

Commissioners at the said Conference reason on the heads of the ceremonys, and how far ministers may medle with civil affairs, and if they may vote in Councill and Parliament," that is, to defend The Book of Discipline in those points, and answer the Courtiers if they insisted on them; and not, as the Doctor would have it believed, as if this was a Conference soly upon those heads, or as if the Assembly wer willing to have ceremonies, civil burdens, and vote in Parliament bro't on ministers, wher indeed ther was no such thing. I find by the Registers of the Assembly conveened at Glasgow, Aprile, 1581, Sess. 7, that "The Assembly think it meet that Mr. Alexr. Arbuthnet be placed in the Ministry of Aberdeen, and that he demitt his place in the College in favour of Mr. Nicol Dalglish," but I do not find whether this took effect.

Litle more offers till Mr. Arbuthnet's death. There was a peculiar friendship betwixt him and Mr. George Buchanan, our celebrated poet and historian. Mr. Calderwood nottices that the learned Buchanan dyed upon Friday, the 28 of September, 1582, in the 68 year of his age, and was buryed upon Saturday, attended by a great company of the faithfull, and cites Mr. Smeton's character of him: *Orbis terrarum non tantum Scotiae decus,* and, *Seculi nostri decus, antiquae virtutis et pietatis exemplar, summae eruditionis miraculum, doctorum et doctrinarum omnium principem et parentem.* Mr. Buchanan, at his death, left, Dr. McKeinzie says, the revising and printing his History to Mr. Arbuthnet, and he published that History, which, he adds, gave great offence, both against the author and Mr. Arbuthnet. The learned will judge what ground of offence was given by either. The admirers of Popery and arbitrary government, and the lovers of slavish principles, wer grated with this noble History; but I belive all good judges, either of stile or matter, recon that History and its author an ornament to our nation, and think themselves obliged to Mr. Arbuthnet for his care about it. In the unhappy year 1584, when our young King was under such managers as the Earle of Arran and Archbishop Adamson, who wer hurying him headlong to his own and the Kingdome's ruine, a picked Parliament was conveened, who, in a very few dayes, and very hastily, endeavoured to strick at the root of the liberty of the Church of Scotland, and almost quite overturned what had been done in our Reformation since we separated from

Popery. This meeting, indeed, found "That the buikes of the *Chronicles* and *de Jure Regni Apud Scotos*, made by umquhile Maister G. Buchannane, and imprinted longsyne, conteines sundrie offensive matters worthie to be deleete," and order the copys of those twa volumes to be brought in to the Secretary, that they may be perused and purged of the offensive and extraordinary matters specifyed therin, under the pain of 2000 pounds of every person failzing. The wordle would have been oblidged by a detail of those offensive and extraordinary matters; but they are suppressed, and till we see them we can make no judgment. It was really an honnour, and not a conjure [censure] to Mr. Buchanan and Arbuthnet to be thus taken nottice of by such people, and in such a manner. And ther is no need at this time of day of a vindication of the History and *Jus Regni*, especially from so mean a hand as mine.

Next year, Mr. Arbuthnet was transported, by the sentence of some judicatory, from the Colledge of Aberdeen to be Minister of Saint Andrews, and, as I take it, to be Principall of some of the Colledges there. The King and Council interposed, and gave out letters of horning discharging him to remove from Aberdeen. I have not met with the circumstances of that affair fully related, and, therefor, I can only set down what I meet with in the Assembly records upon it. The Assembly, in October, 1583, in their Articles and Complaints to the King, they regrate "That His Majesty frequently interponed his authority be letters of horning, to stop the execution of the Acts made in the Generall Assembly, in matters properly belonging to the Kirk, and nothing twitching the civil estate". In their instructions to those sent to present the Articles they give this instance: "Mr. Alex. Arbuthnet is charged, against the Acts of the Kirk, to remain in the Colledge of Aberdeen, under pain of horning". Many such attacks were now made upon the proceedings of the Assembly at this time, as may be seen in our printed historians. The King, in his answers to the Assembly's Articles upon this head, gives this return: "The ii. head is very generall, and for the only one example that hath been spoken of to His Highnes, twitching the removall of the Principal of the Colledge of Aberdeen to be Minister of Saint Andrews, His Majesty trusts that the Assembly will not think that matter (the circumstances well considered) either so proper to the Kirk or so improper to the civil estate, but that

His Highnes and his Council had good grounds and reason to direct his letters as he did upon the generall state of the North Countrie, wherin none was prejudged, seing ther was nothing conteaning power to denounce at first, but either to do the thing required, or to appear and show a just cause in the contrair". Dr. McKeinzie's innuendo here is very idle and ill grounded, and can only land upon the King, since it's evident the Assembly could have no such mean view. He says the King suspected the Assembly ordered Mr. Arbuthnet to remove from Aberdeen to Saint Andrews only to have his advice in their factious proceedings, Saint Andrews being nearer the capitall city, where the Assembly met, than Aberdeen. This needs no refutation. The odds 'twixt Saint Andrews and Edinburgh, and Aberdeen and Edinburgh, is not worth while in the supposed case. Ther could be no difficulty in getting Mr. Arbuthnet's advice whenever it was needful; but the Doctor, who, I belive, has coined this fine reason of the King's opposition, forgetts that the Principall of Aberdeen was as oft a member of the Assembly as the Minister of Saint Andrews.

However, I shall agree with the Doctor that this contraversy was soon removed by Mr. Arbuthnet's death. It was, indeed, an inexpressible loss to the Church of Scotland, and one of the threatening tokens of evil coming fast on the Church and land, when he and severall other good men wer taken away from the evil to come, and safely housed from the black cloud, which came on this Church for about two years, the like of which they had not mett with since they lost Popery. He dyed at Aberdeen, on Wednesday the 16, and was buryed the 17 of October, as Calderwood has it, and the 20 as Bishop Spotswood sayes, in Colledge Church there,[1] being 45 years of age. Mr. Andrew Melvil's epitaph on him and Principall Smeton has been insert in Mr. Melvil's Life. His warm and affectionat epitaph on Mr. Arbuthnet deserves a room here.

" Flere mihi si fas privata incommoda, si fas
　　Publica, nec tua mi commoda flere nefas:
　Flerem ego te, mihi te ereptum, pater Arbuthnete,
　　Et pater, et patriae lux oculusque tuae.
　Flerem ego te Superis carum caput Arbuthnete,
　　Et caput, et sacri corque animusque chori.

[1] Note 82.

  Flerem ego: nec flenti foret aut pudor, aut modus, eheu!
    Flerem egote, te eheu! Flerem ego perpetuo?
  Deliciae humani generis: dulcissime rerum:
    Quem Musae et Charites blando aluere sinu.
  Cujus in ore lepos: sapiens in pectore virtus:
    Et Suadae et Sophiae vis bene juncta simul.
  Cui pietas, cui prisca fides, constantia, candor,
    Et pudor, et probitas non habuere parem.
  Sacras et Themidis, medicas et Paeonis artes,
    Et potis immensi pandere jura poli.
  Vis animi, vis ingenii, vis vivida mentis
    Et terram, et pontum, et sidera perdomuit.
  Talis erat hic aevum agitans: nunc aethere summo
    Celsior, et summo non procul inde Deo.
  Perfrueris vera in patria caeloque Deoque
    Felix; haec tua me commoda flere nefas."

          Delitiæ Poet. Scotorum, vol. ii, p. 120.

 I know nothing published by this learned person but that book, mentioned by Doctor McKeinzie, *Orationes de Dignitate et Origine Juris*, quarto, Edinburgh, 1572, on which Mr. Thomas Maitland has a beautifull poem among his elegys, Numb. 7, which, because it conteans a very just and yet high character of this great man, I shall likewise take in here.

  "Tempus erat, cum glans dura Jovis arbore nata,
    Et facilem vilis praebuit herba cibum.
  Cumque foret vini nec adhuc bene cognitus usus,
    Sedavit gelidi fluminis unda sitim.
  Ast ubi Trinacriis errans dispersit in oris
    Frugiferae messis semina flava Ceres:
  Et cum pampineos proles Semeleia colles,
    Laetaque pinxisset vitibus arva suis:
  Amplius insuaves iam nemo ex ilice glandes,
    Ex rivo gelidam nemo petebat aquam.
  Hinc Cereri tribuit Cerealia festa vetustas,
    Sacra Deae Cnidiae non violanda jocis.
  Sacra racemiferi sic et Trieterica Bacchi,
    Æra puellari queis sonuere manu.

Sic quondam nobis, praeclara scientia Juris,
    (Precipites error sic malus egit avos ;)
Non bene culta fuit, nec enim gens effera legum,
    Constringi passa est libera colla jugo.
At tu doctarum spes Arbuthnæe sororum,
    O Decus O patriae splendor amorque tuae ;
Eloquii postquam monstras velut amne citato,
    Gentibus humanis commoda quanta ferant :
Fallimur ? an legum reverentia sancta nepotes
    Obstringit, quae vix ante tenebat avos ?
Et nudor assuetis cohibens fera pectora frenis
    Justitiam referet, barbariemque premet.
Nec Cereris laudi, aut Bacchi tua gloria cedet,
    Si modo jus potius frugibus atque mero est.
Quod si forte tibi sacra Arbuthnæa negantur,
    Nomine nec niteant templa dicata tuo :
At celebris memori tua fama sacrabitur aevo,
    Factaque posteritas grata stupenda canet.
Macte igitur juris cultor doctissime, perge
    Caelicolum laudes aequiparare tuis."

Delitiæ Poet. Scot., vol. ii, p. 153.

Bishop Spotswood gives Principall Arbuthnet a very fair character, and tells us his death was a great loss both to the Church and country; that he was greatly beloved of all men, hatted of none; and in such account, for his moderation with the cheif men in the North, that without his advice they could almost do nothing, which put him in great fasherie [annoyance], wherof he did often complean. Pleasant and jocund in conversation; in all sciences expert; a good poet, mathematician, lawer, and in medicine skilfull; so as in every subject he could promptly discourse, and to good purpose. Doctor McKeinzie, who has as litle good, as may be, to say of any of our Reformers, gives us indeed the Bishop's character of him, but then it might be seasoned with innuendos, which, however designed to Mr. Arbuthnet's disadvantage by the Doctor, yet with better judges than he, I belive they will be reconed for his honnour. He tells us Mr. Arbuthnet was consulted by all the General Assemblys in the affairs of the Church, and tho' he was of the same principles with Buchanan and Mr. Andrew Melvil, yet he was much more moderat; and if he was not so good a poet as Buchanan, or so great a master of the purity of the Roman language, yet he was a more learned and more universall scholar. Paralels are frequently needless (except when a writter, as here, inclines to disparage both), and often odious. Neither of them had any principles that they need be ashamed of, nor Mr. Melvil; and I belive all the 3 wer very universall scholars and singularly learned; and Calderwood recons Mr. Arbuthnet among the learnedest in Europe at that time. Bishop Spotswood and the Doctor are both out in terming him moderat, if they do not mistake the idea of that word as used by them. He was a most zealous opposer of Popery and all the remains of it, both in doctrine, worship, government, and practise. He was an early and firm opposer of Tulchan Bishops. He had a considerable share in The 2d Book of Discipline, and in setting up of Presbiterys in this Church. He was a vigourous opposer of the encroachments made by the Court on the libertys and priviledges of this Church, and our Reformation rights; an intimat friend of Mr. Knoxe's while he lived, of Mr. Lawson, Mr. Smeton, and Mr. Andrew Melvil; and had the same principles and views they had. If this be what they mean by moderation, they and I shall not differ in our sentiments. I wish I had more concerning this excellent person handed down to me.

COLLECTIONS UPON THE LIFE OF Mr. JAMES LAWSON, SUB-PRINCIPAL OF THE COLLEGE OF ABERDEEN AND MINISTER AT EDINBURGH.

Mr. Lawson was the person Mr. Knox fixed upon for his successor at Edinburgh; and besides the divine direction that dying saint implored in this important manner, which is cheifly to be considered, everyone that knows Mr. Knox will allow he was a good judge who was fitt to take the charge of that principall watch-tower upon him, when he was hasting to the end of his labours, and Mr. Craig was about to leave that town. Indeed, the event justifyed Mr. Knoxe's choice, and for twelve years, Mr. Lawson was a burning and shining light in that place. His Life, that I know of, has not been essayed by any; tho' his memory deserves to be preserved, not only as a faithfull, usefull, and succesfull servant, but as a remarkable sufferer for the truths of Christ and our Reformation principles, to banishment, and even to death, in a forraigne land. I will, then, essay to recover what yet remains concerning this worthy person, and give some account of him from Mr. Calderwood's History, our MS. Acts of Assembly, and other writings of that time.

He was born about the year 1538. I have nothing of his parents or the place of his birth, save that it was near Perth, and that when a boy he was in very mean circumstances and great penurie. Thus the Lord, in His providence, for wise and glorious ends, hath raised up some of the greatest men in all the ages of the Church from the dunghil, as it wer, to eminent services; and brought them throu no small straits and difficultys in their education. Mr. Lawson's inclinations to learning wer strong, and his capacity great. Those are generally indications of the future designs of Providence, and enable such, for whom God has after work in view, to graple strangly [strongly] with their hardships. When Mr. Lawson came in first to the Grammar School of Perth, he was glad to receive his meat by going about with the rest of the scholars, till his excellent master, Mr. Andrew Simson [1]—afterward Minister at Dunbar, and author of our old Latine Rudiments, which begin with *Quum Literarum*—began to observe his singular genius for learning, and took him into his house. By him he was well founded in the languages—the great key to usefull learning.

From Perth School he came to the University of Saint Andrews, and was in the same class with his (afterwards) intimat freind Mr. Alex. Arbuthnet, Principall at Aberdeen. Their freindship began early, and Providence cast their lotts much together in Saint Andrews and Aberdeen; and afterwards, in the Generall Assembly at Edinburgh, Mr. Alex. lodged still in Mr. James his house; and ther was but a year betwixt their getting to heaven, wher their freindship is perfect, elevated, and everlasting. After Mr. Lawson had taken his degrees with applause, he was pitched upon by the Countes of Crawford to take the care of her three sons, whom she sent to France, as was then usuall, for travelling and forraigne education. There, we may be sure, Mr. Lawson improved himself in proportion to the advantages he had, and laid the foundations for his vast progress in all the branches of solid and usefull learning, for which afterwards he was celebrated.

About the year 1567 or 1568, he returned to Scotland; and, having made himself master of the Hebrew tongue abroad, to show his gratitude to the University wher he had his education, and, at the earnest desire of the Masters, he taught that language for some time at Saint Andrews. As far as I can find, he was among the first who, since the restoration of learning in Europe, taught the Eastern languages publickly in Scotland, and may be termed to restour the Jewish [?] learning among us.

Upon the Laird of Dun's Life, we have seen the reformation of the University of Aberdeen, 1569; and, when Mr. Alex. Anderson and others of the Popish Masters wer justly turned out for not subscribing our Confession of Faith, a new sett wer bro't in, who wer a great blessing to the North, and the whole Church of Scotland. Mr. Arbuthnet, as we shall see on his Life, was made Principall, and Mr. Lawson was pitched on to be sub-Principall, in the King's College there. And about that time, I recon Mr. Lawson was also admitted to the holy ministry;

---

[1] Note 83.

at least, I find him a member of the General Assembly, July, 1570, and put upon the committy for decision of questions referred to the Assemblys, wher severall of the most learned and knowing members of the Assembly generally wer put, because the nature of their work required this. He continued at Aberdeen about three years, wher he was singularly usefull in training up the youth, and putting them into a quite other way of learning than had been used before by the Popish Masters.

In Mr. Knoxe's Life, the reader will see that about September, 1572, Mr. Knox and the town of Edinburgh, with advice of those appointed by the Assembly, fixed their eye on Mr. Lawson to be collegue, or rather successor, to Mr. Knox, there. Mr. Knoxe's warm and moving letter to him, with his admission by Mr. Knox (November 9) are notticed, and this was Mr. Knoxe's last publick work. In Edinburgh, Mr. Lawson continued twelve years in the ministry, with very great asistances from his Master—Christ—acceptance among the people, and many seals of his ministry, till the end of his life—when he was called to suffer. I have the most part of my materialls from the Registers of our Generall Assemblys, wher Mr. Lawson acted a wise, prudent, and faithfull part; and I shall nottice the hints there, as the best vidimus I can now give of this good man.

At the next Assembly, March, 1573, Mr. Knox being now resting from his labours, and Mr. Craig gone from Edinburgh, joyntly with his Session Mr. Lawson addressed the Generall Assembly for a collegue. The Session of the Kirk of Edinburgh give in a petition " Requesting the Assembly to appoint any one of the ministers underwritten to be joyned with Mr. James Lawson already placed, to wit, David Ferguson at Dunfermline, John Brand at Holyrood House, or George Scot at Kircaldie. The Assembly giveth commission to their loving brethern, John, Bishop of St. Andrews, John Erskine of Dun, Mr. John Spotswood, Superintendent of Louthian, and John Winraime, Superintendent of Strathern, with advice of the Session of the Kirk of Edinburgh, to chuse one of the fornamed, or otherwise satisfy the desire of the said Session of Edinburgh, and sicklike another for the Kirk of Jedburgh; and whomsoever they shall happen to chuse, the Assembly shall cause him to enter, and this to be done before they leave the town." What was the reason I know not, whither from the backwardnes of those named to leave their flock, or some other cause, none of them wer transported to Edinburgh, as far as I find. But Mr. John Dury, this or the next year, was bro't in from Leith, as may be seen on his Life; and the number of professors, communicants, and inhabitants in Edinburgh encreasing, next year after, 1575, Mr. Walter Balcanquell was setled ther. Those 3, with Mr. Davidson, who frequently preached after this in Edinburgh, wer those Ministers of that town till the 1589, when the most part of the honest ministers of the Church wer forced to remove or abscond for a season.

The Earle of Mortoun, Regent, with what view is pretty evident, signifyed his desire to this Assembly to see the Registers of the Generall Assemblys hitherto holden, that he might understand how many of them wer perpetual and how many only temporary. This was gone into; and Mr. Lawson; Mr. David Lindsay, Minister of Leith; Mr. Brand, Minister of Hollyrood House; Mr. John Spotswood, Superintendent of Lothian; Mr. Robt. Pont, senator of the Colledge of Justice; and Mr. Clement Litle, advocate, wer appointed to meet with His Grace and Secret Council to oversee the Acts of the Generall Assembly according to the Regent's desire. I find no more upon this subject, save, as is to be seen in Mr. Craig's Life, some appointment to collect into one body the Acts of standing force and generall use, which, because of the continouall troubles and changes in the country, never, as far as I perceive, came to any bearing.

After the Reformation, our Generall Assemblys took particular nottice of the few presses then in Scotland,[1] and wer carefull that nothing should be published, at least by ministers, till it wer communicat with their bretheren, and revised by some appointed by them; knowing well what influence, either good or bad, the productions of the press have upon morals and religion. That next year, the Assembly, March, 1574, appoint the Superintendant of Lothian, Mr. Clement Litle, advocate, Mr. Robert Pont, Mr. James Lawson, Mr. David Lindsay, Mr. Alex. Arbuthnet, and Mr. Patrick Adamson, or any four of them, to revise and consider the reply made by John Duncanson, Minister of the King's house, against Mr. James Tyrie's last book[2]; and what the said bretheren find therin to report again to the Assembly, to the effect

[1] Note 84.   [2] Note 85.

it may be understood whether the said reply be committed to print or not. And in like manner, that the saids bretheren, or any four of them, peruse and consider a book presented to the Assembly by the Earle of Glencairn, set out by a brother, and entituled *Of God's Providence*. I have seen none of those in print, and doubt if they wer published.

At this Assembly, ministers wer sensible more and more of the hazard and corruption like to come into the Church by the conclusions taken at the Convention at Leith, two years ago, and none was more zealous against those than Mr. Lawson. At the last Assembly, the Laird of Dun and others had been appointed to conferr with the Regent, who supported the Tulchan Bishops, as we have seen on his Life. Their commission was given up at this Assembly; and the ministers, who wer earnest to have the Regent coming in amicably to a reformation, dealt with the Earle of Mortoun to be present in the Assembly and hear their reasonings, that so the Estates, at present conveened, might ease them of their burdens by some better provision. To prevail the more with him and some of the principall of the Estates to meet and receive light from their reasonings, Mr. Lawson and Mr. David Lindsay, with the Commissioners from Edinburgh and Perth, wer sent to the Regent with the following supplication, which I insert here, because it's but short, and conteans some facts not elsewhere to be had, and because I guess it was formed by Mr. Lawson :—

"Unto our Lord Regent's Grace and Lords of Privy Council, with others of the Estates conveened with His Grace, the Generall Assembly now conveened wisheth everlasting health in Christ.

"It is not unknown that Holy Mystery of God, That hath chosen to Himself a Kirk, and that from the beginning, which shall continue for ever, and this same is the congregation and company of faithfull professors of Jesus Christ; and in His book God hath appointed His Holy Mysterys to be ministered, and calleth men to be ministers of the same, that be the same ministry the elect of God may be called, regenerat, and nourished, to the everlasting life. For preservation of the holy ministry and Kirk in purity, the Lord hath appointed Assemblys and Conventions, not only of the persons appointed to the ministry, but also of the whole members of the Kirk professing Christ; the which Kirk of God hath continoually used, and useth the same Assembly, sanctifyed by the word of God, and authorized by the presence of Jesus Christ. It is also not unknown to Your Grace and Lords that, since the time God hath blessed this country with the light of the Evangell, the whole Kirk most godly appointed, and the same be Act of Parliament authorized, that two godly Assemblys of the whole general Kirk of this Realme should be ilk year, as well of all the members therof in all estates as of the ministers; the which Assemblies have been since the first ordinance continoually keeped in such sort, that the most noble and of the highest estate have joyned themselves be their own presence in the Assemblies, as members of one body, concurring, voting, and authorizing all things by their proceeding with their bretheren. And now, at this present, the Kirk is assembled according to this godly ordinance, and look to have the concurrence of their bretheren in all estates, and wish of God that Your Grace and Lords of Privy Council will authorize the Kirk in this present Assembly by your presence, or others having commission from Your Grace and Lordships' names, as members of the Kirk of God. For, as Your Grace's presence and the nobility should be to us most comfortable, and so is most earnestly wished of all, so Your Grace's absence is to our hearts most dolorous and lamentable; wherof followeth a want of the great part of the members, which cannot be well absent from the treating of those things which appertain to the Kirk and policy therof to be handled by advice of all together in the Assembly; and to which end the Assemblys are appointed; the authority wherof Your Grace knoweth to be such, as the contempt of it tendeth to the very dishonnour of God. And, therfor, as ye esteem yourselves members of Christ and of His Kirk, show the fruites therof, of the which this is not the least to joyn yourself to the Kirk, not only in hearing the Word and receiving the Sacraments, but also in conveening with your bretheren in the holy Assemblys, the which to do we give you admonition in the name of the Lord, extending this our admonition to every person of whatsomeever estate, that are present with Your Grace and Lordships; and especially we admonish the bishops, and such as are of the ministry, to joyn with us according to their duty, otherwise they will be thought unworthy of the office they bear. The time that the Assembly will sit will be short, and time would not be neglected; yet the Assembly is not so rigorous but that men may, after their presence given in the Assembly, have liberty, as time requires, to await upon their lawfull bussines. And this admonition we give Your Grace with all reverence and humility, and that cheifly in respect Your Grace by your own Articles and Questions sent to the Assembly desireth first to be admonished charitably, whensoever offences rise, befor the samine be otherwise traduced."

This petition is built upon a fact then well known, otherwise it's not possible they would have insisted upon it with the Regent, who, they knew, was not so very favourable to the power of Assemblys: that, by Acts of Church and State, Assemblys wer appointed twice a year, and with them professors of all ranks joyned themselves with the ministers; and Mr. Calderwood observes that there wer scarce ever a larger convention at an Assembly than this. The Regent at first gave them a hard answer, and asked them "Who gave them power to convocat the King's leidges, without his advice who was in authority?" He well enough knew the law gave them power, and had not forgot, probably, what had passed as to this very point about ten years before, in Mr. Knoxe's case, as may be seen in his Life. But he put this sudden question, which the ministers did not expect, to dash [intimidate] them. It was surprising at first, but one of them—probably Mr. Lawson—soon replyed: "We are conveened at the commandment of our Master and Head of the Kirk, Jesus Christ, Who hath ordeaned, when His Kirk is [in] any trouble, the members therof to conveen, and set the Kirk at rest and quietnes, and purge the same of all filth and corruption". The Regent coloured upon this; but, however, they got not that answer to their petition they expected.

When the Regent and many of the nobility declined to meet with the Assembly, they went on to consider the jurisdiction of the Kirk, and appointed the Bishop of Glasgow, the Superintendants of Angus and Strathern, Mr. Robt. Pont, Mr. Row, Mr. Arbuthnet, and John Duncanson, to meet next morning, in Mr. Lawson's house, and bring in write the Heads and Articles concerning the jurisdiction of the Kirk to the Assembly, which, when aproven by the Assembly, were to be presented to the Regent; which they did as followes: "Anent the jurisdiction of bishops in their ecclesiasticall function, the Assembly hath concluded the samine shall not exceed the jurisdiction of superintendants which formerly they had, and presently they have; and that they shall be subject to the discipline of the Generall Assembly, as members therof, as the superintendants have been heretofore, in all sort. That no superintendants nor commissioners of Kirks have, or shall have, collation of benefices, nor admitt ministers without the asistance of three of the qualifyed ministers of their province, who, also, shall give their testimonials to the Superintendant or Commissioner subscribed with hands in signe of their consents therunto. And in like manner, that no bishop shall give collation of any benefice within the bounds of superintendants in his diocis, without their consent and testimoniall subscribed with his hand; and that bishops within their own dioces visit by themselves, wher no superintendants are, and give no collation ordinar on benifices, without consent of three well-qualified ministers, as said is, in the case of superintendants and commissioners." And in the next session, they ordean the persons who brought in that to reason with the Regent and Council on this subject. But it was to no purpose; he stuck by his bishops, and the Assembly went on by steps against them, as is to be seen in Mr. Craig's, Mr. Andrew Melvil's, and the Laird of Dun's Lives.

In May 28, 1574, Mr. Lawson was preaching before the Regent in the Kirk of Edinburgh. That day, the Session had ordeaned Robert Gourlay, one of their elders, a dealer for the Earle of Mortoun, to be rebuked for transporting wheat out of the county when the straits of the country would not allow of it. When the elder was called upon to make acknowledgement of his offence, the Regent answered out of his seat: " I have given him license, and it appertaineth not to you to judge of that matter". The ministers at this time wer very particular in their reproving, and zealous in bearing down all open vice. The Regent tho't them too severe; and, being haughty when his own vices wer touched, he indeavoured to usurp over the ministers and the Kirk. He called Mr. Lawson, the Laird of Dun, Mr. Lyndsay, and some others, and appointed the Justice Clerk, Mr. David Borthwick, Sir James Balfour, the Laird of Whittinghame, and some others, to reason with them, before himself in Hollyrood House, upon the differences betwixt him and the Kirk. They had many meetings for thirteen or fourteen dayes; but the ministers being perfectly joyned, and making an unanimouse stand against his proposalls, he dissolved the meeting with[out] coming to any conclusion.

We had one instance of the care of the Assembly about the printing of books just now. In Agust, 1574, Mr. Lawson and some others are appointed to oversee all books that are published. Their Act runs thus: "For so meikle as be imprinting and putting to the light works repugnant to the truth of God's Word, or conteaning manifest error, the truth may be heavily prejudged, and the weak seduced from the truth; therfor the Generall Assembly, presently conveened, have all in one voice given power to their loved bretheren, Mr. Robert Pont, Provost of the Trinity Colledge; Mr. James Lawson, David Ferguson, Mr. David Lindsay, Mr. Clement Litle, one of the commissioners of Edinburgh; John Brand, Minister of Holyrood House; or any three of them, conjunctly to visit and oversee all manner of books and works that shall be proponned to be printed, and to give their judgment therupon, if the same be allowable and approved by the law of God or not; and they are to give their judgment and opinion therupon be their subscription and handwritt, for reliefe of such as shall read the said works, which commission of oversight forsaid the Generall Assembly willeth to endure firm and stable".

At the same time, they appoint a particular comitty for revising Mr. Adamson's paraphrase upon Job—I suppose because it was a poem—in this termes: "For revewing and sighting *The History of Job*, compiled by Mr. Patrick Adamson, in Latine verse, their loved bretheren, the Right Honourable Mr. George Buchanan, Keeper of the Privy Seal; Mr. Peter Young, Pædagogue to our Soveraigne Lord; Mr. Andrew Melvil, and Mr. James Lawson, Minister of Edinburgh, to take travell in perusing of the said work; and if the same be found by them agreable to the truth of God's Word, to authorize the same with testimony of their handwrite and subscription". And to cast all I have met with on this subject [together], the Assembly (1583) "ordeans Mr. Andrew Melvil, Mr. James Lawson, and David Ferguson, to visit the books set out by George Scot and report". I find no more about them. Ther was one of this name we have seen was minister of Kircaldy. Whither this was he I cannot tell.[1]

Mr. Lawson and some others, in the next Assembly, March, 1575, wer appointed to form an Act about apparrel.[2] It may be the reader that is curious may incline to have it here, it never having been published, I suppose. The Assembly's recommendation to them

[1] Note 86. [2] Note 87.

followes :—" Seing not only it becomes the true messengers of the Word of Salvation to bear in their conscience a good testimony of their unfeigned humility and the simplicity of their hearts, but also in externall habit and behaviour to represent the sobriety and humility of their minds, that the mouths of the godless generation, which are opened to blaspheme the godly calling of the ministry, may be shut up from just accusation and slandering of the same; therfor, by determination of the whole Assembly, it is statut and ordeaned, that all who serve within the Kirk apparrell themselves in a comely and decent cloathing, as becometh the gravity of their vocation; and that they conform their wives and families therunto, that no slander nor offence arise to the Kirk of God therthrough; and, to the effect it may be notified to the whole bretheren what ought to be eskewed in apparell, the Assembly hath enjoyned their loved bretheren, the Superintendants of Angus and Fife, the Commissioners of Renfrew and Aberdeen, with Mr. James Lawson, to advise therupon and report." Their report I find not till next Assembly, when Sess. 3—" The bretheren, appointed to pass their judgments anent the habits of ministers and their wives, presented the same to the Assembly, which was found reasonable; and all the bretheren ordeaned to conform themselves therunto." The tennor wherof followes:—" For sa meikle as a comly and decent apparrell is requisit in all, namely ministers, and all that bear function in the Kirk: First, we think all kind of broudering unseemlie, all bagaries[1] of velvet in gowns, hose, or coats, and all superflous and vain cutting out, and steetching with silk; all kind of costly sowing in pastments,[2] or sumptous and large steeking with silks; all kinds of costly showing and variant hewes in sarks; all kind of light and variant hewes in cloathing, as red, bleu, yellow, and such like, which declareth the lightnes of the mind; all wearing of rings, bracelets, buttons of gold, silver, or other mettal; all kind of superfluity of cloath in making of hose; all using of plaids in the kirk be readers or ministers, namely, in the time of their ministry, and using their office; all kind of gowning, coating, doubletting, or breeks of velvet, satine, taffety, or such like; all costlie guiltings [gildings] of whingers, knives, and such like; all silk hatts, and hatts of diverse and light collours. But that their whole habit be of grave collour, as

[1] Stripes of a different colour or material sewed on.   [2] Fringes or trimmings.

black, russet, gray, sad brown, or sarges, worset, chamelot, grograme, lylis[1] worset, or such like; and, to be short, that the good Word of God be them and their immoderatness be not slandered; and the ministers' wives are to be subject to the same order."

Ther fell in a case of discipline before this Assembly, wherin Mr. Lawson was concerned, which deserves a room here, to show how strict our ministers after the Reformation wer in admitting persons to the Sacraments; and how near they came to the vigorous exercise of discipline in use during the First Ages of Christianity, as far as the different circumstances of time and persons allowed. And I chuse the rather to make this observation, wher soe the learned Father Le Courayer, threw misinformation and ignorance of the practise of the Reformed Presbiterian Churches, suggesting a totall overthrow of discipline among us, in his letter to Mr. Williams, prefixed to the English edition of *Courayer's Defence of the Validity of the English Ordinations* (London: 8vo, 1725). After some complements upon the learning of the Church of England, he is pleased to commend them for *their strong aversion to that totall overthrow of discipline, introduced into the Presbyterian Churches.* I wish, indeed, that the exercise of Christ's institution of ecclesiasticall discipline wer better looked to in Presbiterian Churches, and regrate our slacknes in the impartiall administration of it. But, then, I think, I have ground to say, that we ought not to be charged with a totall overthrow of it; and that charge falls heavier upon some other Reformed Churches than us of the Presbiterian denomination; and the Scripturall rules prescribed are nowher so closely observed as among Presbiterian Churches; and in Popish countrys it's evident that Christian ecclesiasticall discipline is turned to merchandize, and a plain trade for amassing of money, and prying into the secrets of familys and princes. The best among the Reformed Prelaticall Churches heavyly regrate the almost totall overthrow of discipline; and it's strange to me that the learned Courayer did not know that the Presbiterian Churches are blamed for an exces in the matter, and that the strictnes of our discipline in Scotland has been one of the things, which have brought persons of a loose conversation to dislike and oppose the Presbiterian Constitution of the Church. On the whole, they must be perfect strangers to our history, after the

[1] Note 88.

Reformation, who know not with what vigour and impartiality discipline was exercised.

The instance I am now concerned in is this: Mr. Thomas M'Ralzean, an advocat, and at this time, as I take it, one of the senators of the Colledge of Justice, and a ruling elder, had continoued in Edinburgh, 1571 and 1572, when the town and castle wer hold out against the Regent and for the King's mother, and probably had made some complyances with that side. All who had done so wer obligded to satisfy for the offence they had given by this complyance, befor they could be admitted to the Lord's table. When the times changed, Mr. Thomas came in heartily enough to the Regent; and probably, considering his station, expected to be overlooked without a publick acknowledgement of his complyance. Mr. Lawson and the Session of Edinburgh would not break in upon their rules. The gentleman compleaned to the last Assembly. They remitted the matter to some neighbouring ministers, who wer not able to bring it to an issue, so it comes before this Assembly, whose Act will give us a full view of the affair, and is as follows: "Anent the supplication given in to the Generall Assembly by Mr. Thomas M'Ralzean of Crichtonhall, one of members of our Soverayne Lord's Colledge of Justice, making mention that whereupon his late supplication, presented in the last Generall Assembly, toutching his not admitting to the holy Sacrament of the Lord's Supper, they be their Act and Ordinance ordeaned Mr. Rob. Pont, Provost of Trinity Colledge, the Ministers of Leith and Cannongate, with the Kirk of Edinburgh to take tryall, if his remaining in Edinburgh a certain time of the late troubles, was by compulsion, and, if it was so found, to mitigat their Act. For taking of which tryall he hath insisted oftentimes, and they, conveening together, have put no end therunto, but for some good considerations, as he suppones, hath remitted the cause unto their Wisdomes; wherfor, most humbly beseeking them, since his remaining within this town, is notoriously known to have proceeded from compulsion, just fear and dreadour, that they would take such order as he may be admitted to the next Communion, which is to be celebrated in this town. The said Mr. Thomas being personally present, and the Commissioners appointed by the last Assembly for taking tryall if the said Mr. Thomas remained in the town for fear and dreadour, which might fall in a most constant man, compearing be Mr. James Lawson, Minister of Edinburgh, and their proces being read and considered in open assembly, the said Mr. James, in name of the Kirk of Edinburgh, being enquired why the said Kirk admitted not the said Mr. Thomas to the Communion, answered for two causes. First, because the town of Edinburgh admitted none that remained within the town of Edinburgh in time of rebellion without first compearing before them and their submission to the Kirk; and secondly, that he was an elder and bare office within the said town. The Assembly, notwithstanding, having considered the qualifications of the said Mr. Thomas remaining within the town [were] just fear, votted and concluded that the said Mr. Thomas' oath to be taken, if upon just fear he remained within the said town, and bear office, as said is, who, being called on and re-entering, declared on his conscience that he remained, as said is, within the said town, and bear office therein for most just fear and dreadour, which might fall in a constant man. Therfor, the said Assembly, taking to consideration the said Mr. Thomas' declaration, as said is, ordeans the Kirk of Edinburgh to admitt the said Mr. Thomas to the next Communion and participation of the Sacrament, to be celebrat within this town, the said Mr. Thomas appearing before the pulpit of Edinburgh in his own gown, and making repentance for his said offence in the face of the congregation, and therafter giving to the poor the gown wherin he maketh the said satisfaction, or else the price therof." I am apt to think not a few in this age will rather blame the severity of this act of discipline, than think that Presbiterians have subverted discipline totally.

That same Assembly appointed Mr. Lawson joyntly to visit with Mr. Spotswood in his bounds, by their following order: "The brethren, having consideration that their brother, Mr. John Spotswood, Superintendent of Lothian, is become sickly, and not altogether able, in his own person, presently to visit the whole bounds allotted to him in commission, and understanding that their brother, Mr. James Lawson, Minister at Edinburgh, is purposed to pass throu the country and visit the said bounds, have thought meet, and ordeaned the said Mr. James to support the said Mr. John in his office of visitation, and to make such supply to him therin, as goodly he may, till the next Assembly".

At this Assembly, the brethren, who wer appointed to travel and write their judgments concerning the discipline of the Kirk, are appointed to meet together in Mr. Lawson's house, and conferr their labours and writings, that they may be presented to the Assembly. Nothing was yet finished, but this was the beginning of The 2d Book of Discipline, wherin Mr. Lawson has a considerable share. As we shall see, great pains wer taken, and much care used, in compiling that body of rules, as I have frequent occasion to observe in this Work. Mr. Lawson, as hath been notticed in Mr. Andrew Melvill and Mr. Craig's Life, was one of the 3 appointed to reason upon the office of bishops as now exercised in this Church.

Next year, 1576, Mr. Lawson having been named to receive the collections gathered for the French Protestants, made his report to the Assembly and his discharge. The Minutes of Assembly thereanent bears that "Mr. Lawson reported to the Assembly and Commissioners therof an acquittance and discharge of the money collected and gathered for the help and supply of the exiled bretheren of the French Kirk in England, with a roll of the names of the persons contributing therunto, and the quantity of every man's contribution, desiring the one and the other to be enregistrat and booked in the Register of the Kirk, *ad perpetuam rei memoriam*, which desire the Assembly tho't good, and ordeand the same to be registrat among the Acts of Assembly, to be a testimoniall to the posterity and age to come of the good mind and zeal of the charitable persons, that succoured the necessity of their said bretheren in the day of their extremity; and the Assembly ordean the said Mr. James to keep in his hands some further money, collected since by the diligence of the visitors and superintendants, till further order be taken therwith".

In the Assembly, Aprile, 1577, which was conveened cheifly to receive the returne of the bretheren imployed in forming The 2d Book of Discipline, their joynt labours wer presented; and by the report I find one Head was presented by Mr. John Row, being penned by him, one of whose Articles was referred to further disputation; another Head was penned and presented by Mr. Lawson, and approved. The Head given to the Laird of Dun being tho't by him obscure and mystick, he was desired to conferr to-morrow morning with the rest of the Commissioners. The remanent Heads, being prolix and amply written by the Commissioners, wer tho't good to be contracted in short propositions and conclusions to be presented to publick reading therafter.

And, after long publick reasoning and an approbation in the Assembly, 1578, it was ordered to be presented to King and Council by the Laird of Dun, Mr. Lawson, and the rest concerned in forming it. With some others, as is to be seen in Dun's Life, they wer impoured to conferr and reason upon the Heads of it, and also upon the Head of the ceremonys, and how far ministers may medle with civil affairs, and if they may vote in Council or Parliament. The result of all is to be seen in the Laird of Dun's Life.

In the year 1579, after the King's taking the Government into his own hand and the jarrs among the nobility wer a litle calmed, the King, on the 17 of October, made a splendid entry to the town of Edinburgh. Mr. Calderwood gives a very large account. At the Port, Mr. John Sharp welcomed him in a Latine oration. The magistrates, with about 300 citicens in velvet satine and silk, attended the King up the town. In the Bow, a litle boy came out of a globe, and presented the keys of the town in silver to the King. At the Old Tolbooth, 4 young virgins, representing Justice, Temperance, Fortitude, and Prudence, had orations to the King. When he came over against the Great Kirk, Dame Religion shewed herself and desired his presence, which he obeyed, and lighted at the ladye's steps, and went into the Kirk, wher Mr. Lawson made an exortation on the 2nd Psalm (v. 10) and exhorted both the King and subjects to do their duty and to enter into a league and covenant with God, and concluded with thanksgiving. After sermon was sung the 20 Psalm.

I find Mr. James Lawson, Moderator of the known Assembly, 1580, July 12, at Dundee, wher the office of bishops, as exercised of late in this Church, is declared unlawfull in itself, and all bruiking [holding] it are charged to demitt *simpliciter*, and abstain from all ministerial work till *de novo* they receive admission from the Generall Assembly, and that, under the pain of excommunication. Vigourous steps were taken against the alienators and masters of the rents and patrimony of the Kirk. The readers are appointed to be examined *de novo*, and those that in two years time have not improven their time and profited, so farr as to be found fitt for preaching the Gospells, are ordeaned to be deposed. Vigourous steps wer likewise taken against the growth of Popery, and applications made to the King, which issued in the framing of the Nationall Covenant, as may be seen in Mr. Craig's Life.

In all which, and other excellent constitutions of this zealous Assembly, the Moderator had no small influence, who was all along a firm opposer of Prelacy and other corruptions.

Mr. Lawson, being a person of great learning, and having been some years abroad and acquainted ther with learned men, cultivat this by a closs correspondence with eminent divines in forraigne Protestant Churches. This fell to his share in Mr. Knoxe's elder and declining years, and especially after his death; and when Mr. Andrew Melvil came to Scotland, who caryed on a most closs correspondence with learned men, this did not lessen but rather extended Mr. Lawson's acquaintances. The laborious Mr. Strype takes notice of letters that passed this year betwixt the learned Beza and Mr. Lawson, whom, had Mr. Strype known better, he would not have writ so diminutively of him. In his "Annals" on this year, he observes that Beza's book, *De Triplici Episcopatu*, was translated to English by Mr. Feild, one of the cheife Puritan ministers. Mr. Stryp adds that Beza divides bishops into three sorts—those of God, viz., thir elders at Geneva; those of men, or by human appointment, as ours in England; and those of the devil, or the Popish bishops. He affirms that all bishops but those who have an equality among them should be sent a packing, and that the cheif elders should be admitted to be present in Parliament, as the bishops wer, to deal in spirituall causes and answer in the place of God. If this last point be Beza's opinion, he hath not many Presbiterians to follow him. He adds, the same year, 1580, Beza wrote to one Lawson in Scotland, who had informed him of an attempt made there in behalf of bishops (perhaps for restoring them) and how it was defeat by the Reformers, Beza expressing his infinite joy at it, and begins his letter, though he was sick, '*Beasti me*, &c.' He cites Bancroft's *Survey* (p. 50, edit. 1593), which I have not at hand for this passage. The same Mr. Strype, in his *Life of Whitgift*, p. 405, gives a large letter of A. B. Whitgift to Beza, dated Feb. 1594, wher I find this passage, "While we hoped all things wer a litle pacifyed, my friend Beza, your book of a 3 fold Episcopacy sent to this island, and not long after translated into the English Tongue and privately printed, with your Letter to Lousanus, a Scot, written the same year, but flying through the hands of many, set a new torch to the flame that was before almost quenched; in which Epistle among other things you wrote thus: *In humanam potestatem sed Satanicam potius tyrranidem, &c.;* that is, *I am wont by very good right (unless I am very much mistaken) to call that false episcopacy not a human power so much as a Satanicall tyranny, which as heretofore it destroyed the Church, so now at least it hindereth at least its restoration from the miserable state in Germany and the country nearer you; I wish Scotland may be seasonably enough sensible of it.*" The Archbishop adds that here he (Beza) seemed scarcely to be able to bear that episcopacy, which here he calls Satanicall tyranny, should be esteemed for human episcopacy, as he stated it elsewhere, and that under the name of *that nearer miserable country* to Lowson he did not obscurely point out England. I have, for my more curious readers, added in the Appendix Beza's Letter to Mr. Lawson (copy Bancroft's *Survey of Discipline*, edit. 1593, p. 50) and Beza's letter to Archbishop Whitgift, in defence of his book, *De Triplici Episcopatu*, App. n. (copy *Whitgift's Life*, by Strype, Appendix, Book iv., n. 17).[1]

Upon Mr. Durie's Life, I have taken nottice of Mr. Durie and Mr. Balcanquell their prosecution for a sermon, in September, this year. Mr. Lawson, the Sabbath before, had taken nottice of the present dangers to religion from Papists and France. He notticed the tyranny of Frenchmen when last in Scotland, and how the English drove them out and set us at liberty, both in body and soul; adding, that now, what they could not attain to by force, they seek to compass by slight, and have sent in wicked Monsiours, now in the King's minority, when he hath got the authority in his own hand, to subvert religion, and to break the unity betwixt the two Realmes. Mr. Lawson was not summoned, tho' the plainest of all the three Ministers of Edinburgh, at this time—the reason I cannot give—one would think they could not with any decorum attack and confyne all the three Ministers of the town at once. I have frequent occasion to nottice that thir free warnings wer only given by the ministers, when Popery was breaking [out] and Popish councils prevailing, and civil and religious interest in the greatest hazard, as in the two or three last years of Queen Mary, and won under the King's minority, when D'Aubigney and Coll. Stewart had the King in their management, and wer in a most dangerous plott with France and the Queen Mother; and afterwards when the King fell into measures with Popish earles, and dependants upon the Pope and Spain,

---

[1] These appear to be lost.

as may be seen in Mr. Davidson, Mr. Andrew Melvil, and Mr. Bruce's Life. And I nottice that during all the four Regents' government—even Mortoun's, who bore hard enough upon the libertys of the Church, but was a firm Protestant — ther are not complaints of ministers' sermons, save once, for preaching against acknowledged vice. The plain reason of this was, during their regency they wer under no fears of Popery from the Court; but when that was making wide and daring steps, and our all, as men and Christians, at stake, we need not be surprised to find the ministers using freedomes in publick, which at another time they would not have done.

By The 2nd Book of Discipline, Presbitrys wer declared to be necessary, and after the engagment of the generality of Protestants throu the Kingdom to a constant adherance to the discipline established, which possibly could be no other than Presbiterian, by Sessions, Presbitrys, Synods, and General Assemblies, by the Nationall Covenant; much of the work of the Assemblies, in concert with the King, was to form the plan of the erection of Presbitrys throu the Kingdom, in the year 1581. Mr. Lawson I find much imployed in the necessary work. The first plot [scheme] was agreed to that year; but it afterwards underwent severall necessary alterations. Severall ministers in different corners wer appointed to make necessary proposals for alterations, wher they wer necessary, and all their papers wer to be transmitted to Mr. Lawson, who was to draw up all in form for the more regular procedure afterwards: it took some years before this good work was compleated, a dark cloud coming on this Church next year.

In the beginning wherof, the Duke of Lennox and Earl of Arran, prosecuting the Earle of Mortoun's steps, tho' they wanted his real concern for the Reformation, and they had far worse views than he was capable of, in forcing in bishops, particularly Montgomery upon Glasgow, took such measures as alienated the King from the ministers, his firmest friends, and open breaches fell in betwixt them ; as is observed in Mr. Durie's Life, and Mr. Davidson's, In June, the Earl of Argyle, convinced of the evil designes of the Duke, wrote a letter to Mr. Lawson that he would stand to the defence of the Reformation and Gospell now preached; and severall well-affected gentlemen found it proper to give the like assurance to support the ministers in their present struggle with the corrupt Courtiers. In the beginning of June, the Duke desired a conference with Mr. Lawson and some others of the ministry, which was granted, as occasionall, but not with any power from the Kirk. The Duke compleaned the King and his servants wer ill-used by the ministers; Mr. Lawson and Mr. David Lindsay justifyed the conduct of the late Assembly and ministers, and compleaned that the Church had no redress of her grievances now for many years. They come to no issue in this conference.

In the time of the meeting of the Generall Assembly, June, 1582, on Mr. Dury's affair, as is to be seen in his Life, after Mr. Dury had been charged by the Magistrates, and upon that charge left the town of Edinburgh, Mr. Lawson, in his sermon upon Friday, June 30, regrated very heavily Mr. Durie's treatment in being forced out of the town, and the more, as he said, because he understood this came by some of his hearer's procurement, meaning the Magistrates, who wer too much upon the Duke's party. Mr. Calderwood narrates a free conference after this sermon between some of the ministers and Magistrates, which I insert here, to show the impartiall plaines used at this time by the ministers with persons of all ranks. After sermon, the Provost, coming out of the Council House with Henry Nisbit, met with Mr. Davidson, Andrew Melvil, Mr. Balcanquell, and Mr. Lawson, in the litle yeard near Mr. Lawson's house. Mr. Melvil fell pretty foul on the Provost in conversation, and affirmed the Council of Edinburgh had done most unworthily in Mr. Durie's affair, for which they had been justly reproved in the sermon; adding that they wer unworthy of any faithfull minister among them, who had so treated that man who had so long and so faithfully travelled among them; adding severe threatenings if they repented not. The Provost coldly replyed —" Mr. Andrew, you know not the matter," adding some disdainfull words, upon which Mr. Davidson struck in with his usual fervency, and said—" What brazen faces must those be who despise the threatenings of the servants of God, who are sent furth from His throne? I say to you, except you repent, your banishing of Christ in yon man's person, wherof you have been instruments, the Lord will pull you out of your thrones with shame and confusion. Who dare be so bold, for the pleasure of any flesh, so to entreate the servants of the living God?" The Provost was not a litle dashed. Mr. Charters said— " The matter was not so great as men made it; and if the cause was knowen, they (the Magistrates) wer not to be blamed ". Mr Davidson said—" Was the charge ye got wicked or not ? " The other answered he could not allow of the charge. Then said Mr. John—" If the command be evil and wicked, what think ye of the obedience to it ? What case are you in that have been doers, and obeyed the same command; and Pilat's absolving, and yet condemning ? Because ye pretend some reason for your doings, I tho't good to meet you after this manner. Indeed, I am sorry for you, Henry, that it should have fallen in your hand." The Provost said—" I have been as forward to advance the Evangell as ever you have been ". " I am the more sorry for you," said Mr. Davidson, " to see you make such a bad conclusion. God grant you repentance." So they left them with Mr. Balcanquell, who reasoned a litle with them to the same effect, but a litle more cooly. He told them if they had been charged to give 20 pound to the King, you would have sent and seen, whether it had been the King's will or not. How much more should ye have shown your diligence in so weighty a matter ? In the afternoon, Mr. Lawson and Mr. Balcanquell gave in a Bill to the Assembly, desiring liberty to remove themselves from Edinburgh, as occasion should offer, befor they wer compelled to it, as their colleague (Mr. Durie) had been. Their desire was not granted because of severall inconveniences that might follow; but all ministers wer discharged to enter in Mr. Durie's place till the Assembly should determine in that affair.

In this moneth of June, the Duke's designes began to open out, and one branch of his plott was against Mr. James Lawson. Mr. Calderwood sayes of the Duke of Lennox [who] laid this plott, that, unles Glencairn, Boyd, Bargany, Mar, the Abbots of Cambuskenneth, Dryburgh, Paisley, Lochleven, Lindsay, the Master of Glames, and Abbot of Dumfernline, were out of the way, who favoured the Douglasses, ther was no surety for him and his; and that Mr. James Lawson, Mr. David Lindsay, Mr. And. Hay, Mr. Thomas Smeton, Mr. Andrew Polwart, and Mr. And. Melvil should be warded in sundry places beyond Spey.

A stop was put for a season to the evil projects of the Duke of Lennox and Earle of Arran by the firm Protestant lords and gentlemen their placing themselves about the King, commonly called the Road of Ruthven, on the 23 of Agust. When the Duke got nottice of this, he applyed to the Magistrates of Edinburgh for their concurrence to keep the town and castle till he got orders from the King. The Magistrates wer not in the present juncture too forward, as the Duke expected, and put him of with dilators, and sending a messenger to the King to know his own will. They had been formerly too friendly to the Duke, and they saw not yet how matters would end ; and the Duk's purposes began to be disclosed, as afterwards, on his flight, they wer more fully knowen, that upon Monday next, Agust 27, he was to have keeped a Court of Chamberlanarie at Edinburgh, brought in all the forces of Maxwell, · Livingstoun, Seaton, Herries, Hume, Scot, Newbatle, Pharnihurst, and others, his freinds, occupyed the ports of Edinburgh and street, discharged all citizens, except such as wer called for to appear. 40 citizens wer to be fyned in 1000d. pounds per head, 40 others to have been forfaulted and hanged, and the ministers to have been dealt with as they carried [demeaned themselves] to the Bishop. On the 26, the Provost sent to Mr. Lawson, desiring him to be sparing in his sermons that Sabbath. He returned answer that, whatever the Lord put in his mouth, he would speak, as his text offered occasion. The Duke was indisposed that day, and came not to sermon as he designed. Mr. Calderwood gives the following account of Mr. Lawson's sermon :—" He preached on the beginning of the 6th chapter of Zechariah, and showed the two hills of brass ther wer to be understood the providence of God everlasting and immutable, which was compared to two hills, because those are two things in His providence, to wit, His will and His power to put in execution, so that wher His will is not obeyed, power must needs follow with execution. By the diverse colloured horses was signifyed the manifold executions of God, some bloody, some craftie hypocrites, some false teachers, some fals brethreen : good men wer signifyed by the white horse. He declaimed against the Duke of Arran and their counsellors, whom he compared to the black horse, howsoever they had subscribed, professed, and communicat ; yet their deeds testifyed that they wer enimies, violators of discipline, annullers of excommunication, setters out of proclamations to traduce the best of the nobility and ministry, and setters up of Tulchan Bishops, theron unsatiable covetousnes. He charged the Duke with raising uproars in the Kirk, troubling the Commonwealth to sustean his intollerable pride, introducing prodigality and vanity of apparrell, superfluity in banqueting and delicat chear, buying and deflouring of dames and virgins, and other fruits of the French Court; and vexing the poor country with Airs and Chamberlanerie Courts. He exorted Edinburgh to be thankfull for their deliverance from what was intended in a day or two, if God in His mercy had not prevented; otherwise, a greater plague was abiding them; adding—it becometh thee, O Edinburgh, to sing—*Laqueus confractus est et nos liberati fuimus.* But he cheifly came to the Duke's charge, that he made the King the author of all his faults, and laboured to corrupt him."

Upon Friday, the 31 of Agust, Mr. Lawson earnestly exhorted the nobility present at the sermon to concur with the rest in a through reformation; and proved that it was highly unreasonable that one man, even the best, should have all the credit of the King and whole Realme; and that to suffer such a thing was to suffer tyranny. He had formerly proven the necessity of a further reformation. Those sermons helped to prevent the Duke's evil designes in Edinburgh, and strenthened the firm Protestant lords now about the King's person.

Upon the 23 of January, next (1583) year, came a French ambassador in room of La Mott, who was ready to depart. The ministers and sincere Protestants wer troubled at La Motte's coming in the beginning of this moneth, knowing his dangerous errand, as may be seen in Mr. Davidson's Life; but they got more ground when they saw another coming to stay sometime, when they hoped to have been rid of French counsell; especially when they knew that this Monsieur Monnigill or Manningvill was a virulent Papist, and the first who devised the League in Piccardie against the Protestants. His errand was to prevail with the young King to take the Duke back again, to which he was not unwilling, and then to keep him under French influence, and cary on the designes on foot in favour of Popery and the Queen Mother, and break the amity at present with England. At his first audience, he craved to be treated as an ambassadour from so great a king, and required food to his soul, *i.e.*, the Mass publickly, as well as to his body. The King rounded somwhat in his ear, and desired him to be easy. On the 25 of January, Mr. Lawson, having ended his sermons on Malachy, the day before, pitched upon the history of the ambassadors from the King of Babylon in Esai [Isaiah], and discoursed from it what was very seasonable at that juncture. Misreports went of this sermon to the King, and he proposed to the Council that they might take nottice of it, being, as he was informed, chosen out of pick [pique]. He was told that he had immediately before ended the book he had preached upon, and was at liberty to take any particular text, till he fixed on another book to go throu.

Upon the 28, Monsieur La Mott took his leave of the King, and recommended Monsieur Mannigil, who was to reside some time. On the first of February, the King sent a letter to the Magistrates of Edinburgh, requiring them to give a splendid entertainment and banquet to Monsieur La Motte befor he left the town. The Magistrates called for Mr. Lawson and Mr. Durie, and communicat the letter to them, and desired them to communicat it to the Session of the Kirk for their opinion. The Session met on Friday, and gave their opinion that such a banquet was very unmeet in the present circumstances, which called rather for fasting and mourning than sumptous feasting. However, the Town Council went into the proposall, alledging the Kirk had not given their judgment directly against it. Upon nottice of this, the Ministers went at night to the Provost and endeavoured to break him of from the designe, but in vain; the matter was concocted, and they resolved to please the King, and put hounour on the French, the present great plagues to the King and religion, and the fountain of all our disorders and dangers. On the Lord's Day, in the morning, the Session conveened, and concluded that in case the designe went on to feast the ambassadours, that the congregation should meet to-morrow for fasting and prayer, as what the Lord in providence was calling them to, and that this should be intimat after sermons; which, accordingly, was done. Accordingly, when nothing would divert the Magistrates from their banquet, the congregation met on Monday 'twixt nine and ten hours, and continoued in prayer and hearing the Word till two of the clock. Mr. Lawson preached on 2 Cor. vi. 14—" Bear not in an unequal yoak," &c.; Mr. Dury, on the 9th of Ezra; and Mr. Balcanquall, on the 4th of Esther. Betwixt the exortations ther was reading some parts of the Scripture and singing of Psalmes. Mr. Lawson in his sermon declared the sinfulness of banqueting the Ambassador: it was a token of love he said, and if they meant truly, they sealed up by this feast their fellowship and true love with the murderers of the people of God; if they dissembled, it was hypocrisy. That afternoon, Monsieur La Mott went to Seaton, and from thence by England home.

I have given the larger account of this, because the ministers, and particularly Mr. Lawson, are blamed by the Prelatick writters for their carriage at this time. Bishop Spotswood gives a very byassed and ill-natured account of this matter of the banqueting the ambassadours: he speaks, as I take him, of a feast ordinarly given to ambassadors at parting, which had never been used, at least by the town of Edinburgh: he sayes, to impede the feast the ministers proclaimed a fast to detain the people at the church that day the feast was appointed. The Bishop could not but know the ministers had no such designe; they knew well enough that their fast would not impede the feast, nor hinder such who were necessary to be there, who would not be hindered by that day of prayer; it was only upon supposition of what they thought sinfull, and what without repentance and supplication might justly draw down Divine wrath on the town, that they appointed this fast, on view of what he calls the feast, and not as that they tho't they would hinder it. The case was plain, the Session of Edinburgh reconed this singular honnour done to the French ambassadors, who wer come for the ruine of the King and country and religion, and strenthening the present wished designes of Papists, and not merely to renew the ancient amity, as Spotswood would make us think. [It] was a publick homologation of those designs, and consequent a branch of defection from the Reformation and the Solem Covenant for its defence, lately entered into. This, and many other things in the present state of affairs, called for humiliation before the Lord. They had just authority to call their flock to this work that was so evidently their duty at such a juncture. They fixed on the Monday for it, not to hinder the feast and keep the people at the church, but because it was the day following, and the thing, as they judge, did not allow of delay, and to bear the plainest testimony against what they judged sinfull and a present defection from religion. What followes in Spotswood, that the preachers thundered curses against the magistrates and noblemen who waited on the banquet by the King's direction, is neither true, nor comes it well from the pen of one who professed a regard for God's ordinance of preaching His Word: they showed the sinfulness, indeed, of ane open profession of amity and friendship with murderers of the people of God, as Mannigval, or Menivil, as the Bishop calls him, litterally was; and declared the Scripturall denunciations of the Lord's wrath against the Magistrates. What he adds, that the ministers' folly stayed not here, but they pursued the Magistrates with the censures of the Kirk, because they waited not on their fast, and with difficulty wer stayed from excommunicating them, is so full of spite, ignorance of facts, and false, in fact, that I wonder how the Bishop could fall into it. The ministers never expected the Magistrates were to joyn with them; and, as far as I can observe, passed [not] the least censure on them for not observing their fast, nor entertained any tho't of excommunicating any of them. All this is gross, ill-natured fiction, and may teach us how litle regard is to be given to the Bishop's accounts of Presbiterian ministers.

The King was much fretted at the removal of the Duke of Lennox, and continoually stirred up against the lords now with him by Colonell Stewart, Earl of Arran; and the nouse [news] of the Duke's death in France hightened all. Therefor, in concert with the Colonel, upon the 27 of June, he withdrew himself to the Castle of St. Andrew's, quit the lords that formerly wer with him, and fell in [with] very severe measures against them, being now for two years or more intirely managed by the Colonell and Mr. Patrick Adamson in Church affairs. Upon the 18 of July, the Presbytery of Edinburgh sent Messrs. Lawson, Davidson, Pont, and Lindsay to conferr with the King, and warn him against innovating matters, and crediting everything as told him, till he examined matters and knew the truth. What passed at this conference stands in Mr. Davidson's Life. I only nottice here that Mr. Lawson was sent for by the King to Falkland, the day before, and blamed for saying that, as the Duke thirsted for blood in his life, so he dyed in blood, of a bloody flux; and the King let him see Alexander Clock, Provost of Edinburgh his letter, informing him of this. Mr. Lawson vindicat himself of this aspersion.

The King slighted the advice of the ministers at this conference, and went on under the Earle of Arran's conduct; and, upon the last of July, published a proclamation at Perth, reflecting upon the Lords concerned in Ruthven Road and removing the Duke from him. Heavier things wer in view against them, as this was but a beginning. Great pains wer used to bring in the ministry to the present courses, and to approve the King's proclamations against the Lords and gentlemen who had been about the King. Mr. Lawson, Durie, Lindsay, Hay Smeaton, Ferguson, and Galloway, wer called to the King at Saint

Andrews, Agust 22. It was generally tho't the Court designed to bring them in to approve the present procedure against the firm Protestants the King had now lost. When they could not be gained, the ministers wer called before the Council, and interrogatorys wer proposed to them upon severall Heads. The ministers in this criticall juncture craved liberty to give in their answers in writ, a safer way than to deliver them in word; and I shall here insert them from Calderwood, the rather because I take them to be drawen by Mr. Lawson, and for anything I know, they may not have been published.

"Answers by certain ministers, conveened at the King's Majesty's desire at Saint Andrews, Agust 23, 1583, to certain Heads propounded, partlie by His Majestie, and partlie by the general commissioners appointed to reason with them.

"1. Concerning that which fell forth the last year (Ruthven Road) for the preservation of the Kirk of God, the King's Majesty's person and Commonwealth, we simply submit our judgments to an Act made by the General Assembly theranent.

"2. Touching the estate of things present and to come, in uprightness of conscience we protest that we mind nothing but quietness and peace, under the obedience of our good God and the King's Majesty, whereof we have been, and shall be, procurers, according to the Word of God, our own callings, and duty to His Grace and Commonwealth.

"3. As to the late proclamation declaring the King's mind of his Grace's estate the last year, it appertains not to our vocation curiously to enquire threof. Neither know we any of our number that have transgressed in that point, neither do we purpose in time coming rashly or unadvisedly to speak of that proclamation, or any other, and solemnly protest that whatsoever we speak we shall lean upon the warrand of God's Word, conteaning ourselves alwise within the bounds of our calling.

"4. For as much as we are heavily burdened by wrongous bruit made, as well of the whole ministry in generall, as of some of us in speciall, we most humbly crave that His Majesty and Your Lordships would not suddainly credit every report, but use diligent tryall, wherby we are assured that our innocence, and the ungodly minds of our accusers, shall easily appear.

"Lastly, because we are come here in few number at His Majesty's desire, without any commission from the General Assembly, and, therfor, may answer only for our own parts, if His Majesty would crave any further good, it wer to cause propound the same to the General Assembly, wher with advice and consent of the whole number resolution may be had."

From those answers we may easily guess what the Courtiers insisted on with Mr. Lawson and the rest, and how cautiously they caried. The Court was exceeding grated at the Generall Assembly's Act concerning the enterprize of Ruthven approving it, which they did not go into till they sent a message to the King to know his mind in that affair; and after the King's earnest desires that they might declare it good service to religion. They did so, and indeed they tho't it was so, and certainly it was; and the King, in his answers to the English Ambassadour, Walsinghame, greives (which with the King's answers I have insert App. copy Cald., v. 3 p. 259-63).[1] They decline to approve the late proclamations, and desire the calumnies raised against them to be tryed, and a Generall Assembly called for full resolution.

Towards the end of the year, matters went on with more and more rigour against all concerned in Ruthven Road. The ministers by no means could be bro't in to approve thir present courses. Dec. 13, Mr. Lawson and Mr. Durie wer called before the Council, just as the 3d bell tolled. The King told that he had called them, that he might declare the falsnes of the rumors that wer going that he was going to take some of their lives and medle with their blood, and that he might speak somwhat to John Durie before Mr. Lawson; and him he blamed for making a distinction that the effect of the Road of Ruthven was good, however it was done. They reasoned long upon that. The King asked if they tho't that effect good that he was keeped prisoner, and his servants and kinsfolk taken. They answerd those wer not the effects they meant. They wer removed, and the King and Council concluded that Mr. Durie had contraveened the Act made against those concerned in Ruthven Road, and therfor was to be punished at the King's will. Being called in, the Act was read unto them, and their opinion of it asked. Mr. Lawson said it was purely civil, and had no relation to them. Mr. Durie said the same, but expressed himself

---

[1] Vide Cald., Vol. III. p. 725. Wodrow Society Edition.

unwarrily that he had nothing to say against the Act—yea, allowed it. This the Courtiers took hold of, and minuted that they both allowed the Act, and gave out the accounts that the ministers approved the procedure. But Mr. Davidson's sermon next day, of which nottice is taken in his Life, soon convinced the hearers this was a misreport.

I come now to the last year of Mr. Lawson's life, when he was forced to leave his native country and retire to England for safety, wher he got to his rest. The particular occasion of this was after the Parliament—if that meeting deserved that name—had clandestinely and hastily passed the iniquous Act against the Church, in May. Upon the Saturday, May 23, before the Acts wer proclaimed, the King and his violent Counsell, suspecting that the Ministers of Edinburgh would declare the sinfulnes of those Acts, sent a charge to the Provost and baileys to take the ministers out of pulpit and cast them in prison, in case they spoke anything against their Acts and proceedings. Upon the Lord's Day, May 24, Mr. Lawson and Mr. Balcanquell, tho' they knew of the orders, resolved to run the utmost hazard before they would be silent, when such open attempts wer made upon the Reformation and libertys of the Church, and spoke very freely against those iniquous awes and proceedings. The magistrates, tho' not very friendly to the Ministers, yet agreed to delay executing their commission till the Acts wer proclaimed, which was done Munday, May 25, at the Cross, when, as we shall see in Mr. Robt. Pont's Life, he and Mr. Balcanquell openly protested against those Acts with all due formes. When the Earle of Arran heard of this, he blamed Mr. Lawson for all, and made many vowes that, if his head wer as great as a hay stack, he should cause it leap from his hause (throat or shoulders). When Mr. Lawson and Balcanquell heard his threatenings, and knew the warrand already given to aprehend them, after they had consulted with the Presbitry and the best of their flock and some well affected barrons and gentlemen about, and they being all positive as to their removing for a season, the two ministers withdrew themselves secretly to Berwick, and got safe there, the 27 of May. The King went that week over the watter to Falkland, and left orders with Coll. Stewart to aprehend them; but they wer out of his reach before he knew of their flight.

Upon the 2d of June, Mr. Lawson and Balcanquell sent a letter to their flock at Edinburgh, declaring the reasons of their leaving them, dated at Berwick, June 2nd, which, conteaning a very distinct view of matters at this juncture, as well as the pressing causes of their flight, I have inserted App. n. (copy *Cald.* v. 3, 377-81).[1] When this letter came, John Cairns, Reader, presented it to the Council at Edinburgh. At the persuasion of Henry Nisbit, a favourer of the Earle of Arran's, they sent it to the King at Falkland, wher Bishop Adamson penned answer to it in name of the congregation of Edinburgh, which stands also App. n. (copy *Cald.* v. 3, p. 382, 3).[2] This was sent over to the town of Edinburgh with the King's command to signe it, and send it to their ministers. The most part refused to signe it, and for this a considerable persecution was raised in Edinburgh by Colonell Stewart. Many wer imprisoned; and Edward and James Cathkins, with Robert Mark, wer banished. Many papers wer writt at this time, severall of which as reasons for not subscribing Mr. Adamson's own letter to Mr. Lawson and Balcanquell, to which they returned a most pointed answer, with the ministers' answer to the answer sent them by some of their flock, and a letter in name of Janet Gutery and Margaret Majoribanks, spouses of Mr. Lawson and Balcanquell, to the Bishop's letter to them—all those are in Calderwood MS., but too long to be insert in the Appendix.[3] Bishop Spotswood gives us a lame abstract [of] the ministers' letter and his predecessor's, drawn for their flocks at more lenth, and owns that the terms of fugitives, rebells, wolves, laid in it on their ministers, wer so odious to all good men that with difficulty 16 wer got to signe it. He adds that when it came to Mr. Lawson, he fell into such sorrow, and thereby contracted a sicknes that ended in his death. If this be true, his death may be well charged on the Bishop of Saint Andrews; but I question if greif for this letter, so much as the lamentable views he had of the present state of religion, sunk him. Whatever was the cause he was removed from all his sorrows this year.

While in England, Mr. Lawson was sometime with the Earle of Angus, and Marr, Mr. of Glames, and other Protestant lords, now banished and remaining in England, and preached to them; and after he went south to London, and with his bretheren, Mr. And. Melvil and the rest, visited the Universitys and afterwards came back [to] London. Meanwhile, in September, the fury of the Court reached the

---

[1] Vide *Cald.* IV. p. 73, &c. Wodrow Society Edition.
[2] Vide *Cald.* IV. p. 79, &c., as before.
[3] Vide *Cald.* IV. p. 126, &c.

wives of the ministers who had retired from the storm; and in September, Mistresses Lawson, Balcanquell, and Durie, were obliged to sell their furniture very hastily, and remove out of their houses, the keyes of which they delivered to the Magistrates. The King's charge to the Magistrates in so singular a case deserves to be preserved, with the observation, that nobody was settled in their husbands' rooms, nor preached in the town of Edinburgh, that I can observe, till the happy turn next year, save the Bishop of Saint Andrews and some he employed. But none wer settled; so that it was meer spite to turn the good woemen from their houses, when guilty of no fault, and no body was needing the houses. The charge, such as it is, followes:

"Trustie freinds, we greet you well, being most carefull to remoove the slander of your want of preaching, by appointing of godly, learned, quiet spirited pastors to supply the deserted places of your late ministers; and finding it most necessary for the better commodity of their habitation, that the houses appointed for your ministry, presently possessed by those men's wives and families, be made void and rid of them, to the effect they may enter in immediately therunto, have, therfor, directed our letters charging the said ministers' wives to remoove them and their families furth of the said houses to the said effect, and therwith another charge to some woemen (Janet Adamson, Janet Henderson, Janet Gilbert) within your town worse affected to the obedience of our late Acts of Parliament, to retire them be north our watter of Tay, for a space, till they give further declaration of their disposition to our obedience; which charges, if they be sisten by the said persons, it's our will, and [we] command you that of your office you see the same obeyed and both the one and the other remooved without further delay than is accorded to them by the charges; as ye will answer to us upon your obedience, and will be comptable to us upon the contrair. Subscribed with our hand at Falkland, Sept. 8, 1584.

"Arran.   "JAMES R.
"Montrose."

In July, after his journey to Oxford and Cambridge with his bretheren, and conference with the godly and learned there, Mr. Lawson and they returned to London, wher, partly through fatigue and travell, which he did not agree with, partly through the alteration of the air, and also being of a melancholy temper, with too much griefe for the misbehaviour of his flock in their letter to him and his collegue, and especially being oppressed with the present hazard of the whole Reformation, he fell into a sicknes, which ended in a dyssenterie, which, by no medicine, could be cured.

When he began to turn weak, he dictat his testament in Latine, and desired Mr. James Carmichael to help him if he went wrong, and to perfect it. Mr Calderwood observes that he signifyed at that time that, had the Lord been pleased to have spared him any time, he was minded to have written his own Life, at least such parts of it as he could now recover: that he would not have been ashamed to have expressed his mean education and penurie when he entered in Perth, glade to receive gains of the hands of the scholars, till his good master, Mr. Andrew Simson, received him into his house: that he would have set down all that he could remember, and nothing but the truth, that God might have His Own glory in raising him up from the dust, and not be spoiled of any part of His praise for His carefull providence towards him, and would not have forgotten God's work in bringing him to London after his work was ended at Edinburgh; and removing him from an ungratefull party there, who, since the coming of D'Aubigney to Scotland, very much withstood the good and flourishing state of the Gospell; and for their own particular gain and merchandise with France, inclined more to the new and forraigne than amity with England; for the defence of which (for the safety of our Reformation priviledges), both in pulpit and more privatly, he susteaned the hatred of the French Court and all the Aubignists in Edinburgh. It's no small loss to us that succeed, that his strenth did not allow him to begin and finish this account of his Life, and the state of things in his time. Few in this period, if any, could have done it so well since Mr. Knox ended. And I recon it one of the greatest losses we have in understanding the true state of affairs in Church and State, that men of integrity and ability, who have their hand in affairs, and knew the true state and springs of what passes in every period, set not down memoires of what passes within their own reach.

Upon the 7 of October, he caused read over, and subscribed, his testament; and, since it conteans his dying sentiments, under his views of eternity, as to his soul's state and the present circumstances of things in Scotland, I chuse rather to insert it here than to turn over to the Appendix, and I give it as Mr. Calderwood has preserved it in English.

> "At London, in Honielane, Cheapside, in Mr. Anthony Martin's house, upon Wensday, Oct. 7, 1584.

"I, Mr. James Lawson, Minister of God's Word, of the flock of Christ at Edinburgh, with grace, mercy, and peace from God the Father, and from the Lord Jesus Christ, with the continouance of the Holy Spirit, to all those that fear the Lord and love His blessed Evangel, giving to understand to whom it apperteans, that being whole in mind, but finding my God summoning me by His messenger, sicknes, wherwith He has laid me to bed, to put an end (as appears) to my course, in this my transitory life, have thought good to commit my testament and latter will to write as followes :—

"First, I thank my God, through Jesus Christ, my Saviour, Who has not only of His unspeakable mercy, wherof I confess myself most unworthy if He should deal with me according to my deserts, plucked me out of gross ignorance and blindnes of superstition, Papistry, and idolatry, especially since the time I did hear that nottable servant of God, Mr. Knox of blessed memory, impugne with great authority of doctrine that antichristian tyranny, but also of His great goodnes from time to time has moved me by His sacred Word and instruction of His Holy Spirit to dedicat myself and the small talent, which His wisdom concredit to me, to the edification of His people in the holy ministry ordeaned of His Kirk, and has blessed also the same, first in the congregation of Aberdeen, and last in the town of Edinburgh, testifying to the whole worlde that, as I have felt from time to time the working of His Holy Spirit kindling in my breast a bent and ready will to discharge my own conscience in teaching the word of God purely and sincerely, without fearing the faces of men, and also to procure the establishment of that ecclesiasticall discipline revealed and set down in the Holy Scriptures of God, according to the measure of the knowledge given to me ; so, do I feel of God's speciall love, a delectation, a zeal and thirst sealed up to my heart, to persevere in the same as the infallible truth of God, and to continou in the same, if it shall please God to prorogat my dayes. Albeit, Lord ! far be it from me to boast or glory in anything in Thy presence, before Whom the angells are not able to plead their innocency, but in the cause of Thy Son, Jesus Christ, seing the want of sufficient zeal, diligence, and ability in the said office, and the many infirmities and imperfections staying me in the performance therof, as it became me, I have my refuge to the throne of Thy Grace, acknowledging, after all my irksome travells wherwith I am broken, me to be an unprofitable servant, referring the whole praise of my weak ministry to the glory of Thy holy Name, be Whom I have my being and moving, craving in the meantime pardon of all my offences and sins, being now assured of the remission therof through the merits of the death and passion of Jesus Christ, with Whom I am conjoyned in His everlasting covenant by lively faith, wherby I presently possess His mercy, attour I render most hearty thanks unto His gracious goodnes that He has not only used me as a poor instrument to communicat His heavenly counsels unto others, but also has called me to that honour, to suffer for the constant defence of His truth and ecclesiasticall discipline conteaned therin, and has of His carefull providence given lively experience of the performance of that promise, which His Son, my Saviour, made: that whosoever shall forsake houses, father, mother, bretheren, sisters, wife, or children for His name's sake, or the Gospell's, should receive an hundredfold more now at this present, and life everlasting in the wordle to come, not only to the most godly learned bretheren and sisters among the strangers, and especially in the godly family wherin the Lord brought me, wherin I have been most lovingly enterteaned at my heart's desire, but also of so many of my bretheren and fellow-labourers in the Evangell with me of my own country, whose kindnes, courtesie, and good offices towards me showen, I wish the Lord to requite to the one and to the other. And now, turning my exertion to my faithfull bretheren, whom God has called to dispense His Holy Mysterys of His Word and Sacrament, whose dayes it shall please the Lord to prolong after my departure, I beseek them all in the bowels of Jesus Christ that they take heed that they imploy their whole studies, in whatsomever time shall be granted to them in the face of the earth, to prosecute their good cause, to feed their people committed to their care by preaching the glad tydings of salvation, in season and out of season, neither for lucre nor for the fashion, but earnestly, zealously, and with a ready mind in removing, planting, and advancing that holy ecclesiastical discipline in the House of God, which is established in His Word, and so much the more valiantly and constantly to stand in defence therof, that Satan his supports *pseudo-episcopi*, grievous wolves, are entered in and impiring [domineering] as they wer lords over God's heritage, whom neither the Apostle Saint Paul nor any part of the Word of God did ever allow maliciously to impugne the same. And, as concerning the flock of Edinburgh, howbeit this body of mine has greatly wasted, yet I repent me nothing of my travaill there; being assured that the Lord has there a Kirk, who unfeignedly fear His Name, and for whose salvation the Lord has made my ministry profitable; therfor, from my very heart I leave my blessing to all the faithfull there, who dearly love the coming of our Lord Jesus Christ; and my God, blessed for ever, blesses them, not only with true and faithfull labourers in the ministry and to preserve them from ravenous wolves, but also with continouall increase in all godlynes and perseverance in that true faith and doctrine, which I have taught among them; and at last with everlasting life in heaven, wherby both they and I shall mutually rejoice: and for a few others, whose names of charity I suppress, who, as they grieved my heart oftentimes, while I was present with them, by resisting the upright and godly course and assisting the wrong, so now, since my departure from them, through their subscribing that false and infamous lyball, set out against us their pastors, and sundry other unthankfull dealings, which we neither merited nor looked for at their hands, they have done that in them lay to wound the same; for my part I forgive them with my heart. And, seeing they would collour their facts under the shaddow of obedience to that superior power, I beseek the Lord to forgive the King for obtruding of that letter, injuriously exacting their subscriptions therunto, and to give them both the repentance therfor, and not to lay the burden therof to their charge, nor crave at their hands my blood. May the same Lord open the King's eyes to behold in what hazard he has brought the true religion, his own person, fame, and state, together with the best and most obedient subjects within his realme; and give him grace in time to withdraw himself from those pestilent and wicked counselors, wherwith he is invironed, and leave that unhappy course, wherwith he has wrapped himself most fearfully to the great danger of his body and soul, unles he repent. Amen:

Amen. And now I commend my soul into the hands of my Heavenly Father, Creator therof, and of Jesus Christ, my only Redeemer and Saviour, by Whom the parts of heaven are made patent unto me, willing my trustie and dearly-beloved bretheren, insert witnesses of this my will, to cause bury my body in that place, and after that manner which shall seem good unto them, there to sleep untill the day of the joyfull Resurrection to life everlasting, when my soul and body being joyned together shall have the full fruition of His face, with the bodyes and souls of all the faithfull. And, now concerning the ordering of my family, seing the possession of earthly things is not able to enrich the posterity, I desire, as God is the Father of the fatherles, and Comforter of the widow's case, by the riches of His blessing to supply their poverty; and, touching the portion of goods given unto me, I put the same in the hands of my most speciall friends, Robert Fairly of Braid, Mr. John Lindsay, senator of the Colledge of Justice; John Johnstoun of Elphingstoun, burgess of Edinburgh; with my loving spouse, Janet Guthrie, whom I constitute executors of this my testament; and they with common consent chuse one or mo of their number, [to] whose fidelity the intromissions shall be committed upon sufficient security, that all things shall come to the use of my children, which burden I most earnestly request them to take upon them, for the love and familiar conjunction that has been betwixt us in Christ; giving power to them to make and subscribe an inventure of my books, household gear, and other moveables left behind me in Scotland, wherever they shall be transported; and, also, praying my beloved bretheren, the witnesses underwritten in this my testament, to make and subscribe another inventure of my books, cloaks, and other moveables which I have in London, and deliver them to be keeped by my brother, Mr. Walter Balcanquell, the whole books, cloaths, and other moveables, and household gear whatsomever conteaned in the two said inventures to be sett to reasonable prices and to be sold, at the sight and appointment of my said executors and intrometters; and that part therof, which shall of right be judged be them to appertean to me, shall be divided into four equal portions to my wife and three children, to bring them up in the fear of good of the schools in such company as their wisdomes shall think most meet and expedient. And, as touching the gold and silver presently in my possession here, the whole to the number of 76 pieces—to witt, a Portugall doucat, 11 rose nobles, 30 crowns, estimat to 72 pound; 22 angells, and a half angell, 3 other new angells, and 2 doucats, a double pistole, 2 unicorns, with half an unicorn, a litle Scottish peice, valued at 26 shillings Scottish; another litle piece with Jehovah on it; item, 6 pound 13 shilling 4 pennies of English coin, which peices of gold and summ of English silver I have committed to the credit of my faithfull brother, Mr. Walter Balcanquell, to be disposed as followes:—Imprimis, ye shall deliver to the French Kirk at London 3 angells to be distributed to their poor; item, to Mrs. Vannell, who keeped me in my sicknes, ane angell; item, I will that my loving brother, Mr. James Carmichael, shall bow [bend] a rose noble instantly, and deliver it to my dear brother and loving friend, Mr. Walter Balcanquell, who has been so carefull of me at all times, and especially in time of my present sicknes, to remain with him, as a perpetuall token of my speciall love and thankfull heart towards him; item, I will, the said Mr. Walter, deliver, in my name, to my dear and well-beloved spouse, Janet Guthrie, beside other provision made, or that may fall, unto her be my testament, the Portugall ducat, in signe of my lovingkindnes, which she has well deserved, as a faithfull brother gave the same to me as a pledge of his singular love towards me. And, touching the peices of gold and English silver resting of the summ forsaid, I will that the said Mr. Walter deliver the same, *bona fide*, to my said executors, together with the said inventure, goods, and gear therin conteaned, he receiving sufficient discharge therof for his warrand from the said executors, bestow in the manner following:—Imprimis to my sister, Christian Lawson, the summ of 20 pounds Scots, and all the rest to be equally parted betwixt my 3 bairns in 3 portions, providing alwise that the recompense of the physicians, apothecaries, and whatsoever expenses necessary, shall be made in time of my sicknes, or shall be aught and [due] be me in London, when it shall please God to call me out of this valley of misery, which is only debt, and which I am owing presently, or expense in transporting my graith home be first payed be my brother, Mr. Balcanquell, at the sight of the said bretheren, of the readiest of the said summ, which shall be defalked therof, by the saids executors, after the sight of the ticket therof, be the said bretheren, which I will shall be a sufficient discharge unto him for the same. Last, I earnestly requeist of my loving bretheren, Mr Andrew Melvil, Mr. John Davidson, and Mr. James Carmichael, to concurr with my brother, Mr. Walter Balcanquell, in revising my writebooks, and papers, as well at London as elsewhere, and use the same as they may think may best serve for the glory of God and comfort of the Kirk; and my will is that my said executors deliver them thankfully into their hands; giving power alswa to my said executors to put this my testament, if need bees, in more exquisit and ampler form, with all clauses requisite, the substance alwise being restant within the premises, and in confirmation of my testament, written, at my request, by my brother, Mr. James Carmichael, I, the said Mr. James Lawson, hath subscribed the same with my hand, and desires my good and trustie freinds, Mr. Andrew Melvil, Provost of the New Colledge of Saint Andrews; Mr. James Carmichael, Minister of God's Word in Haddington; Mr. John Davidson, Minister of God's Word at Libbertoun; and Mr. Walter Balcanquell, my collegue in the ministry at Edinburgh, to testify the same by their handwrites, the which also they did, in my presence, after we had all heard the same distinctly read, day, moneth, year, and place forsaid. Sic subs.

"J. LAWSON, called
to the Lord."

"Mr. Andrew Melvil,
"Mr. James Carmichael,   Witnesses to
"Mr. John Davidson,   the premises."
"Mr. Walter Balcalquall,

When Bishop Adamson of Saint Andrews heard of Mr. Lawson's illnes, he formed a ludicrous testament in his name, made up of a great many falshoods and acknowledgments contrary to his knowen principles, with a good many letters, pretended to be writt by Mr. Lawson, to the most eminent ministers, full of satyre and bitternes and false insinuations, to the King, Queen Elizabeth, and the Scots nobility and bishops. Whither Bishop Adamson designed those as ludicrous jests on this good man and the other faithfull ministers, his bretheren, or if he designed they should pass for Mr. Lawson's personall deed, in case he had not formed and signed a real one at London, I cannot say. The first was mean, and unsuitable to the gravity and decency of a man or Christian; the other was villainous, and an imposing on the wordle in the gravest matters; and yet this composing and fathering such cheats as those has been too usuall from the Prelatick quarter, as in Mr. Calderwood's Recantation, Mr. Alex. Henderson's Declaration on his death-bed, and other instances, which may come in in this Work. Mr. Calderwood has given himself the trouble to transcribe the whole of those in his History, and they fill up 10 or mo sheets of paper. I doe not take them to be worth preserving in this Work. I find by a letter of the abandoned Earle of Bothwell to the Ministers of Edinburgh, 1592, that Bishop Adamson, on his death-bed, charged all those ludicrouse papers on Chancellor Maitland, but neither the Bishop nor the Earle deserve any great credite, and they father themselves on the Bishop.

During Mr. Lawson's sicknes, it was his own mercy, and more that of those about him, that his tongue served him till his departure; and Mr. Calderwood observes that he uttered many heavenly and comfortable speeches to the hearers. His death was most dolourous to the godly, as he lived most godly and sincerely through the whole course of his life. Speaking still to edification, far from all slanderous, vain, or idle words, as all who wer with him in conversation, yea, the very enemies of Christ and His Gospell, behoved to confess, soe gave he an evident proof that the true fear of God was deeply seated in his heart, and yielded up his spirit unto God, dying as he lived, uttering most comfortable and zealous speechs to the consolation and admiration of all his hearers, who felt it true which Jesus the Son of Syrach sayeth: It is better to be in the house of mourning than in the house of banqueting, for a most precious lesson might there be learned, as a most lively pattern how to dye, and not to fear death. Ther are many to be seen, who have a show of godlynes in their life, who, when they are put to a sharp proof by sicknes, declare their profession to have been mere hypocrisy, and utter nothing but blasphemous, slanderous, and injurious speeches; but Mr. Lawson, being tryed as in a fiery furnace for the space of 34 dayes, never pronounced out of his mouth so much as one impatient word, but most comfortable, constant, and zealous sentences, with his eyes lift up to heaven and his hands stretched out, more moving than any gesture or behaviour of a most zealous preacher in pulpit can express, not only preaching as if he had been in a pulpite, but also singing of psalms, and provocking others to sing with him. 3 dayes before his death, he caused sing the 103 psalme and the 124 psalme, and a few hours before it the 130 psalm; and, when voice would not serve, his lips were well seen pronouncing the same words that wer sung. No doubt he was under the comfortable reflexions of the presence the Lord had given him through the course of his ministry, and in the close of it [while] he taught at Berwick, to the great consolation of all his hearers, who testifyed with many tears with what joy and comfort they heard the doctrine of salvation out of his mouth, and when at London, albeit by the injury of the times, he had no acces to preach in publick, yet undoubtedly his 34 dayes' teaching with authority in his sicknes and bed won some to Christ, and confirmed many in the truth, who either received out of his own mouth, or by the faithfull report of the godly present, who at all occasions reported his most nottable sentences to their familys and acquaintances. This provoked new confluence to him to be partakers of their comfort. Those exercises undoubtedly procured and confirmed many disciples to Christ, as appeared in many who accompanyed him to his grave with love and affection, at which time, conference and repetition of his sentences and godly admonitions allured many to love him, who had never seen him. However, it was burden to him that he had not an opportunity to preach; and he desired the Lord to be mercifull to those who would neither enter into the kingdome of God themselves, nor suffer others to enter therein.

Mr. Lawson ended his dayes, the 12 of October, 1584, in the 46 year of his age, in Mr. Anthony Martine's house, in the upper chamber, in presence of Mr. Melvil, Carmichael, Davidson, and Balcanquell, Mr. John Coupar, George Douglas, Mr. David Hume, Patrick Forbes, Mr. Wilson, Tylour, Mr. Strachan, Mr. Guthry, Robert Garrow, Scottishmen; besides English men and woemen. The time of burial being appointed next day, which was Wensday, at two afternoon, he was carryed in a coffin, covered with a small lining cloth and a black cloath, by six, as was appointed by the four bretheren before, by Mr. Melvil and Davidson, before, Mr. James Carmichael and Mr. Balcanquell, behind, Mr. Check and Mr. Gardiner, in the midst—all preachers. Those wer soon releived by Mr. David Hume, George Douglas, Mr. Archibald Moncreif, Patrick Forbes, Mr. Robert Lauder, Mr. Morison,

Mr. Guthrie, Mr. Lik, Mr. Harrison, Schoolmaster of Paul's. Those wer releived by Mr. Strauchan, Mr. Forsyth, Mr. Wilson, Patrick White, Mr. Hundson; and so by many godly bretheren, ministers, and citicens, who most covetously and gladly offered themselves in that work, so thickly, comley, and courteously, as if he had been best knowen to them, and of their chief kinsmen of greatest authority in the town. I transcribe thir litle circumstances from Calderwood, because as thir incidentall things want not their own use in historicall matters, so they show the great and universall esteem in which Mr. Lawson was. He further observes, that at this buriall thir was an unaccustomed frequency even of the cheifest men of the city; for the most part thir used to be but 30 or 40, seldom 100; here there resorted of gentlemen, honest burgeses, and godly matrons, above 500 persons; preachers—Mr. Travers, Suddick, Check, Gardiner, and Baptist ministers—Mr. Fountain, Castole, Lane; three ministers of the French Church, and many Frenchmen; Doctor Bright, Mr. Smith, Esk and his wife; authores—Martine, Potter, Font, Allane, Doctor Cruke, Mr. Barbour, Mr. Wood, deprived, Egertoun, Mr. Feild, Mr. Edmunds, Mr. Colins and his wife, Robert Garrow, Mr. Smith, elder, Barbour, Smith, Surfleit, Mr. Brian, Mr. Cout, Mr. Brown, Schoolmaster at Saint Anthonies; Mr. Bodle, Mr. Hornbie, Mr. Bacon, gentleman; Mr. Pope, Secretary Walsingham's gentleman; Mr. Hiet, merchant; Mr. Mortingtoun, Sturt, Evant, Culver, Mr. Whitebread, gentleman, married to the Bishop of Elie's wife's daughter; Mr. Evecole, gentleman—all sound Christians and professors of the Evangel; of matrons—Alderman Martine's wife, who had bestowed 20 grains of unicorn's horn upon Mr. Lawson, beside other things, so carefull was she of his health and restoring; Mrs. Johnstoun, Mrs. Martine, Anthony Martine's wife—all careful mothers and sisters for him; Mrs. Harrison, Overtown, Vantrellier, Mrs. Vannane, and Mr. John Davidson's wife. He was buried in the new churchyeard at Bedlem: Bishop Spotswood adds, he was buried at the side of Mr. Deering, a famous preacher in England.

He was, as we have seen, married to Janet Guthrie, and left behind him three children very young. I have not seen anything of his published; tho' it appears that he designed some of his papers should have been published, if his bretheren found them proper; and that he had a view of writing the remarkable passages of his own

Life. As we have seen, he had a share in "The 2nd Book of Discipline".

His character may be gathered from what is above. Bishop Spotswood sayes: "He was a man of good learning and judgment, of a pious and peaceable disposition, great gratitude, and a preacher at Edinburgh 12 years, in great esteem and reputation, untill those unhappy times which bereaved his Church and country of him and his labours". Yet he escapes not a lash of the Bishop's pen, who throws in to lessen what he had said of him, that he was carryed too much away with the idle rumors of the people. Everybody almost that was firm against Prelacy must have innuendo from the Bishop, be their ability never so great. What the import of this innuendo against Mr. Lawson is, I do not fully know; if it be that he was credulous or caryed away with the popular attempts at that time, I cannot say, but his gravity, learning, and singular piety made him proof against both, and very far from being chargable with this imputation. Mr. Calderwood gives him a short, but a very just character: "Mr. James Lawson was not only an excellent preacher, but also a profound scholar, and a holy and zealous man".

Let me conclude my account of this great and good man with a note of a sermon of his I find in an old MS., which conteans extracts of sermons of the ministers after the Reformation; had it been dated I should have brought it in on its proper place. I think it's worth (?) preserving. Its title is, *Mr. James Lawson's note;* "God has yet His own servants in His awin Kirk, wha threaten judgments against stubrone sinners; and evin in the Edinburgh, He has awin servands and messangers, teacheirs of His Word, some in ane kynd and some in anuther kynd: some with greater vehemency and some with the spirit of lenity; for God moves not the heart of all alike alwyse, whidder we teach with the spirit of severitie or with the spirit of levitie. Blasphimous are they that misreports the servands of God, seing they have the testimony of an upright conscience, and God's Word for their warrand. They that thinks it behooves the servands of God to follow ane only course in teaching, they are altogether deceived in thinking that the servands of God sould not threatin and cry out against wickednes. Sall we cease from threatinings when wicked men and women will not cease from their wickednes and rebellioun against the Majesty of God? Wherfor, yet repent in time, and yet abhor the works of darkness, and look upon the Light shining amongst you, give ye wold escape the plague of God. This is the only way to be sure—follow this remedie, in the name of the Living God."

Mr. James Melvil, in his own Life, sayes that for gifts and estimation he was cheif among the ministry. He adds this character of his wife: that she had most rare and excellent gifts of knowledge and devotion; that she was tender, zealous, and most loving to all God's servants and the lovers of Christ, and an example to posterity of all that is good. She was come the lenth of Berwick in her journey to London, and some farther, when the nouse of his death came, upon which she was brought back to the House of Hutton Hall, of which family, Mr. Melvil gives a great character for godliness and usefulness. Upon this melancholy occasion, Mrs. Lawson discovered her being a Christian indeed in a calme resignation. She lived about 9 years after her husband—a true widow and relict of such a husband. In fasting, prayer, and meditation, abounding in the works of mercy and love, instructing the ignorant, admonishing offenders, comforting the afflicted, visiting the sick and diseased in body and mind, persevering with them in prayer to the end—her pleasure and satisfaction was in those exercises. Her death was as much lamented by all ranks, especially the poor, as any woman in her time.

COLLECTIONS OF THE LIFE OF Mr. ROBERT HOWIE, PROFESSOR OF DIVINITY AT SAINT ANDREWS.

Mr. Howie was a man of some learning; but his being put in very irregularly, and contrary to the inclinations of most part concerned, in Mr. Andrew Melvil's room, exceedingly lesned his character. Indeed, a man's abilitys had need to be extraordinary who succeed a person like Mr. Melvil. He was long in the Chair at Saint Andrews, first as Provost, and then Professor of Divinity in the New Colledge upwards of 40 years; and yet it's but litle about him hath come to my hand.

I know not whether he was any time in the ministry, or if he had any pastorall charge before he was brought into the University of Saint Andrews; neither have I anything as to his parentage or education. When he was setled at Saint Andrews, I have not learned; it seems to have been after the year 1584, since I do not find him signing Mr. Andrew Melvil's testimoniall given by the University that year, and before the year 1591, since that year, his dissertations wer printed at Basil, and it's probable he would be professor a year or two before he would print anything. In the year 1598, I find him named in the Records of Assembly among our doctors of Divinity, that is, teachers of it. In the year 1598, after the General Assembly had concluded that the number of the votters in Parliament in name of the Kirk should be equall to the number of votters in the Papisticall Kirk—that is, 51—and that the election should be mixed, partly in the Kirk and partly in His Majesty, for want of time, the rest of the questions as to votters in Parliament—that is, *de modo eligendi*, of his rent, continouance, whither chosen *ad poenam* or not, of his name, and the cautions and restrictions for preventing him from corruption—wer referred till another Assembly. Meanwhile, to prepare things for a conclusion at next Assembly, it's ordeaned "that every presbitry be ripely advised upon the heads above written, and therafter convocat their synodall assemblys upon the whole Realme, upon one day, which shall be the first Teusday of June next to come; and, thereafter new advisement with the forsaid particular head, that every synodall shall choice out 3 of the wisest of their number, who shall be ready, upon His Majesty's advertishment—which shall be upon a moneth's warning at least—to conveen with His Majesty and the doctors of the Universitys, viz., Mr. And. Melvil, John Johnstoun, Robert Rollock, Patrick Sharp, Robert Howie, Robert Wilkie, Sir James Martine, what day and place His Majesty thinks convenient, with power to them to reason and conferr upon those; and, if they agree, to conclude all that concerns the vote in Parliament; but, [in] case of discrepance and variance, to referr the whole to the next Generall Assembly".

It seems Mr. Howie was at this time on the King's side, and a favourer of the votters in Parliament, and so I find him chosen at the next Assembly, which mett at Monross, Aprile, 1600. The case was this. The consideration of what was yet undetermined as to ministers, votters in Parliament, was remitted to the Conference before it came to the Assembly, and that being very numerouse, that so the force of the arguments against votters might be knowen, and the best answers that might be prepared against the matter came in to the Assembly. This privy Conference, in order to peace and agreement, named 4 on every side, to reason the matter fully; and it was said, if they could agree, all would soon come to harmony. So upon the King's side wer named, as we have seen on severall of their Lives—Mr. George Gladstanes, Mr. Ja. Nicholson, Mr. Robert Howie, and Mr. Alexr. Douglas, and Mr John Spotswood to be their scribe. For the other side—Mr. Patrick Sharp, Mr. Patrick Simson, Mr. James Melvil, and Mr. David Barclay, with a scribe. This lets us see Mr. Howie was valued, by the side who chose him, as a person of ability.

Mr. Howie still continoued on the same side, and I find he is called up in the year 1606 to London, when Mr. Melvil and the 7 others who stood for our discipline, wer written for to London, on pretext of a conference before the King. On the same side with Mr. Howie wer Bishop Gladstanes, and Law, and Spotswood, Mr. James Nicholson, Mr. Patrick Sharp, Mr. Andrew Lamb. What passed stands in Mr. Andrew [and] James Melvil's Lives. Perhaps ther was another reason of Mr. Howie's journey to London at this time, viz. to prepare him for succeeding to Mr. Andrew Melvil in teaching Divinity in the

New Colledge; for, though this was not yet spoke out, it seems to have been resolved that Mr. Andrew Melvil should no more teach in Scotland.

Accordingly, as hath been notticed in Mr. A. Melvill's Life, in July, 1607, ther was a visitation of the University of Saint Andrews; the members [being] some of the corrupt side of the ministry, some of the Privy Council, and some gentlemen about. They found Mr. Melvil's room as Provost of the New Colledge vacant, meerly upon the act of the English Council confyning him to the Tower, and for nothing done in Scotland, though the Masters wer not wanting to load him with their own faults in the oeconomy. The current year's stipend was promised to Mr. Andrew by the favour of the counsellors and gentlemen, and not the ministers, who showed no great favour that way. And Mr. Robert Howie was charged, under pain of horning, to accept of Mr. Melvil's place, and a new meeting for his reception was appointed upon Agust 3.

This day was anticipated, probably because the Parliament met Agust first, and the Primat could not be wanted there. Therfor, upon July 27, Mr. Howie was placed in Mr. Melvil's room by Bishop Gladstains. Mr. Calderwood gives the following account of this, which comes in here:—" Upon the 27 of July, Mr. George Gladstanes, Bishop of Saint Andrews, conveened the University within the school of the New Colledge, the scholars being almost all gone to the vacance, and there declared His Majesty's will that Mr. Robert Howie should be placed Provost in that Colledge, in room of Mr. A. Melvil, who, for treasonable words, was put in the Tower of London; and, therfor, removed from his place in the Colledge. So Mr. Howie was placed there, in the King's name, and during His Majesty's pleasure. Protestations wer made in the contrair, in respect no process of deposition has been intended against Mr. Andrew. But all was repelled by minacing speeches;—'Take heed to speak for traitors, least you be closed up with him,' &c. Mr. Howie refused to accept of the place, unless he had it given him *simpliciter, et ad vitam*. But the Bishop imperiously commanded him to accept of it, for it should be no otherwise than he (the Bishop) had spoken. So Mr. Howie took documents and entered. The whole action was ended in less than a quarter of an houre."

Very soon after Mr. Howie's admission in Mr. Melvil's room, he writes a letter to the King, probably in concert with his patron, Bishop Gladstains, wherin he appears to be uneasy under the thoughts of Mr. Melvin's still having a title to his post and his own being a deput and lyable to be turned [transferred]. I shall take no nottice of the flattery and servil, selfish spirit that seems to run through the letter, but rather let the reader make his own remarks upon it, as it stands from the originall in the Lawers' Library. "Sacred Soveraigne, may it please Your most excellent Majesty, as nothing hath been more dear to me next God than Your Majesty's royall person, estate, and the furtherance of Your Majesty's wise and princely designments in Church government, wherin I have not only followed Your Majesty in all our sincerity (notwithstanding of any misconstruction in the contrair, which I hope God in His own time will disclose), but also the light of God and my own conscience, so have I, at Your Majesty's direction and commandment, undertaken the Provestry of the New Colledge, a work full of difficulty and envy, wherin I have no assured stay but Your Majesty's unchangeable favour and countenance to me, so long as I continou Your Majesty's faithfull servant. My case was quiet and wealthy, according to the fashion of this country. Now the zeal of Your Highnes' service hath forced me to forsake my calme, and to committ to the hazard of most violent tempests. Sir, for my honest service done, and to be done, I crave no more, but that Your Majesty may command that I may have formall surety of this place, according to the commone order, and not to be a viccar or a depute for an *interim*; since my heart is devoted, both in my own actions and in the formation of this seminary of youth, to the promotion of Your Majesty's honour, estimation, and service, with most upright affection. And, Sir, I will not dissemble to you; I will be more frank and forward to take hazard in Your Highnes' service, when I have ane formall provision, than when I have only a changeable place. Thus referring to Your Majesty's incomparable wisdom to give order to my Lord Archbishop of Saint Andrews, whom I present as my surety in the premisses, and the remanent visitors, I beseech God to bless your most excellent person, estate, and progeny ever more, and am,

"Your Majesty's most humble servand and devoted orator,
"Mr. ROBERT HOWEY.

"Edinburgh, 9 of Agust, 1607."

When Mr. Howie entered upon teaching, his inferiour abilitys to his predecessor wer noture, and the subjects he chose rendered him still more and more unacceptable. To please the King and bishops, the subject he handled was the superiority of bishops over presbiters. When he had had severall discourses on that subject, his auditors professed plainly they wer rather confirmed in their former opinion than in the least shaken with his arguments. When the Presbitry of Saint Andrews heard of this, they sharply censured him. Mr. Melvil had left scholars there able to defend the truth and the doctrine he had taught; and Mr. David Dalgleish, at this time a probationer, and afterward minister at Coupar, offered both in privat to himself, and before the Presbitry, to disput that subject in publick with Mr. Howie.

At the Conference in Falkland (June, 1608), it was agreed that ther should be no publick preaching or teaching upon the heads that wer contraverted amongst ministers, but all things done that might take away heartburning, and heal the present breaches. This was the proposall of the bishops and those that joyned with them, and for peace' sake was yielded to by Mr. Simson and those on the other side. But Mr. Robert Howie made no difficulty of breaking in upon this agreement. Mr. Calderwood gives us this account of it: " In the end of June, the Earle of Dumbar came down with a great train of nobility, and severall English divines and doctors in company with him. The English doctors seem to have had no other direction but to persuade the Scots that ther was no substantiall difference in religion betwixt the two Realmss, but only in things indifferent, concerning government and ceremonies, which might stand well enough, without any danger of faith or salvation; and to show that it was His Majesty's will that England should stand as he found it, and Scotland as he left it. Severall of them came by land, and Doctor Maxie, one of the King's chaiplains, came by sea. When the English doctors came to Saint Andrews [Mr. Robert Howie], a man of a seditiouse and turbulent spirit, declaimed in his lessons against the discipline and government of the Church of Scotland. The English doctors, upon this, uttered their mind in very plain termes. This was a manifest breach of the Conference, and no order taken with it. This was the policy of the aspiring bishops to cry ' Peace! Peace!' and to crave silence from their opposites; while, in the meantime, they took all advantages as occasion proved."

Mr. Row his MS. History, gives much the same account :—" After the Meeting of Falkland, the Earle of Dumbar came down with a magnifick Commission of Lieutennandry for the north parts of Scotland. A rumor was made to go that, if the King got not his will of the Kirk, he would, by virtue of his prerogative royall, discharge all presbitrys, and assemblys. At the same time, ther came down with the Earle some English deans, as the Dean of Winchester (Doctor Abbot), who was afterwards Archbishop of Canterburry, and the Dean of Rippon, and some doctours. Their errand was to persuade all who would be persuaded by them, that ther was no difference between their Kirk in England and ours, but only some few indifferent things, and chiefly concerning the government of the Kirk, they being governed by bishops, and we by presbitrys and assemblys, and some ceremonies they used, whilk we wanted, and wer ἀδιάφορα [things indifferent]; yet they never talked openly of thir purposes till they came to Saint Andrews, and heard Mr. Robert Howie, who was now Principall of the New Colledge in Mr. A. Melvil's place. He taught in the schools, and confirmed, as well as he could, the authority and jurisdiction of bishops above ministers, for which lesson the Presbitry of Saint Andrews did sharply censure him; and a plain and full refutation of that lesson of his came out, to his great disgrace, penned by one who had been Mr. Andrew Melvil his scholar, and at this time was an auditor of Mr. Howie. Thus the King, having forgotten his covenant, in sending hither deans and doctors to tempt us, was a breakneck to many; and Doctor Howie became quickly infamous among honest men for so soon quitting his covenant, and being so opposite to his worthy and learned predecessor."

At the next Conference in Falkland, May, 1609, Mr. Howie was chosen to reason for the bishops. The account of their proceedings stands in the printed Calderwood, and I'le only set down the persons named to conferr on both sides. For the bishops—Mr. George Gladstanes, John Spotswood, Alexr. Lindsay, Alexr. Forbes, Patrick Sharp, Robert Howie, Jo. Mitchelson, Henry Philip, and George Hay. For the ministers—Mr. Patrick Galloway, John Hall, William Scot, Archibald Oswald, Jo. Knox, John Carmichael, John Weems, William Couper, and Adam Ballantine. I have observed that many, such as Mr. Galloway, Hall, Couper, and Ballantyne, who could not be depended on, wer mixed in with the rest.

In the Assembly, 1616, the Confession of Faith was presented by Mr. Hall and Adamson, and ordered to be revised by Doctor Howie, the Laird of Corse, Mr. George Hay, and Mr. William Struthers, before it wer printed.[1] In *Bishop Gladstane's Life*, we have seen that Mr. Howie, though by his station a doctor of divinity, yet was solemly created doctor of divinity by the University with some others, somtime before this. We heard also on *The Laird of Corse his Life*, that the Assembly imploy Doctor Howie, with others, to meet with the bishops and form a body of discipline and cannons. The same Assembly "appoint that a Form of Divine Service be set down to be used in churches, and that ther be a consideration of the prayers conteaned in the Psalme-Book". The Assembly do not, by any minutes of theirs I have seen, nominate the persons.

I have, on Mr. Hall, the Laird of Corse, Mr. Struthers, and others, considered what was done in consequence of this Assembly's appointments, as to a Confession of Faith and Catechismes. If I may be allowed to guess, I suppose that the pressing of Perth Articles, next year, put a stop to this appointment about a Form of Prayer and Service, because, upon the receiving the English ceremonies, it would be proper to give formes of prayer suited to those holy days and significant ceremonies. This makes me imagine that, though Mr. Howie, according to what was laid upon him, did draw up forms of prayer, yet Perth Articles, with the debates about them, put this and what this Assembly order about discipline and canons out of head; and ther was no more done about them till the 1635, when the New Book of Canons and our Scots Liturgy, framed under the direction of Archbishop Laud, wer pressed on us, and brought on the great Revolution 1637 and 8. However, I have in my hands, in MS.—and it seems an originall and first draught—a forme of service entituled "Howit's Form of Service," because I find the Doctor severall times termed in Calderwood, Doctor Howit. I at first took this to be the Doctor's draught. But when I look into the printed Calderwood, I am ready to think I am in the

[1] Note 89.

wrong, and the drawer of it is Mr. Petter Howit, Minister at Edinburgh, who was next year deposed by the High Commission for his share in the supplication to the Parliament, with Mr. Calderwood, Mr. Arch. Simson and others. The Assembly's appointment runs thus: "It is statute and ordeaned that an uniform order of Liturgie, or Divine Service, be set down to be read in all kirks on the ordinary dayes of prayer and every Sabbath before sermon, to the end that common people may be acquainted therwith, and by custome may learn to serve God right; and to that intent, the Assembly have appointed Mr. P. Galloway, Mr. Peter Howat, Mr. John Adamson, Minister at Libbertoun, Mr. Will Erskine, Minister at . . . , to revise The Book of Common Prayer conteaned in The Psalm-book, and set down a common form of ordinary service to be used at all times hereafter, which shall be used in time of common prayers in all kirks where ther is exercise of common prayers, as likewise by the minister before sermons, wher ther is no reader".

And tho' I be led to this in a mistake—of Mr. Peter Howat for the Doctor—yet, since I have no materialls for his Life, and this is a part of our Church story not so well knowen, I'll go on here to give some account of the MS. I take to be original, in my hands. It's intituled on the loose leafe *A Form of Service*, and at the end *Howat's Form of Prayers*. Its generall title is "A Form of Service to be used in all the Paroche Churches of Scotland upon the Sabbath day by the readers, wher there are any established, and wher ther are no readers, by the ministers themselves before they go to sermon". It begins with the 4th commandment; then Psalm 19, v. 14. Then ther is an exhortation to prayer, confession of sins; then the 92 Psalme to be sung; then a prayer; then the chapters to be read of course; then another prayer; next, the 89 or 103 Psalm; then the Creed to be recited; then followes the last prayer; then prayers for the King, Queen, Prince Charles, Prince Palatine, nobility and council, the clergy, schools, for the sick, in famine, in dearth, in pestilence, seed time, in harvest; then all ends with a list of prayers in the old Psalm-Book which may be yet reteaned. This Form of Service and Prayers is a curiosity, and may be of some use; and, therefor, it may stand in the App. (copy MS. 4to, v. 20, n. 11).[1]

[1] Note 90.

Only Mr. Calderwood in his MS. sayes :—"On the 15 of Jan., 1623, Mr. Robert Howie, Principall of the New Colledge, Doctor Wedderburn, and Doctor Melvil wer directed, by a letter from Doctor Young, in the King's name, to use the English Liturgy morning and evening in the New Colledge, wher all the students wer present, at morning and evening prayers, which was presently put in execution".

This same year (1623), probably, upon the conformity of the Masters to the English usages, Mr. John Murray of Lochmaben, gentleman of the King's bed chamber, gives a complement of books to the library at Saint Andrews, upon which Doctor Howie and some other of the Masters, in the name of the rest, send him a letter of thanks, which I give from the originall in the Lawyers' Library. "Right Worshipfull, please your Worship, *per* Mr. Doctor Young our most humble duty of service being commend to your Worship, [in respect] of ten pounds sterling worth of books, to be given by your Worship, to our Bibliotheck, for whilk cause we think ourselves greatumlie addebtit to your Worship, and not only we, but all those that love learning in this kingdom ; and because we are not able to requite your Worship's sa great liberality but be thankfull rememberance, we shall, God willing, make the memory of it continou sa long as this University stands, or learning continoues in this kingdome. Beside that, we shall pray to God for the continouance of your estate and weelfare ; and, if ther be anything wherin our service can be steddable to your Worship, your Worship shall have us alwise to command, as

"Your Worship's most humble and dutyfull servands,

"ROBERT HOWIE, Doctor and Rector.
"PETER BRUCE, Doctor, Dean of Faculty.
"DAVID BARCLAY, D.D., and Minister Standreis, Doctor Divinity, and
"JAMES BLAIR, Professor Ordinary therof.

"St. Andrews, Agust 28."

I know he outlived that change ; at least, have been told so, and complyed with the reformation brought in at that time. So that I suppose he lived till about the 1640 or 41. If ever I write Mr. Rutherford's Life, I'll have occasion to narrate a passage that hapned after a prayer of Mr. Howie, as the eldest Master, before the casting of a lot in the choice of a Regent, wherein Mr. Rutherford had what he took as a check from heaven to him. But the precise time of his death I know not.

Mr. Charters, in his Catalogue of Scots writters, sayes:—" Robert Howie, D.D., Professor of Theology at Saint Andrews, wrote *De Reconciliatione Hominis cum Deo; De Communione Fidelium cum Christo; De Justificatione Hominis coram Deo*, printed together at Basil, 4to, 1591. Obiit circa Anno, 1540."

Mr Wm Forbes.

COLLECTIONS ON THE LIFE OF Mr. WILLIAM FORBES, MINISTER AT ABERDEEN AND EDINBURGH, AND BISHOP OF EDINBURGH.

Mr. Forbes is celebrat for learning and piety by the writers of the Episcopall side. We shall just now see he was a person of very great passions, and violent for all the innovations that wer thrust in upon this Church. He was a great follower of Bishop Laud, and by his interest advanced to be the first Bishop at Edinburgh, upon the erecting of the new Diocess; and, I imagine, had Monsieur Baile knowen his attachments to Bishop Laud, he had not given him the encomiums he bestowes on him in his Dictionary; but, I imagine, those hints wer given to M. Baile or his bookseller by Doctor Garden, or some of our Scots Episcopall Jacobites in Holland, at the time his Dictionary was printed. Be that as it will, I would not overlook him in this Work. Some hints about him are in Calderwood's printed History, while he was minister at Edinburgh; from his MS., and Mr. Row, and severall other originall papers in my hands, I shall gather what I can concerning him.

I find nothing about his parentage, birth, and education, save what I gather from Mr. Andrew Stephens, schoolmaster at Fetteresso, his poem upon him, which shall be afterward notticed. He was born at Aberdeen, of parents that wer of no great rank,[1] if we may believe the ill-natured epitaph that follows. He was taught Latine, probably there by one Mr. Cargill, and made great progress in the languages, and especially in the Hebrew.

After he had finished his philosophicall studys, he was made Master of Arts when but 16 years of age, and such was his reputation for learning, that that very year he was chosen Regent, and caryed through a class of scholars 4 years, till they ended their philosophicall

[1] Note 91.

[course], with very much applause. He was a zealouse defender of Aristotle's method against Ramus and his followers. When he had taught 4 years, he chose to accomplish himself in all branches of literature by forraigne travail and conversation with learned men abroad. He was the next four years of his life mostly in the Universitys of Germany, wher he made great progress in Theology and the Hebrew Tongue. From Germany he came down to Leyden, wher he stayed some time, and was much esteemed by the learned men in Holland. There, I doubt, he got his first tincture of Arminianisme. The ill state of his health hindered him from making a tour to France and Italy, as he designed; and obliged him to think of coming home and returning by England. Such was his reputation for learning, that the University of Oxford did him the honnour of making him an offer [of] the Professorship of Hebrew there. His physicians wer of opinion that his health required his going to his native air.

And after his return, he was first minister at Alford, probably after that people had lost all hopes of receiving back again their exiled minister, Mr. John Forbes, whose Life stands in this work. From that he was taken to the parish of Monymusk, and from that transported to the town of Aberdeen, wher he graduat Doctor in Divinity, and was Rector in the Colledge, and was very usefull in enlarging and bettering the fabrick. I want the dates of those different changes in his pastorall work. From Aberdeen he was transported to Edinburgh, and from that to Aberdeen; and, at last, came back to Edinburgh as their bishop. So many changes in a minister, unles his aimes be single and straight, are no great commendation, in my poor opinion.

Monsr. Bayle in his Dictionary sayes that, "Such was his estimation for learning and knowledge, that Mr. Forbes got not leave to stay in Alford. He was called into Aberdeen, wher he acquitted himself as a true minister of the Gospell ought to do. There he was created Doctor in Divinity, I suppose, about the 1616." Mr. Bayle sayes:—"The labours of his office and his fervent preaching much weakned his health; and, therfor, as what was less toylsome, he was made Principall of the Marischal Colledge in Aberdeen, wher he had 3 publick lessons a week, according to the Statutes, and was chosen first Dean of Faculty, and afterwards Rector of that Colledge".

He was minister at Aberdeen, in the year 1622, when called thence to Edinburgh. He was pitched upon by the bishops as a fit man for the town of Edinburgh to push on conformity with the Articles of Perth now, when the inhabitants and ministers wer in a considerable flame upon the pressing of those ceremonies, the Session generally dissenting, and the Magistrates and Councill, at present under intire subjection to the bishops, consenting. Mr. Calderwood in his MS. takes nottice of the irregularity, and forced nature of his election to Edinburgh. In the beginning of December, 1621, the Magistrates, old and new Council, with the old and new Sessions, conveened to chuse a minister, as I take it, in Mr. John Hall's room, from the lites which had been formerly agreed upon. Upon the lites wer two Conformists, Ministers—Mr. Theodore Hay and Mr. James Leighton, and two not so favourable to the course of conformity—Mr. Andrew Cant and Mr. William Arthure. The plurality chose Mr. Andrew Cant after he and the rest had been heard severall times. This was displeasing to the Bishop of Saint Andrews, and, consequently, the Magistrates would not go in to it. Upon the 12 of December, David Aikenhead, Provost, conveened the old and new Council, and obteaned all their consents to call Mr. William Forbes, Minister at Aberdeen, recommended by the Primat, but never heard by the town, only 7 or 8 disagreeing. The day following, the Provost named Mr. Forbes to the Session of the Kirk, and desired them to consider upon the proposall. The Magistrates met privatly after the Session, and agreed that warning should be given next Sabbath by the ministers to the old and new Councill, and the old and new Sessions to meet and form new lites. The ministers gave warning accordingly. Mr. Galloway, in great anger, beat upon the pulpit, and said a few fantasticall persons hindered the calling of a minister, who would have none but men after their own humors, such as will preach against the King and the Assembly. And Mr. Thomas Sydserf seconded him. Nixt Thursday, on the 18 of December, they met, and [the] Provost proposed Mr. Forbes, saying—"Let us chuse one that can be had". Many withstood, but the Magistrates and Ministers prevailed by votes. No one wer allowed to vote but the members of Councill and Session. The other side alledged an honest man, Mr. A. Cant, was already chosen ; if the Bishop and Magistrates and Ministers would impose another, they protested he was not their choice ; and, as for Mr Forbes, they had not heard him preach. The plurality of votes in Council and Session was thought enough, though ther were present 200 citizens, who wer not admitted to vote as was alwise done in elections formerly, and they wer against Mr. Forbes. Dec. 21, John M'Naught and William Nimmo wer sent from the Council to invite Doctor Forbes to come to them in all hast. This is Mr. Calderwood's account.

In another MS. Collection, from the 1589-1641, I find this account of Mr. Forbes' election: "Upon the 18 of December, 1621, ther was a great meeting in the Little Kirk of the Provost, Baileys, old and new Sessions, and a great number of the honest neighbours, for electing another minister in room of Mr. Cant, whom the Bishop of Saint Andrews had showin could not be received. The Provost had beforehand so plotted the matter, as to prevail with the most part of Councill and Session to elect Mr. William Forbes, minister beside Aberdeen, without hearing or leeting, according to the usual order; and, albiet the body of the honest men, who wer conveened to the number of 2 or 3 hundred, and a great many of the Council and Session dissented, the said Mr. Forbes was chosen. The inhabitants' votes wer still sought at former elections, but now they wer not allowed to vote. This was to the great discontent of all the good people of the town, and with such murmuring as was marveilouse to hear."

Doctor Forbes, being thus invited, came to Edinburgh and preached, Jan. 13, 1622. His text was Rom. 14, v. 17. He affirmed confidently that the ceremonies wer matter of moonshine: that the King might command them, and ought to be obeyed. He was advised by the rest of the ministers not to be over vehement in defence of the ceremonies at his first entry, and, upon Teusday next, he tempered matters a little in his next sermon. Mr. Calderwood adds that, on Thursday, the 21 of March, the Bishop of Saint Andrews preached, and received him minister at Edinburgh. The Provost, Magistrates, Bishop and Ministers after sermon went to a banquet prepared for them, and sat so long that the Session could not meet that day for discipline. But the godly had sorrowfull hearts, both for the form of his entry and his corrupt disposition, which was not long concealed, but burst forth from time to time with such bitternes and fury that he fostered the malcontentment of the better sort; but in time he wearied, and went from Edinburgh in as unorderly a manner as he came to it.

Upon the 28 of Aprile, 1623, Mr. Forbes, preaching upon Phil. 2, inveighed against those that would not communicat with their ministers that kneeled. He said they refused their own salvation, served the Antichrist, and should never get Christ; that they wer ignorants, and had ignorant teachers, whom they received in their houses; and did write and instruct them, that none wer so bold and pert as those who least could defend what they did affirm; that none could instruct the auditory so well as he and his bretheren; that kneeling at the receiving of the Sacramentall Elements hath been received since the dayes of the Primitive Kirk; that all who teach the contrair would be scourged out of all schools of learning for ignorance and want of learning. And yet the braggadoceo never set pen to paper for defence of the contraverted ceremonies, and at disputing he was soon put to silence: he had nothing at this time but bitter railing and naked assertions without proofes. While other ministers wer much silent now, as ashamed of their conformity, under the prospect of the danger to the whole Reformation from the Popish match of our prince with Spain[1], Mr. Forbes —more Popishly disposed, if not altogether so, than the rest of his collegues—he would not conform with the rest, nor let the ceremonies vanish away. Thus Mr. Calderwood sets down this matter. The author of the Collections just now cited—one who lived in Edinburgh, as I guess by many things he narrates peculiar to that town, and probably Mr. Forbes' hearer—sayes: " Upon the penult of April, being Teusday, Mr. William Forbes preached on Phil. 2, wher Paul was purposed to send to the Phillipians their own pastor, Epaphroditus, for their comfort, because they wer troubled with enimies without and within. Upon this, he said this Kirk was troubled with Papists without, and unskilful and ignorant men in the ministry, who carryed away the people and filled them with wind, in so far that they stood at kneeling in communicating, wheras standing or kneeling wer but trifles. He called those ministers ignorants, adding that, Papists now being rising, if learned men and Jesuits came among us, they would draw us away and make a nose of wax of us; that those ministers would be mocked and whipped out of the schools. He found great fault with the people that went out of Edinburgh and communicat at other kirks sitting. He said that, because they communicat not with their own pastors, they

[1] Note 92.

did not communicat at Christ's table. Yet in this, his sermon, he never offered to clear the matter of sitting, but only uttered those assertions."

Mr. Row sayes that before the Communion in Edinburgh, 1624, at the meeting which ordinarly they had in session for removing of differences—when the Session, upon the minister's removall, gave their opinion as to their minister's life and doctrine—when Mr. Forbes went out, some of the session gave in against him some points smelling of Arminian and Popish doctrine, adding, "Those things do not agree with our Catechisme and Confession of Faith, and we desire our minister to explain himself and clear us in those particulars, all which he uttered in publick". When he came in, all the explication, clearing and contentment he gave, was railing and upbraiding them as going beyond their line. After that, adds Mr. Row, the ministers of Edinburgh had no more meetings of that kind.

Mr. Calderwood gave a larger account of this matter. Upon Teusday, the 23 of March, the Magistrates, Council, and Sessions met according to the customs in Edinburgh since the Reformation, and the Ministers removed themselves willingly to see if any had anything to observe against their life and doctrine, that they might utter their minds the more freely. The Provost caused Mr. John Hay, clerk, ask if any man had anything to object against their Minister's life, doctrine, or conversation, before the Communion. After he had asked once or twice, John Dickson, merchant, asked liberty of the Provost to speak, and he granted it, on which John said, ' My lord, my speech is against one of our pastors, whom I wish no more evil to than my own soul. There soundeth an uncouth voice in our pulpit, which we never heard before. Mr. Forbes affirms in his doctrine, that we and the Papists may be easily reconciled in many of the points contraverted betwixt us and them. This is contrary to the doctrine we have been taught, and to that [of] Mr. Struthers, to witt, that ther can be no agreement 'twixt us and the Papists, more than betwixt light and darkness, betwixt Christ and Beliall, between the Kirk of God and idols. My lord, this would [need] be taken heed to.' John Fleming added, that Mr. Forbes said that Papists and Protestants might be easily reconciled, especially in the head of Justification. When the Ministers came in, at the Session's desire, without Mr. Forbes, the case was stated, and the Ministers' advice desired what to do in it. They made a common cause of it, and said they wer no judges of their doctrine, and they removed willingly out of custome, but would not subject to their judgment. The printed Calderwood gives a full account of what passed, and the complaint the Ministers made to the King, and the examination of the objectors against Mr. Forbes by a committy of the Counsell, and what followed, and so I do not insert it here, only I'll give what past upon Thursday, the 25 of Aprile, at the next session, from an originall paper in my hand, written by one of the elders that heard what passed; and it's a sad instance of the height and violence [that] unbridled passion may lead a man otherwise of learning and sense to. The paper runs, " Edinburgh, Thursday, March 25th, 1624, by Mr. William Forbes, in the Session of the Kirk of Edinburgh, sa meikle as I remember. The occasion was this: It was proponned by the Moderator, that the elders and deacons should attend and wait on about the celebration of the Lord's Supper, and for the mair security their names wer desired to be read. And because, at the first reading of them, they thought ther was not a sufficient number to serve the turn, it was ordered that they should be everyone in particular called upon again, that the Ministers might not be disappointed. And because a number refused, Doctor Forbes denounced great judgments and threatnings of the vengeance of God that should light upon the refusers for their contempt and disobedience, and in particular, he spake to those persons following. He said to John Dickson, that he wanted wit and should be catechized; and the 2nd time, he said to him, he was a vagarer, an ignorant, and got over-much liberty to censure the doctrine of his pastors, and that he must be catechized. John said, Mr. Forbes should remember the love that he spake of in his sermon, that day. But he said again (Mr. Forbes), ' Love and knowledge! man, ye must be catechized'. Further, he said to James Nairn, that he must be catechized, for he was an ignorant, and the 2nd time, he called him a recusant, and should be punished; he was but a bairn, though he had hair on his face, and therfor he must be catechized. He said to John Smith, he was but a bairn, and should be catechized, and he said to him the 2nd time, he was but a bairn, and should not speak, but should be catechized. He said to Bailzie William Rig, he was a debauched vagarer, and he should be catechized. The Bailzie said he had been catechized by very honest, learned, worthy men, of whom, some wer with the Lord, and some wer alive yet. The Doctor, in great rage, as he was in all the time, said he was learneder than they, and would catechize them that catechized him, they wer but mercenary men and pensioners, and bad the Bailey bring out his Gamaliell, and produce him if he wer in his house, that we may see him. The Bailzie said, they were freer of those imputations than himself. The Doctor used many irreverent, reproachfull, mislearned, taunting and scornfull words, as, O! Mr. Bailzie, O! Mr. Rigg, O! Mr. Bailey, ye are a great magistrat, O! a great clerk! In end he bad all come; 'Come,' said he, 'all down to me to Magdalen Chappell, that I catechize you'. All this he delivered, with intollerable rage and choler, like one bereaved of his wit. He said they should all smart for it." They did so; as witness— they wer warded, confyned, declared uncapable of their offices in town, prodigiouse fines of 50,000^d merks threatned, and otherwise dreadfully harassed; and the Ministers wer by all charged as the unrelenting causes of this heavy persecution, as may be seen in the printed Calderwood. King James' death next year, put a stope to this rigour, and Mr. Forbes was so much misliked, that soon after he left Edinburgh.

The writer of the forsaid Collections tells us that, "Upon the 23 of March, 1625, Mr. Forbes, preaching the 1 Epist. John, 3 chapter, fell upon the love of the brethren, and how every one should love another, and that a calumniator is a murderer. Thence he took occasion to reprove so vehemently some ministers deprived by the High Commission, especially one whom he said he would not name, but all understood that he meaned Mr. David Calderwood, an excellent, learned man, now out of the country, who had written diverse learned and godly treatises, for the confirmation of the discipline of this Kirk, before the ceremonies came in, as also against them. On the word calumniator, Mr. Forbes calumniat Mr. Calderwood and his writings; he avowed him with great vehemency to be a calumniator; that his writings had neither piety or learning in them; that he perverted both the Scripture, antiquity, and the Fathers, quoting them as falsely as the Devil. This uncharitable censure upon a minister made his auditory admire his inmodesty. He vehemently pressed his hearers to look on all that man's writings as calumnies; and yet pretended not to give one single instance, but builded all on his own single assertion. At the same time, he commended some Jesuits highly for learning, to the offence of many."

At Michaelmass, 1626, Mr. Forbes gave over his ministry in Edinburgh, and went back to Aberdeen with his wife and family. All the arguments the Magistrates could use did not prevail with him to stay. He was despised at Edinburgh because of his violence and passion. His auditory still lessened, and it was very thin, and this he could not easily bear.

I have nothing concerning Mr. Forbes while at Aberdeen. I have a paper which I take to be his, which was once in Mr. Calderwood's hands, and is quoted on the back, *Forbes on Apparell*. It may, perhaps, be Doctor John Forbes of Corse, his father probably being dead before anything cast up in Scotland upon habites and ministers' apparell, at least, that I have observed. When the King came down to be crowned at Edinburgh, 1633, the violent conformists, Mr. Mitchel and Mr. Sidserfe, I see changed their apparell in preaching, and conformed themselves to the English mode to ingratiate themselves with Bishop Laud and the King. Indeed, in King James' time, about the 1616, ther was orders came down, about the bishopes' apparell, and that of the Lords of Session, and others; if this paper was writt then, it's probably Mr. Patrick Forbes of Corse his writing. But I do not find any debates then about ministers' apparel, and therefore I guess it rather to be writt about the 1633, by Mr. William Forbes. However, I thought it was worth preserving, and it stands App. N (copy MS., fol. 44 n 17).[1] It's writt at the desire of some bishop, and conteans remarks upon Mr. Henry Bullinger's answers to the questions of the English pastors, as to ministers' habit and apparell in their administration.

I come forward to the last stage of Dr. Forbes' life, as Bishop of Edinburgh, which, though but short, yet conteans some pretty remarkable passages, which, for anything I know, have not been published, and, therfor, I'll give them at the greater length from Mr. John Row his MS. History, and the above mentioned Collections. And when the King was in Scotland, summer, 1633, Doctor William Laud, Bishop of London, and very soon Archbishop of Canterbury, came down with him, and was close by him his great adviser, while in Scotland. It was agreed upon, as is generally thought, at the motion of Bishop Laud, that Edinburgh should be erected into a Bishop's See,

---

[1] This paper appears to have been lost.

(as Mr. Row thinks in imitation of his own), [the] Bishoprick of Edinburgh. I'll transcribe Mr. Row's words, which contean a black, but I fear too true character of Bishop Laud, and some passages about him while in Scotland, that are not much knowen. " Soon after the King's return to England, Bishop Abbot dyed, and Bishop Laud succeeded him in the See of Canterbury. If ye part Bishop Laud's religion in four, two parts will be found Arminian, a third part Popery, and scarce a fourth part Protestant. Being in Scotland with the King, when he was made burgess in Saint Johnstoun he refused to swear to defend the true Protestant religion, as is their constant custome there to exact of such as they admit burgesses; and shifted it with this, 'It's my part rather to exact from you ane oath for religion, than yours to exact it of me'. When he was in the kirk of Dumblain, and looking at it, he said it was a goodly church. ' Yes, my Lord,' said one standing by, ' this was a brave kirk before the Reformation.' ' What, fellow?' said the Bishop; 'call it Deformation, not Reformation,' reconing the demolishing and casting down of some kirks and abbacys, a greater evil than the pure preaching of the gospell was a good. Any man may think it ominous that the Bishop of Canterbury, *alterius orbis papa*, his name VVILL. LaVD is just 666, the number of the name of the Beast, Rev. 13, 17, 18. This Popish, Arminian, Protestant Bishop made great changes and alterations both in Scotland and England. In England, conformity was more urged than before, which made sundry ministers and others, good professors, to leave England, and to go to New England in America; and in Scotland, whoever would be at preferment, behoved to vent in public some Popish or Arminian doctrine, else no preferment for him. So Bishop Laud ruled the King fully; so that he was in effect Primat, Patriarch, or Cardinall, call it what ye will, of all Brittain and Ireland. In the end of this year, the King sent down a charge to the Magistrates of Edinburgh, to cast down the partition wall of Saint Geils-Kirk, which divided the Great Kirk from the Litle one, and had been built 50 years ago, that the Kirk of Edinburgh might be one, fair, spacious, Cathedral kirk (Antichristian bishops had a great care of all gorgeouse outwards, but unpreaching prelates wer never carefull to fitt Kirks for hearing the word of God), because the King at Laud's suggestion was now to erect a Bishoprick in Edinburgh, as many thought, in imitation of London, which had its own Bishop."

Upon the first of December, those nominated by the King to be the Chapter of the Bishoprick of Edinburgh met there, and having read the King's letter recommending to them Mr. William Forbes, lately Minister of Edinburgh, and now Minister of Aberdeen to be chosen, they elected him their Bishop, and agreed upon the time of his consecration, which election, sayes the writter of the Collections, was esteemed in the judgement of all judicious men, to be a strange novation, especially the same not being done by any Act of Parliament, as matters of that importance ought to have been done, and ever used, yea, [of] things of far less importance. Mr. Row observes that this was reconed a great innovation, ther not being a Bishop in Edinburgh even in the time of Popery.

Upon the 17 of December, the Doctor came to Leith, and next day, to Canongate, wher he lodged. Many went to wait on him, and next day, the Magistrates went in a body and welcomed him. This was displeasing to many of the better sort, considering that so laitly he had been one of their ministers, and left town without their allowance, and [in] discontentment at the Magistrates and people.

Upon Teusday, January 28, 1634, he was consecrat and received Bishop of Edinburgh in the Chappell of Halliroodhouse. The Bishop of Dunblain preached the sermon; and [there] were assisting at the consecration the Bishops of Saint Andrews, Murray, Ross, Brichen, Glasgow, Galloway, and Dunblain. After all the ceremonies of that action wer over, the Magistrates, officers of State, ministers of the town and others wer at a large dinner and feast prepared for them. The Bishop had his first sermon in the New Kirk at Edinburgh, lately much enlarged. But the Bishop being sickly and his voice weak, scarce a hundred of all the hundreds present heard him.

Upon Wensday, the 19 of February following, Mr. Thomas Sidserf, one of the ministers of Edinburgh was consecrat, received, and admitted Dean of Edinburgh. Mr. Alexander Thomson, one of the ministers of the town preached a sermon, and the Bishop gave the Dean many admonitions concerning the charge given unto him. All was done in presence of the Magistrates, several other bishops, and a numerous company of spectators. After the solemnity was over, the Bishop, Mr. Sidserfe and many others wer feasted by the Magistrates.

In March following, the time of giving the Communion drew near, and this new Bishop resolved to shew the great zeal for conformity to the ceremonies now for some time in the Church. But the observation of them had not been so violently urged in Edinburgh and round about as once it was. Upon the 5th of March, he wrote a letter to the Presbitry of Edinburgh, and all the other presbitrys within his Diocess, full of threats and boasting, and imperiousely enough urging all the bretheren he now reputed to be under his Dioces to strict conformity to the order established. It was delivered to the Presbitry of Edinburgh, March 5, and it runs thus:

"BELOVED BRETHEREN,—It is not unknowen to you what evil effects this long continoued schisme brings forth in our Kirk. All good Christians among us are touched therwith, and so they should. But none more than you, whose calling in particular is to keep Christ's Body from renting, and to build up the breaches therof. Herefor, I desire you earnestly to think upon all good means for bringing back our peace; and, being persuaded that, for the present, one of the most powerfull means will be your conformity in your own persons to the laudable Acts of our Church, in giving the Sacraments, I require you by thir presents, that ye all, who are the Bretheren of the Exercise of Edinburgh, fail not to give the Communion, this next ensuing Pasch day (which will be the 6th of Aprile), every one of you in your own churches, and that you take it yourselves upon your knees, giving so good an example to the people; and likewise that ye minister the Elements out of your own hands to everyone of your own flocks. I have desired the Moderator to cause you to signify your consent by write hereunto in a paper, which he shall present to you, that you put your names thereunto, and report me answer within 14 days; certifying you, that such whose names I find not in the write, I will take them as refusers to conform, and maintainers of our schisme, against whom I will be forced to proceed with ecclesiasticall censures, seing both you have had so long time to inform yourselves, and also many of you are bound to conformity by your own promise and oath at your entry to the ministry. I desire you likewise, whenever you administer the Sacraments after this, to admitt none to it but those of your own parishes, for the want of which ther has been great profanation of this Holy Mystery; and for this cause I have willed you to give it altogether at one time; and I pray you see to this, for the breach of it I account as worthy of censure as the other;

and, last of all, I require you to preach of Jesus Christ His Passion for our Redemption upon the Friday before Pasch, and that according to the Canon of our Church. So expecting your answer, I committ you to God's best blessing, and rest,

"GUL. EDINBURGEN.

" From Hallirood House, this morning."

Mr. Row makes the following remarks upon this letter :—" In this letter observe, all that adheres to the covenant and oath of God, and who will not perjure themselves by apostatizing with perjured prelats, are separatists, schismaticks, mentainers of a schisme, enimies to the peace of the Kirk. Three men entered into an oath and covenant to go to London by the high road, and not to quitt that way either for terror or alurement. Yet shortly, two of the three, hearing of some gain to be had at a market, leave the high road way, forgets their oath, forgets their covenant, mocks and nicknames the 3d man, who would not for any gain quit the remembrance of his oath and covenant. It is applyed already. Next observe, the Bishop buries the memory of Presbitry, having set up Prelacy in its room, and only termes them the Bretheren of the Exercise. And, lastly, ye see how tyrannicall and imperiouse is this late Lord Bishop, boasting [threatening] men if they will not consent to perjure themselves."

This letter was sent to all the other presbyterys of the Diocess as well as that of Edinburgh. In the Presbitry of Edinburgh itself, ther wer but a few gave their consent. The form of their consent deserves to be preserved, with the names of the subscribers and it followes ;—

" The within written letter being produced from the Right Reverend Father in God, William, Bishop of Edinburgh, we, the bretheren of the Presbitry thereof under subscrib, and oblidge ourselves, and promises to obey the whole contents of the said letter, by thir presents subscribed by our hands at Edinburgh, March, 1634, as after followes.

" James Hanna	David Mitchel	Thomas Sydserfe
" William Myrton	James Fairly	Andrew Ramsay
" John Adamson	William Wishcart	Alexander Thomson
		Henry Rollock."

Very soon after this letter came to be knowen, ther was a counter letter and admonition, to counter the Bishop's letter, written by a very good hand, and spread through all the presbitrys in the Synod. Whither this helped subscription in the termes of the Bishop's letter, I know not; it's [not] probable it would, for it's penned in a very strong and homely way. The copy of this Admonition deserves to be preserved here, and it's addressed "To my revered Bretheren of the Ministry within this new Dioces," and it followes:

"Ye are not ignorant, dear bretheren, that this new Dioces is not as yet erected by authority of Parliament, or consent of the General Assembly, or people of the Diocis, as also that our new Chapter had no power to elect any bishop at all. Beside that, all elections by chapters of bishops is discharged by Act of Assembly, 1578, under pain of perpetuall deprivation. A Form of Election was agreed upon, anno 1600, for electing a minister votter in Parliament, whether he was to be stiled Bishop, Abbot, or Prior, which is not observed; but none, either by chapter or otherwise, at that time or since, to the office of a consecrated Bishop. Therfor, howsoever our new chapter-men conveened, and observed an inauguratory form of election, or rather, consented to the receiving of Mr. Forbes, yet their presumptous usurpation is of no force to bring them under his subjection in any case whatsomever. Therfor, you wrong yourselves, and make light account of the libertys of the Kirk, if ye acknowledge him. As much may be said of the rest of his fellowes, but that the Parliament hath established their election by chapters, which is not sufficient, it being done without consent of the General Assembly, yea, contrary to their Act, and unto an office never allowed by our Kirk, since it was damned. We ought to have a respect to the Acts of the Kirk in ecclesiasticall matters, more than to Acts of Parliament made without their consent, yea, contrary to their determination. Ye know the bounds of the power granted by the Act of Glasgow, to the bishop votter in Parliament, and only upon assurance that he shall be lyable to the censure of ordinary and set Generall Assemblyes; which failing, their limited power faileth also. What power hath he by that Act? or whence otherwise lawfully, to send directions to presbitrys, or to urge ministers with subscriptions? What need ye then to subscribe? If ye will be so servile as to acknowledge him your Ordinary, notwithstanding of the just exceptions ye see ye have against his entry; yet why will ye yield to him more than he can claime by the Act of that same pretended Assembly? He cannot depose any supposed delinquent without associating to himself the ministers of the bounds where the delinquent serveth, that is, without associating to himself the presbitry where the delinquent serveth, according to the meaning of that pretended Assembly, forbearing the terme *presbitry*, only because it was alledged that it would offend the King. Who supposes the presbitry wer so perversly set as to assist him to the rigor? Yet ye cannot be found delinquents for not celebrating the Communion kneeling; for the Act of Perth is conceived *per modum consilii* non *per modum præcepti*, as the pretended bishops themselves acknowledged in a conference with some ministers at Saint Andrews, anno 1619. The Act of Parliament, it's true, ratifyed that Act with a sanction of civil pain, which was a wrong, yet what have they to do with the execution of any Act of Parliament, especially such as exceed to bounds of ratification? If you subscribe, ye quitt all those defences which ye might use in case he would proceed against you, and do nowise rely on God's providence. What know ye but he may be shott to death before he execute any sentence. If ye be cited before the Holy Commission, and other bishops assist him, ye know that court is not authorized by Parliament; and further, that you are discharged by an Act made May, 1584, to obey or acknowledge any jurisdiction and judgment, not authorized by the King and the Estates. Will ye use no defences, though never so relevant, because you think it will not avail? Then ye wrong the cause, ye cover their tyranny, and harden them in their usurpation. Consider how hainouse a sin it is, to bring in that abomination in your congregations, wher the worship of God hath been preserved in purity ever since the Reformation. Consider further, that the urger is Popish, and under pretence of conformity and obedience to an Act of pretended Assembly, (howbeit he hath entered himself without any regard to Act of any Assembly), he seeketh to be avenged upon all orthodox and sound preachers and professors, and aimeth at further than obedience to some Acts of pretended Assemblys. Ye may perceive wher the present course doth tend. The Lord give you hearts to call instantly and sincerely for wisdom and courage, and hearts to encourage others.

"Your brother in Christ.

"' Facile est vincere non repugnantes.'"

We may easily think this letter and advertisement, full of plain facts and strong reasonings, would very much, when spread among the ministers, mar the influence of the Bishop's letter, however positive and blustering it is; and Mr. Row tells us that, "At this time ther was an admonition penned to warn this new bishop not to be so violent in his courses, and the brethren of the presbitryes, not to yield to any corruption, proving by many good reasons, that they would hurt their own consciences if they did so, and after many reasons the writer asks them, why should ye fear a mortall man? What can ye tell but he may [be] shoot to dead before he can get any of those wicked designes accomplished?" I make litle doubt but Mr. Row has the paper just now insert in his view. Accordingly, in other presbitrys, (we have seen what passed in Edinburgh), there were few or none who subscribed. Some of them answered both wisely and modestly that they could not conform, and gave in their reasons for their refusall. Some excepted against Mr. Forbes as not being their ordinary Bishop, and therfor said they would answer their ordinary Bishop; others took the matter to advisement, and some few utterly refused to conform; neither thought they it expedient or advantagious to the cause of God to take the matter to advisement.

The Presbitry of Dunce in the Merse sent a very positive refusall to the Bishop, and ordered their Moderator, Mr. David Hume, Minister at Greenlaw, their Moderator for the time, to return an answer in their name, and to denounce the Lord's wrath, as coming certainly upon him, if he should insist in such a vehement manner, to urge the Bretheren of the ministry to do anything in the work of God, wherein they had no warrand from God's Word; and that they could not be answerable to God, in a good conscience, to do that wherof they wer sufficiently informed of the contrary's being their duty, and the Bishop's death following after this peremtory denountiation of hasty vengeance upon him, was the more observed by many.

When Pasch came, at which his Diociss should have given proofes of their conformity, the Bishop himself, being very tender and sickly, would go out and give the Communion on that solemn festivall. But he was so unmeet for anything of that nature, that he was not able without help to put the cup to his own mouth. After he had served two tables, he turned so sick that he behoved to be helped out of the kirk, and went home and took his bed, and for anything I can observe, never came to the street again. The writter of the Observations nottices that the Bishop, when in the church, observed the people not so ready to communicat kneeling, as he looked for, said that if he lived, he should make the best of them who refused kneeling to yield, and be content to do so, or then he should quitt his gown; and soe he did, and his life also, and got not this done as he desired.

He was very tender for some weeks before, but neither he nor others apprehended his death to be so near as it was, though he was told by persons of skill that it was near; and, on Saturnday next, about 11 of the clock at night, he departed this life, being the 12th of Aprile. Mr. Row observes that he enjoyed the sweet fruites of that new coyned dignity, which his brother Bishop, Mr. Cowper, of Galloway, said never grew on the Tree of Life, only but two moneths and a half. Next day, being Sabbath, was the last Sunday of the Pasch Communion at Edinburgh, and through the country, from which the Bishop got so much obedience to his injunctions, the Sacrament was dispensed. The Dean of Edinburgh, Mr. Sidserf, and others who favoured the Bishop, wer wonderfully greived at his death. The Dean regrated the loss from the pulpit, and said one of the greatest lights in Scotland was removed; but, for that time, he said he would not enlarge on his learning, life and conversation. The Bishop had got medicine that day he dyed, but was not able to keep it; the weaknes of his stomach brought him to a violent vomiting, and soon after he dyed. Many of the better sort, sayes the writer of the Collections, said God was not content with the doings of the bishops and their followers. They wished them eyes to perceive so much, and leave off their course as troubling people upon thir matters; seeing the Bishop had brucked that place so short a time, to which he came so unorderly, and was taken away to eternity even before that Communion was quite over.

Upon Wensday, the 23 of Aprile, Mr. Sydserf preached his funerall sermon from John 5, 35, 36. Mr. Row sayes he therin extolled the Bishop above John the Baptist, and compared him to Christ in several things. The writter of the Collections sayes he commended his piety and learning; he preffered him to all of the clergy in this land, formerly or now living; he called him the bright star of Israel, and compleaned heavily of the loss susteaned by his death. When he compared the light of John the Baptist with the Bishop, he observed the Bishop continoued for longer a light than John, and was not only the offerer of the Oblation, but the Oblation itself—meaning his dying in the time of the Sacrament, which expression not only raised discontent, but many said it was blasphemy, and derogatory to Christ, the only Oblation. The Dean also termed Mr. Forbes the *Great Bishop*, so that the Bishops of Saint Andrews and Dumblane, who were present, could not forbear checking Mr. Sidserf disdainfully after sermon; and spoke to severals in privat, shewing their displeasure with his discourse. After sermon, the Bishop was burryed in Saint Giles Kirk, Edinburgh, at the East end therof, which was lately called The [Little] Kirk till the downtaking of the wall, which divided the Litle Kirk and the Great Kirk, at the back, wher the pulpit stood, in the Litle Kirk, betwixt and the East wall. He was burryed with no great pomp, the Magistrates, Ministers, inhabitants, some of the nobility, the Bishop of Saint Andrews, with some two or three more bishops [attending].

Mr. Row gives him this character: " If Mr. Forbes had left in legacy a confession of his faith, ye would have seen a strange miscellaneous farrago and hotch potch of Popery, Arminianisme, Lutheranisme, and what not. Mr. John Maxwell, Sydserf, and Mitchell wer never heard to utter any unsound doctrine and heterodoxy, except in relation to Prelacy and ceremonies, till Doctor Forbes came to Edinburgh. But then it was taught, *that the Pope is not Antichrist ;—that a Papist living and dying such may be saved ;—that Christ descended locally into hell ;—that he dyed for all intentionally, to redeem all ;—that ther is an universall Grace ;—that the same may fall from grace finally aud totally ;—that Christ is realy present in the Sacrament, verbum audimus, motum sentimus, modum nesciumus, tho' as yet they would not as yet speak out either consubstantiation or transubstantiation ;—that in honorem sacerdotii, a minister may medle with secular affairs, be upon Parliament, Court Council, Session, Exchecker, Commission &c ;—that ministers' doctrine should not be examined by the people ; but seeing they watch for their souls, as those that must give account, the people should believe what they preach to them ;* and those points, and many more have we heard with our ears preached in that most eminent watch tower of this Kirk. Mr. Sydserf thought to have succeeded him; but Mr. David Lindsay, Bishop of Brechin, was nominat."

He was generally disliked, and some of that sort wrote this for his epitaph.

" Here lyes Bishop Forbes who never did good,
A degenerat gentleman of no great blood,
A traitor to Christ and souldier of Rome,
Here lyes his corpse till the day of doom."

Upon the other hand, he was as much extolled by his friends, as we have in part seen. Ther is in my hands, and it looks like the originall, at least it's very carefully written, a poem written by Mr. Andrew Hepburn [Stephens?], schoolmaster at Fetteresso, and dedicat to the Primat, Aprile 16, 1634, intituled " Eximii animi dotibus, et in Dei vinea cultoris fidelis, Domini Gulielmi Forbesii, Edinburgeni Episcopi VITA". It's not long and seems not an ill Latine poem. How true, I leave to other, and so I'll insert it in the Appendix N (copy 4to, v. 20, n. 6).[1]

Mr. Charters in his List sayes, " Mr. William Forbes, Minister at Aberdeen, thereafter at Edinburgh, and first Bishop there, was a very learned man. Scripsit Considerationes Pacificas et Modestas de Iustificatione, Invocatione Sanctorum, Christo Mediatore, Purgatorio et Eucharistia. Lond. 8vo, 1658; he inclines much to Popery." Save the remarks upon Bullenger, I have met no more of his; upon this book of his I shall bring in what I have further about him from Monsr. Bail's Dictionary.

I have not seen the Bishop's Considerationes Modestae, nor the Elenchus Vitae Gulielmi Forbesii, that is prefixed to it, and therfor I must hold myself by Monsr. Bayle's Hints from it. His Considerationes Modestae are in 8vo, and consist of 466 pages.[2] The writer of the Elenchus tells us, that the occasion of the Doctor's leaving Edinburgh, as we have seen, was the debates about Episcopacy. The Doctor taught in his sermons that bishops were above presbiters. His hearers did not believe this doctrine, being wedded to the Genevan Discipline and Constitution which made all ministers equall. Mr. Forbes mentained in his sermons modestly and solidly that the superiority of bishops is not by humane lawes only, but is founded on the Word of God, the Apostles' practise, and that of the Primitive Church. His hearers dislicked this doctrine, reproached him and charged him with Popery. This writter either knew not, or would not tell us, that he was charged

---

[1] This Poem has not been found among Wodrow's MSS.   [2] Note 93.

with Arminian doctrine, blamed for compleaning to the King of his people and other things; and his mere preaching Episcopacy would not have gone far, since it was now common. But to return to the author of the Elenchus. He adds, when Mr. Forbes perceived his labours among his flock wer turning useles, and the seed he sowed cast on barren ground, he resolved to leave that charge, and the rather that his lean and extenuated body did not agree so weel with the smoaky air of Edinburgh, and found himself in an ill state of health, he returned to Aberdeen where he was passionately desired. He preached before the King, in 1633, about the time of his coronation, with so much eloquence and learning, that all his auditory admired him, and the King was soon convinced that he could not fill his new Bishoprick of Edinburgh better than with him. Mr. Forbes' Considerationes was reprinted at Helmstadt, Anno 1704. The writter of the Elenchus gives this character of this book: "Opus hoc posthumum quod jam in lucem prodiit est pacati ingenii et moderati animi ingens specimen et indicium; in quo, tanquam alter Cassander et Catholicus Moderator, rigidas et austeras, utriusque tam Reformatae quam Pontificae partis, opiniones in quibusdam [religionis] contraversiis componere saltem mitigare satagit. Quanti moderationem fecerit, ostendens, dicto illo frequenter ab ipso usurpato, si plures fuissent Cassandri et Wicclii, non opus fuisset Luthero aut Calvino." Monsr. Bayle observes those last words will displease zelates, as being a tacit censure on Luther and Calvin. The writer of the Elenchus observes, that Doctor Forbes had writt down marginall notes and remarks upon his copy of Bellarmius Works in 4 folios. Those notes appeared so just and judicious to Doctor Barron, his successor, in the Divinity chair at Aberdeen, that he preferred them to all that had been written against the Jesuit Cardinall. He designed to have published them had not his death prevented. The writter of the Elenchus adds, "Pauca scripsit; scire enim maluit quam scribere, et hoc dicterium scripturienti cuidam, et ei magnos labores ostentanti, lepide sed solide usurpavit, 'Lege plura et scribe pauciora'". W. Bayle remarks that Mr. Forbes' counsell would have been fuller, if he had put in meditation with reading, and tells a passage concerning Monsr. Claud to a person who was a prodigiouse reader; he advised him to give over reading for 4 years or therby, and spend that time in thinking and meditation, adding, "You have eat too much, labour to digest it". Monsr. Bayle observes in the last place, that Monsr. Le Fevre, Doctor of the Sorbonne, made an ill choice of Doctor Forbes as one of his proofes that the Calvinists did not hold by the decisions of the Synod of Dort, and Monsr. Arnauld failed not to make an advantage of this. Monsr. Arnáuld, in his large book *Renversement de la Morale*, had asserted that the Indesertibility of Grace was one of the opinions of the Calvinists according to the Acts of the Synod of Dort. Monsr. Le Fevre opposeth this assertion, and asserts that the Calvinists wer at liberty in this matter, and cites severall Protestant writters, who taught that ther might be a totall and finall falling from Grace, and particularly cites Mr. Forbes. Monsr. Arnauld in his *Calvinisme convaincu de nouveau* makes his reply: " The title itself of Doctor Forbes' book might have convinced Monsr. Le Fevre that he was no wise and proper voucher to bring against what I had said. He was one of the most moderat and equitable of the Episcopall pacifick writters; and ardently wished for a union between Protestants and Catholicks, and made no difficulty to declare himself for the Catholicks against the Calvinists when he thought the Calvinists wronged them, and he thinks the Catholicks are wronged by them in most of the points he handles. For this reason, the writter of the Abstract of his Life, before his dissertations, calls him another Cassander. Doctor Forbes' friends durst not publish his dissertations till the year 1658, 20 years and more after his death; and while alive, for many years, he was reconed by the Calvinists an Arminian, and mentaining against them the Defectibility of Grace; and indeed he could not conceal his sentiments this way in his sermons, and when the Presbiterians, supported by the rebellious Parliament of England, wer ejecting Episcopacy, one of the reproaches they cast on the unhappy Archbishop of Canterburry, Laud, was that he favoured Arminianesime; and one proof they brought for this was that he advised the King to fill the bishops' sees in England with persons who had nothing else to distinguish them from others but that they were zealouse Arminians; and instanced Doctor Forbes made Bishop of Edinburgh by Laud's influence. The liberty the Doctor took to oppose the opinions of Geneva sunk the Doctor's reputation so much among the Calvinists, that, when Minister in Edinburgh before he was Bishop, the Puritans there could not bear with him, and used to call him a Papist." The reply that Monsr. Le Fevre makes, *Replique à Monsieur Arnauld*, ch. 7, was far from mending the matter; indeed it's too noture that Bishop

Forbes was no Calvinist, and, as Mr. Charters hath observed, was exceedingly favourable to the Papists.

I shall conclude with Bishop Burnet's character of Doctor Forbes in his Life of Bishop Beddell. The words are, "One of the Doctors of Aberdeen, William Forbes, was promotted by the late King when he was in Scotland, 1633, to the Bishoprick of Edinburgh, then founded by him; so that that King said on good grounds, he had found out a bishop that deserved that a see should be made for him. He was a grave and eminent divine. My father that knew him long, and, being of counsell for him in his law matters, had occasion to know him well, hath often told me that he never saw him, but he thought his heart was in heaven, and that he was never alone with him, but he felt in himself a commentary on those words of the Apostles, 'Did not our hearts burn within us while He yet talked with us, and opened to us the Scriptures.' He preached with a zeal and vehemency that made him often forget all the measures of time; two or 3 hours was no extraordinary thing for him. Those sermons wasted his strenth so fast, and his asceticall course of life was such and he supplyed it so faintly, that he dyed within a year or so after his promotion. So he only appeared there long enough to be knowen, but not long enough to do what might have been otherwise expected from so great a prelat. That litle remnant of his, which is imprint, showes how learned he was. I do not say but his earnest desire of peace and union amongst all Christians has made him too favourable to many of the corruptions of the Church of Rome; but though a charity that is not well ballanced may cary one to very indiscreet things, yet the principle from whence they flowed in him was so truely good, that the errors to which it caryed him ought either to be excused, or at least, to be very gently censured."

Since the writting what is above, I meet with an abstract of Bishop Forbes' Life and his character in Doctor Garden's Life of Mr. John Forbes of Corse, who was a great admirer of his. That I may give my readers all I find as to this first Bishop of Edinburgh, I shall translat the Doctor's account of him. "Among Mr. Forbes of Corse contemporarys was the eminent Mr. William Forbes, well knowen to the learned wordle by his posthumouse book—'*Considerationes Modestae et Pacificae Contraversiarum &c.*,' as among the learned of the first rank. His father was Thomas Forbes of Corsindae, a worthy citizen of

Aberdeen, a grandchild of the barrons of Forbes, of whom the lairds of Corse descended. His mother was full sister to Doctor James Cargill of Aberdeen also, a celebrated physician, mentioned honourably by Baulinus Lebonius, and other botannicall writters. He had his education at Aberdeen, wher he was born. When he was about 20 years, he went abroad, invisited the most eminent Protestant universitys in Germany, Holland, and England. He looked into their well furnished librarys, read the Fathers, and conversed with their learned men. After 5 years spent this way, he returned to his native country, as the bees do, when loaden with honney and wax gathered in diverse fields and flowers, return to their hive, and disburden themselves for the common benefit. So did he with strong desires to promot God's glory, the salvation of souls, and the benefite of his country. He was a presbyter in this church about 25 years, first, in the country parishes of Alford, and then of Munnimusk, in the Diocess of Aberdeen; then in Edinburgh, the capitall town, but longest in the place of his nativity, the city of Aberdeen. There for some years he was Principall of the Marischall Colledge. In the year 1633, when the King came down to be crowned, Mr. Forbes was chosen first Bishop of Edinburgh, which the King erected in a Bishoprick as a lasting monument of his piety and regard. The King on this occasion said, he had found a man worthy to have a bishoprick erected for him. He was soon taken away from the malice of the wicked: when he had not been bishop for more than 3 moneths, he fell under heavy sicknes, and sweetly fell asleep in the Lord, in the Kalends of Aprile, 1634. He was a person who might be numbered with the best primitive Christian Fathers, for his sanctity of life, humility of mind, gravity, modesty, temperance, frequent prayer and fasting, the practise of good works, care of the poor, frequent visiting the sick and comforting them, and all Christian virtues. In preaching, he was so fervent so as he ravished the minds and hearts of the hearers; [of] eminent doctrine and learning, of an elevated judgment, of such a strong memory, that it was ordinarily said, he knew not what it was to forgett anything; he was a lover of truth and peace, and consequently, after a full pondering of the moment of every contraversy, being byassed to no side, he endeavoured to compose, or at least, to mitigat differences. He deplored the lamentable state of the Christian wordle, the horrible schisms, the bitter contentions prevailing; he regretted the mutuall hatreds and reproaches of partys, not only betwixt the Reformed, but even those between the Reformed and Church of Rome so barbarously prosecuted on all hands, that, when they pretend to defend Christianity, they appear to have laid aside human nature. He blamed the leaders of each party and their contraversiall writters, that they heightened the flame, and unfairly represented the opposit doctrine, and magnified above measure the errors of such as differed from them. He frankly declared that the Bishop of Rome's tyranny, setting up to be universall Bishop, Christ's Viccar General, and the Infallible Interpreter of the, Scriptures, and his pretences to be the Church's Head and Monarch, together with his and the Romish clergy their iniquity in coining new creeds, and imposing them upon others by force and armes, as necessary to salvations—that all this was the principall cause of the schisme, and cheif impediment unto a Catholic unity and peace. In his Theologicall prelections, in the Marischall Colledge, he endeavoured to state impartially the modern contraversys, without any bias to sides, that he might bring back men to follow truth, peace, and charity, without which, no man can see God. Some of those prelections, more than 20 years after the author's death, were published under the title of 'Considerationes Modestae,' full of errors in the printing. The author hath suffered much from the most part of the Reformed writters, as having in that book he had quitt the Protestants, and gone over to the Popish doctrine; although till his death he remained in communion with the Reformed Church, and enjoyed publick holy offices among the Protestants, and he was a person much removed from all hypocrisy. In those prelections, not a few of the Romish errors are notticed and confuted, not without some warmth. The author's love to truth and peace made him ready to embrace, and openly to profess, the verity on whatever side he found it; the same principle leading him to discover errors in his freinds, especially wher hurtfull to salvation; and he did not spare what to him appeared, even in such who wer on his own side, that tended to sett opinions, even of adversarys in a wrong light, and charged them with things of consequences which they did not allowe; hence therby mutuall hatred and reproach were spread. This learned man wrot also elabourat and nervouse Animadversions upon Bellarmin's 4 tomes, of the Paris edition, in 3 volumes, and filled the margins of those, above and below, and everywher with learned animadversions. Those, his successor, Doctor R. Barron, valued so much that he preferred them to all that had been writt against Bellarmine; and had not death prevented, he resolved to have printed those animadversions. But when Doctor Barron, by the persecution of his countrymen, was forced to retire to Berwick, he dyed there, and Mr. Forbes' animadversions are lost. Certainly such egregiouse wrong Bishop Forbes, when they make him a Roman Catholic; he needs no more to vindicat him from this than his sermon befor the King at Edinburgh, 1633, which is printed, and ye abstract given by Doctor Garden."[1]

[1] Note 94.

COLLECTIONS ON THE LIFE OF Mr. CHARLES FERME OR FAIRHOLME, MINISTER, AND PROFESSOR AT FRAZERBURGH.

This holy and very learned man was one of the most burning and shining lights in his time. He was the head and only teacher of [the] little, learned Colledge, or Schola Illustris, in one of the most remot corners in Scotland. He was the first teacher of Philosophy and Divinity at Frazerburgh, and for anything I find, that nursery of learning not long at least continoued after he was torn from it by prelaticall fury. He was a great and long sufferer, confyned, and sometimes in great straites for near 10 year; he was a most pious and zealous person. It's pity I can recover so very litle about so great a man. It's only a few hints I can cast together out of Mr. John Adamson's preface to his Commentary on the Romans; a book too much neglected, and which I have heard some not ill judges reacon to have brought as much solid light to that important and difficult Epistle than many far larger commentarys have done; and some further accounts of him from Mr. Calderwood and Row's MS. Historys, and some others not printed.

Mr. Ferme, or as Mr. Calderwood, his scholar, frequently writes him Fairholme, was born at Edinburgh, in the year 1567. When he had learned his Latine at the Grammar School there, and made himself very much master of the Latine Tongue, he was so happy as to come under the instruction of the learned, pious Mr. Robert Rollock, lately set over the new erected Colledge of Edinburgh. He was one of Mr. Rollock's first scholars, and by him probably recomended to the new erected Colledge at Frazerburgh to lay the foundations of a new seminary of learning there, as Mr. Rollock did at Edinburgh. Under Mr. Rollock's inspection, he soon made himself master of the Greek grammar and the writters in that excellent language which he took a particular pleasure in. He entered to Mr. Rollock's instructions in the year 1584, and finished his Greek and Philosophy, and was graduat Master of Arts, 1587. In his own teaching he loved to follow his master, Mr. Rollock, whose method was this: after his scholars wer weel founded in the Greek, he taught them Ramus' Dialectick. This was much valued, sayes Mr. Adamson in his preface, by Mr. Rollock, as the best help young scholars could have to understand analysis and genesis; and he used to say that such who understood not Ramus, might do some small thing in composition, but could never do anything in analysis or exposition. After Ramus, he taught Galen's Retorick, Aristotle's Logicks, Physicks, and Ethicks, our countryman Sacrobesco, or Holywood de Sphera, Ursius Catechisme, some common-places in Divinity, and some short Analysis of the Apostolicall Epistles, and the rudiments of the Hebrew Tongue.

In the year 1589, Mr. Ferm gave himself wholly to the study of Divinity, and attended closely on Mr. Rollock's lessons, and made himself master of the Hebrew Tongue. The students at Edinburgh multiplying very much upon Mr. Rollock's rising reputation, the Professor saw it necessary to take in a helper, and pitched on Mr. Ferme as the meetest of his scholars to take care of the new intrants to the Colledge, while he took a general inspection of them once every day likewise; but cheifely confyned himself to take the charge of those who studyed Theology; and so in the year 1590, Mr. Ferme was made Regent to a numerouse class of students of Philosophy. Them he caryed through their studyes, and in the year 1593 he laureat them, and presided when they took their degree as Masters of Arts. After this, he taught another class, and brought them through their course of studyes with approbation. He entered upon the 3d course of teaching, but his reputation for piety and learning, and much skill in teaching, growing very much, he was pressed to enter into the holy ministry, and with that also to take the care of instructing of the youth in Frazerburgh, and complyed with ane earnest and clear call he had to that work.

Since the writting of what is above, a MS. of the learned Mr. Thomas Crawford, giving a distinct account of the Masters of the Colledge of Edinburgh, is come to my hand. From this, I am able to give a more exact and distinct account of Mr. Ferme while a member of that learned society. Here I find that, "Agust, 1587, Mr. Rollock laureat the first class in that Colledge, which had passed under his charge, after every one of them had subscribed the Covenant, among whom wer many able witts; namely, Mr. Charles Ferme, Mr. Philip Hislop, Mr. Henry Chartaris, Mr. Patrick Sands. In January, 1589, Mr. Charles Ferme, who in the disputation for the Regent's place had been declared 2d in abilitys, was elected Regent to have the charge of the next class to enter in October following. He was a man of obscure parentage. Born about Edinburgh, and brought up in Mr. Alexander Guthry (the town clerk) his family, and of good age when he entered to the Colledge; but was exceedingly piouse, industrious and learned. He was therafter called to the ministry at Frazerburgh in Buchan, where there was a beginning of ane University, over which he had the charge, and dyed ther, having been much persecut by the prelates. Agust 12, 1593, the 6th class, educat under the care of Mr. Charles Ferme was laureat 19 in number. Amongst them, John, Earle of Gourie, both defended the theses, disputed upon them, and subscribed the Covenant. In the year, 1598, Mr. James Knox was elected to succeed Mr. Charles Ferme, who then had a call to the ministry at Frazerburgh, to which he removed next winter, Mr. James succeeding to his charge."

The town of Frazerburgh lyes in the Shire of Aberdeen, and Presbitry of Deer, a place remote from education very much. It was attended with difficultys to send the youth from the Shires of Caithnes, Inverness, Murray, and Ross, to the Colledges at Aberdeen, lying at a considerable distance. In that country, Popery was not yet much rooted out, and ther was great need of a learned ministry, and a carefull education of the youth of the nobility, gentry, and better sort of the inhabitants in literature. This was justly reconed one of the best means to root out barbarity, superstition, and Popery, from that more remote part of the nation; and, therfore, a litle Colledge and Seminary for all kinds of learning was set up at Frazerburgh, to answer those good purposes. I cannot give such accounts, as I incline, of this pious and excellent foundation. Begun about the year 1599, for what I know, it has been for a long time sunk, and I have not met with any teachers who wer remarkable in it after Mr. Ferme was forced from his work. I know many mortifications and donations of public spirits, for excellent uses and purposes through Scotland, in former times, through negligence, mismanagement, the iniquity of the times, and unforseen incidents, have gone to nothing. The Laird of Philorth, a piouse and learned gentleman in that neighbourhood, was the great benefactor and founder of that litle Colledge, and I doubt not but other weel disposed persons encouraged so good a designe.

The only account I meet with of the erection of this nursery is in Mr. Rowe's MS. History. If any other of our historians have notticed it, I have overlooked it, when giving account of the Generall Assembly, which convened at Monross, March 18, 1600, the King being present, Mr. Robert Wilkie, Moderator—our 64 Generall Assembly since the Reformation. Mr. Row gives their Act, fixing Mr. Ferme there thus;— "Anent a supplication given in by the Presbitry of Deer, making mention that Philorth had erected a Colledge at Frazerburgh, and had agreed with Mr. Charles Ferme to be both Minister of the town and Master of the Colledge, whilk Mr. Charles refuses to accept, except he be commanded by the Generall Assembly. Wherfor, the General Assembly, considering the necessity of the work and ability of the man, ordeans the said Mr. Charles Ferholme to undertake the said charges, and to await on them." Thus, this new nursery hath the approbation of the King present in the Assembly, and that of the Church interposed.

Accordingly, in the year 1600, Mr. Ferme entered upon his work as Minister in the town of Frazerburgh and Master of the Colledge there, and continoued a burning and shining light, singularly usefull in that place and to the country round, for 17 years, but sadly interrupted by the persecution of prelates, for more than half that time. Mr. Adamson, who was one of his scholars, tells us that in his teaching he was very happy. He took care with learning to instill piety; he taught them modesty and industry with the closest application. That his verball instructions wer excellent, but his example, life, and manners wer yet more effectuall upon them than his words.

Many of his scholars wer not a few piouse, learned and excellent men; who was singularly usefull in the Church of God, and appeared eminently in the learned wordle. It's naturall for persons to remember their school and colledge accquaintances, and Mr. Adamson upon this occasion names severall of his condisciples under Mr. Ferme, who indeed made a considerable figure afterwards. He does not distinguish betwixt his teaching at Frazerburg and Edinburgh; but I suppose most he names wer Mr. Ferme's scholars at Edinburgh. It's not forraigne to this work I am on to mention them. Mr. Adamson begins with Mr. David Calderwood, whom he termes *accerrimus pseudo-espiscoporum hostis*, a strenuous adversary to the prelates, who in his *Altare Damascenum* takes the name of Edwardus Didoclavius by anagrammatisme. This part of our biography from the Reformation to King James' death is mostly taken from this great and good man's MS. History. Mr. Calderwood was obliged to conceal his name in that Work, least he should fall into the cruell hands of the bishops, to whom Mr. Adamson gives the harsh name of *orci satellites*, which is too rough for me to translate. Another of Mr. Ferme's scholars was Mr. Robert Scot, Minister at Glasgow for a good while, and there saved his own soul and many that heard him. Next to him, he names Mr. William Craige, who taught Divinity in the Protestant College of Saumure, not [without] very much reputation.[1] Next to him, Mr. Oliver Colt, who after he had taught the Belles Lettres, particularly the Greek, for some time in the Colledge at Edinburgh gave himself wholly to the study of Divinity, and was ordeaned Minister at Fulden, wher after many and faithfull labours he dyed. Mr. Edward Brice, who both in Scotland and Ireland was highly honoured to convert many to Christ by His Gospell. The reader will allow me to add Mr. John Adamson, whose Life I designe to write, who publishes the acccount of Mr. Ferm, and made a considerable figure in this Church. All those, or many of them, I suppose, wer under that great man Mr. Robert Rollock's care in their studys in Theology.

Those wer but a few of Mr. Ferme's scholars. Many other excellent persons singularly usefull both in Church and State might be added. The whole North of Scotland knew with what zeal, diligence, and succes Mr. Ferm taught publickly, and from house to house. As a Professor he was singularly usefull amongst his scholars, and, I apprehend, followed Mr. Rollock's example and method. His Analysis upon the Romans is a specimen of his method in explaining the Scripture to his scholars, and making them to understand it. His usefulnes amongst his flock was great, and his labours in teaching his scholars did not hinder him from a closs minding of his pastorall charge. He took a speciall care and pleasure in dealing with the young of his flock, and little boyes and girles wer by his pains, and his exact

[1] See page 56.

oversight of the English school in the town brought to give ane account of their faith and knowledge in the foundation truths of Christianity, in a most distinct manner, and not without some early sense of religion.

He was miserably interrupted in this his work by the prelates, as I shall more particularly narrate. Mr. Adamson tells us the bishops, because Mr. Ferme termed them plants not planted by God, and that, therfor, they should be rooted out, and because he charged them with breach of covenant and perjury, exerted all their influence to be rid of him. He was often torn from his congregation and imprisoned, but no threatning nor the greatest terrours could keep him from what he reconed the faithfull discharge of his office. He bore the rage of his persecutors with an intrepide mind, and invincible courage, and was unshaken like a rock in midst of a storm. He was of a weakly, frail constitution of body, but of a heroick spirit. At lenth, his body gave way, macerated with indefatigable study and incessant labours and diligence, and through the rich grace and mercy of Christ, he at lenth happily changed his suffering, troublesome, miserable life for a blessed and happy immortality. This is the short hint Mr. Adamson gives us of this great man.

Let me now add some of the more remarkable passages of his life. His work as a Master and Minister was so large and extensive, that we must not look to find him taken up much in the affairs of the Church. And, indeed, our Judicatorys wer now fast filling with corruptions, and he had no great pleasure in attending our Generall Assemblys, those few we had after his ordination; yet upon particular occasions, when the necessity of the Church called for it, he forgot his flock, and the youth under his care, and made more publick appearances, and suffered a great deal.

I'le begin with his appearances against Popery. That was now mightily prevailing in his neighbourhood, in the Shires of Aberdeen and Murray, especially by the influence of the family of Huntly, the great support of Popery in the North since the Reformation. The two last Generall Assemblys before the King left Scotland, had made great shewes to bring over Huntly and other Popish noblemen by conferences, which wer laughed at by the Papists. Huntly knew the interest he had with the King, and tooke his hazard of all that the ministers could do. Ther was no Assembly since the 1602, and little prospect of any more.

The Synod of Aberdeen, that is, such hearty, zealouse ministers as Mr. Ferme, Mr. John Forbes, and many others, reconed that now the more lay upon them to do in a Synodical capacity, and soe the Synod of Aberdeen brought the process of excommunication against the Earle of Huntly to the point of pronouncing, upon which, the Earle got letters against them to compear before the Council to answer to a complaint my Lord Huntly gave in against them. Mr. Calderwood tells us, " Mr. Charles Fairholme or Ferme, and Mr. John Forbes, in February, 1605, compeared before the Council, against the Earle of Huntley, to justify their proces of excommunication against him; upon promise of his offers to be made to the Synod of Aberdeen, the matter was deferred for some time. The Lord Newbotle, Vice-Chancelour for the time, produced a vile letter directed from the Laird of Laureston to the Council, for letters of horning, warding, and bannishing the bretheren of the North (no doubt, a speciall eye was upon thir two who had been most active) if they would not desist from their proceedings against the Marquise, so reasonable a man. The Earle did nothing but mock the ministers. In making his offers, he would not subscribe himself, but ordered his servant to subscribe the Confession of Faith for him." We see Laurieston, the King's Commissioner in ecclesiastical affairs, has demand upon the Councill, for severitys against Mr. Ferm and Forbes, for their zeal against Popery. It's scarce to be doubted but the influence of Papists at this time was not small upon [the] Council and other Judicatorys; and when Mr Forbes and Mr. Ferm wer prosecute for the Assembly at Aberdeen, their zeal against my Lord Huntly was no doubt remembered. Mr. Forbes, as we see on his Life, went up to the King, in March, to represent this affair truely to him, and Mr. Ferme signes the address of the Synod to the King, sent up by Mr. Forbes, February 21, 1605.

Upon Mr. John Forbes and Mr. John Welsh, fellow sufferers with Mr. Ferm, in their Lives, I have given a large account of the process against them and the rest for their conveening in the Assembly at Aberdeen, July, 1605. Mr. Ferm came up to which meeting of the Assembly from the Presbitry of Deer, and joyned with his brethren in what was done there, which indeed was nothing but naming another dyet, with Laurieston, the King's Commissioner's consent, upon the 3rd of October, 1605. He was called before the Council, and acknowledged his being at the forsaid Assembly, and stood to the lawfullness of it in his opinion, but subjected his judgment in that to a future Generall Assembly, the only proper judge of such matters. For this, and his refusall to condemn that meeting till a Generall Assembly condemned it, he was by the Council ordered to be imprisoned with Mr. John Monroe, Minister of Tain, in the Castle of Tain. Five others were imprisoned in other places for the same cause.

He and the rest of the warded ministers in Blacknes, Dumbartane, Stirling, and Down Castles, wer summoned to appear before the Council, October 24. The tennor of their summonds stands in the printed Calderwood, and the ministers' carriage before the Council, with the answers and defences, under a protestation and declinature, subscribed with all their hands, October 24, stands in Mr. Forbes and Mr. Welsh [their Lives], upon which they wer all warded again in their different prisons. The six ministers warded at Blacknes, Mr. Forbes and the rest, wer singled out and processed for treason, though Mr. Ferm and the rest had joyned in the declinature as well as they.

Mr. Ferme continoued in the Castle of Tain till October, 1606, when the sentence was passed upon the six ministers warded in Blacknes, bannishing them the King's dominions for ever. Then, as Bishop Spotswood tells us, the King, by a letter to the Council, ordered the rest of the ministers in their different wards, to be sent unto the Highlands, Islands, and remote places, and confyned there. "By the King's letter to the Council, Mr. Charles Farum was ordeaned to be confyned to the Isle of Bute; Mr. John Monroe to Kintyre; Mr. Robert Youngson in the Isle of Arran; Mr. James in Orkney; Mr. William Forbes in Zetland; Mr. James Greg in Caithnes; Mr. Nathaniel English in Sutherland; Mr. John Ross in Isla." This was done at the proposall and desire of our Scots bishops, now inured to hardships upon their bretheren. The severity of confyning good and usefull persons, for no fault but adhering to the legall constitution of yearly Generall Assemblys, to desolate, barbarous places of the Highlands, where they wer under great straits, and understood not the language spoken, needs not be exposed. The bishops wanted to be rid of their presence and arguings in their ecclesiastical meetings; but it had been much more mercifull to have confyned them to their own parishes, or some parts of the nation, wher they would have had some company and accomodation.

The clamour was very great against this harsh procedure, and so the Council referred the matter to the wisdom of the bishops, and after much solicitation and influence used, the bishops at lenth yielded to the liberating from their wards and confyning to their own parishes 5 of them; so, July 2, 1607, Mr. Nathan English, Mr. James Greg, and Mr. William Forbes came before the Council, and wer prevailed with to subscribe as followes: "For as much as our proceedings, at the Assembly of Aberdeen, and the ratification thereof, wherin we intended not to have offended His Majesty, have been conceived by His Highnes and your Lordships to be an offence, we are sorrie, and come in His Majesty's will for the same". That same day, Mr. Robert Youngson and Mr. James Irvine wer called before the Council. They stood to their opinion of the lawfulness of the Assembly at Aberdeen; as for the write of the Commissioners, and letters from the Counsell, they professed they tooke them not to import disobedience, but if their Lordships find it to be so, they are content to underly punishment. Upon this, they wer permitted to return to their flocks and familys. Whither Mr. Ferme, and Mr. Monro, and Mr. John Ross, whose wards wer in desolat, remote islands, wer offered the benefite their bretheren gets upon the like declaration, I cannot say, or whither, they had not clearnes to make any such declaration, but I find that Mr. Ferme and Mr. Monro wer continoued in their wards.

The hardships Mr Ferm continoued under [in] his confynement will stand best, from his own words in a letter to Mr. R. Bruce,[1] at this time also confyned in Inverness. Mr. Calderwood has preserved them to us;— "About the same time (Feb., 1608) Mr. Charles Fairholme, Minister at Frazerburgh, a holy and learned man, one of the ministers who was confyned in the Highlands for the Assembly holden at Aberdeen, in a letter sent to Mr. Robert Bruce, hath those words:—'I have to this hour been relieved by the comfort of no creature, neither have to whom I may go. A thousand deaths has my soul tasted of, but still the truth and mercy of the Lord have succoured me. The Lord to the end perfect His Own work in me.' But little care had the King and his bishops. To what straits they drew good men, providing they might attean to their purposes!"

How long he continoued in Mull [Bute?] I know not, or how he

---

[1] Note 94.

was liberat. My worthy predecessor,[1] Mr. M. Crawford, in the short hint of him he gives, taken from Mr. Adamson's preface, sayes, he was near 20 years Minister at Frazerburgh, and for his zealouse opposition to prelacy and ceremonies obtruded upon this Church, he was severall times imprisoned and torn from his flock, and by the intercession of freinds returned to them again. He dyed when about 50 years of age.

By Mr. Archibald Simpson's account of his death, it would seem he was about two years under confynement. He got to gloriouse reward of his service and sufferings, upon the 24 of September, 1617. Mr. Simpson's words are: "Hoc anno, duo in Christo, et honorabiles et fidelissimi Dei servi, Carolus Fermeus, Frazerburgensis pastor, fere biennio abhinc, propter ecclesiæ Scoticanæ tuitionem incarceratus; nec non Robertus Walesius, Fani Andreæ pastor, inde violentia expulsus, et in Tranent Lothianæ opidulum ductus, et ad mortem illic inclusus; ambo, inquam, hoc anno moriuntur". Having room enough, I will not grudge to set down Latine verses Mr. Simson composed upon both their deaths, and more particularly on Mr. Ferme's. Upon both he sings:

"Valesius moritur, sic Fermeus imbribus istis;
   Hujus opus Boreas illius Auster habet;
Quos pietas dedit esse pares, carcerque fidesque,
   Immature etiam mors dedit esse pares".

Upon Mr. Ferme, Mr. Simpson wrote what follows: "*In Carolum Fermeum Frazerburgensem verbo et opere stigmatibus insignem, Archibaldi Simsoni συνπρεσβυτερου και συμματυρος Epicidium.*

"Quid tibi vita fuit, nisi mors? Quid mors nisi vita?
   Ferme, ergo vivis, Ferme, etiam morieris,
Cum tibi jam Christus mag[num] est in funere fœnus
   Vita etiam Christo victima sacra tuo.
Carole, tu vivas, aut tu moriare, perinde est
   Tum vivens morieris quum moriendo viges."

[1] In the Parish of Eastwood.

"Anagramma ejusdem.
Carolus O clarus!
Cum pietas sincera facit te, Carole, clarum
Vero ergo a claro nomen, et omen habes.
Epitaphium Caroli Fermei.
Non hic marmoreo condendus episcopus antro,
Sed viridi tantum cespite contegitur,
Non ventri aut veneri aut mundo servit ut ista
Aetas produxit plurima mancipia,
Petro successit zælo, pietate, labore,
Carceribus, nec non vulnere sanguineo.
Mitram armenta gerunt stolam fatuique cuculi,
Et terra nati regia sceptra possunt,
Carolus igne Dei Borealia frigora solvit,
Et verbo et vita lumen erat Boreæ,
Flet Boreas tanto privatum lumine se esse,
Tam Superis amor est quam Boreæ dolor est."

The reader will find Mr. Ferme's scholar, Principall Adamson's poems upon his death, before his Commentary on the Romans. I shall not transcribe his Latine ones, but only add to my English readers the principall English elegie on his death. He gives it the title of a *Funeral Elegy and Elogie, in memory of that faithful servant of Jesus Christ, Mr. Charles Ferme.*

"If learning, grace and godlyness,
Could lenthen humane life,
So soon then had not Atropos
Drawen forth the fatal knife
To cut the short thread of thy dayes,
Scarce fifty years out spunne;
Nor should another mortall thee
In lenth of life outrun.
But, since thy ghost is gone and left
Its litle house of clay,
Let all surviving souls be sure
That here they cannot stay."

I have seen none of his works in print save his Analysis on the Romans, published by Mr. Adamson. Its title is, *Caroli Fermæi, viri undique doctissimi, Analysis Logica in Epistolam Apostoli Pauli ad Romanos: In qua omnia verba, sententiæ, et phrazes difficiliores ex Sacris Scripturis exacte et dilucide explicantur.* 8vo, 1651. Mr. Crawford seems to speak of his Book on Esther as printed, but I have not met with it. Mr. Adamson, in his preface, which is now wholly insert here, says that Mr. Ferm left diverse learned works behind him, but only two of them had reached him, both of them very much discovering the author's hidden learning, singular piety, and his zeal for God—his lessons upon the Book of Esther, and the Analysis upon the Romans. He belives that the knowing readers will be of opinion, that hitherto no commentary upon the Romans has been published which comes up to the analiticall logicall rules, and is so accurat as this. He adds, the worlde is oblidged to a learned youth and minister of the Word, Mr. William Riross, for the recovery of those two books of Mr. Ferme. I shall ende my account of Mr. Ferme with Mr. Riross' epitaph on him.

" Carolus hic situs est Fermæus, servus Jesu,
 Quo nemo vixit doctior aut melior."

M. G. Rirosius, V.D.M.

COLLECTIONS ON THE LIFE OF Mr. JOHN JOHNSTOUN, PROFESSOR OF DIVINITY IN THE UNIVERSITY OF SAINT ANDREWS.

Ther is a very learned person of this same name, and I recon of Scots parents, though born in Poland, and so he designes himself in his books Joannes Johnstonus Polonus, who was a physitian, if I be not misremembered, and lived after our Professor of Divinity. I have 3 of his books full of vast reasoning and literature, *De Naturæ Constantia*, 12mo, Amstelodi, 1632, wher he refutes what he recons a vulgar error, that the course of naturall agents, the earth, elements, &c., are still decaying and growing weaker and worse, *Historia Orbis Civilis et Ecclesiastica ad Annum* 1633, 12mo, Amstel., 1633, and *Thaumatographia Naturalis*, 8vo, Amstel., 1661, a very curious book.

It's but very litle I can give of this learned Professor of Saint Andrews. He was colleague to Mr. Andrew Melvil at Saint Andrews, after (as I take it) his nephew, Mr. James, entered into the ministry. I do not find that either Mr. Andrew or he had any particular pastorall charge. Ther wer doctors which our 2nd Book of Discipline make to be one of the standing offices of the New Testament Church, and the Apostle Paul's teachers (Eph. 4, 11,) and under this character, they wer members of our Church Judicatory, and generally sat and judged in our Assemblys. Whether, upon the incoming of prelacy, 1610, he left his native country and taught at Sedan, I cannot tell. Ther, I find some of his books printed. But his friend and colleague, Mr. A. Melvil, might do that for him there. He was a zealous and strict adherer to our Reformation Constitution in this Church, and of the same principles and temper with Mr. Andrew Melvil. He was highly esteemed by forraigne divines, and consulted upon incidentall debates and disputes on the most important heads: as we shall see, he was valued, and corresponded with, by no less persons than Beza and the Lord Mornay Du Plessis.

So that I much regrate that I can give so few and lame hints about him from Mr. Calderwood's MS., and some papers fallen into my hands. I wish others may add to them.

Mr. Johnstoun is by Mr. Charters in his list called *Aberdonensis;* and I think I have somewhere read that the learned physitian, and famed Scots poet, Arthur Johnstoun, at Aberdeen, was a brother or a near relation of his.[1] My worthy predecessor, Mr. Crawford, in his short hints of our Scots Divines, seems to have had other informations, that he was born and educat at Saint Andrews. I know no more than what he hath about Mr. Johnstoun till he was Professor. I'le take in Mr. Crawford's whole account of him here, in the entry, since it's very short.

"Mr. John Johnstoun was born of honest parents, and, after he had passed his course in the Colledge of Saint Andrews, made Master of Arts; he went abroad to France, and from thence to Geneva, wher he studyed Divinity, and became very familiar with Beza and other forraigne Divines, as appears from Beza's letter to him before his treatise, *De Vocatione Efficaci*,[2] and about the 1590, was made Professor of Divinity in the New Colledge of Saint Andrews with Mr. Andrew Melvil, by whose labours Popery was strongly beat down and extirpat, and piety and learning advanced, so that the fame of that University drew many strangers both out of France and Germany, who gave a large testimony to the doctrine and order of the University, as appears by Piscator's epistle before his Theses Theolgical. *p*. 5. After he had done much good in the University, he dyed in the Lord, Anno. . . ."

In the end of the year, 1592, or begining of the 1593, Mr. Johnstoun was received as Professor of Divinity in the New Colledge of Saint Andrews. Mr. James Melvil in his own Life gives us this account of it. "The winter following, God provided in the place of Mr. John Robertson, one of the Masters of the New Colledge, a godly, honest, and learned man, Mr. John Johnstoun, who, after diverse years' peregrination for the study of good letters in Germany, Geneva, France and England, came home, and was contented to take part with my uncle, Mr. Andrew, in the said Colledge, and who sensyne has been a great help and comfort to my said uncle, and ornament to the Colledge and University. Mr. John Caldelough withstood his election, and troubled the Colledge and

---

[1] See Introductory Notice.   [2] Note 95.

University very much, and at last raised summonds and called us before the King and Council, but was sent home the greater fool, wher, for his violation of the Acts, and troubling the University, he was deposed from all office-bearing within the same."

I take it to be a proof of the opinion the Church had of Mr. Johnstoun's judgment, solidity and skill in discipline, that he was named upon a committy by the Generall Assembly, June, 1595, to extract the Acts of a publick nature, and which might be generally fitt to be knowen, in order to their being printed. I believe I have taken nottice of the Act upon the Lives of some others named with him, and, indeed, the Act is so worthy of imitation, that I wish somewhat of that nature wer yet done as to our Acts of Assembly from the Reformation to this day. "In the 9th session, the Assembly ordean that the Acts of Assembly be sighted, and special Acts serving for practice be extracted and joyned with the Book of Discipline, either in write or in print, that none pretend ignorance, and that Mrs. Robert Pont, Thomas Buchanan, James Melvil, John Johnstoun, with the clerk, meet for that effect." I am apt to think the reason why nothing was done in this matter after many appointments, was, that next year the change began, and corruptions came in apace, which behoved to be struggled with, and that keeped back the sincerer part of the ministry, who had this and many other usefull things in view, from doing anything, and in some years, such an extract would have been a satyre upon the courses many wer rushing to, and yet this made it so much the more necessary.

Next year, Mr. Johnstoun's correspondence with the learned Beza at Geneva began, which continoued till Beza's death. I have mett with none of the letters which passed, save Beza's first. It's printed by Waldgrave, before Mr. Rollock's book, "De Efficaci Vocatione," as what conteans Beza's sentiments upon some of Mr. Rollock's former books printed by Waldgrave. I have before me an old MS. copy of this letter, with some variations, indeed, of no great importance, from Waldgrave's copy, and it's worth preserving here.

"Spectatæ tum pietatis tum doctrinæ viro, Domino Joanni Johnstono, amico summe observando, Edinburgi vel Andreapole.

"Serius ad tuas literas, ut sero mihi redditas, respondeo, mi Johnstone, ex quibus pergratum mihi fuit intelligere te salvum ad tuos reversum, ecclesias vestras in beato et tranquillo statu comperisse, quem illis perpetuum et securum in longos annos exopto. Et quidni sic futurum confidam? Quum et tam præclare jam inde ab initio fuerint a magnis illis et vere fidis servis Dei, jacta earum fundamenta: et qui supervenerunt, non stipulas neque fœnum, sed aurum et argentum, et lapides vere pretiosos, superstruxerint: imo sanctis eorum laboribus sic Deus manifeste faverit, ut quicunque ad hoc aedificium impegerunt, non modo suis conatibus exciderint; verum etiam procul, velut ipsius Dei manu sint dissipati, et jam quasi in tenebras exteriores projecti. Ad hoc accedit rarissimum et pretiosissimum Dei donum illud, quo vos est idem ille Deus dignatus, concesso vobis eo rege, et in tot, tantisque periculis admirabiliter conservato, qui ad illud singulare pietatis tuendae, et conservandae puritatis ecclesiarum studium, tantam Christianæ religionis ex ipsis fundamentis cognitionem adjunxerit, ut in eo pene Dominus, et Regiae Majestatis, et sacri ministerii dignitatem videri possit simul contulisse, ut Scotiæ jampridem nihil deesse videatur, unde optima et maxima quaeque sint illi speranda, si modo, quod sane futurum non immerito confidimus, tanta haec dona agnoscere; et sicut adhuc fecit, illa pergat ad rectum illum summum finem et scopum, *i.e.* ad ipsius omnium bonorum Authoris gloriam dirigere. Hanc vero beatam sortem, tibi, ceterisque istis venerandis fratribus, hisce literis gratulandi gaudeo praebitam mihi occasionem, tum ab eo vestrate, *Domino Davide Dromenio*, viro pio et non indocto, cujus presentia aliquot dierum nobis hic fuit jucundissima, ad vos revertente, cui has literas commisi: tum ex eo quod hoc ipso tempore mihi contigit thesaurum nancisci, qui nescio quo sinistro fato, quamvis hic in omnium aliorum conspectu versaretur, me tamen adhuc subterfugerat. Thesaurum, enim, cur non appellem, et quidem prætiosissimum, illos honorandi summe fratris Rolloci, tum in Epistolam ad Romanos, tum in Epistolam ad Ephesios [utramque] inter Apostolicas omnes Epistolas celebratissimam, commentarios? Sic, enim, ego quidem de iis apud me statuo (quod absque ulla specie adulationis dictum velim) nihil adhuc legisse me in hoc interpretationis genere brevius simul, et tum elegantius, tum iudiciosius scriptum, ut ipse me, iis inspectis, continere nequiverim, nec etiam, opinor, debuerim, quin et Deo, de hoc utilissimo procul dubio quam plurimis futuro labore, gratias magnas agerem; et tantum hoc vobis bonum, vel toti potius Ecclesiæ concessum gratularer, Deum precatus, ut hunc hominem novis subinde donis auctum fæliciter conservet, hoc præsertim tempore, in quo propter tantam operariorum in excolenda ecclesiae Dei nostri vinea raritatem, et paucissimos ex veteranis illis exercitatissimis superstites, triumphare jam sibi de oppressa veritate Sathan cum suis videbatur. Cæterum, quod ad hujus Ecclesiæ et Scholæ statum attinet, perstamus quidem adhuc illa vere, ipsis etiam nostris hostibus admirabili omnipotentis Dei et Servatoris nostri manu, velut ex ipsis mortis faucibus erepti, sed solis adhuc καθ' ἀνθρωπον induciis cum hoc anno finiendis freti, et ab iis necesario pendente nostro statu, quae tandem in illo nunc Rothomagi coacto coetu, vel de bello, vel de pace, (in qua nos æquis conditionibus comprehendamur) inter ipsum Galliae regem et vicinum nobis principem brevi decretum iri speramus. In hoc autem tam incerto statu, illud nos plane solatur, quod sciamus istud quantumvis tenue et fragile filum, a quo veluti suspensi nunc pendemus, ipsius Dei nostri manu teneri, nunquam passuri ut falsum comperiatur quod, et ex Apostolo didicimus, et toties reipsa sumus experti, omnia viz. eorum qui Deum diligunt bono cedere. Vos autem interea nostri in assiduis precibus vestris memores esse quaeso pergite. Ego vero jam ab aliquot mensibus, etsi neque febri, neque calculo, non denique podagra, vel acribus illis morbis vexor, quae senectam fere consequuntur; tamen ita me sentio debilitatum, ut ab utroque publico munere meo pene cogar prorsus abstinere, me domi continens, ac totus ad ἀναλυσιν illam optatissimam intentus, quo me 78 annum jam agentem, aetas ipsa vocat; qua in re tuas et piorum omnium præces requiro, et quidem venerandi mihi fratris D. Melvini, itidemque D. Petri Junii, quem, nisi me fallit memoria, D. Scrimgerus beatae memoriae, sibi cognatum hic olim appellabat: quibuscum, adjuncta meo nomine officiosissima salutatione, peto ut has tibi communes esse literas velis; Deum precatus, mi suavissime frater, ut vos istic omnes, quam potentissime et felicissime adversus omnia pericula domi et foris tueatur. Bene vale. Genevae, Kal. Novembris, vetere nostro calculo, 1596.

"Tuus Theodorus Beza totus."

After the unhappy change, in the end of this year, Mr. Andrew Melvil, and Mr. John Johnstoun, so much valued abroad, wer trampled upon at home, and turned out of our pretended Generall Assemblys, because of their steady adherence to the government of this Church, and because it was hard grapling with them in point of argument. Thus it was convenient to be rid of them. I have given a pretty particular account of this on Mr. Andrew Melvil's Life, and shall not resume much here. By the Act of the High Commissioner, if we might call it so, or the commissioners of the Generall Assembly and King, the Professors of Divinity wer laid under restrictions not to come to the Generall Assembly, and when chosen to it, the King charged them off. When the Assembly met at Dundee, March, 1598, to handle the great question of Ministers' Vote in Parliament, Mr. Andrew Melvil and Mr. Johnstoun came up, as reconing their office led them to be present in debating such important points, and being chosen: in the entry, the King being present, alledging they wer contrary to the restrictions laid on them, and so they wer confyned to their rooms in the town. But that did not satisfy; they had opportunity to assist their bretheren with arguments, and so the King caused charge them off the town, upon pain of horning. Mr. John Davidson, as we see in his Life, compleaned of this in open assembly, and told the King he had wronged the Church in discharging Mr. Melvil and Johnstoun. But in vain: the King authoritatively said "Not one word of that". Upon this, the writter of the latter joke upon Laud, which stands in the Appendix, is pretty satyricall. The passage relative to this runs thus: "As to the discharging Mr. A. Melvil, Mr. J. Johnstoun, Mr. Patrick Melvil, and the rest of that sort (daft precise men, who, though God has more nor any king of kings, cannot suffer kings to borrow from Him, greedy men of God's gear, of fiery humours, enimies to monarchy and seditious persons, as courtiers termed them, who can tell if all may be sealed that they say?) as for those men, I know them not well, but we hear say herabouts of them, that those men, whom they so term, are as upright with God, Whose commissioners they are, as any in this land, the King's commissioners not excepted, whom some call His Majesty's led horses when His Majesty rideth in the affaires ecclesiasticall; and further, concerning those men, they say, that in God they love His Majesty as well as any of his commissioners do; and some say, were they put to the proof concerning their true love to His Majesty, they should be found the most faithfull subjects His Majesty hath in this land, as His Majesty has sometimes esteemed of some of them; and it's esteemed by the godly that those men shall die in peace, cease from their labours, and their works shall follow them, to their great praise and commendation ".

We have seen on some other Lives, that the remains, undetermined by the Assembly next year, of the questions about the voters in Parliament, wer referred, to be prepared by the Doctors and Professors in Universitys, and Mr. Johnstoun, among others, for another meeting. Mr. Johnstoun still continoued to oppose the innovations' bringing in, and he, with his colleague, wer consulted by forraigne divines in some controversy that cast up among them, particularly in the flame that was like to arise in the Church of France, as to Piscator's doctrine anent Justification, who confyned it to the passive obedience of Christ. Their letter upon this head I'le insert, if once I had the reader in to the state of this matter, which gave a rise to this their letter.

The learned and pious Doctor J. Piscator, Professor of Divinity, at Herborn, took a particular whim in his head, to depart from the rest of the Reformed Churches, in the great Article of the Imputation of Christ's active obedience throu his life unto us in Justification, granting, however, the Imputation of Christ's sufferings and propitiatory death, as the sole foundation of Justification from sin, without any mixture of the merite of good works from the Papists, or of evangelicall obedience and grace from the Pelagians, Semipelagians, Arminians, and others, who I hope go not their lenths. This made a great noise in the churches of France, which lay nearest the infection, particularly in Dauphiny, when the National Synod met at Gap, 1603. When they came to read and explain their Confession of Faith, which they did every Generall Synod, and considered the state of doctrine in that numerous Church, and at the end of reading it, as I take [it], the members signed and subscribed it, at least, they did so at this Synod, upon the 18, 20, and 22, Articles concerning our Justification. Before God the Synod expressed their detestation of those errors nowadayes vented to the contrary; in particular their errors, who deny the Imputation of Christ's active and passive obedience (by which He hath most perfectly fulfilled the whole law) unto us for righteousness; and they require Provinciall Synods, Colloquies and Consistorys, shall have a carefull eye on those persons who are tainted with that error; and by the authority of this Assembly they shall silence them, and in case of a wilfull stubborn persisting in their errors, that they depose them, if they have a pastorall charge in the Church, from the ministry. Mr. Quick adds, that they further order letters to be writt unto Mr. Piscator, entreating him not to trouble the Churches with his innovations and new opinions, as also that letters be writ from this Assembly to the Universitys in England, Scotland, Leyden, Geneva, Heydleberg, Basil, and Herbourg (in which Piscator is Professor), requesting them to join in this censure, and in case Piscator shall pertinaciously adhere to his opinions, Mr. Sohnes and Ferrier are to prepare an answer to his books, and that it be ready against the next meeting of the Nationall Synod.

Let me only by the by take nottice, because it's new to me, and probably will be so to many of my readers, that, upon what occasion I know not, this Synod give their sentiments on the meaning of the word Superintendant in The Confession of Faith drawn up by the Church of France and subscribed, which was formed by Calvin. That Church assert Article 29, that the officers of the Church are a *pastor's elders and deacons*, and in Article 30, that *all pastors have all the same authority and equal power among themselves*, under Jesus Christ, the only Head. And Article 32, *we believe that it is expedient that they who be chosen* SUPERINTEN-DANTS *in the Church, should wisely consult among themselves by what means the whole body may be conveniently ruled, yet so as they do not swerve from that which our Lord Jesus Christ hath institute.* This doth not hinder, but that in some Churches ther maybe those particular constitutions which will be more convenient for them than others. From those Articles it's very plain, that the Reformed Church of France was just as much Presbyterian in its constitution as we in Scotland, and that the necessary, temporary office of Superintendants was what they had, as well as we; and it may be we went into it the rather that they had gone in to it; neither they nor we had any notion of proper Praelates being the same with Superintendants. Whither any motions wer on foot at this time in France, now when our King was bringing in the English Government among us, I do not know; but from that, or somewhat of that nature, I suppose this National Assembly at Gap declare *that the word* SUPERINTENDANT *in the* 32 *Article of their Confession, is not to be understood of any superiority of one pastor above another, but only in general of such as have office and charge in the Church.* And this declaration is indeed nothing but an application of the 30 Article of their Confession, and shews their sentiments to have still been that a Superintendant was never meaned by them of an office distinct from the pastor, but an extending of their care and charge by the Church. This is a digression, but it will be pardoned, since I do not see it notticed in our debates about Superintendants. I return now to the affair of Piscator.

Letters wer writ according to the Synod's orders, and the opinions of not a few wer returned to the next Nationall Synod at Rochell, 1607. I have a collection of papers befor me, which would give a good deal of light to this debate upon Justification, wer they not too large. They are copyes taken by the R. Mr. Robert Baillie, from transcripts sent of them from France. I'le only give the titles of them. *Monsr. Anthonie Regnant, Minister at Bourdeaux his Representation to the Synod at Rotchell, February 20, 1607.* It is a paper of many sheets in French, wherin he gives a long account of a journey he made by order of the Synod of Vapinci in Dolphing to Hidlberge, Geneva, Basil, and other Churches in Germany, and to Holland, and what passed between the divines and him upon the recomendation of the Synod of Gap as to Piscator's doctrine; and another Article from that Synod about the Pope's being Antichrist; next, ther is another representation to the said Synod by Mons. Anth. de la Fay. It seems mostly to be about the Article concerning Antichrist. Then followes: *Litteræ Senatus Hydlbergensis Ecclesiæ Synodo Vapinci-Dolphinatus, Jan. 3, 1604;* next, *Literæ Electoris Palatini Synodo supradicto, Jan. 1604.* Followes [next] *Version Francoise des Lettres patents de Mons. Elector, touchant Difference de Sr Piscator, Feb. 1604;* next, *The letter of the ministers of the 5 classes, Lausanne, &c., to the Synod on the same subject.* Next, *The letter of the professors at Hydlberge to the same Synod on the same head.* Next, *The letters of the ministers of Hanover to the same Synod.* I take all those to have been presented to the Generall Synod at Rotchell by Mons. Regnant. And, lastly ther stands in this collection, Piscator's own letter to the forsaid Synod, in this affair, that I imagined was worth preserving [in] this nice affair. It is directed, *Reverendis amplissimis et doctissimis viris, dominis, pastoribus Ecclesiarum Gallicarum, eis, qui nuper Vapinci-Dolphinatus in Synodo Nationali congregati fuerint, dominis et fratribus honorandis atque in Christo dilectis,* and I have put it in the app. n. (copy M.S. 4to, vol. 22, n. 9,) as conteaning Piscator's own opinion. It's dated Jan. 24, 1604. [This Paper has not been found.]

How the Synod of Gap's letters came to our Scots Universitys, I cannot tell, but I imagine it was by a correspondence Mons. Duplessis had in Scotland; at least, Mr. Melvil and Johnstoun's return is directed to the Lord Morney, *Domino Morneo*, as one of the two copys I have of their letter bears. It conteans their sentiments of the debate with Piscator, and breaths all peace and forbearance, which was the road the Church of France took with this learned man. It will best speak for itself. I believe it's not yet published, and, therefor, I imagine it's Mr. Johnstoun's draught rather than his; one of my copyes wants, and the other hath, the following title :—

Epistola ad Dominum Morneyum.

"S.P.D—Facit communio nostra in Christo, *vir illustrissme*, ut te in communi Christi et ecclesiae causa, etsi in facie minime tibi noti, confidentius in hoc tempore appellamus; facit insignis pietas tua, ut quae ad pietatis publicum commodum, ex sincero pietatis studio, et effectu, ad te allaturi sumus, ea in optimam partem abs te acceptum iri speremus, ut minime opus arbitremur speciosa apud te excusationis praeoccupatione. Res autem ita se habet. Literis amicorum a plurimis locis transmarinis ad nos perlatum est, et passim percrebuit rumor, in proxima superiore Synodo Gallicana, sententiam Joannis Piscatoris, qua asserit Justitiam Christi passivam sive obedientiam Christi in morte imputari duntaxat nobis in Justitia nostra coram Deo, publice damnatam. Haec, cum nobis nuntiata essent, non parum nos et pios hic fratres commoverunt, etsi minime dubitamus prudentissimis et piissimis viris, quibus Gallicana abundat Ecclesia, hujus consilii atque facti constare rationes, neque temere eos quodquam in tam gravi negotio pronunciavisse. Tamen, cum tempora circumspicimus, temporumque et rerum expendimus circumstantias, veremur ne res in manifestam abeat controversiam; atque ex ea in Evangelicis Ecclesiis triste oriatur dissidium; nisi Dominus ex ingenti misericordia sua praevertat, per providos pios et moderatos viros. Nonne dissidiarum et turbarum plus satis est? Nonne hostes ubique, parati et intenti in omnem turbandae pacis occasionem? Quod si studiis partium contraversia in publicum prorumpat, quis non videt miserabile ex ea oriturum incendium? Quare, communibus votis orandus est nobis Deus, ut hoc malum, ab Evangelicis Ecclesiis averruncat; cum vero tua auctoritas ob pietatem, prudentiam, et divini ingenii aeterna monumenta, aliaque illustria in rem Christianam, mente in Ecclesia Gallicana, emineat. Te valde vehementerque rogamus, ut in hac causa authoritatem imponas tuam, et per te omnes istuc pios fratres obsecramus, ut operam quoque suam et concilia, ad pacis et concordiae studium mature conferant, priusquam ad contentionem et turbas res perducentur. In Articulo ipso Justificationis per Dei gratiam, nulla dissentio est sed in explicatione Articuli, utraque sua sibi videtur habere fundamenta, in quibus, etsi sit dissimilitudo quaedam sententiarum, tamen ejusmodi non videtur esse, quae animorum pariat dissentionem, quae Ecclesiam Christianam distrahere, aut pacem turbare debeat. Quod si quis aliter sentit, hoc quoque Deus revelabit. Quare nos et nostro et communis Ecclesiae nostrae nomine, per viscera D.N. Jesu Christi vos rogamus, et obtestamur, ut omnes rationes pacis et concordiae stabiliendae procuretis: Ecclesia nostra in hac causa, pro mediocritate sua, omnem operam suam studiaque in Christo defert. Atque hoc ipso nomine ad Dominum Piscatorem scripsimus, quem minime refractorium fore arbitramur; literas, etiam, dedimus ad Ecclesiae Genevensis et Basiliensis doctores, ut operam, et authoritatem suam, et consilia, in commune conferant. Has literas, studii officiique nostri testes, cum ad communem causam Ecclesiae vestrae spectent, eas (si tibi visum) cum Synodo vestra communicare digneris, rogamus. Quod super est, Deum Patrem D.N., Jesu Christi comprecamur, ut Ecclesias Evangelicas Spiritus Sui Sancti praesidio tueatur, et in unitate fidei confirmet Evangelii pastores et doctores, pacis et charitatis vinculo inter se colligatos. Potenti Suo Verbo et Spiritu Suo Ille rogat, ut eadem secundum Spiritum et Verbum ipsius sentiant et loquantur, ad propagationem regni Christi in terris. Amen. Vale, vir illustris. Floreas in Christo Domino, Qui te Ecclesiae, reipublicae, et nobis diu servet incolumem. Andreapole in Scotia, posteridie Iduum Octobris, 1604, tuae eximiae pietatis et verae in Christo unitatis studiosissimi, caeterorum apud nos fratrum nomine,

                        "ANDREAS MELVINUS SCOTUS,
                        "JOANNES JOHNSTONUS."

This letter seems not to be written, as I thought till I better considered it, in answer to the application of the Synod of Gap, but we see it is the effect of a large correspondence those two large professors had with forraigne divines in Germany. They seem to have had more favourable uptakings of Piscator's sentiments on Justification, than the French pastors had; and, perhaps his denying the Imputation of Christ's life of Righteousness to us has been keeped up from them; otherwise I incline to think, that they would not have said the difference was only as to wayes of explaining the Article, and that ther was a full agreement in the Article itself. Whatever be in this, they are all, we see, for moderat and amicable measures, which letts us see thir divines wer not so fiery in these theologicall matters, as at least Mr. Melvil is generally represented.

To complet this account, lett me from Mr. Quick's Synodicon give the procedure of the next Nationall Synod at Rochel, 1607, in this affair. "Whereas, Doctor John Piscator, Professor in the University of Herborn, by his letters of answer sent him by the Synod of Gap (which stand in the appendix), doth give us an account of his doctrine in the point of Justification, as that it's only wrôt out by Christ's death and passion, and not by his life and active obedience, this Synod, nowise approving the dividing causes, so nearly conjoyned in this great effect of Divine grace, and judging those arguments produced by him for defence of his cause, weak and invalid, do order that all the pastors in the respective churches in this kingdom, do wholly conform themselves in their preaching, to that form of sound words which hath hitherto been taught among us, and is conteaned in the Holy Scriptures, to wit, that the whole obedience of Christ, both in his life and death, is imputed to us for the full remission of our sins, and acceptance unto eternal life; and in short, this being but one and the self-same obedience, is our intire and perfect Justification. And the Synod further ordeans, that answer shall be made unto the letters of the said Doctor Piscator, propounding to him this holy doctrine, together with its principall foundations, yet without any vain jangling, and with that devotion which becomes the singular modesty expressed by him in his letters to us, wherin ther is not the least bitterness nor provocking expression; leaving to God, Who can, when it pleaseth Him, reveal the defects which are in the doctrine of the said Piscator, as also to assure him that he hath exceeding satisfyed the said Assembly in his explications on the topick of Repentance." Some other things follow in Quick, vol. 1., p. 265, that I shall refer the reader to, and add what Mr. Quick wants, and, [which] I suppose was never printed—the Synod's letter to Piscator. Though pretty long, it's a valuable paper on such a subject, app. n. (copy MS. 4to, vol. 22 n. 11). [This Paper has not been preserved.]

When Mr. Andrew Melvil was insidously called up to London, 1606, the care of the New Colledge of Saint Andrews lay on Mr. Johnstoun, but he had litle satisfaction after his removall. In Mr. Howie's Life, who was thrust in as his collegue, I have notticed what hapned on this occasion. The enimies to Mr. Andrew Melvil, and the Bishop of Saint Andrews, wer in a strait what to do, when they had resolved that Mr. Melvill should not return. They found Mr. Johnstoun would not yield to Mr. Howie's being in the superior place in the New Colledge. It was once proposed the Bishop should be Provost, and Mr. Johnstoun and Mr. Howie on the same foot in teaching under him, but that was not gone into. When, the next year, the Colledge was visited, the Bishop proposed to lay aside Mr. Johnstoun from his office, alledging he was disaffected, and his chamber a receptacle for all evil affected persons, but the University rejected the motion unanimously, and the Bishop could not accomplish his designe.

How long Mr. Johnstoun continoued at Saint Andrews after Mr. Howie was placed in Mr. Andrew Melvil's room, I have not found, or how long he lived, I know not. Some of his books I find printed in France after this; whither he went over to Mr. Melvil there, I cannot say, but after the removall of those two great lights, that University sank much in their [its?] reputation.

It would seem he dyed about the year 1615, at least, Mr. Charters in his list, places his death at that year,[1] and gives us this list of his works :—" Joannes Johnstonus, Abredonensis, Professor Theologiae Andreapolitanus. He wrote Inscriptiones Historicas Regum Scotorum. *Item*, Heroes Scotos, 4to, Amstel., 1602. *Item*, Consolationem Christianam sub Cruce, et Iambos de Felicitate Hominis cum Deo reconciliati, 8vo, Lugd. Batt., 1609. *Item*, Tetrasticha et Lemmata Sacra. *Item*, Cantica Sacra. *Item*, Icones Regum Judae et Israelis, Lugd. Batt., 1612. *Item*, Iambos Sacros, Salmurii, 1611. *Item*, Sidera Veteris Ævi,

[1] This is a mistake. Charters places Johnston's death under the year 1612.

Salmur., 1611." His "Subscriptiones Regum Scotiae" and his "Heroes" are printed in the first volume of the Deliciae poetarum Scotorum, and among the Scotos Heroes he mentions severall persons eminent for learning, as the famous Creighton, and with him in the introduction, Sir James Sandilands of Calder, William Kirkcaldy of Grange, Alexr. Boyd, an eminent poet, 1601, and others. I shall conclude my account of him with Mr. Rowe's hint in his MS. History: "Mr. John Johnstoun was a godly, learned man, commended by Theodor Beza in his epistles. He was one of the Masters of the New Colledge of Saint Andrews with Mr. Andrew Melvil. He set out a treatise in print, concerning the Government of the Church, in 2 books. In the first, he improves the unlawfull Government of the Kirk by bishops; in the 2nd, he approves and confirms the true government of the Church by presbitrys and assemblys; and all by plain and clear testimonies of Scripture, and unanswerable arguments drawen from the same."

Since the writing of what is above, I have met with some original letters of Mr. Johnstoun's, which clear the latter part of his life, and setle the time of his death. In the Lawers' Library, I find a letter from him to the King, desiring his concurrence to a petition he presented. Whether he succeeded, I know not: it's scarce probable he did. The letter runs "It is not knowen to Your Most Excellent Majesty what have been my endeavours and travails in advancing the colledge living; wherupon my colleagues have advanced themselves with litle or no regard to me:—in respect wherof, with consideration of my affection and travails approved by Your Majesty, in setting forth the memories of Your Majesty's most noble progenitors (he means I suppose his Inscriptiones Regum Scotorum), it may please Your Highnes to put your royall hand to this my present suit to encourage me in my calling, and for releise of my household and family; and hereby to remember Your Maist Excellent Majesty in my humble prayers for Your Heines' long and prosperouse reigne.

"Your Most Excellent Majesty's most humble Orator,
" MR. JOHN JOHNSTONE.
" Donininon, the 13 of March, 1606."

In Mr. Boyd, of Trocherig's Life, Mr. Johnston's letter to him, May, 1600, stands. Ther, he compleans of the failing of his health, and tells him he is going through his papers and putting them in order, and about to print some of them, and declares himself on the side of the sincere sort of the ministry. Mr. Boyd visited him when in Scotland, 1610, and had a high value for him, and May, 1611, Mr. Johnstoun sends over his Iambi Sacri and some other of his poems to be printed at Saumure by Mr. Boyd and Mr. Will. Craige's care. Mr. Johnstoun seems to have dyed in the 1611, soon after this his last letter, and Mr. Boyd speakes of him as dead, March, 1612, and sends a 100 copies of his poems, printed at Saumure, to Mr. Johnstone's relations. Those letters and hints stand at full lenth in Trochrege's Life, and I referr to them.

NOTES AND ILLUSTRATIONS.

Note 1, Page 1.

SPOTSWOOD, otherwise Spottiswoode, the historian and archbishop, was the elder son of John Spotswood, one of the pillars of the Reformation and Superintendent of Lothian, Merse and Teviotdale. John, the historian, was born in the year 1565, and educated at the University of Glasgow. Having made choice of the clerical profession, he, on the death of his father, succeeded to the incumbency of Calder, in the year 1586, in which station he obtained so good a reputation, that he was chosen to accompany the Duke of Lennox as his chaplain in his embassy to France, in the year 1602. From this connection he naturally cast in his lot with the Episcopal party, and became a devoted adherent of the King. For this he was rewarded by being first made Archbishop of Glasgow, and afterwards Archbishop of St. Andrews. He was regularly consecrated along with Lamb, Bishop of Brechin, and Hamilton, Bishop of Galloway, on 21st October, 1610, in the Chapel at London House, by the Bishops of London, Ely, and Bath. He, in 1615, was preferred to the See of St. Andrews, which he held till he was deposed and excommunicated by the General Assembly of 1638, and forced to flee into England, where he died the following year, and was buried in Westminster Abbey. He is disliked by the Presbyterians, says Dr. Cunningham, as the chief agent employed by the King to force Episcopacy on the country, and though, it appears, some of the violent measures of the Court were taken against his better judgment, yet he is, perhaps, on that account, the more culpable, as he gave such violent courses his active support. While, doubtless, conscientiously preferring Episcopacy to Presbyterianism, he scrupled not to sacrifice his country's faith to his own ambition. He wrote a small treatise in Latin, *Refutatio Libelli de Regimine Ecclesiæ Sotticanæ*, London, 1620, in answer to Calderwood; also, a *History of the Church of Scotland*. This work, though uncritical and biassed, as all the histories of that time were, is yet a most respectable production. Destitute of marks of genius, it everywhere evinces sound judgment, moderation, and research. The best edition is the one undertaken by the Spottiswoode Society, in 3 vols., 8vo. It contains a full notice of the Life and Works of the Archbishop, written from a strongly Episcopal point of view. Keith's Catalogue of Scottish Bishops. Cunningham's Church History of Scotland. Calderwood.

The Records of our Assemblies. The most ancient Records of the Church of Scotland, contained in three volumes, and embracing the period from 1560 to 1616, are no longer in existence, having been destroyed in the fire which consumed the Houses of Parliament, on the 16th October, 1834. The history of these volumes is curious. They were known under the name of the *Booke of the Universal Kirk*, and though produced at, and attested by, the famous Assembly of 1638, had afterwards been purloined, and by some unexplained way came into the possession of Campbell, Bishop of Aberdeen, and were by him eventually deposited in Sion College in London. During the investigations which were instituted by a Committee of the House of Commons on the subject of Church Patronage in Scotland, in the year 1834, these volumes were produced for the consideration of that Committee. Their authenticity was established by Dr. Lee and other competent judges; and the Committee having suspended its investigations and made a report of the evidence which it had obtained, these books were left in keeping of the clerks, and perished in the conflagration by which the Houses of Parliament were consumed.

For a full account of the ascertained facts relative to the history of these documents, see the editions of the *Booke of the Universal Kirk of Scotland*, published by Peterkin and by the Bannatyne Club. The prefaces to these, especially that of the latter, give full information how the loss of the Records has been supplied, and also of the origin, nature, and authenticity of what now passes under the name of *The Book of the Universal Kirk of Scotland*. The subsequent Records of the Church are accessible to all in the various forms of Collections, Abridgments, Compendiums, &c.

David Calderwood, the most industrious and useful of all our Scottish Church historians, was born in the year 1575. Not much of his early history is known, but it is pretty well established that he was come of a good family. He took his degree of A.M. at the University of Edinburgh, 1593, and having been early destined for the Church, he devoted assiduous attention to the requisite studies, and became possessed of much theological learning. He became Minister of Crailing, near Jedburgh, and, during those stirring times, appeared a conspicuous member of the Church Courts. Calderwood was of a very different spirit from Spottiswoode, and soon came into collision with the King and Episcopal party, and, in 1617, was imprisoned, and finally banished the kingdom. After visiting various places abroad, he returned to Scotland, about 1624, and was eventually appointed Minister of Pencaitland, in the county of Haddington, continuing through all vicissitudes a most redoubtable champion of Presbyterianism.

He died at Jedburgh, on the 29th of October, 1650, at the age of seventy-five. His public life is to be found in his own History and in other public records of the time. Dr. Irving has written an appreciative notice of him in his *Lives of Scotish Writers*. Calderwood devoted many years to the preparation of a *History of the Church of Scotland*. In 1648, the General Assembly voted him a yearly pension to enable him to continue and complete his design. He left behind him an historical work of great extent, valuable not as a finished literary production, but as a huge storehouse of authentic materials for the general history of the country. He has with great research and industry incorporated many original documents, which are not otherwise now preserved, and recorded an immense multiplicity of facts which illustrate the civil and ecclesiastical annals of the period to which his work relates. An abridgment, which appears to have been prepared by himself, was published after his death in 1678. The materials of his History, as at first collected and arranged by him, filled six large volumes of closely written manuscript. These he afterwards with great industry re-arranged, curtailed, and improved, and this recension, or second version of his History, has been edited with collations and extracts of the larger manuscript for the Wodrow Society in eight vols., 8vo. This edition contains also the most authentic notices of Calderwood's Life and literary Works. Dr. Irving's Lives. Wodrow Edition of Calderwood's History.

Row's MS. History. This History has been published for the Wodrow Society under the competent editorship of the late Dr. David Laing. John Row, the historian, was the third son of John Row, the reformer, who died Minister of Perth in 1580. Our historian was born at Perth, towards the end of the year 1568. Of his early history and education he has left an interesting sketch, which appears to have been written during the last year of his life. and which has been inserted by Dr. Laing in his edition of Row's History. He seems to have been a precocious child, as under his father's instructions he was able to read, when seven years of age, a chapter of the Hebrew Bible when the family dined or supped. From his early proficiency in learning he was able to act as tutor to the children of his uncle, Bethune of Balfour; and, in 1586, he accompanied them to Edinburgh, and entered as a student the newly erected college, and took his degree of A.M. in 1590. After being two years schoolmaster of Aberdour, Row, about the end of the year 1592, was ordained Minister of Carnock. The church, he tells us, was in a very "evill condition," being thatched with heather; and, on one occasion, when he happened to be confined to the house by sickness and had no person to officiate in his stead, the roof of the church fell in, and would no doubt have proved fatal to some of his hearers had there been service that day. He married a daughter of David Fergusson, Minister of Dunfermline. As Fergusson had taken an active share in all ecclesiastical affairs from the time of the Reformation till his death, in 1598, he was in possession of numerous documents and memoranda, which came into Row's possession, and proved of the greatest service to him in the composition of his *Historie of the Kirk of Scotland*. Row died Minister of Carnock, in 1642, and such was his interest in parochial matters that the minutes of his kirk session were written with his own hand till within eight days of his death. His second son, John, who became Principal of King's College, Aberdeen, continued the History to July, 1639, and his transcript of his father's revised and enlarged copy has been adopted as the basis of the Wodrow edition by Laing. For a full account of Row's ministry at Carnock, with notices of his family and much subsidiary information, and also a fair estimate of his value as an historian, the reader is referred to the edition above-named.

Note 2, page 1.

For a notice of his parentage and early life, see introductory remarks on Craig.

Note 3, page 6.

"Magdalen's Chappell is still in existence. It stands in the Cowgate, Edinburgh. The Chapel of St. Mary Magdalene, in the very heart of the old city, still raises its tower above the meaner roofs; but its destiny is hardly worthy of its traditions. It has passed into the possession of a body known as the 'Protestant Institute,' and is no longer one of the National Churches. Although it has suffered from mutilation and neglect, it is not beyond the reach of careful and intelligent restoration." Lecture on John Craig (privately printed) by the Rev. Dr. Story of Glasgow University.

Note 4, page 7.

Craig's ministry and sojourn in Aberdeen have already been noticed in the Introduction. In regard to his predecessor in Aberdeen, Adam Herriot, we may shortly remark that he was born in 1514; but of his parentage or of his early years nothing is known. Having embraced a monastic life, he became a canon regular in the Augustinian Abbey at St. Andrews. He employed his leisure in the study of scholastic theology, but his researches resulted in weakening his belief in the Catholic Church. After some hesitation and vacillation, which gave no small scandal, he finally cast in his lot with the Reformers, and, in 1559, made a public profession of his adherence to the Protestant faith. When the ministers of the new creed were distributed over the country, Herriot was sent to Aberdeen, "in which," says Spottiswoode, "there lived divers addicted to the Romane profession ". From Herriot's proficiency in scholastic learning, he was considered peculiarly suited to that place. He was well received by the citizens, and, besides various gifts, received a stipend of £200 a year—a salary equal to that which Knox received from the corporation of Edinburgh. Premature old age, weakness, and disease, assailed Herriot. His labours were partially relieved by the appointment of James Lawson to the care of St. Machar's; but as he stood in need of still further assistance, in Nov., 1570, Walter Cullen was appointed Vicar and Reader of New Aberdeen with an annual stipend of twenty pounds. Herriot's sickness still increasing, he finally resigned his charge in the summer of 1573, and died on the 28th August, 1574, of apoplexy, in the sixtieth year of his age, greatly lamented. He was interred in St. Nicholas Church, and his grave is marked by a blue tombstone, the inscription on which has long been obliterated. His memory has been consecrated in Latin verse by the famous John Johnston, Professor of Theology at St. Andrews. These verses have been published (along with a complete account of Herriot's ministry in Aberdeen, in a History of the Reformation in Aberdeen, written by the late Dr. Joseph Robertson) by Messrs. Edmond and Spark, Aberdeen, 1887. Scott's Fasti.

Note 5, page 9.

James Anderson was the son of the Rev. Patrick Anderson, a non-juring minister, who had been ejected from his charge of the Parish of Leamington, and imprisoned for a time on the Bass Rock, at the Restoration. James was born in Edinburgh, 5th August, 1662, and, on completing his education at the University of that city by graduating A.M., 1680, he chose the legal profession, and served his apprenticeship in the office of Sir H. Paterson, an eminent member of the Society of Writers to the Signet. Anderson's intimacy with Capt. Slezer, author of *Theatrum Scotiæ*, as well as his professional duties, formed in him a taste for the study of antiquities, which he afterwards prosecuted with much success. His first work which gained him celebrity was *An Essay showing that the crown of Scotland is Imperial and Independent*. This work was written in refutation of a pamphlet, published in 1704, by a lawyer named Attwood. Anderson's Essay was very popular in Scotland, and the Scottish Parliament voted him thanks and a sum of money as a reward. Mr. Anderson was now encouraged to engage in engraving a series of fac-similes of the royal charters previous to the reign of James I., and of seals, medals and coins from the earliest times to his own age. This undertaking put him to expenses which were never fully defrayed by Government, but as a compensation he was appointed in 1715 Postmaster General for Scotland, a situation which he retained only about two years. He was allowed, however, to retain the salary by way of pension. He published, in 1727, *Collections relating to the History of Queen Mary of Scotland*, in four volumes quarto, a valuable and impartial work. He seems to have lived an unhappy life from matrimonial differences, and his financial difficulties obliged him to pledge the plates of his intended work. Anderson died suddenly, on 3rd April, 1728, having finished the collections for his great work only a few days before. This work was afterwards published by Ruddiman, Edinburgh, 1739, folio, under the title of *Selectus Diplomatum et Numismatum Scotiæ Thesaurus*. Note in II. vol. of Wodrow's Correspondence. Dictionary of National Biography.

Note 6, page 12.

David Lindsay was son of Robert Lindsay of Kirkton, a younger son of the family of Edzell. Having travelled in France and Switzerland, he imbibed the principles of the Reformation, and was one of the twelve originally nominated by the leaders of the newly reformed Church of Scotland for the chief places of the kingdom, and was appointed to Leith, 19th July, 1560. Henceforward he became one of the most prominent figures in the ecclesiastical and political world. A full account of his services, and the offices he held is contained in Scott's *Fasti*. He was a great favourite with James VI., and baptised two of his children, the Princess Margaret, and Prince Charles, afterwards King. He was promoted to the Bishoprick of Ross in 1600, and took his seat in Parliament, still retaining his parochial charge, though living in the neighbourhood of Dundee. He died the father of the Church, 14th August, 1613, in the 83rd year of his age, and the 54th of his ministry. Scott (*Fasti*) says: "During his lengthened incumbency there was a constant succession of change. The discipline and government of the Protestant Church had to be defended and put in a regular train; the spirit of toleration was totally unknown, liberty of the person was frequently abused, and very different opinions were entertained of the line which separated civil and ecclesiastical power. By his prudent and judicious conduct, however, he steered through them all, respected and generally esteemed, acquiring for himself, in the language of two of his brethren in Edinburgh, who knew him best, the character of 'a wise and learned man'." Keith's Catalogue. M'Crie's Life of Melville.

George Buchanan is so well known that it is perhaps unnecessary to refer to him farther than to mention, that his Life has been lately written anew by Mr. P. Hume Brown. Time, a more correct literary taste, and higher demands in public and private morality than were once current, have dealt very unkindly with Buchanan's reputation, and greatly diminished its proportions. The Athenæum, when lately reviewing Mr. Brown's book, very pertinently asks what is Scotland's debt to Buchanan that he should be ranked amongst her greatest sons? Buchanan was born in 1506 near Killearn in Stirlingshire, of a family more respectable than opulent, and died at Edinburgh, 28th Sept., 1582. His early life, his struggles for his education, his adventures and wanderings, his employments abroad and at home, are all admirably set forth by his most recent biographer—to whose work the reader is referred for ample information on these points. Some, perhaps most, persons, will think Mr. Brown less happy when he sets about establishing Buchanan's claims as poet, historian, political writer, and reformer, and still less successful, when he vindicates his subject from the charges of private immorality and untruthfulness, of inconsistency and venality in his public life, and of gross ingratitude to those who assisted him in time of need. As it is impossible to enter on these and kindred topics, in the compass of a note, the reader is confidently referred to Mr. Brown's Biography for ample materials for forming an estimate of Buchanan as a man and a writer. This only may be added, that out of the whole mass of Buchanan's verses on professedly sacred subjects, Trench could find nothing worthy of insertion in his charming volume of sacred poetry. Indeed, it may be asserted without fear of contradiction that there are exhibited more poetry and piety in almost any one of the hymns of nameless authors in any given breviary than in the whole volume of Buchanan's stilted, cold, classicalities, purporting to be a translation of David's Psalms into Latin.

George Hay sometimes styled Parson of Ruthven, and, at other times, Parson of Eddilston, was a brother of Andrew Hay, Parson of Renfrew, who filled for many years the office of Rector of the University of Glasgow. Calderwood, quoted by Dr. McCrie in his Life of Melville. An account of Hay's Answer to the Abbot of Crossraguel is given by the last named writer in his Life of Knox. In April, 1576, " Certane brether appointit to oversie the booke wrytin be Mr. George Hay contra Tyrie ". Buik of Univ. Kirk. Other notices of Hay may also be found in Calderwood, and in McCrie's Lives of Knox and Melville.

Note 7, page 13.

John Winram or Wynram, brother of Mr. Robert Wynram of Ratho, was enrolled as a student in St. Leonard's College, St. Andrews, in 1513, and took the degree A.B., 17th March, 1515. About 1528, he belonged to the Augustinian Monastery of St. Andrews, in which he held several offices in succession. He assisted at the trials for heresy of Sir John Borthwick, in 1540, of George Wishart, in 1546, and of Walter Myln, in 1558, but, shortly after joined the Reformers, and was nominated Superintendent of Fife, in 1560. He was a member of the first General Assembly, 20th Dec., 1560, and one of those whom they found " prepared for ministering and teaching ". He is mentioned as Superintendent of Strathern at the Assembly of March, 1572, which office he demitted in the Assembly of March, 1573. We find the Assembly of March, 1574, again committing to him the office of Superintendent of Fife and Strathern. As Prior of Portmoak, he attended the convention at Holyroodhouse, 5th March, 1574, and was one of those named for drawing up the Second Book of Discipline. He died, 28th September, 1582, aged 90. Scott's Fasti. Dr. Scott adds, " Though early converted to the Protestant cause, he yet retained his situation and emoluments in the Romish Church. It seems doubtful, therefore, if he was not actuated by a sordid and selfish spirit, as much as by a love of the truth. He attended about thirty-six assemblies, but does not seem to have had much share in their management, or to have stood very high in the esteem of his brethren." He was the author of a Catechism of which no copy is known to be in existence. Further notices of Wynram are found in Lee's Church History, and in McCrie's Life of Knox.

Alexander, that is, Alexander Gordon, of the house of Huntly, previously in the See of the Isles, was translated to the See of Galloway, 1558, after the death of Bishop Durie. He accompanied the lords who were in arms in defence of Queen Mary to Edinburgh, in 1570, and at their desire preached in John Knox's pulpit. When Protestantism seemed established, he came over to that faith, " but," says Keith, " yet for all his obsequiousness, not only was he not allowed to exercise his functions as a bishop, but he had the mortification of once to be suspended from his office as a private minister by the Assembly of the Kirk ; and at another time, when he humbly craved to be appointed Visitor only of the Churches within the diocese of Galloway, he was rejected, and another minister preferred. Yet notwithstanding all this harsh treatment, he always retained the title of Archbishop of Athens and Bishop of Galloway ; and the benefice of this latter See he still considered as his own private property, insomuch as when he was a-dying, in the year 1576, he made a resignation thereof by consent of the Queen to his own son, John Gordon, by Barbara Logie, his wife. Thus went the ecclesiastical benefices in that period." Keith's Catalogue.

Adam Bothwell, Bishop of Orkney, son to Mr. Francis Bothwell, one of the senators of the College of Justice, was preferred by Queen Mary, in 1562, to that See. He was one of the four bishops who embraced Protestantism at the Reformation, but he does not appear to have afterwards exercised any ecclesiastical jurisdiction. Though he performed the ceremony of the Queen's marriage to the Earl of Bothwell, yet he was one of those who afterwards persecuted her Majesty with the utmost virulence. He was also one of the judges in the Court of Session. He died 23rd Aug., 1593, at the age of 72. Keith's Catalogue.

Besides the four Catholic bishops who conformed to the principles of the Reformation, a great number of ecclesiastics of inferior rank embraced the same cause, and, from their unfitness for ministerial work through ignorance and other reasons, these converts were long a source of much trouble and weakness to the reformed party.

Note 8, page 21.

See notice of Craig in the Introduction.

Note 9, page 21.

Tulchan Bishops. "There be three kinds of bishops," said Adamson with severe irony, " My Lord Bishop, My Lord's Bishop, and The Lord's Bishop. My Lord Bishop was in the Papistry; My Lord's Bishop is now, when My Lord gets the fat of the benefice, and the bishop makes his title sure; The Lord's Bishop is the true minister of the gospel." The term Tulchan, applied to bishops, arose thus: It was once the custom in Scotland to set up a stuffed calf's skin before cows when being milked, under the belief that the cow was thereby induced to give her milk the more readily. This stuffed calf was called a *tulchan*. The coarse humour of the nation found vent in nick-naming the new race of prelates "tulchan-bishops," as they were thought no better than stuffed calves, set up to make the benefice yield its revenues to their lord. Of course these tulchan or titular bishops were properly speaking not bishops at all, not having received due episcopal consecration. Melville's Diary. Calderwood's History, cited in Cunningham's Church History.

Note 10, page 22.

It has not been thought expedient to reprint this Confession here, as it may be found in Dunlop's *Confessions*, and otherwise. Dr. Story, in his lecture above cited, thus characterises this Confession. "This 'powerful protest,' as Mr. Law says, is perhaps the most remarkable and characteristic document which ever emanated from the Church of Scotland. It was written in English for home use, and in Latin for circulation abroad. With Ernulphian comprehensiveness, and yet with most lawyer-like precision and brevity, it sets forth the doctrines and usages of Rome, each and all of which it binds its subscribers to 'abhor, detest, and refuse': while it also engages them to defend 'with their gear, bodies, and lives, the king's person in defence of Christ's evangel, the liberty of the country, the ministration of justice, and the punishment of iniquity'. The Deed has a unique historical interest, as containing the substance of all later Scottish documents of a kindred intention. It appears in the years 1590 and 1595, and, as the National Covenant, was signed again by all sorts of persons in 1638 and 1639; and it was accepted and subscribed by that eminent defender of the faith,

Charles II., twice before his coronation at Scone in 1651. The world has not yet learned the futility of such subscriptions, although the sight of Lennox's name, next to the names of the King and Craig, might have suggested the lesson three hundred years ago."

Note 11, *page* 23.

This Confession, pronounced by Calderwood to be forged, is contained in his History, vol. iii. p. 511, &c.

Note 12, *page* 23.

This New Confession is set down in Calderwood's *History*, vol. vii. pp. 226 and 233. It was signed by the Marquis of Huntly on his being restored to the King's favour. Dr. Sprott (*Scottish Liturgies*) pronounces it more Calvinistic than Knox's Confession of 1560. This is only partially true; its deliverances on the priestly office and on the Sacraments are much more developed than those of the old Confession.

Note 13, *page* 25.

The Confession referred to here is that drawn up in the year 1560. When the Scottish Parliament met, in the month of July that year, a petition signed by a number of barons, gentlemen, and ministers was presented to the Estates, craving a reformation of the doctrine and discipline of the Church, and that its patrimony might be devoted to the support of the ministry, the encouragement of learning, and the assistance of the poor. In answer to the first of these requests (that the corruptions of doctrine might be condemned) Parliament called upon the barons and ministers who had subscribed the petition to draw out and exhibit to them, under plain and distinct heads, the sum of the articles of belief which the petitioners wished to be established. In four days the Confession was produced as the declaration of their united judgment concerning the chief points of doctrine. This earliest Scottish Confession is inserted at length in the Histories of Knox and Calderwood, in the Acts of the Scottish Parliament for 1567, in Dunlop's *Collection of Confessions*, in Niemeyer's *Collectio Confessionum*, in Irving's *Confessions of Faith*, &c., *anterior to the Westminster Confession*, and in Schaff's *Confessions*. Perhaps the best and fullest account of it is contained in Principal Lee's *Lectures on the History of the Church of Scotland*, vol. i. p. 106, &c. See also the Church Histories of Cunningham and Grub.

Note 14, *page* 28.

The first Book of Discipline (*The Book of the Policie and Discipline of the Church*) was drawn up by a Commission—probably the same that drew up the

First Scottish Confession of Faith—consisting of Wynram, Sub-Prior of St. Andrews; Spotswood, Parson of Calder; John Willock, formerly a Franciscan friar; John Douglas, Rector of the University of St. Andrews; John Row (hitherto a priest at Perth), and John Knox. This book, though not formally approved by the Parliament, was subscribed by a great number of the nobility, gentry, and members of the Privy Council. Dr. Lee questions if an altogether correct copy of this production is now in existence, as the book which passes under that name appears to be an awkward translation into English. On the contents of this work, and other matters relating to it, Dr. Lee's *Lectures on the History of the Church of Scotland* may be most advantageously consulted. Also Grub, vol. ii. p. 91, and Cunningham, vol. i. p. 356.

The Second Book of Discipline was prepared by more than twenty brethren nominated by the Assembly, 1576, to meet in different parts of the country to prepare an overture on the Policy and Jurisdiction of the Church. Correct copies of this *Second Book of Discipline* are to be found in Calderwood's *History*, Pardovan's *Collections*, Dunlop's *Collection of Confessions*, Peterkin's *Booke of the Kirk of Scotland*, and Irving's *Confessions*, &c., *anterior to the Westminster Confession*. Ample discussions regarding its contents, &c., are to be found in the historical works of Lee, Grub, and Cunningham.

Note 15, page 30.

Episcopacy being now (1633) established by the persevering and generally illegal action of James and of Charles, it was conceived a great defect in the Church of Scotland that it had no suitable Liturgy nor Book of Canons. The new bishops were, accordingly, required to prepare draughts of both, that they might be submitted to the revision of the English prelates. It would have gratified both Charles and his ecclesiastical adviser, Laud, if the Scottish bishops would have adopted the English Liturgy without any alteration; but they represented that, as the Scots were jealous of their independence, it would be much easier to reconcile them to a set of forms composed by their own bishops than to the imposition of foreign ceremonies (Lee). It has too often been supposed that Scotland at this period had no liturgy of her own, and that the Scottish clergy and people were opposed to all liturgical forms whatever. This is a mistake. Scotland had never been without a *Book of Common Prayer*. Even before the Reformation was established by law, the *Service Book* of Edward VI. was used in many of the parishes where Reformation principles prevailed. After Protestantism became the creed of the nation, the *Book of Common Order*, used by the English congregation at Geneva, came into use, was sanctioned by several Assemblies, and continued the authorised form of worship up to this time

(Cunningham). By a blunder on the part of Charles and his advisers, the *Canons and Constitutions Ecclesiastical: gathered and put in forme for the Government of the Church of Scotland. Aberdene. Imprinted by Edward Raban*, appeared in 1636, before the *Booke of Common Prayer* was published. This latter, the famous and ill-fated Liturgy, was printed at Edinburgh in the year 1637 by Robert Young, printer to King Charles the First. It is generally known as "Laud's Liturgy," and was prepared by Maxwell, Bishop of Ross, and Wedderburn, Bishop of Dunblane, and then submitted to the Archbishop of Canterbury for revisal. Without entering further on the extensive and debated subject of Liturgies in Scotland since Reformation times, we may be permitted to refer the reader for ample information to the historical works of Lee, Grub, and Cunningham, to Dr. Sprott's Introductions to *Scottish Liturgies of the Reign of James VI.*, and the *Book of Common Order*, to Bishop Dowden's Introduction to *the Annotated Scottish Communion Office*, and to Baird's *Chapter on Liturgies*.

Note 16, page 30.

Without going minutely into details, we may notice that even before the General Assembly of 1602, which was held valid by Presbyterians, Prelacy was virtually introduced into the Scottish Church, and after that date it was openly established by a series of Acts of Parliament and by the exertions of the High Commission set up by the King. The Assemblies mentioned in the text were all Episcopalian, as is evinced by the whole course of procedure in these conventions. They were one and all contrary to the ancient constitution of the Church, convoked and packed by the King, and were, indeed, held merely for the purpose of registering his edicts and giving a quasi-legal aspect to them, as having received ecclesiastical sanction. The last of these so-called General Assemblies is remarkable for being the one in which the "Perth Articles" were adopted by the subservient bishops and clergy. No General Assembly was legally called, according to Presbyterians, after 1605, till the Assembly of 1638, which met at Glasgow, and overturned at one swoop the whole edifice of Scottish Episcopacy which James and Charles had been for so long industriously building. This Assembly sat for several weeks, and passed a large number of Acts of the utmost importance. They annulled the six preceding so-called Assemblies. Lee, Cunningham, Grub, and authorities cited by them.

Note 17, page 30.

Robert Montgomery was translated from the ministerial charge of Dunblane to Stirling, in 1572. Either through influence, or by a simoniacal agreement with

Esme, Duke of Lennox, he was promoted to the Archbishopric of Glasgow, after the death of Boyd, in the year 1581. Besides accepting this office of a bishop, contrary to the law of the Church, Montgomery was also accused on various charges relating to doctrine and practice by the General Assembly. The Assembly, being required by the King to stay their proceedings against him for accepting the See of Glasgow, then resolved to consider the charges against his life and doctrine. These charges against Montgomery were proved by eight witnesses, but the Assembly, unwilling to proceed against him in his absence, remitted the case for fuller investigation to the Presbytery of Stirling. In the meantime, he was ordered to remain Minister at Stirling and not to aspire to the Archbishopric of Glasgow. The Presbytery suspended him, and the Synod were about to depose and excommunicate him, when the King again interposed, summoning the members of Synod before the Privy Council. The Synod, as Wodrow relates, appeared, but declared that they declined the jurisdiction of the Council in a case so purely ecclesiastical. The General Assembly, to whom the case was again referred, disregarded a similar attempt to interfere with their spiritual functions; and, after some delay, in consequence of overtures of submission from Montgomery, by which, however, he did not abide, the Assembly proceeded to excommunication, which was pronounced by Mr. John Davidson, in Liberton Church. The affair occupied several successive Assemblies, and was one of the great causes of dissensions between the Court and the Church (Lee). This excommunication was declared null and void by Act of Parliament, 22nd May, 1584, and Montgomery was absolved from it by the Commissioners of the Assembly in 1587, and was afterwards settled at Symington, Ayrshire. Scott's Fasti. Keith's Catalogue. Calderwood.

Note 18, *page* 31.

James Lawson was Knox's colleague and successor. His Life, as written by Wodrow, is contained in the present volume of Collections.

David Lindsay. See note 6.

Robert Pont. He had entered the University of St. Andrews under the name of Kynpont, but is much better known under the name in the text. He appears as Minister of Dunkeld in 1562, afterwards Commissioner of Moray, then Minister of St. Cuthbert's, Edinburgh, and for twelve or thirteen years a senator of the College of Justice, as well as a minister. He was afterwards nominated to the Bishopric of Orkney, but he refused to accept the dignity without the approbation of the Church. When a new translation of the Scriptures was proposed, in 1601, he was ordained by the Assembly to revise the metrical translation of the Psalms. He died, 8th May, 1606, in his 82nd year, and the 44th of his ministry.

Publications—*Parvus Catechismus*, Andreap., 1573, 12mo (Translated, with notice of author, Wodrow, *Miscel.*, Vol. I.). *Three Sermons against Sacriledge*, Edinb., 1599 ; *A Treatise on the Right Reckoning of Yeares and Ages of the World*, Edinb., 1599, 4to; *De Unione Britanniae*, Edinb., 1604, 8vo; *De Sabbaticorum annorum periodis*, London, 1619, 4to; *Chronologia de Sabbatis*, London, 1626, 4to; *Translation and Interpretation of the Helvetic Confession*, 1566 ; *Contributions to Second Book of Discipline* ; *Six of the Metrical Psalms*, Edinb., 1565. Livingstone's Scottish Metrical Psalter. Lee's Lectures. Scott's Fasti, with the authorities there cited.

Walter Bulcanquell or Balcanquall was admitted, Whitsunday, 1574, Minister of St. Giles. He was elected to the chaplaincy of the altar called Jesus, 20th Nov., 1579, was called before the Privy Council for a sermon against the French influence at Court, 7th Dec., 1580. Having reflected on the Court in a sermon, 24th May, he fled to Berwick with his colleague Lawson, to avoid apprehension. In 1586, he was one of eight to whom was committed the discipline of Lothian by the General Assembly. To avoid a second apprehension he escaped to Yorkshire, 20th Dec., 1596, and was put to the horn, but was permitted to return next year ; and, in 1598, on a new arrangement of the Edinburgh charges was admitted to the Trinity College Church. Scott's Fasti, with authorities cited.

Nicol Dalgleish had been for many years a regent in St. Leonard's College, St. Andrews, which he left in the year 1577. He went to France and remained for some time at Bourges. After his return to Scotland, he was nominated by the General Assembly, in 1581, as a fit person for being made Principal of King's College, when it was proposed to remove Arbuthnot to the ministry of New Aberdeen, but no vacancy took place. Openly sympathising with his exiled co-presbyters, he was tried for treason and condemned to death, and a scaffold was erected for his execution, but the matter ended in his being confined in the Castle of St. Andrews. Afterwards, on his petition, he was pardoned and released. He returned to his former charge, from which he was translated to Pittenweem, in 1589. M'Crie's Life of Melville. Scott's Fasti, with authorities there cited.

John Davidson, formerly Minister of Liberton, successively Minister of St. Giles, 1589, and the Canongate Church, 1590, was finally translated, 1595, to Prestonpans. Scott's Fasti. Notices of him are given in Dr. C. Lee's St. Giles'.

John Duncanson had been Principal of St. Leonard's College, St. Andrews, from 1553, and was a member of the Chapter, prior to the Reformation. He was appointed by the Assembly, 1563, to assist in planting kirks in Menteith, demitted his office as Principal in 1566, and was therein succeeded by George Buchanan. He was then appointed Minister of the King's House, or Dean of the Chapel

Royal of Stirling. In 1574 he was Commissioner of Galloway, and with others had a hand in drawing up the *Second Book of Discipline*. He died in 1601, aged about 100. He wrote a reply to the Jesuit Tyrie's *Refutation of Knox's Answer* to a former work, which reply was appointed to be revised by the General Assembly, March, 1573. Scott's Fasti. Lee. McCrie's Life of Melville.

Note 19, page 31.

Patrick Adamson, otherwise Constan or Coustone, was born in the town of Perth. Having been first licensed to be a preacher, he afterwards studied law, which study he prosecuted several years in France. On his return home, he resumed his clerical functions, and became successively Minister of Ceres and Paisley, from which latter place he was taken into the family of the Earl of Morton whilst Regent. His patron, Morton, made him Archbishop of St. Andrews, 1576; but Adamson was never consecrated. He seems to have been a man of good literature, and was much employed by the Court party to argue against the Presbyterians. He fell into debt and deep distress, so that the King became ashamed of him, and granted the life-rent of the See of St. Andrews to the Duke of Lennox. He died in the year 1591, and it is said that he on his death-bed recanted his Episcopalian tenets. He was the author of several books, as noticed by Wodrow. He was charged with mutilating the Records of the General Assembly to serve the King's views. A most bitter, malevolent, and coarse, attack on Adamson, entitled *The Legend of the Bishop of St. Andrews Lyfe, &c.*, is printed by Dalyell in his *Scotish Poems of the 16th Century*. Keith's Catalogue. Lee. M'Crie's Lives of Knox and Melville.

Note 20, page 32.

The choice of these ambassadors from the Church was eminently judicious; Craig being cautious, courtly, and an experienced diplomatist; Davidson, impetuous and intrepid, and both eloquent and honest.

Note 21, page 33.

John Durie occupies a place in the present volume of Collections.

Hume. This seems to have been Alexander Hume or Home, Minister of Dunbar. He was admitted minister there, 1582, and demitted his charge some time previous to May, 1601. Scott's Fasti. About the same time, there was another Alexander Hume in the Church, viz., Alexander Hume or Home, Minister of Logie, near Stirling, and author of *Hymnes or Sacred Songs*, and is mentioned as "Sone to umqle Pat. Home of Polwart". M'Crie's Life of Melville.

Note 22, page 34.

Nothing shows the mean and vindictive spirit of King James more than the persecution of these ministers' wives when he could not reach the husbands. Calderwood iv. p. 200, says: "The honest weomen sold the movables which they could not keepe, and delivered the keyes to the magistrats. Farther, there was another charge givin to some weoman within the toun, evill affected to the late Acts of Parliament, to retire them be-north the water of Tay for a space." Lee, also Cunningham's History, vol. i. p. 467.

Note 23, page 34.

Andrew Blackhall was formerly one of the conventual brethren of the Abbey of Holyrood-house, and, in 1567, became Minister of Ormiston, having at the same time charge also of Cranstoun and Pencaitland, with a stipend of one hundred pounds. In 1570, he removed to Cranstoun. Scott's Fasti. Frequent notices of him occur in Calderwood's History.

John Brand was formerly a monk in the Abbey of Holyrood, and was employed by Archbishop Hamilton to carry a message to John Knox, "That howsoever he had introduced another Form of Religion, and reformed the doctrine of the Church, whereof it might be there was some reason, yet he should do well not to shake loose the Order and Policy received, which had been the work of ages, till he was sure of a better to be settled in place thereof". Brand was examined, and admitted to the charge of Holyrood-house, afterwards the Canongate Church, by the Superintendent of Lothian, in 1564. After some other preferments by the King, he died in 1600. Scott's Fasti. Lee i. 293, note, notices that it fell to Brand to proclaim the marriage of Queen Mary to Darnley.

John Herries or Hereis was in 1576 appointed Minister of Ormiston, whence he was translated in March, 1584, to Newbattle. He was presented by James VI., 11th March, 1586, to the parsonage and vicarage of Melvile or Melville, a now suppressed parish, and died sometime before 8th Aug., 1620. Scott's Fasti, with authorities.

Note 24, page 35.

Andrew Hay, son of the Laird of Tallo, was Rector and Parson of Renfrew, in 1558, but joined the Reformers in 1559. He took an active share in the ecclesiastical transactions of his time, being a member of thirty-four of the forty Assemblies held before 1590. He was twice moderator. He attended the Conventions of 1571 and 1588. He was named Dean of the Chapter of Glasgow at the former. For several years he discharged the duties of Commissioner of Clydesdale, Renfrew, and Lennox, besides holding several other offices. He suffered for his principles, and was several times "in ward". We find him in office in 1591. He had the character of being an "honest, zealous, and frank-hearted gentleman, who never liked bishopricks". Scott's Fasti. J. Melville's Autobiography.

Andrew Polwart, after studying at Geneva for the ministry, was appointed to Paisley, in 1574. In the same year, he was named by the Church one of those who were to revise and correct the English edition of the Bible, then being printed by Arbuthnot and Bassandyne. He was, in 1578, translated from Paisley and presented by James VI. to the sub-deanery of Glasgow. By the Assembly of 1581, he was one of those appointed to see after the constituting of presbyteries, specially in the districts of Clydesdale, Renfrew, and Lennox, and was also " one of the brethren for reconciling the great and many divisions and deidly feids ryseing among parties in the western district". He served the Church on various commissions, and died at Glasgow in 1587. We are informed that "there was in his studie buikis estimat to iii^c marks. He leiffs in legacie to Adam Boyde of Pinkill his French Bible and his hagbute." It was reported of him that in his sermons he insisted much on Protestants laying aside their several differences and cultivating a spirit of mutual unity. Scott's Fasti. Lee's Memorial. Calderwood. Melville's Autobiography.

Patrick Galloway was first settled as Minister of Perth, from which charge he was promoted to be one of the King's chaplains. He is mentioned as in the Great Kirk, in 1610, and on the division of the city, in 1625, he was nominated to the north-west quarter in the High or Great Kirk. So effectually did he ingratiate himself with the King that his son was created a peer by the title of Lord Dunkeld. Lee ii. p. 157, note. Scott's Fasti. His name often occurs in the history of that period. Notices of Galloway are also to be found in Dr. Cameron Lee's St. Giles'.

James Carmichael studied at St. Leonard's College, and graduated A.M. at St. Andrews, about 1564. He was appointed master of the Grammar School there, an office which he held about six years, and was then, in August, 1570, admitted Minister of Haddington. From April 16, 1572, he combined with his ministerial functions the office of schoolmaster, with a salary of forty-two pounds, but the Town Council, 28th May, 1574, resolved "that in no time coming the minister of the Kirk should be admitted schoolmaster of the burgh". Carmichael thereupon relinquished that office in 1576, receiving a hundred pounds as compensation. He took an active part in ecclesiastical business, and must have been a man of great business aptitude and scholarly accomplishments, as he was appointed by the Assembly one of four for preparing the *Acts of the Kirk* for more general use, and also one of six for overseeing every book before it was printed. When the *Regiam Majestatem*, with notes by Sir John Skene, was put to press, "finding non so meit as Mr. James Carmichael, minister at Haddingtoune to examine and espy and correct such errors and faults therein as usuallie occurs in every printing that first cumis from the presse," the lords of the Privy Council applied to his presbytery to excuse his absence from his charge "the space of tua monethis or thereby". Note, M'Crie's Life of Melville, p. 391. Scott's Fasti. Spottiswoode. Calderwood. Carmichael's Life is also contained in Wodrow's Collections.

Note 25, page 35.

Robert Pont. In addition to what is stated in Note 18, page 31, it may be remarked, that however incongruous it may appear now for a clergyman to form one of the College of Justice, it was not so looked upon when that Court was first established. When the Court of Session was instituted in 1532, its constitution was to be composed of fourteen judges—one half selected from the spiritual and the other from the temporal estate, over whom was placed a President, who was always to be a clergyman. Accordingly the first President was Alexander Myln, Abbot of Cambuskenneth. It has, however, always been a principle of the Presbyterian Church of Scotland that the ministers of religion ought not to be distracted from the duties of their office by holding civil places. The first General Assembly (1560) petitioned the estates to remove all ministers of religion from civil offices. It was only at the express request of the Regent Mar that the Assembly allowed Pont to act as a Lord of Session on account of his great knowledge of the laws. Tytler. M'Crie's Life of Knox, with authorities cited.

Note 26, page 36.

Adam Johnston, in 1569, entered as Minister and Provost of the Collegiate Church of Crichton, to which were afterwards added the Churches of Fala and Soutra. He was appointed by the Assembly, in 1579, joint Commissioner with John Spottiswood over the province of Lothian. Afterwards he was employed in several Commissions by the Presbyterian party. In 1587, he was named for visiting the dangerous parts of the North, and was also sent against the Catholics in the South and West. He was afterwards, in 1590, appointed by the Privy Council, one of three for the maintenance of true religion within the bounds of his presbytery, to which office was subsequently conjoined the visitation along with a colleague, of the ministers in the Merse. After an active and consistent life, Johnston died in 1596, in the twenty-eighth year of his ministry. Scott's Fasti. Wodrow Miscellany. Calderwood's History.

William Pourie was successively Minister at Errol and Abercorn. He was presented to the vicarage of the latter by James VI., in 1595, and died in 1632, in the forty-seventh year of his ministry. Scott's Fasti.

Andrew Simson taught at Perth, between 1550 and 1560. At the establishment of the Reformation, he became Minister of Dunning and Cargill, from which he was translated in 1566, to Dunbar, where he sustained the double office of Minister of the parish and Master of the Grammar school. He was the author of the Latin Rudiments which continued to be taught in the schools of Scotland until the time of Ruddiman, and was much esteemed by that accomplished scholar. M'Crie's Life of Knox, with authorities cited. See also Lee i. p. 261 *et seq.* Scott's Fasti.

Patrick Simson, after serving the charges successively of Spott, Tranent, and Cramond, was translated to Stirling, in 1590. He was elected to Edinburgh, 1596, but refused the charge. He died in 1618, in his 62nd year. Works: *A Short Compend of the Historie of the First Ten Persecutions, &c.*, Edin., 1613-16, 4to; *A Short Compend of the Growth of the Heresies, &c.*, Edin., 1616, 4to. Scott's Fasti. M'Crie's Life of Melville.

John Clappertoun, a native of Berwickshire, was, in 1570, Exhorter at Livingston, whence he was successively translated to Hutton and Coldstream. After trimming sometime between the Presbyterians and the Court party, he finally cast in his lot with the latter, and was, by the Assembly of 1606 appointed Constant Moderator of his Presbytery. He continued submissive to the measures of the Court till his death, which took place in 1617, in the forty-first year of his ministry. Calderwood says of him: "The man was ambitious, and readie to embrace any preferment". Scott's Fasti. Calderwood's History.

Patrick Kinlowrie, otherwise Kinlowie (Kinloquhy) or Kinloch, a canon of the Augustinian Monastery at St. Andrews, previous to the Reformation, was settled Minister at Linlithgow sometime in 1561, and was presented to the vicarage by the King, in 1574, having charge also of Kinneil, Carridin, and Bynnie. He was a member of Assembly, in 1578, when the *Second Book of Discipline* was confirmed. After an abortive attempt to make him one of the ministers of Edinburgh, he was cited to appear before the Privy Council for nonobedience to his Ordinary, on which occasion he read answers for himself and his brethren; yet before the month closed he gave in his submission. He was engaged by the King, in 1586, along with two of the court ministers, to hold communication with his recusant brethren with a view to their submission. He seems to have pleased the court party, for in 1589 he was appointed, by the Privy Council, one of the Commissioners for the maintenance of true religion in the Sheriffdom of Linlithgow. He was in 1608 still one of these Commissioners, and died a few years after. Scott's Fasti.

Note 27, page 39.

It may perhaps be not altogether impertinent to call attention to the remarkable paper here reproduced by Wodrow; the style so simple, manly, terse and, for the period, wonderfully good. Well may the writers characterise as "nottable" the sentence: *That they who were not true to God would never be true to man.*

Note 28, page 44.

Among the peculiarities of the so-called Episcopacy then set up, was the fact that the bishops were subject to the various judicatories of the Church. These, specially the General Assembly as the Supreme Court, could try, suspend, depose, and even excommunicate, those ecclesiastically superior to the constituent members. In 1580, the Synod of Fife, having revived an old process against the Archbishop of St. Andrews, and having found him guilty, not only of the charge brought against him, but of the additional one of contumacy, excommunicated him. Adamson published an appeal from this sentence which was answered by James Melville. Adamson, as noticed in a previous note, having lost the Court support, was reduced to penury and made humble submission, and at the King's instance received a conditional absolution. Lee ii. p. 89. Calderwood iv. p. 504.

Note 29, page 45.

This letter may be found in James Melville's Autobiography and Diary, p. 200, Wodrow Society Edition.

Note 30, page 46.

William Aird was minister of the West Kirk, beside Edinburgh, otherwise called Sanct Cuthbert's Kirk. His fellow labourer was Mr. Nicol Dalgleish. "William Aird, before his calling to the ministrie, was a maisson, and mareid. He learned first of his wife to read English, and thereafter, by himself, he studied to Latine, Greeke, and Hebrewe languages, attended upon the Colledge and the Exercise, and studied Divinitie. He profited so weill in few yeeres, that he was called to the ministrie, and proved a notable instrument in the Kirk of God." Calderwood iv. p. 237.

Note 31, page 46.

Confession of Helvetia, or Confessio Helvetica. There are two documents bearing this name which are not to be confounded. The former, drawn up by Bullinger, Myconius Grynaeus, Leo Juda and Grossman, and composed in Latin, was dated 1536. It was submitted to and approved by the

Conference at Basel held that year, and also by the Assembly at Wittemberg, and by a meeting of Protestant princes at Smalkald in 1537. This Confession was translated into English by George Wishart the martyr. This translation is supposed to be the only literary production of Wishart extant. It is reprinted, with introductory note, in Vol I. *Miscellany of the Wodrow Society.* The latter document, known by the name of the Later Confession of Helvetia, is the one referred to in the text. It was composed by Henry Bullinger, in the year 1562. It is sometimes known also as the Confession of the Church of Zurich, and was translated into English by Robert Pont. The General Assembly of 1566, after deliberating on it, ordained it to be printed with an epistle sent by the Assembly approving it, providing a note be put in the margin, where mention is made of some holy days. Lee. This confession declares superiority of ministers to be a human appointment, and Confirmation to be a device of men which the Church may want without any disadvantage. It disapproved prolix public prayers hindering the preaching of the Word, canonical hours, heaping up ceremonies to the prejudice of Christian liberty; and the observation of days dedicated to the saints, but it retained the festivals commemorative of Christ's Nativity, Circumcision, Passion, Resurrection, Ascension, and the effusion of His Spirit on the day of Pentecost. These, as well as the Saints' days, were objected to by the Scottish Church, which was so far from observing any of them (says Calderwood) that it oftentimes held its Assemblies on the day kept by many Churches in remembrance of Christ's Nativity. Lee i. 286. The texts of both Confessions in Latin are contained in Niemeyer's *Collectio Confessionum.*

Note 32, page 52.

This Letter from Hume told in homely, but expressive phrase that all the ministers betwixt Stirling and Berwick, all Lothian, and all the Merse, had subscribed, with only ten exceptions (there were more according to Wodrow's text); that the Laird of Dun, the most venerable champion of the Kirk, had so far receded from his primitive faith, as to have become a pest to the ministry in the North; that John Durie, who had so long resisted, "had cracked his curple" at last, and closed his mouth; that John Craig, so long the coadjutor of Knox, and John Brande, his colleague, had submitted, and that the pulpits in Edinburgh were nearly silent—so fearful had been the defection, except, said he, a very few who sigh and sob under the cross. Tytler's History of Scot. iv. p. 97.

Note 33, page 52.

Robert Boyd, of Trochrodge or Trochrig, was the son of James Boyd, Archbishop of Glasgow. He was Professor of Divinity, first at Samur, in

France, and afterwards at home, both in Glasgow and in Edinburgh. He wrote a Commentary upon Ephesians. Keith's Catalogue. Boyd's Life has been written by Wodrow, and forms one of the most valuable of all his Collections, as he had free access to the family papers. This Life has been published with other of Wodrow's Collections by the Maitland Society.

Note 34, page 53.

As Calvin's Catechism was the first adopted by the Church of Scotland, a slight notice of it may not be uninteresting. Calvin or Cauvin was born at Noyon in Picardy, 10th July, 1509, and died at Geneva, 27th May, 1564. In 1536, he was elected by the Genevese not only preacher, but also doctor (teacher) of sacred letters. He lost no time in setting about carrying out his duties. He had lately published his Institutions, the book that wrought Craig's conversion; and followed up that work in the same year with a summary of its doctrine. This production afterwards became Calvin's Catechism. It was composed originally in French, for adults and not for children, and was not in the form of question and answer. In this respect compare the Catechism of the Council of Trent and the Catechism of Archbishop Hamilton, the last effort at reformation of the Catholic Church in Scotland. Beza states that in 1541 Calvin composed a Catechism in French and Latin, differing little from the former: only fuller, and divided into questions and answers. Soon after its publication, it was translated into many languages and adopted in various countries. In England it probably formed the basis of Nowell's, the one authorised at the Reformation by the Church of England. Calvin's Catechism in English was first printed at Geneva by John Crespin, in the year 1556. This was reprinted at Edinburgh, in 1564, by Robert Lekprevik. The Latin Catechism is included in Niemeyer's *Collectio Confessionum*, and the English translation in Dunlop's *Confessions*, 730, as stated by Wodrow. The English translation has also been reprinted by Dr. Horatius Bonar, London, 1866, in his *Catechisms of the Scottish Reformation*, with a valuable preface and notes, from which the substance of this note has been chiefly drawn. At the end of Calvin's Catechism there was printed an abstract entitled, "The maner to examine children before they be admitted to the Supper of the Lord". This work went by the name of *The Little Catechism*, and was "read and learnit in Lectors' Schools". Included also by Dr. Bonar in his *Catechisms, &c.*

Note 35, page 54.

Wodrow has here fallen into a curious blunder from his ignorance of the existence of Craig's earlier and larger Catechism, confounding it with an abstract of it published by Craig himself, about ten years later, at the request of the General Assembly. The former and larger Catechism of Craig was composed by him, when resident in Aberdeen, and was published at Edinburgh, in 1581, by Henry Charteris, under the title of *A Shorte Svmme of the whole Catechism, Wherein the Question is proponed and answered in few wordes, for the greater ease of the commoune people and children.* It is addressed: "To the Professovres of Christis Evangell at Newe Abirdene, M. Johne Craig wisheth the perpetual comfort and increase of the Holie Spirit, to the end of their battell". A most beautiful fac-simile reprint of this rare work was executed, 1883, at the desire and under the direction of the late Mr. James Gibson Craig, by Mr. Thomas Graves Law, Edinburgh, with a valuable Introduction, which embraces perhaps almost the whole authentic information we have regarding Craig's history. This earlier Catechism was reprinted in London by John Wolfe, in 1583, by Robert Waldegrave in 1584, by Thomas Orwin, in 1589, and by Robert Harrison, in 1597—which last was the edition followed by Dr. Bonar in his reprint contained in his *Catechisms*. The first edition (1581) is of the greatest rarity, only two copies being known to be in existence; and this scarceness may account for the fact that it was unknown to Dr. H. Scott, Dunlop, Tytler, and others. Mr. Law's Introduction. This larger and earlier Catechism has been confounded by Wodrow with an abridged work of a similar character, first published by Craig, in 1591-2, entitled, *Ane Forme of Examination before the Communion*, and prepared by him, as above stated, by the direction of the General Assembly, 1590. This "forme" has been often reprinted: by Dunlop, in his *Confessions*; by E. Irving; by Dr. Bonar; and by others. Dunlop describes it as Craig's Catechism, being ignorant of its predecessor's existence.

The Honourable Mr. Archibald Campbell mentioned in the text was second son of Lord Niel Campbell, second son of Archibald, Marquis of Argyll. According to Dr. Johnson, as recorded by Boswell, he was engaged in the rebellion of his uncle, the ninth Earl of Argyll, in 1685, and on its failure made his escape to Surinam. Though a violent Whig in his early years, " he afterwards," Johnson states, "from keeping better company, became a violent Tory". He changed not only his politics, but his church principles also, and at the Revolution adhered to the ejected Church in Scotland, and even refused to communicate in the Church of England, or to be present at any place where King William's name was mentioned. On 25th August, 1711, he was consecrated a bishop at Dundee by Bishops Rose, Douglas and Falconer, but continued to reside in London. With some other non-juring clergymen he entered into negotiations for a union with the Eastern Church. The proposal was, however, found impracticable. In a letter to the Chevalier, Lockhart thus refers to the Bishop: "A. Campbell (who, though adorned with many of the qualifications necessary in a bishop, and remarkable for some things inconsistent with the character of a gentleman, was most imprudently consecrated some time ago) is coming here from London with the view of forming a party". The result of his visit to Scotland was that, on 10th May, 1721, he was chosen by the clergy of Aberdeen their diocesan bishop, upon which the College of Bishops wrote signifying their approval, on condition that he would undertake to propagate no new doctrine or usage not sanctioned by the Canons of the Church. After his election, Campbell still continued to reside in London, but was, notwithstanding, of considerable service to his fellow-churchmen. On account of a divergence of views in regard to certain usages, he resigned his office in 1724. He afterwards attempted to constitute a communion distinct from the Sancroftian line ; and, to ensure its permanence, he ventured upon the exceptional step of a consecration by himself without any assistance. His small non-juring sect soon became extinct. Campbell died in the year 1744. His connection with the Ancient Records of the Church of Scotland has already been referred to in Note 1. He wrote a treatise, referred to by Wodrow, *Doctrine of the Middle State between Death and the Resurrection*, also several controversial works. Bishop Dowden of Edinburgh says Campbell was not only a man of curious and varied learning, but possessed much intellectual power. The length of this Note prevents us from quoting Craig's sentiments on the Eucharist, or referring to Campbell's criticisms thereon. Dictionary of Nat. Biography, Bishop Keith. Dowden's Introduction to the Annotated Scottish Communion Office.

Note 36, page 54.

The Palatine Catechism, that is "A Catechism of Christian Religion, composed by Zachary Ursin, approved by Frederick III. Elector Palatine, the Reformed Church in the Palatinate, and by other Reformed Churches in Germany, and taught in their Schools and Churches . . . translated into English and printed *anno* 1591, by public Authority for the Use of Scotland". Dr. H. Bonar. Bonar adds, "I have not been able to discover any Act of Assembly authorising this Catechism, nor any reference to it in the history of our Church. One would like to know how and why Calvin came to be superseded by Ursin, Ursin by Craig, and Craig by our present Westminster Catechism". The Catechism was composed in 1563. The text at full length, both in German and Latin, is to be found in Niemeyer's *Collectio Confessionum*. There are various English translations of the Catechism, *e.g.* in Dunlop's *Confessions;* in Bonar's *Catechisms* already referred to. Bonar, to his reproduction, has added an instructive preface and notes, to which the reader is referred for further information.

Note 37, *page* 55, *seee Note* 24.

Note 38, *page* 55.

Henry Blyth studied at St. Andrews and, in 1598, was appointed by the Presbytery of Edinburgh to officiate occasionally in the room of Mr. Brand, and translated to the first charge of Holyrood house in the Canongate, in 1601. Afterwards, espousing the cause of the persecuted ministers Forbes and Welsh, he was warded for some time in Blackness Castle. In 1620, he was deprived of his charge by the High Commission, it being his Majesty's will that he "wald give obedience in some vther place". He was afterwards, in 1622, presented to the Church and Parish of Eccles, and died at Edinburgh, in 1635, aged about 62 years. Scott's Fasti. Calderwood.

J. Fairfoul was a student of St. Andrew's, in 1569, exhorter at Aberdour, 1571, school-master at Dunfermline, 1584, and Vicar of Dalgatie and Beath before 1594. In 1598, he was translated to Dunfermline. For sympathising with the ministers banished in 1606 for holding the Assembly of Aberdeen, Fairfoul was confined for a time in Dundee. Ultimately he became Minister of Anstruther-Wester, and died in 1626, aged 80 years.

Peter Ewart, Ewat, Hewart, Howat, Hewet, for under all these forms does his name appear, was one of the ministers of Edinburgh, and in 1612 had a gift from the King of the Abbacy of Crossraguel, which entitled him to a seat in Parliament. Siding with the Liberal party, he was, in 1617, deprived by the High Commission, and died at Maybole in 1645. For his liturgical services, see Dr. Sprott's Introduction to the *Scottish Liturgies of James VI*. Scott's Fasti. Calderwood.

Andrew Lamb was sometime Minister of Burntisland, afterwards translated to Arbroath, thereafter to South Leith. In 1610, he was consecrated at London, Bishop of Brechin, and in 1619, was transferred to the See of Galloway. He died in the year 1634. Keith's Catalogue. Scott's Fasti. Lee.

James Nicholson, Parson of Meigle, was preferred to the See of Dunkeld, in the year 1606. He was chosen to preside in the Assembly at Linlithgow, 10th December, 1606. He died next year, on 17th August. Keith's Catalogue. Scott's Fasti.

James Law became Minister of Kirkliston, in 1585, was made Bishop of Orkney, in 1605, and, having been Spottiswoode's "old companion at football, and com-presbyter, was, by his influence, admitted his successor at Glasgow". He died in 1632. Dr. Sprott's Introduction to S. Liturgies, &c.

John Spotswood—the future archbishop and historian, already noticed, Note 1.

Note 39, page 55.

Rev. Laurence Charters was an episcopal clergyman, and previously Professor of Theology, in the University of Edinburgh. He drew up for the use of his friend, Sir Robert Sibbald, a Catalogue of Scottish Theological writers, with some notice of their works. This Catalogue was published with an Introduction giving some notices of Charters and his works, along with some other documents relating to Scotland, by the late Mr. Maidment, under the title of *Catalogues of Scottish Writers*, Edinburgh, 1833.

Note 40, page 55.

John Livingstoun, son of W. Livingstoun, Minister of Lanark, was born in 1603, and was educated at the University of Glasgow. He early showed a spirit of nonconformity in disobeying the Perth Articles. He was licensed a preacher in 1625, and was often in trouble on account of his principles. He was settled Minister of Stranraer, in 1638, from which place he was translated to Ancrum, in 1648. Here he remained till 1662, when he was forced to leave the country. He went to Rotterdam where he ended his days, in 1672, in his seventieth year. He wrote an account of his Life, which has been published along with some of his letters and other memoranda concerning him, by the Wodrow Society. Vol. I. *Select Biographies.* See also Scott's Fasti.

Note 41, page 56.

Rollock, the well known first Principal of the University of Edinburgh. Notices of his Life and works are to be found in Vol. I. of his selected works, edited by Dr. Gunn for the Wodrow Society.

Note 42, page 56.

T. Crawford, or Crauford, author of a *History of the University of Edinburgh*, was educated at St. Andrews, and graduated there M.A., in 1621. In 1626, he was appointed Professor of Humanity in the College of Edinburgh, and in 1630, Rector of the High School there. On the visit of Charles I. to Edinburgh, Crawford was conjoined with Principal John Adamson and Drummond the poet, in devising the pageants and making the speeches and complimentary verses with which the monarch was entertained. These were published in 1633. Crawford was afterwards appointed to the Chair of Mathematics, and died 30th March, 1662, leaving the reputation of having been a great grammarian, a profound philosopher, and deep theologian. His *History of Edinburgh University from* 1580 *to* 1646, was published in 1808. See Histories of University of Edinburgh, by Dalziel and Grant; also Dictionary of Nat. Biography.

Note 43, page 58.

Weems was translated, in 1562, from Ratho to Glasgow. His Life is contained in one of the volumes of Wodrow's *Collections*, edited, with an interesting Appendix to the Life, for the Maitland Society. For full particulars regarding Weem's troubled life, see in addition to the work mentioned, Scott's Fasti.

Note 44, page 58.

The Convention at Leith took place in 1571-2. Dr. Cunningham states that it is unknown by whom it was convened. It was not a regular assembly, but it assumed to itself the strength, force, and effect of a General Assembly, and it was attended by the superintendents, barons, commissioners to plant kirks, commissioners of provinces, towns, kirks, and ministers. *Booke of the Universal Kirk*, quoted by Cunningham. This Convention appointed certain commissioners to meet and confer with certain other commissioners chosen by the Privy Council. These joint committees formed what has been called the Concordat of Leith, by which a modified Episcopacy was introduced. The bishops appointed under this arrangement were called in derision, Tulchan Bishops. See on this subject, among others, the Church Histories of Cunningham, Lee, Calderwood, Grub, &c.

Note 45, page 60.

The "Agustan Confession" was the famous document presented by the Lutherans to the Emperor Charles V. at the Diet of Augsburg, in 1530. This Confession, afterwards giving rise to various differences, had published in its defence what was called *Apologia Confessionis*, and this was followed later by the Smalcald Articles, and the Form of Concord. These failed to secure harmony and union among the Protestants. The Council of Magdeburg was called by John Cassimir, Prince Palatine, to bring about a union between the Lutheran and Reformed Churches, which Council did not however meet. Representatives from the Churches of England and Scotland were invited to attend; a proof of the intimate communion subsisting between the reformed Churches of Britain and those of the Continent. Mosheim. Calderwood.

Note 46, page 64.

The Laird of Fintry was David Graham. He was executed, 16th February, 1592-3 for carrying on negotiations with Spain against the Protestant religion in this country. Row. Calderwood.

Note 47, page 64.

William Gordon, the last Popish Bishop of Aberdeen, is thus noticed by Archbishop Spottiswoode in his History, vol. i., page 210: "William Gordon, son to the Earl of Huntly, succeeded in the place. This man, brought up in letters at Aberdeen, followed his studies a long time in Paris, and returning thence, was first parson of Clat, and afterwards promoved to the See. Some hopes he gave at first of a virtuous man, but afterwards turned a very epicure, spending all his time in drinking and whoring; he dilapidated the whole rents by fewing the lands, and converting the victual-duties into money, a great part whereof he wasted on his base children, and the whores their mothers,—a man not worthy to be placed in this catalogue. He died in the year 1577." A hollow in the road, which winds northwards along the base of Benachie, is still pointed out where an unsuccessful attack was made on a body of the Earl of Huntly's retainers, returning to the Castle of Strathbogie, laden with the spoils of the Cathedral and Bishop's Palace of Aberdeen. This hints pretty distinctly where part of the ecclesiastical plunder of Aberdeen went. See also Keith's Catalogue.

Note 48, page 66.

Herriot was succeeded, not by Blackburn, but by John Craig, as has been already stated in the introductory notice of Craig.

Note 49, page 66.

"The fatall turn of things in the 1597." On the 17th December, 1596, a tumult arose in the Streets of Edinburgh [see Calderwood v., p. 510] "which was made the pretext for the alterations in the government of the Church afterwards introduced by the King. The King, either in real or pretended alarm, retired to Linlithgow, and unjustly ascribed the uprising to the sermons of the ministers. James made this the pretext for issuing an order enjoining all ministers to subscribe a bond, acknowledging the King as their judge, not only in all cases of sedition and treason, but in all complaints of their speeches which may import these crimes". Lee. In pursuance of this policy, the Court prepared fifty-five queries concerning Church government to be submitted to a Convention of ministers summoned by the King to meet at Perth, in Feb. 1596-7. Great pains had been taken by the Court to secure a large attendance of the Northern ministers, as being less under the influence of the extreme Presbyterians of Fife and Edinburgh, and more likely for other reasons to support the King's policy. The King succeeded in getting all his measures carried. The regular meeting of the General Assembly, which had been appointed to be held at St. Andrews, was attended by very few, and was disowned by the King, who called another Assembly to meet at Dundee, on the 1st of May. This Assembly proved quite subservient to his wishes. Besides other measures, he prevailed on them to consent that "such ministers as his Majesty shall at any time please to provide to the office, dignity, and title of bishop, abbot, or other prelate, shall have vote in Parliament". The number of what Wodrow calls contemptuously "ministers' votters" was fixed at fifty-one, the same as in the time of the Catholic Church. Lee and Cunningham.

Note 50, page 67.

The Government was frequently in the way of appointing commissions to visit the various Universities to inquire into their teaching, discipline and administration of funds. The Scottish reformers also, who were specially interested in the cause of education generally, and its diffusion among all classes of the community, through committees appointed by the General Assembly, often made similar investigations regarding the doctrine, morality and suitability of the regents and other officials in these seminaries. In the year 1578, when great exertions were made in behalf of the various centres of education, measures were recommended by a Government Commission for restoring the dilapidated funds of King's College; and at the same time a new plan of instruction was drawn up for it, similar to those new schemes introduced into St. Andrews and Glasgow. This "new foundation" *inter alia* appoints a principal, sub-principal, three regents, and a teacher of grammar, and defines the duties of these officials. One of the new recommendations was that the teachers henceforth were to confine themselves in their tuition to one special branch of study, and not to carry their pupils through the whole curriculum of study as heretofore. In 1581, Parliament appointed a Commission to "treate and conclude on certane articles," one of which was "Reformatioun of the College of Abirdene". The following were some of the steps taken regarding this "new erection". In April, 1583, George, Earl Marischal; Robert, Commendator of Deer, and certain brethren, who had charge of the King's Commission, presented a petition to the General Assembly, desiring it to visit the College of Aberdeen to take trial of the travels they had taken in the said matter, and "to depute some persons to take trial of the members thereof, that they be sufficient and qualified to *conforme to the new erection*". To this the Assembly agreed, and ordained Mr. James Lawson and others "to consider the proceedings of the said Commissioners touching the said erection; and, if they find the same allowable and weel done, to give their testimony and approbation thereof to be presented to the Erle Marshal, that his Lo. may travel for the king's M. confirmation thereof". Nothing having been done in the affair, the Assembly, which met in October that year, renewed the appointment of the Committee. It appears from a letter, published by Dr. M'Crie, that this measure met with opposition from the Crown. Public opinion also seems to have been against the new erection, as Wodrow mentions that there was a "hazard of the scholars skailing to St. Andrews". The question as to the legality of the new foundation was afterwards warmly disputed in the College between the years 1634 and 1638. M'Crie's Life of Melville. Lee. Calderwood's History. Book of the Kirk of Scotland, Peterkin's edition. Records of the University and King's College, Aberdeen.

Note 51, page 68.

The King at this time fell under the influence and guidance of the Duke of Lennox and the Earl of Arran, whose views on ecclesiastical matters were widely different from the Presbyterian leaders.

Note 52, page 70.

"The excommunicat earles" were the Earls of Huntly, Errol and Angus, the two first being specially obnoxious to the Presbyterian chiefs on account of their adherence to the Catholic faith. James seemed to have a lurking favour for Huntly, and some time after created him Marquis of Huntly.

Note 53, page 71.

These men—tried leaders, and the most eminent for ability, learning and worth in the Church—formed what may be styled a standing committee for the safety of the Church. Their appointment, however, seems to have created some scandal, as being contrary to Presbyterian parity and the government of the Church by the usual judicatories of Presbytery, Synod and Assembly. But the measure was only a temporary one, and called forth by the special exigencies of the times.

Note 54, page 71.

David Black studied at St. Andrews, but afterwards left the country for a time. On his return to Scotland he was, through the influence of Andrew Melville, appointed, in 1590, minister of St. Andrews. In October, 1596, while the country was agitated by the report of the return of the Popish Earls, Black from the pulpit boldly denounced the Governments of both England and Scotland in the strongest terms. This gave offence to the King, and Black was summoned before the Privy Council, 18th November, 1596. He, however, declined their authority to judge in matters spiritual, which declinature was adhered to by his whole brethren of the ministry. The trial, notwithstanding, proceeded. The Court found itself competent to try the case, as the crimes charged in the libel were of a treasonable and seditious nature. The King, knowing how powerful the ecclesiastical interest was in the kingdom, was unwilling to proceed to extremities, and would have willingly accepted a nominal fine, could Black have been prevailed on to plead guilty; but to do so would have yielded up the whole point of spiritual independency. As compromise was found impossible, the libel was found proven, on 9th December, and Black was charged to enter himself in ward "in a part by-north of the North Water, and to remaine and keepe waird by-north the said water, upon his owne expences; . . . ay and whill His Hienesse declare his will and minde towards him". The Synod of Fife, 8th February, petitioned His Majesty that Black might be reponed, but unsuccessfully, as the King removed him in July, 1597, to Arbirlot. Black died at Dundee, on his way to Perth, while stretching out his hand after having given thanks at a meal, on 12th January, 1603. On Black's life and case, see Calderwood, Spottiswoode, Tytler, Scott's Fasti, and Cunningham, especially the last on the question of spiritual independence.

Note 55, page 73.

The tumult already referred to in Note 49 arose from the excitement arising from Black's case.

Note 56, page 74.

William Scot was Minister of Kennoway, whence he was translated to Cupar, in 1604. Laing says he was born probably about 1558, and derived his origin from the Scots of Balwearie, a family of great antiquity, in Fife. He signed the protest, with forty-one others, against the introduction of Episcopacy, 1st July, 1606, and was one of the eight ministers summoned to London by King James's letter, 21st May preceding. Dr. Scott (Fasti) says his prudence and counsel were very serviceable to his brethren in London, and prevented the English Court and bishops from getting any advantage over them. With a view to his conversion to the principles of Episcopacy, he was committed to the charge of Dr. Dove, Bishop of Peterborough, but his principles were too deeply rooted for him to entertain the idea of change. He seems, however, to have gained the good opinion of the English bishops, and, on his petition, he was allowed to return to his parochial charge. After being conversant with most of the ecclesiastical matters of his time, Scot died in the year 1642. His works are: *The Course of Conformitie*, 1622, 4to; *Apologetical Narration of the State and Government of the Kirk of Scotland*, which was published, along with a notice of Scot's life by Dr. Laing, by the Wodrow Society, 1846, 8vo. For other notices of Scot, see Scott's Fasti.

Note 53, page 36.

The book referred to is one entitled "A Facile Traictise, contenand first ane infallible reul to discern trew from fals religion; next, a declaration of the nature, number, verteu and effects of the Sacraments, togider with certain prayeres of devotion. Dedicat to his soverain Prince the King's Maiestie of Scotland, King James the Saxt." [*Catalogues of Scottish Writers*, Edinburgh, 1833.] Hamilton's Life has been written by Lord Hailes, q. v. along with Lee's remarks on Hailes' sketch, i. p. 345.

Note 57, page 76.

A few particulars only need be given here respecting these sufferers for the sake of the truth, as their names and doings are largely recorded in the Annals of the Church of Scotland. John Forbes, brother of the equally well known Bishop Patrick Forbes, the third son of William Forbes of Corse, was born about 1566. Laing says he was probably educated at King's College, Aberdeen, but Dr. Scott states definitely that he studied at St. Salvator's College, and had his degree from the University of St. Andrews, in 1583. From the relationship between the Forbes family of Corse and Andrew Melville, and the fact that Bishop Forbes was educated under the care of Melville at Glasgow, John Forbes would likely have the same advantage of Melville's oversight as his brother Patrick had. Melville was transferred from Glasgow to St. Andrews in 1580, and John Forbes probably entered that University at that time. Forbes was settled Minister of Alford about 1593. He was named by the General Assembly of November; 1602, as one of those from whom his Majesty might select for nominating commissioners from each presbytery to parliament. This scheme was not carried out, but it paved the way for the erection of Episcopacy. He was commissioned by the Synods of Aberdeen and Moray, in 1605, to wait upon his Majesty anent their proceedings against the Marquis of Huntly. When the Assembly met at Aberdeen, contrary to the King's wishes, in July, 1605, Forbes was chosen Moderator. For this he was banished to France, where he spent the remainder of his life. He went to Sedan in 1607; after that became minister to a congregation in connection with the Church of Scotland at Middleburg; thence removing to Delft in 1621, he was displaced by the interference of the British government, and died about 1634. His works are: *The Saints' Hope and Infallibleness thereof*, Middleburg, 1608, 8vo; *Two Sermons*, Middleburg, 1608; *A Treatise on Justification*, Middleburg, 1616, 4to; *A Treatise how God's Spirit may be discerned from Man's own Spirit*, London, 1617; and several sermons. He wrote also *Certain Records touching the Estate of the Kirk in* 1605 *and* 1606, which was edited with a full notice of Forbes's Life, by Dr. Laing, for the Wodrow Society. See also Scott's Fasti, McCrie's Life of A. Melville, Cunningham, and the other Church Historians.

John Welch, or Welsh, or Welsche, the son of the laird of Collieston in Dunscore, was born in 1570. After certain wild youthful escapades, he was sent to the University of Edinburgh, where he took his degree in 1588, and was the first minister settled who had studied there. He was nominated one of three by the Privy Council for maintaining and preserving true religion in the Forest and Tweeddale, from which duties he was translated first to Kirkcudbright, and then to Ayr, about 1601. Though he did not arrive at Aberdeen till two days after the Assembly had been held (July, 1605), he zealously approved of that meeting's proceedings, and has been considered one of its chief supporters. For his Presbyterianism and his holding strictly the principle of spiritual independence, he was imprisoned in Blackness Castle, and being charged with treasonably declining the authority of the Privy Council, he was found guilty and sentenced to perpetual banishment from his Majesty's dominions. After long imprisonment, Forbes, Welsh, and their four fellow exiles, were brought to the pier of Leith, at two o'clock on a stormy November morning for embarkation for the land of their exile. An affecting account of this leave-taking of their friends and country is given by James Melville in his Autobiography. Cunningham thus shortly describes the scene: "A large concourse of people had already assembled on the sands to bid them farewell. Welsh, for the last time on Scottish soil, lifted up his voice in prayer, and few men could pray as he did; the whole multitude then joined in singing the 23rd Psalm, and when the hopeful words of the last verse had died away, the exiles, for conscience sake, tore themselves from their weeping friends, and were soon steering their course down the Forth on their way to France". Welsh, on his arrival in France, studied the language with such zeal and success, that in fourteen weeks he was able to preach fluently in the French language. It is pleasing to find that his old parishioners in Ayr still continued to regard him as their minister, and to make regular remittances to him for his support. Welsh ministered first at St. Jean d'Angely, where he stood a siege, but was protected, on its capture, by the express precautions of the French King when he took the town. Welsh next removed to Rochelle, but his declining health induced him to return to England, in 1622. At London, his wife, in a personal interview with the King, urgently solicited leave for her husband to return to his native air. James replied that he might return, provided she would persuade him to submit to the bishops. Mrs. Welsh, a daughter of John Knox, lifting up her apron towards the King, replied, "Please your Majesty, I'd rather kep (receive) his head there". Welsh died shortly after this in London, in the fifty-third year of his age. Scott's Fasti, M'Crie's Life of Melville, Melville's Autobiography, and the various Scottish historians who treat of Welsh's period.

Mr. Firm, *i.e.* Fairholme, or Ferme, Minister and Principal (designate) of the proposed college at Fraserburgh. A notice of his life is contained in this volume of Collections.

Note 59, *page* 76.

The various districts embraced by the Diocese of Aberdeen had been, for long, in a chronic state of warfare arising from the feuds between the Irvines and the Keiths, the Gordons and the Forbeses, the Leiths and the Leslies, and other barons and lairds. This state of matters was intensified by the two chief houses of Gordon and Forbes taking different sides in the civil war between the party of Queen Mary and that of her son James. During this conflict, which perhaps might be correctly described as private hostilities between the two chief families and their allies and dependents, various battles were fought and many atrocities, for example, the burning of the Castle of Towie, were committed. Property was so insecure that the Town Council of Aberdeen, in accepting the lands of Ardlair for the maintenance of the Bridge of Dee, stipulated to be relieved of their burden if they should cease to hold peaceably the said lands. If the talented young writer, who contributes to Henderson's *History of Banchory-Devenick*, a chapter on the history of the Bridge of Dee, had taken a due estimate of the troubled state of the country and the locality of Ardlair—on the borders between Kennethmont and Clatt, in the dividing district between the Forbeses and Gordons, and surrounded by Leiths and Leslies, he would not have found occasion to rally the Fathers of the City for their excessive caution. Aberdeen itself had not infrequently a taste of what it was to offend one of the county magnates.

Note 60, *page* 76.

John Strathauchine, or Strachan, a name said to be found spelled in twenty different ways, was presented, in 1582, to the vicarage of Kincardine O'Neil by James VI. He was Moderator of the General Assembly, in 1602, and of the Synod of Aberdeen, in 1606, and was "named by the Assembly, December, 1606, as one of those for writing to the brethren condemned for holding the Assembly at Aberdeen, and advising them to submit to his Majesty". Scott. He was appointed by that Assembly, Constant Moderator of his presbytery, and his co-presbyters were charged by the Privy Council to accept him as such, under pain of being held guilty of rebellion. He was also a member of the Court of High Commission, in the years 1610 and 1619. He died before 27th February, 1636. Scott's Fasti, with authorities there cited.

Note 61, page 77.

This mission of Forbes to the King in regard to the excommunicated Huntly and the growth of Roman Catholicism in the North has been already referred to in the Note on John Forbes. An account of Forbes's Commission, of his interview with the King, and a copy of the Synod's letter, are to be found in the volume published by the Wodrow Society containing Scot's *Narration* and Forbes's *Records*. See also M'Crie's Life of Melville and Row's History.

Note 62, page 79.

Alexander Forbes, of the house of Ardmurdo, near Inverurie, was first Parson of Fettercairn, in the Mearns, and then promoted to the See of Caithness, 12th November, 1606, where he sat till he was translated to the Bishoprick of Aberdeen. He died in 1618. Keith's Catalogue. Spottiswoode.

Note 63, page 80.

This son was the celebrated Dr. John Forbes, sometime Professor of Divinity, King's College, Aberdeen, and probably divides with the Presbyterian Cameron the reputation of being the most learned theologian produced by Scotland. The materials for forming an estimate of Forbes's life and works are ample; so there is no need for referring to either at any length here. He was the second son of Bishop Patrick Forbes, and was born on the 2nd of May, 1593. After studying at Aberdeen, he was sent to the University of Heidelberg, and enjoyed the advantage of studying divinity under the celebrated David Pareus. Forbes studied also at Sedan, then a famous seat of Protestant learning, and at various other Continental Universities. Having returned home, he was in his twenty-sixth year appointed Professor of Divinity in King's College. He filled this office with much ability, and added to his own stores of erudition by assiduous study. The country was, however, much distracted by religious differences, and, to assist in obtaining peace, Forbes wrote and published at Aberdeen, in 1629, his earliest work, *Irenicum*, to the lovers of truth and peace in the Scottish Church. On the death of his father, Bishop Patrick, Dr. Forbes succeeded to the family estates, as his elder brother had died some years before. Dr. Forbes, being naturally of a peace-loving disposition, next published *A Peaceable Warning to the Subjects in Scotland : given in the yeare of God, 1638; Aberdene*, 4to. The doctor, along with the other Aberdeen doctors, was soon involved in hot controversy with the leaders of the Covenant. Forbes was for a time treated with some degree of tenderness, as the Covenanters were anxious to gain over to their side such a convert, the more especially as a delegation of the General Assembly, after examining him, declared him free from the taint of Popery and Arminianism. Declining, however, to sign the Covenant, he was deprived of his office; and, anxious to prosecute his studies in peace, he soon afterwards embarked for Holland. Dr. Forbes resided for the most part at Amsterdam, where he prepared for the press his great work, *Instructiones Historico-Theologicae de Doctrina Christiana*, a work of vast erudition and of the greatest value. It was published in 1645 at Amsterdam. After a residence of two years in Holland, Dr. Forbes returned to Aberdeen in 1646, and was permitted to reside peaceably at his country seat of Corse, where he died, 29th April, 1648. A collective edition of Forbes's works in Latin was published in two volumes folio at Amsterdam, with a copious Life of the author and his associates by Dr. George Garden. His Life has also been written by Dr. Irving in his *Lives of Scotish Writers*. To these the reader is referred for full information regarding this good and great man.

Note 64, page 80.

This work is now very accessible, having been printed for the Spottiswoode Society, 1845, and edited, with biographical memoir and notes, by Charles Farquhar Shand, Esq., advocate.

Note 65, page 80.

Doctor George Garden, already referred to as the editor and biographer of Dr. John Forbes, appears, as Dr. Irving remarks (*Lives of Scotish Writers*), to have been "a very amiable and estimable man. He was a regent of King's College, and afterwards minister of St. Machars, but was ejected from his living on the restoration of the Presbyterian discipline." Garden was afterwards (1701) tried by the General Assembly and deposed from the ministry for Bourignianism. Cunningham, C. H. ii. p. 324 *et seq.* Maidment, from information supplied to him by the late Dr. Joseph Robertson, gives, in his *Analecta Scotica*, vol. ii. p. 234, a list of Garden's works, viz.: " A Sermon preached at the Funeral of the Rev. Henry Scougal, M.A., by G. G., D.D.," appended to an edition of Scougal's works published at London in 1726. He translated *Bourignon's Light of the Worlde*; and published at London in 1699 *Ane Apology for Antoine Bourignon* in 8vo. He wrote also *The Case of the present afflicted Clergy in Scotland truly represented*, London, 1689; besides some communications to the Philosophical Society.

Note 66, page 83.

Wormistoun, or Wilmerston, or Wormiston, for the place has been variously spelled, is in the county of Fife.

Note 67, page 87.

For a notice of Calderwood's life, see Note 1. The protestation mentioned in the text, for sharing in which Calderwood "was prosecute and deprived by the High Commission," was a respectful but earnest protest against a proposition of the King, which, if passed into law, would have practically abolished General Assemblies. The proposition was, "That whatsoever His Majesty should determine touching the external government of the Church, with the advice of the archbishops, bishops, and a competent number of the clergy, should have the strength of a law". A number of ministers met and drew up a strong representation against the proposed measure, as subversive of a polity which they believed to be founded on the Word of God. The King was exceedingly angry with the protestors. Hewat and Simpson, whom he considered ringleaders, he deprived of their offices; and Calderwood, who had joined in the protest and defended it in the presence of the King and the High Commission, was stripped of his ministry and banished the kingdom. Cunningham ii. p. 31, &c.; Row, 312. See the whole case circumstantially and graphically narrated by Calderwood himself in his History, vii. p. 259, &c.

Note 68, page 96.

For an account of "the disput about the Covenant and Episcopacy" which "the doctors of Aberdeen" held with the Covenanting Commissioners from the south, see "General demands concerning the late Covenant, propounded by the ministers and professors of divinity in Aherdeene to some reverend brethren who came thither to recommend the late Covenant to them and to those who are committed to their charge, together with the answers of those reverend brethren to the said demands; also, the replyes of the foresayd ministers and professors to their answers. Aberdeene: reprinted by John Forbes, *anno Dom.* 1662." The papers by the doctors are subscribed by John Forbes of Corse, D.D., Professor of Divinity in the King's College; Alexander Scrogie, D.D., Minister at Old Aberdeen; William Leslie, D.D., Principal of the King's College; Robert Baron, D.D., Professor of Divinity in the Marischal College; James Sibbald, D.D., Minister at Aberdeen; and Alexander Ross, D.D., Minister at Aberdeen. The answers to the demands of the reverend doctors are subscribed by Alexander Henderson, Minister at Leuchars; David Dickson, Minister at Irvine; and Andrew Cant, Minister at Pitsligo. The second paper of the brethren bears the signatures only of Henderson and Dickson. Middleton, in his appendix to Archbishop Spottiswoode's History, says that Dr. Baron "bare the greatest share of that famous debate, *anno* 1638, between the doctours of Aberdeen and the

Covenanters ". On the other hand, Bishop Sage, in a letter to Bishop Gillan, dated 9th March, 1702, remarks that "the demands, replys and duplys of the doctors of Aberdeen, as I was informed when there, though subscribed by six, were all formed and digested by Dr. Seely [Leslie], Principal of the Old Town College". Note in Gordon's *Scots Affairs*, Spalding Club edition, p. 9, &c. For a history of the time, specially of the transactions in this neighbourhood, see, besides Gordon's *Affairs*, Spalding's *Memorials of the Trubles in Scotland*. It may be here remarked that Gordon and Spalding are both prejudiced against the Covenanters. Biographical notices of, and references regarding, the Aberdeen doctors are contained in the Spottiswoode reprint of Forbes's *Funerals*. The "life and times" of Henderson have been written by the Rev. John Aiton of Dolphington: Edinburgh, 1836. Full notices of Dickson and Cant are to be found in the Church Histories of the times, as well as in Dr. H. Scott's *Fasti*. The best account of these Covenanting controversies, written from the anti-Covenanting point of view, is contained in "A Large Declaration concerning the late Tumults in Scotland, from their first Originals, &c., by the King". London, 1639.

Note 69, *page* 98.

This sermon was entitled "Holinesse to the Lord, or A Sermon upon the 36th verse of the 28th Chapter of Exodus, &c. . . . . Preached by James Sibbald, Doctor of Divinity, and minister of Saint Nicola's Church of Aberdeen, April 16, 1635".
woode Society, 1845. See notice of Sibbald's *Life* in the vol. just mentioned,
Funeral Sermons, &c., on Bishop Patrick Forbes. Reprinted for the Spottis-
page 119, &c., with the various authorities there cited.

Note 70, *page* 105.

The editor of Bishop Forbes's *Funerals* for the Spottiswoode Society says, p. 4: "The Bishop's Tomb is now in the open air, the portion of the cathedral within which it stood having been demolished. The inscription is still quite legible, the stone having been lately cleared from moss and earth. The denunciation on the monument against those who shall in any way disturb or interfere with the ashes reposing beneath reminds us of the similar warning on the tomb of Shakespeare.

"It would seem that the family of Corse at this time used the motto—*Salus per Christum*—as it appears on the monument." It may have been a pious motto used only by the Bishop or his son John.

Note 71, page 106.

See notice of Bannantine or Bannantyne in the Introduction.

Note 72, page 113.

The "actuall minister" was Robert Colvill, who died in 1630, and was succeeded by John Duncan. Note to Row's History, page 349. For further particulars of Colville see Scott's Fasti.

Note 73, page 116.

Lord Stirling, the celebrated courtier, statesman, and poet, was the son of Alexander Alexander of Menstrie, in Stirlingshire, and was born some say, in 1567, others, in or about 1580. He ingratiated himself with the Kings James VI. and Charles I., and was successively created a knight-baronet, Lord Alexander of Tullibody and Viscount and Earl of Stirling, and Earl of Dovan, in Scotland. He died in 1640. For an exhaustive account of the poet-statesman see Rodger's *Memorials of Earl of Stirling and House of Alexander.* His poetical works have been reprinted with a memoir and notes in three vols, Glasgow, 1870.

Note 74, page 131.

This refers to John, 4th Earl of Athole, who was sworn into the office of High Chancellor of Scotland at Stirling, 29th March, 1577. He was the chief leader of the party opposed to Morton, the Regent, and his measures. Afterwards a sort of reconciliation, through the mediation of the English Ambassador, took place, and a grand banquet was given by the Regent at Stirling in honour of the event. Athole was present at the entertainment, and immediately thereafter took ill, and, after suffering four days, died at Kincardine Castle, near Auchterarder, not without strong suspicion that he had been poisoned. The doctors who made a *post-mortem* examination of the body could not agree as to the cause of death, and Morton strongly protesting his innocence, was never brought to trial. See Calderwood iii. p. 449, and Tytler iv. p. 21, note and appendix.

Note 75, page 132.

A sudden rumour had arisen, no one knew how or whence, that the Earl of Morton, in 1580, had entered into a plot with some others to seize the young king while he was residing in Stirling Castle and carry him off prisoner to Dalkeith. Due precautions were, however, taken by the king's guardians for his protection, and this rumour, as well as others of various kinds, came to nothing. Morton, at the time and afterwards at his execution, stoutly denied all complicity in these intrigues. See Tytler iv. p. 25.

Note 76, *page* 138.

John Bradford suffered martyrdom in the reign of Mary, Queen of England. The treatise referred to may be "Godly Meditations upon the Ten Commandments, &c. . . . Whereunto is joined a treatise against the Feare of Death, &c.," 1567, or more probably, "Treatise against the Fear of Death, whereunto are annexed certaine sweete Meditations upon the Kingdom of Christ, &c." Various editions; two undated. Lowndes.

Note 77, *page* 142.

Tytler, in his *Life of Sir Thomas Craig* says, page 111 : "We know that a project for a general digest of the laws was suggested in a convention of estates held in the year 1574, under the Regency of the Earl of Morton. . . ." This design is thus referred to by Hume of Godscroft: "The care of this was committed to Sir James Balfoure and Master John Skene, Clerk Register and Master of the Rolls. This work, I am informed, was well advanced, but when he quit his authority they left off any farther proceeding in it." For further details see Tytler *in loco citato*.

Sir James Balfour was one of those versatile, unscrupulous, and ambitious adventurers who frequently manage to raise themselves above their fellows in times of civil commotions. We find him in various and anomalous characters— Parson of Flish, Judge of the Supreme Court, Governor of Edinburgh Castle, Clerk Register, and finally, President of the Court of Session. A sketch of his busy and eventful life may be found in Tytler's *Life of Sir T. Craig*, page 91, *et seq.*

John Skeen, or Skene, afterwards Sir John Skene of Curriehill. For a full notice of this distinguished lawyer and statesman see *Memorials of the Family of Skene*, p. 106 *et seq.*, the first of the books issued by the New Spalding Club.

Note 78, *page* 143.

Montgomery was titular Archbishop of Glasgow. His case is noticed note 17.

Note 79, *page* 161.

The "famous Mr. John Durie" was son of Robert Durie at Leyden. Andrew Melville had considerable correspondence with him. He was remarkable for his exertions to bring about a union between the Lutheran and Reformed Churches. M'Crie's Melville.

Note 80, page 180.

Patrick Hamilton suffered martyrdom at St. Andrews, in 1528, on the last day of February. He was the son of Sir Patrick Hamilton of Kincavil, and Catherine Stewart, an illegitimate daughter of the Duke of Albany. It is uncertain when and where he was born, but when merely a child he was made Abbot of Ferne. He studied at Paris and St. Andrews and made great proficiency in his studies, particularly in music. It seems that when in Paris he imbibed the free sentiments of Erasmus and Reuchlin, and, consequently, when at home he fell under the suspicion of heresy. He accordingly retired again to the Continent and met Luther at Wittenberg. He attended the University of Marburg for some time, and was confirmed in the doctrines of the Reformation. Returning to Scotland in 1527, he was next year brought to trial for heresy by Archbishop Beaton, and was condemned. The affecting details of the execution may be read in Knox's *History* and other particulars on the same subject in Keith's *History*, Appendix. Interesting *Memoirs of Patrick Hamilton* were published by Dr. Lorimer, 1857.

Note 81, page 181.

Thomas Bassandon, or more commonly Bassandyne, a burgess of Edinburgh and a Scotchman by birth, was educated at Antwerp. From this town he seems to have removed to Paris, and afterwards to Leyden, where he learned the art of printing. Returning to Scotland, in 1558, he joined the Reforming party and began business as a printer. Lekprevik, who had previously to this exercised that craft in Edinburgh, having removed to St. Andrews, apparently made over his business to Bassandyne. Bassandyne's workshop appears to have been in the Netherbow, and was a tall, narrow tenement nearly opposite John Knox's house. Bassandyne printed a number of books, and, as the press at first and for long after was under the strict control of the civil and ecclesiastical powers, he fell under the Church's displeasure in 1568 under the circumstances mentioned by Wodrow in the text. Whether it was Bassandyne's object to get the song into circulation under the shelter of the psalm book or to promote the sale of the psalm book by the insertion of the song, or whether the song was inserted by mere negligence or through bad taste—examples of which appear in the *Gude and Godly Ballats*— does not appear, but doubtless Bassandyne had to obey the Assembly's command. He seems to have afterwards regained the favour of the Church, as the title of the following book which he published indicates—" CL. Psalmes of David, in English Metre, with the forme of prayers and ministration of the Sacraments used in the Church of Scotland. Whereunto, besydes that was in the former books, are also added sundrie other prayers, with a new, exact Kalendar for xvi. yeares next to come.

Printed at Edinburgh by Thomas Bassandyne, dwelling at the Nether Bow, 1575. *Cum privilegio.*" Dobson's Bassandyne Bible. For an account of the arrangement under which Bassandyne, in conjunction with Arbuthnot as partner, brought out the first English Bible (an edition of the second Geneva version) in Scotland, see work last quoted. Bassandyne is believed to have died in 1579, and in July that year, the first Bible printed in Scotland was finished and in circulation. Dobson's Bassandyne Bible. Lee's Memorial for the Bible Societies of Scotland. Annals of Scottish Printing by Dickson and Edmond.

Note 82, page 189.

Spottiswoode is in error when he says that Arbuthnot was buried in the College Kirk. Cullen in "The Chronicle of Aberdeen," printed in the second volume of the Spalding Club *Miscellany*, says: " Maister Alexander Arbuthnoitt, prinsepall of the College of Aberden, and persone of Loge [Logie-Buchan] departtit the xvij. day of October, yeir of God 1583 yeris, and was burritt in the pariss Kyrk of Aberden afor the pulpit ". Cullen was vicar and reader of Aberdeen, and died about 1608 or 9,

Note 83, page 194.

For notice of Simson see note 25.

Note 84, page 196.

For an account of the introduction of printing into Scotland with notices of the lives and works of these early printers see the writers above-named—Lee, Dobson, and more especially Dickson and Edmond. The fifth Parliament of Queen Mary, held at Edinburgh on 1st February, 1551-2, passed an Act which gives an insight into the printers' productions at that period. The Act was as follows (transcribed from Dobson):—"Prenters suld prent na thing without license. Item, For-sa-meikle as there is diverse Prenters in this Realme, that dailie and continuallie prentis buikes concerning the Faith, ballattes, sanges, blasphemationes, rimes, alsweill of Kirk-men, as Temporal, vthers Tragedies, alsweill in Latine, as in Englis tung, not seene, viewed, and considered be the Supervisures, as apperteinis to the defamation and sclander of the Lieges of this Realme, and to put ordour to sic inconvenientes: it is devised, statute, and ordained be the Lord Governour, with aduice of the three Estaites of Parliament: That na Prenter presume, attempt, or tak vpone hande, to prent ony buikes, ballattes, sanges, blasphematiounis, rymes or tragedies, outhir in Latine or Englis tung, in ony tymes to cum, vnto the tyme the samin be sene, viewit, and examit be sum wyse and discreit persounis depute thairto be the Ordinares quhatsum-evir, and thaireftir ane license had and obtenit in our Soveraine Ladie, and the Lord Governour, for imprenting sic buikes vnder the pain of confiscatioun of all the Prentaris gudis, and banishing him of the Realme for ever."

Note 85, page 196.

It appears from Maidment's *Catalogues of Scotish Writers*, and from a note in M'Crie's *Life of Knox*, p. 265, that "Mr. James Tyrie's last book" was "The Refutation of ane Answer made be Schir Johne Knox to ane Letter, send be James Tyrie to his vmquhyle brother; set furth be James Tyrie, Parisiis, 1573. *Cum privilegio*." Dr. M'Crie says: "It includes Tyrie's first letter and Knox's answer, but not the other papers originally printed along with that answer. 'Mr. Knox,' says Keith, 'makes some good and solid observations, from which, in my opinion, the Jesuit (in his reply) has not handsomely extricated himself.'" History, Appendix.

Note 86, page 201.

After considerable research, I have not been able to find anything additional to what is recorded in the text concerning George Scot or "the books set out" by him. Dr. Scott, in his *Fasti*, assumes that Wodrow is right in his surmise that Scot was minister of Kircaldy; and states that Scot was brother of Thomas Scot or Scott of Abbotshall, and that he was admitted Minister of Kircaldy before 14th December, 1560. He was a member of the Convention in 1571, and of the Assemblies 1571 and 1572, and one of the electors of the first Protestant bishop of St. Andrews, but he did not concur in the election. In 1574 he was translated to Dysart, where he died in 1582. Scott's Fasti, with authorities cited.

Note 87, page 201.

Scottish ecclesiastics have under most religious systems shown a curious desire to lay down strict rules to guide their order in matters of clerical dress and decorum. In Catholic times, the Provincial Council, which was convened at Linlithgow and adjourned to Edinburgh in 1549 to arrest the growth of heresy, which it declared was the result of (1) the corruption of morals pervading all clerical ranks and orders, and (2) their gross ignorance, proceeded to enact fifty-seven regulations to stop these evils. Among these enactments were precise rules for regulating the dress of the clergy. The Assembly's Act of 1575 was revived in the times (1646) of the supremacy of the Covenanters, who were probably not aware that a Catholic Council, presided over by Archbishop Hamilton, had given strong recommendations to the same effect. Lord Hailes' Historical Memorials concerning the Provincial Councils of the Scottish Clergy. Dr. Lee's Lectures. i. p. 72, &c.

Note 88, page 203.

It would perhaps be useless to hazard a conjecture as to the meaning of this expression when the text is so uncertain. Peterkin, in his edition of the *Booke of the Kirk of Scotland*, gives the passage thus: "But that their haill habite shall be of grave collour, as black, russet, sad gray, sad brown, or serges, wirsett, camlet, growgrame, lytes, worsett, or sick lyke, &c." In the Bannatyne Club edition of the same "booke" the passage is: "Bot that thair haill habite be of grave collour, as black, russet, sad gray, sad browne, or searges, wirsett chamlet, growgrame, lytes wirsett, or sick lyke, &c."

Note 89, page 241.

This Confession is noticed in Note 12.

Note 90, page 242.

"This Form of Service and Prayers" has not been found among Wodrow's MSS. It has, however, been published, with full historical references, by Rev. Dr. Sprott in his *Scottish Liturgies of the Reign of James VI.*: Edinburgh, 1871. Dr. Sprott's Introduction is very valuable.

Note 91, page 245.

For a notice of the parentage of Dr. Forbes, see Introduction.

Note 92, page 249.

The negotiations for marrying Prince Charles to the King of Spain's daughter seem to have given much concern and no little scandal to the Protestant inhabitants generally. Calderwood vii. p. 570, says, in reference to the Prince's journey to Spain: "The King injoyned the ministers of Edinburgh to pray for him, and for his safe returne. They obeyed, but spake never a word of matching with idolaters, and specialliee with the King of Spaine, the Pope's cheefe support. The whole ile of Britaine, speciallie the professours of true religion, were astonished, and feared alteration both in the state of the Kirk and the Commonweale. The formalists themselfs were ashamed of the lavish commendations they had given in former times of the King's sinceritie and constancie in religion, and care to defend the same by word, by writt, and by deed. About the midst of Aprile we heard that he was come safe to Madrede the thrid of Marche, and was honourablie received by the King and his nobilitie."

Note 93, page 263.

The *Considerationes Modestæ* has been published as part of the Anglo-Catholic Library, admirably edited, and accompanied by an English translation, by the late Rev. George H. Forbes of Burntisland, a gentleman who, in connection with the Pitsligo Press, has rendered most important service to liturgical and other students. This edition by Forbes contains prefaces, the bishop's Life by Sydserf, and notes, and is readily accessible.

Note 94, page 269.

This notice of Bishop W. Forbes' Life is contained in Garden's *Life of Dr. J. Forbes*, forming an introduction to the edition of Dr. J. Forbes' works published at Amsterdam, in 2 vols. folio, 1703, by Dr. Garden. This introduction is a valuable storehouse of facts regarding Church affairs and churchmen, especially in the North in the stirring times of Dr. Forbes. Wodrow's is a very free translation of the original Latin.

Note 94A, page 278.

Robert Bruce was not only one of the most distinguished ministers that the Presbyterian Church of Scotland has ever produced, but also one of the most notable Scotchmen of his time. As Dr. M'Crie remarks, his life, which extended from the commencement of the first Reformation down to that of the second, embraces a period of which comparatively little is known. Bruce may be thus said to form the link between Melville and Henderson of whose conversion he was the instrument. A good account of this distinguished man is still a desideratum in Scottish ecclesiastical history. His sermons were reprinted by the Wodrow Society, along with Wodrow's collections for his Life. But Wodrow has merely gathered materials for a biography, which it is hoped may yet be attempted by some competent hand. Only a few particulars of his busy life can be given here. Fuller details may be found in M'Crie's *Life of Melville* and Notes, Anderson's *Scottish Nation*, and Scott's *Fasti*, with the authorities mentioned therein. Robert Bruce, the second son of Sir Alexander Bruce of Airth, was born, some say, in 1554, others, in 1556, and according to Wodrow, about 1559. By descent he was a collateral relation of his great namesake, King Robert Bruce, while James Bruce, the celebrated Abyssinian traveller, was his descendant in the sixth generation. He was destined by his parents for the profession of law, and, after attending for some time the University of St. Andrews, he was sent to Paris, at which University and that of Louvain he studied humanity and the principles of Roman jurisprudence. On his return home, however, after practising as a lawyer with the fairest prospects, he relinquished them all for the study of theology, which he prosecuted at St. Andrews, under A. Melville. In 1587, he was chosen Minister of St. Giles', Edinburgh, and elected the same year Moderator of the General Assembly. Such was Bruce's reputation for ability and honesty, that the King, on leaving his kingdom for his marriage with the Queen, nominated him an extraordinary privy councillor, and requested him to oversee the affairs of the nation, which he did so as to call forth the thanks of King James on his return. He was again Moderator in 1592, and chiefly by his influence an Act of Parliament was passed, on 5th June of that year, which Act forms the great charter of the Scottish Presbyterian Church. By a change in Court policy he sunk much in the King's estimation, and for his opposition to his Majesty's measures was apprehended and cast into prison. On the division of the city into separate parishes, Bruce, after no little vexation, was appointed to the New or Little Kirk. The King's autocratic interference in Church matters found a fearless opponent in Bruce, who was now much harassed by the Court party, and repeatedly imprisoned in Montrose, Aberdeen, and other places. He was, however, indefatigable in preaching the gospel whenever he could find opportunity, regardless of the King's displeasure. Finally, by the King's order he was confined to his own house of Kinnaird, where he died, 13th July, 1631, in the 44th year of his ministry.

Note 95, *page* 283.

The treatise *De Vocatione Efficaci*—On Effectual Calling—was not written by Johnston, but by Rollock, the first Principal of the University of Edinburgh, as is afterwards correctly stated by Wodrow. A copy of this little work referred to in the text is in the Aberdeen University Library, and is a favourable specimen of early Scottish typography.

Holland's translation of this treatise and Beza's letter is included in the selection of Rollock's Works published by the Wodrow Society under the editorship of Dr. Gunn.

APPENDIX.

WODROW'S BIOGRAPHICAL COLLECTIONS IN THE LIBRARY OF THE UNIVERSITY OF GLASGOW.

INDEX OF LIVES.*

John Erskine of Dun, Knight, Superintendent of Angus and Merns (*M.*)	I. 44, XIV. 50, A. III. 49.
Mr. John Row, Minister at Saint Johnstoun	I. 16, XIV. 18.
Mr. John Craig, Minister at Edinburgh, Aberdeen, and to the King's Family (*N.S.*)	I. 44, XIV. 40, A. III. 41.
Mr. John Durie, Minister att Edinburgh and Monross (*N.S.*)	I. 38, XIV. 28.
Mr. James Lauson, Sub-Principal of the Colledge of Aberdeen, and Minister at Edinburgh (*N.S.*)	I. 40, XIV. 28, A. III. 14.
Mr. Robert Pont, Commissioner of Murray, Lord of the Session, and Minister of St. Cuthbert's Kirk (*M.*)	I. 28, XIV. 25, A. III. 12.

* "Lives"—Vols. X., XI., XII., XIII., XIV., XV., XVI., XVII., XVIII. are in Wodrow's handwriting.

"Lives"—Vols. I., II., III., IV., V., VI. are transcripts of the above.

Vols. VII. and VIII. are writings (not autograph) of John Knox.

"Introduction to Our Scots Biography," Vols. XIX., XX. are in the author's handwriting.

"Introduction to Our Scots Biography," Vol. IX., is a transcript of the above.

"Appendix," 4 vols., marked A. I., A. II., A. III., A. IV., are not in the author's handwriting.

The Arabic numerals denote the number of pages which the "Life" occupies.

The transcripts are all folios, the originals and the Appendix are quartos.

(*N.S.*) denotes that the "Life" is printed in the present volume;

(*M.*) that it appears in the two volumes issued by the Maitland Club, in 1834-45.

Mr. Andrew Melvil, Principal and Professor of Divinity, first at Glasgow, next at St. Andrews, and last at Sedan - - - - - - I. 104, XIV. 104, A. IV. 87.

Mr. Thomas Smeton, Minister of Paisley, and afterwards Principal of the Colledge of Glasgow - - - - - I. 20, XIV. 24.

Mr. Alexan. Arbuthnet, Minister, first at Arbuthnet and Logy-Buchan, and thereafter Principal of the King's Colledge, Aberdeen (*N.S.*) - - - I. 12, XIV. 10.

Mr. Robert Rollock, Principal of the Colledge and minister of the Town of Edinburgh - - - - - L 47, XVII. 44, A. III. 22.

Mr. John Davidson, who dyed minister at Salt Preston or Preston Pannes - - I. 44, X. 76, A. III. 64.

Mr. Robert Bruce, minister at Edinburgh *- I. 74, X. 112, A. IV. 100.

Mr. David Black, Minister of the Gospel, first at Saint Andrews, and then at Aberlet - - - - - - I. 52, X. 54, A. IV. 42.

Mr. John Forbes, Minister at Alford, in Aberdeenshire - - - - - I. 64, X. 78, A. IV. 140.

Mr. John Welsh, Minister at Air, and other places - - - - - I. 30, X. 54.

Mr. Andrew Hay, Minister at Renfrew and Commissioner of the West - - - II. 10, XIII. 8.

Mr. John Hall, Minister at Edinburgh and Leith - - - - - - II. 8, XIII. 10.

Mr. James Law, Minister at Kirk-Listoun, and afterwards Bishop of Orkney and Arch-Bishop of Glasgow - - - II. 24, XIII. 30.

Mr. Patrick Galloway, Minister at Perth and Edinburgh- - - - - - II. 40, XIII. 40.

Mr. William Couper, Minister first at Bothkenner, then at Perth, and Dean of His Majesty's Chappell Royall, and Bishop of Galloway - - - - II. 26, XIII. 32.

---

* The substance of this Life appears in *Sermons by Robert Bruce* (Wodrow Soc., 1843).

APPENDIX.

Mr. William Struthers, Minister at Edinburgh - - - - - II. 14, XIII. 20.
Patrick Forbes, Barron of Oneil and Laird of Corse, Minister of Keith, and Bishop of Aberdeen (*N.S.*)- - - II. 28, XIII. 32.
Mr. David Lindsay, First Minister of Leith after the Reformation, and Bishop of Rosse - - - - II. 16, XIII. 16.
Mr. John Gregory, Chaplain of Christ's Church, Oxford, and prebendary of Chichester and Sarum - - - II. 4, XIII. 4.
Mr. John Johnstoun, Professor of Divinity in the University of Saint Andrews (*N.S.*) - - - - - II. 8, XIII. 8.
Mr. John Weems of Lathoquar, Minister at Dunce, and prebend of Durham - - II. 10, XIII. 12.
Mr. Robert Howie, Professor of Divinity at Saint Andrews (*N.S.*) - - - II. 4, XIII. 6.
Mr. James Nicholson, Minister at Meigle, and Bishop of Dunkeld for a few moneths - - - - - - II. 4, XIII. 4.
Mr. George Hay, Minister of Eddilstoun, Minister to the Privy Council, and Commissioner for Aberdeen - - II. 4, XIII. 4.
Mr. David Hume of Godscroft - - - II. 46, XIII. 32.
Mr. John Strang, D.D., Minister at Errol, and Principal of the Colledge of Glasgow - - - - - - II. 16, XIII. 16.
Mr. John Fergushill, Minister at Ochiltree and the Toun of Air - - - - II. 8, XIII. 10.
Mr. James Balfour, Minister at Edinburgh - II. 4. XIII. 4.
Mr. Henry Blyth, Minister in the Canongate, Edinburgh - - - - - II. 4. XIII. 4.
Mr. Nichol Dalgleish, Minister of Saint Cuthbert's, or West-Kirk, Edinburgh - II. 4, XIII. 4.
Mr. John Couper, Minister at Edinburgh and Glasgow - - - - - II. 4, XIII. 4.
Mr. John Duncanson, Minister to the King's House - - - - - II. 4, XIII., 4.

Mr. John Howison, Minister at Cambuslang - - - - - - II. 4, XIII. 4.
Mr. Thomas Hepburn, Minister at Old Hamstocks - - - - - II. 4, XIII. 4.
Mr. William Rou, Minister at Stramiglo in Fife - - - - - - II. 4, XIII. 4.
Mr. Gilbert Primrose, Minister at Bourdeaux, and afterwards of the French Congregation at London - - - - - II. 4, XIII. 4.
Mr. John Rou, Minister of Carnoch in Fife II. 6, XIII. 8.
Mr. David Lindsay, Minister at Dundee, Bishop of Brechen, and then of Edinburgh (*N.S.*) - - - - - II. 8, XIII. 8.
Mr. James Gybson, Minister at Pencaitland II. 8, XIII. 8.
Mr. Charles Ferme or Fairholm, Minister and Professor at Frazerburgh (*N.S.*) - II. 8, XIII. 8.
Mr. John Ross, Minister at . . . in the Synod of Perth - - - - II. 8, XIII. 8.
Mr. Andrew Duncan, Minister of the Gospel at Crail, in the Shire of Fife - - II. 12, XIII. 10.
Mr. William Forbes, Minister at Aberdeen and Edinburgh; and Bishop of Edinburgh (*N.S.*) - - - - - II. 14, XIII. 12
Mr. William Levingstone, Minister at Monyabroch, and then at Lanerk - - II. 20, XIII. 14.
Mr. Henry Scrimgeor, Professor of Philosophy, and First Professor of Law at Geneva - - - - - - III. 12, XVIII. 10.
Mr. David Weems, Minister of the Gospel at Glasgow (*M.*)- - - - - III. 46, XV, 38.
Mr. John Sharp, Minister of the Gospel at Kilmeny in Fife, Professor of Divinity at Die in France, and at Edinburgh - III. 10, XV. 8.
Mr. John Spotswood, Archbishop first of Glasgow, and next of Saint Andrews - III. 190, XVII. 149, A. II. 32, IV. 34.
Mr. John Cameron, Minister at Bourdeaux, Professor of Divinity at Saumure, Principal of the College of Glasgow, and Professor of Divinity at Montauban (*M.*) - - - - - - III. 80, XV. 71.

APPENDIX.

Mr. Andrew Ramsay, Minister of the Gospel at Edinburgh - - - III. 28, XV. 26.

Mr. John Adamson, Minister of the Gospel at North-Berwick and Libberton, and Principal of the Colledge of Edinburgh III. 8, XVIII. 6.

Mr. William Annand, Minister at Falkirk and Air, Viccar of Throuley, and Rector of Leoland, in the County of Kent, in England - - - - III. 10, XVIII. 8.

Mr. Adam Bannantine, Minister at Falkirk, and Bishop of Dumblane and Aberdeen (*N.S.*) - - - - - - III. 12, XVIII. 8.

Mr. Adam Hepburn, Bishop of Orkney, Lord of Hally Rood house, and one of the Senators of the Colledge of Justice - III. 12, XVIII. 8.

Mr. Peter Blaikburn, Minister of St. Nicholas Church, and Bishop of Aberdeen (*N.S.*) - - - - III. 10, XVIII. 6.

Mr. Andrew Boyd, Minister of the Gospel at Eagleshame, and Bishop of Argyle - III. 12, XVIII. 8.

Mr. John Caldcleugh, Professor of Theology, and Minister of New Burgh and Ebdie III. 4, XVIII. 4.

Mr. David Chambers of Ormond, Parson of Suddy, Chancelour of Ross, and one of the Senators of the Colledge of Justice III. 12, XVIII. 8.

Mr. John Colvil, Minister at Kilbride, and Chanter at Glasgow - - - - III. 6, XVIII. 4.

Mr. David Cunninghame, Minister at Lanerk, Monkland, Sub-Dean of Glasgow, and Minister and Bishop of Aberdeen (*N.S.*) III. 6, XVIII. 4.

Sir Adrian Damman of Bistervelt, Professor of Law and Humanity in the Colledge of Edinburgh, and Resident from the States Generall at the Court of Scotland III. 6, XVIII. 4.

William Harlau, Minister of Saint Cuthbert's Kirk, now West Kirk, Edin^r. - - IV. 4, XII. 4.

Mr. Alex^r. Gordon, Bishop of Athens and Galloway after the Reformation, Commissioner of Galloway, and Lord of Session (*M.*) - - - - - IV. 16, XII. 12, A. II. 11.

Mr. John Spotswood, Minister of Calder and Superintendant of Lothian (*M.*) - - IV. 18, XII. 16.
Mr. James Boyd of Trochredge, Tulchan, Arch Bishop of Glasgow (*M.*) - - IV. 20, XII. 18.
Mr. Patrick Constine or Adamson, Minister at Ceres, Paislay, and afterward Archbishop of Saint Andrews - - - IV. 84, XII. 72, A. II. 26.
Mr. James Carmichael, Minister att Haddingtoun - - - - - - IV. 34, XII. 30, A. II. 34.
Mr. John Carmichael, Minister of the Gospel at Kinneuchars in Fife - - - IV. 10, XII. 10.
Mr. Thomas Buchanan, Minister, Ceres in Fife - - - - - - - IV. 8, XII. 8.
Mr. William Scot, Minister at Coupar in Fife - - - - - - - IV. 18, XII. 16.
Mr. John Murray, Minister at Leith and Dumfermline - - - - - IV. 26, XII. 24.
Mr. Andrew Simson, Minister of the Gospel first at Dunning, and afterwards at Dumbar - - - - - - IV. 8, XII. 8.
Mr. Archibald Simson, Minister at Dalkeith IV. 16, XII. 14.
Mr. Patrick Simson, Minister at Spot, Craumon, and Stirling - - - - IV. 36, XII. 34, A. II. 10.
Mr. John Scrimgeour, Minister of the Gospel at Kinghorn - - - - - IV. 20, XII. 16.
Mr. George Gladstanes, Minister first at Aberlott, then at Saint Andrews, and afterward Bishop of Caithnes, then of St. Andrews (*M.*) - - - - IV. 58, XIII. 48, A. II. 4.
Mr. Robert Scot, Minister of Glasgow - V. 4, XV. 4.
Mr. Patrick Sharp, Professor of Divinity in the Colledge of Glasgow - - - V. 4, XV. 4.
Mr. Robert Boyd of Trochorege, in the Shire of Air, and Bailayrie of Carrict, Professor of Philosophy in the Colledge of Montauban, Minister of the Gospel in the Church of Vertuile, Pastor and Professor of Theologie in the University of Saumure in France, and Principal of

APPENDIX.

the University of Glasgow, Minister and Professor of Divinity at Edinburgh, and Minister at Paislay (*M.*) - - - V. 200, XV. 162.

Mr. John Knox, Minister of the Gospell at Edin^r, commonly and justly called the Reformer . - - - - VI. 329, XI. 328, A. III. 292.

Mr. George Buchanan, Principall and Professor of Divinity in Saint Leonard's Colledge in Saint Andrews, Precentor to King James the 6th, Pensioner of Cross-Raguel and Lord Privy Seal - XVI. 134.

Mr. John Willock, Minister sometime at Edinburgh, and Superintendant of the West (*M.*) - - - - - - XIV. 12.

Mr. Walter Balcanquell, Minister of the Gospell at Edin^r. - - - - XIV. 14.

Mr. Alex^r. Douglass, Minister at Elgin and Bishop of Murray - - - - XVIII. 4.

Mr. Patrick Hamiltoun, Nepheu to the Duke of Albany and Earle of Arran, and Abbot of Feren - - - - - XVII. 16.

Alexander Seaton, Dominican Freir, Confessor to King James the 5th, and afterwards Chaiplain to the Duke of Suffolk in England - . - - XVII. 10.

Alexander Alesse [Hales] Professor of Theology at Francfurt and Leipsick - XVII. 16.

Mr. John Fife, Mr. John M'Dowall, Mr. Coo, and John M'Bryar - - - XVII. 4.

Mr. George Wisheart, Minister of the Gospell, and martyre for the Truth - XVII. 36.

John Rough, Minister in Scotland and martyre in England - - - - XVII. 12.

Mr. John Winram, Subdean of Saint Andrews and Superintendant of Fife, and Prior of Portmoak (*M.*) - - XVII. 8.

Mr. John Douglas, Rector of Saint Andreus and Tulchan Bishop there - XVII. 14.

Mr. William Aird, Minister of St. Cuthberts or West Kirk, near Edinburgh - - XVII. 4.

Mr. James Anderson, Minister at Bendochie in Angus - - - - - -	XVII. 4.
Mr. John Carswell, Superintendant of Argyle (*M.*) - - - - - - -	XVII. 4.
Paul Methven, one of our first preachers at the Reformation, and Minr. at Jedburgh	XVII. 8.
Mr. Christopher Goodman, Minister of the Gospell at Saint Andreues - - -	XVII. 12.
Mr. Henry Balnaves of Hall-Hill, one of the first Professors of the Truth, and after the Reformation one of the Lords of Session - - - - - -	XVII. 12.
Mr. Patrick Cockburn, Professor of Languages at Paris and Saint Andreus, and Minister at Haddingtoun - - -	XVII. 12.
David Ferguson, Minister of the Gospell at Dumfermline - - - - -	XVII. 8.
Robert Campbell of Kinzeancleugh - -	XVII. 12.
Mr. John Malcome, Minister at Perth -	XII. 8.
Mr. James Melvill, Professor of Divinity, and Minr. of the Gospell at Anstruther and Kilrinnie - - - - -	XII. 160, A. II. 154.

INDEX.

Abbot, Doctor, Dean of Winchester, 240.
Aberdeen, Bishop of, Patrick Forbes, 80-105.
— Bishop of, Peter Blackburn, 65-79.
— Bishop of Dunblane and, 106-124.
— College of, 188.
— Commissioners of, 202.
— Minister at, John Craig, 1-56.
— Minister at, William Forbes, 245-269.
— Minister and Bishop of, David Cunningham, 57-65.
— Principal of King's College, Alexander Arbuthnet, 180-192.
— Sub-Principal of the College of James Lawson, 192-234.
— Synod of, 275.
— University Library, 342.
Aberdour, 152.
Abernethy, John, 107, 109.
Adam, Bishop of Orkney, 10, 13.
Adamson, Janet, 222.
— John, 155, 242, 257, 270, 271, 273, 274, 275, 281, 347.
— P., Bishop of St. Andrews, 31, 33, 34, 35, 51, 59, 60, 63, 64, 68, 196, 201, 217, 221, 229, 241, 280.
— (or Constine), 347.
Aikenhead, David, 247.
Aird, John, 171.
— William, 46, 349.
— William Calderwood, 316.
Albany (Albanie), Duke of, 20.
Alesse, or Hales, 349.
Alexander, Bishop of Galloway, 13.
Alford, 76, 81, 246, 267.
Allan, Andrew, 110.
Allane, 232.
Alnes, 81.
Anderson, Alexander, 182, 194.
— James, 9, 350.
— Patrick, 301.
Andrew, John, 143, 144.
Angus, 156.
— Earl of, 33, 45, 52, 129, 136, 145, 221.
— Superintendent of, 185, 199, 202.
Annand, Viscount, 111.
— William, 109, 347.
Anstruther, Wester, 83.

Arbuthnet, 66, 67.
— Alexander, first minister of Arbuthnet and Logy-Buchan, and thereafter Principal of the King's College, Aberdeen, 164, 179-192, 196, 199, 343.
— Minister of, 179.
— Viscount of, 179.
Argyle, 26, 143.
— Earl of, 134, 210.
Arnauld, 265.
Arran, Duke of, 213.
— Earl of, 25, 31, 34, 35, 49, 127, 140, 145, 150, 210, 212, 217, 221, 222.
— Island of, 277.
Arthur (Arthure), William, Minister at Saint Cuthberts, 171, 247.
Assembly, General, 10, 11, 27, 57.
Athole, Earl of, 131.
Attwood, 301.
Auchinbreck (Auchinbreack), Laird of, 176.
Auchinleck, Patrick, 184.
Auchterarder, Presbytery of, 110.
Ayr (Air), 52, 59, 124.
— Minister in, 109.

Bacon, 232.
Baithans, Provost of, 38.
Baile (Bayle), 245, 246, 263, 264.
Balcanquell, James, 52.
— Robert, Minister at Tranent, 171.
— Walter, 31, 35, 62, 67, 74, 126, 127, 141, 196, 209, 211, 215, 221, 222, 227, 228, 229, 231, 349.
— Walter. See Scott's *Fasti*, 310.
Balfour, Sir (Mr.) James (laird of Whittinghame), 14, 16, 17, 70, 74, 142, 200.
— Sir James. See Tytler's *Life of Sir T. Craig*, 336.
— Mr. James, minister at Edinburgh, 345.
— William, 52.
Balnaves, Henry, 350.
Bancroft, 208, 209.
Banff (Bamf), 61.
Bannatine Club, 298.

Bannatyne (Bannatine, Ballantyne, Ballantine), Adam, Minister at Falkirk, and Bishop of Dunblane and Aberdeen, 89, 105-123, 241, 347.
Barbour, 232.
Barclay, David, 236, 243.
Bargany, 212.
Barron, Doctor R., 264, 269.
Barton (Bartoun), Robert, 61.
Basle (Basil), 289, 290.
Bassandon, Thomas. See Dobson's *Bassandyne Bible*, Lee's *Memorials for the Bible Societies in Scotland*, and *Annals of Scottish Printing*, by Dickson & Edmond, 338.
Bath, Bishop of, 297.
Beddell, Bishop, 266.
Bedlem, 232.
Bellenden, 26.
Berwick, 36, 44, 45, 51, 83.
Bethune of Balfour, 299.
Beza, 208, 209, 282, 283, 284, 286.
Binning, Lord, 91.
Black, David, 71, 75.
— David. On his life and case, see Calderwood, Spottiswoode, Tytler, Scott's *Fasti*, & Cunningham, 327, 347.
Blackburn (Blaickburn, Blackburne, Blackburn), Peter, 64, 65, 66, 79, 84, 88, 344.
Blackhall, Andrew, 34.
— Andrew, Scott's *Fasti*, Calderwood's *History*, 312.
Blacknes, 35, 277.
Blair, James, 243.
Blantyre, Prior of, 26.
Blyth, Henry, 55, 345.
— Henry. Notice of in Scott's *Fasti*, Calderwood, 321.
Bodle, 232.
Bologna (Bononia), 2.
Bonos (Bowes), 32.
Borthwick, Sir John, 303.
Bothwell, Adam. Notice of in Keith's Catalogue of Scottish Bishops, 304.
— (Bothwel), Earl of, 9, 10, 12, 15, 26, 54, 128, 129, 130.
Baukle, Cuthbert, 38.
Boukle, Michael, 38.
Bourden, James, 110.
Bowes, 132.
Boyd, 212.
— Andrew, 347.
— Alexander, 295, 296.
— James, 348.
— Robert, 52.
— Robert, of Trochrodge, 348. Wodrow's *Collections*, 318.

Bradford, 138.
Braid, Laird of, 181, 184, 227.
Brand, John, 34, 48, 52, 62, 139, 140, 155, 181, 195, 196, 201.
— John. Scott's *Fasti*, 312.
Brechin (Brichen), Bishop of, 165, 255.
Brewton (Brereton), 32.
Brian, 232.
Brice, Edward, 274.
Brichen, Lord of, 117.
Bright, 232.
Brown, 232.
Bruce, 74, 179, 210, 243.
— Sir Alexander, of Airth, 341.
— James, 341.
-- Robert, 278.
— Robert. McCrie's *Life of Melville*, Anderson's *Scottish Nation*, and Scott's *Fasti*, 341-342, 343.
— King Robert, 341.
Buchan, 272.
— Churches of Mar and, 7.
Buchanan, George, Principal of St. Leonard's College, St. Andrews, 12, 82, 187, 188, 192, 201, 349.
Buchanan's, George, Life by Mr. P. Hume Brown, 302.
Buchanan, Thomas, 52, 53, 68, 71, 82, 147, 184, 284, 348.
Bullinger, Henry, 253.
Burn, Nicol, 23.
Burnet, Bishop, 266.
— Laird of Leyes, 93.
Burntisland, 170.

Cadclough (Caldeclough), John, 46, 283, 347.
Cairns (Cairnss), John, 9, 10, 51, 221.
Caithnes, 75, 277.
— Bishop of, 14, 79.
Calder, 295.
Calderwood's MS. History, *passim*.
Calderwood (Caldwood), 1, 14, 26, 27, 36, 38, 49, 50, 57, 66, 68, 70, 72, 74, 79, 80, 83, 84, 88, 89, 93, 94, 105, 106, 107, 124, 127, 144, 154, 163, 179, 184, 187, 207, 211, 213, 218, 221, 223, 228, 229, 231, 237, 239, 242, 243, 247, 248, 249, 250, 270, 276, 283.
— David, 166, 178, 252, 253, 274.
Calvin, 3, 54.
Calvin's Catechism, translated by Dr. Horatius Bonar, 318.
Cambridge, 222.
Cambuskenneth, Abbots of, 212.
Cameron, John, 346.
Campbell (Campbelles), Archibald, 53, 55.

INDEX. 353

Campbell, Hon. Archibald: *Dictionary of Nat. Biography*, Bishop Keith. Dowden's *Introduction to the Annotated Scottish Communion Office*.
— Robert, 350.
Cannongate (Canongate), 13, 14, 18, 204.
Cant, Andrew, 247.
— W., 117, 118, 120, 121, 122.
Carberry Hill, 15.
Cargill, 245.
— Doctor James, 267.
Carmichael, James, 35, 51, 71, 74, 139, 223, 229, 231, 347.
— James. M'Crie's *Life of Melville*, Scott's *Fasti*, Spottiswoode, Calderwood.
— John, 34, 74, 92, 167, 240, 347.
Carnock, Minister of, 300.
Carroll, William, 52.
Carswell, John, 350.
Castle, Edinburgh, 13.
Castole, 232.
Cathcart, Allan, Lord,
Cathkins, Edward, 221.
— James, 221.
Chalmers, 85, 86.
Chambers, David, 347.
Charles I., 97, 114, 179.
— II., 81, 82.
Chartaris, Henry, 272.
Charters, 56, 105, 211, 244, 263, 266, 283.
— Laurence. See Mardment's *Catalogue of Scottish Writers*, 322.
Check, 231, 232.
Cheestlie, J., 26.
Chisholm, Michael, 155.
Christieson, William, 187.
Clappertoun, John, 38, 51, 71.
— John. Scott's *Fasti*, Calderwood's *History*, 315.
Claud, 264.
Clydesdale (Clydsdale, Clydale, Clidsdale), 57, 59.
Clock, Alexander, 217.
Cockburn, Patrick, 350.
Coe, John, 349.
Collier, 114, 116.
Colluthie, Laird of, 155.
Colt, Oliver, 274.
Colvil, James, 26.
— John, 347.
Condon, John, 52.
Corse, Laird of, 80, 241.
Corsindae, 266.
Coupar, 12, 107.
— William, 89, 108, 240, 241, 343.
Cout, 232.
Cowpar (Coupar), John, 52, 64, 231, 345.

Cowper, Bishop of Galloway, 261.
Craig (Craige), John, 1-56, 67, 69, 126, 148, 183, 193, 196, 200, 206, 207, 343.
— William, 56, 296.
Craigievar, 81.
Crailing, Minister at, 298.
Cranstoun, Michael, 52.
Crawford, 34, 156.
— F., 7. See *Histories of University of Edinburgh*, by Dalziel & Grant; also *Dictionary of Nat. Biography*, 323.
— Countess of, 194.
— M., 279, 281, 283.
— Thomas, 56, 175, 271.
Cretch, 85.
Crichtonhall, 204.
Cruke, Doctor, 232.
Culros, 113.
Culver, 232.
Cunningham's *Church History of Scotland*, 298.
Cunningham (Cunninghame), David, 57-65, 72, 75, 79, 347.

Dacres, Lord, 2.
Daill, Thomas, 38.
Dalgleish, David, 239.
Dalglish (Dalgleish), Nicol, 31, 38, 39, 51, 67, 70, 187, 345.
Dalgleish, Nicol. M'Crie's *Life of Melville*, Scott's *Fasti*, 310.
Dalkeith, 83, 145, 146, 152, 169, 170.
Damman, Sir Adrian, 347.
Darnley (Darnly), Henry, lord, 7.
D'Aubigney, 62, 126, 144, 145, 209, 223.
Davidson, John, 31, 32, 34, 62, 67, 139, 142, 144, 146, 150, 196, 210, 211, 212, 214, 217, 229, 231, 287, 343.
Davidson, John. Scott's *Fasti*, Dr. C. Lee's *St. Giles'*, 310.
— Mrs. John, 232.
Davie (Rizzio), 128.
Dee, 81, 97.
Deer, Presbitry of, 272, 273, 276.
Deering, 232.
Delf, in Holland, minister of, 81.
Denmark, King of, 65.
Dickson, D., 96.
— John, 250, 251.
— & Edmond's *Annals of Scottish Printing*, 338.
Dobson's *Bassandyne Bible*, 338,
Dominicans, 2.
Don, 81, 97.
Douglas, Archibald, 128, 129, 130, 140.
— George, 26, 231.
— George, of Lochlevin, 142, 143.
— of Parkhead, James, 35.

YY

Douglas, John, 349.
Douglass, Alexander, 71, 238, 349.
Down Castle, 277.
Dryburgh, 212.
Dumbarton (Dumbartun), 127, 137, 277.
Dumfermline, Abbot of, 212.
Dumfermling, Lord, 151.
Dun, Laird of, 52, 59, 125, 181, 182, 194, 197, 200, 206, 207.
Dunbar (Dumbar), Earl of, 239.
— Minister of, 45.
Duncan, Andrew, 346.
Dunblane (Dunblain, Dumblan), Bishop of, 111, 112, 114, 117, 118, 225, 262.
Duncanson, John, 26, 31, 48, 49, 55, 68, 69, 147, 152, 153, 196, 345.
— John. Scott's *Fasti*, M'Crie's *Life of Melville*, 311.
Dunce, Minister of, 38.
Dundee, Minister at, 165.
Dunfermline, 155, 195.
— R., 26.
Dunlop's Confessions, 305.
Durhame, Alexr., 26.
Dury, George, 125.
Durie (Duries, Dury), John, Minister at Edinburgh and Monross, 21, 33, 36, 62, 124-164, 196, 209, 210, 211, 212, 214, 217, 218, 222, 343.
— John. See McCrie's *Life of Melville*, 336.
— Robert, 52.
Dykes, John, 52.
Dysart, Person of, 109.

East Kirk, Edinburgh, 175.
Eastwood, 279.
Edinburgh, Bishop of, 169.
— Town Council of, 147.
Elgin, 78.
Elphinston (Elphingstoun), Bishop, 97.
Elphinstoun, James, 26.
Elphingstoun, Laird of, 181.
Ely (Elie), Bishop of, 232, 297.
English, Nathaniel, 277, 278.
Enzie, Earl of, 78.
Errol, Earl of, 76.
Erskine, John, of Dun, 195, 343.
— (Areskine), Robert, 26.
— William, 242.
Esk, 232.
Evant, 232.
Evecole, 232.
Ewart, Peter, 55, 166.
— (Ewat, Hewart, Howat, Hewet, Peter. See Sprott's *Introduction to the Scottish Liturgies of James VI.*, Scott's *Fasti*, Calderwood, 321.

Fairfoul, John, 55, 321.
Fairholme or Ferme, Charles, Minister and Professor at Frazerburgh, 270, 281.
Fairly, James, 173, 257.
Fairley, Robert, of Braid, 227.
Falkirk, Minister at, 106, 107.
Falkland, 34, 217, 222.
— Conference at, 108, 239, 240.
Feild, 208.
Fergushill, John, 345.
Ferguson, David, 52, 62, 139, 140, 147, 184, 195, 201, 217, 350.
Ferme (Ferm, Farum) or Fairholme, Charles, Minister, and Professor at Frazerburgh, 270-281, 346.
Ferrier, 289.
Fetteresso, 245, 263.
Fife, John, 349.
— Presbitery of, 91.
— Superintendant of, John Winram, 12, 15, 202.
— Synod of, 73.
Fintray (Fintry), 64, 81.
Fintry, Laird of, 152.
— The Laird of; David Graham. See Row; Calderwood, 323.
Firm, 76.
Fleeming, James, Minister at Caithaness, 171.
Fleming, John, 250.
Floudon, Battle of, 1.
Font, 232.
Forbes, Alexander, Bishop of Aberdeen, and formerly of Caithnes, 87.
— Alexander, of Ardmurdo. Keith's *Catalogue*, Spottiswoode, &c., 331.
— Alexander, Bishop of Caithnes, 79, 240.
— Arthur, 81.
— Arthur, Earl of Grenard, son of Arthur of Corse, 82.
— Bishop, predecessor to Dr. Lindsay, 165, 168.
— David, 81.
— Doctor John, of Corse, 253, 266.
— George H., Rev., of Burntisland, 341.
— John, Minister, 276.
— John; brother of Bishop Patrick, and third son of William Forbes of Corse. See Scott's *Fasti*; McCrie's *Life of A. Melville*, *Cunningham*, 328-329.
— Dr. John, Professor of Divinity at King's College, Aberdeen; Irving's *Lives of Scottish Writers*, 332; Dr. Garden's *Life of*, 341.
— John, minister at Alnes (Alford?), 81.

INDEX. 355

Forbes, John, brother of Patrick of Corse, Bishop of Aberdeen, 84.
— John, of Alford, 76, 77, 246, 344.
— John, son of Patrick of Corse, 80.
— late Bishop of Edinburgh, 119.
— Patrick, Barron of O'Neil, & Laird of Corse, Minister of Keith, & Bishop of Aberdeen, 80-105, 122, 231, 253, 345.
— Patrick, son of John, minister at Alnes (Alford ?), 81.
— Sir Patrick, knight, 81.
— Thomas, of Corsindae, 266.
— William, 105.
— William, Minister at Aberdeen and Edinburgh, and Bishop of Edinburgh, 245-269, 341, 346.
— William, son of David Forbes of Corse, 81.
— William, son of William, son of David, Forbes of Corse, 81.
Forrester, Alexander, 38.
Forsyth, 232.
Fountain, 232.
France, 2, 56.
Frazer, James, 26.
Frazerburgh, 270.
French, Robert, 51.
Fulden, Minister at, 274.
Fyfe, 52.

Gait, Patrick, 38.
Galloway, 261.
— Alexander, Bishop of, 13.
— Bishop of, 255.
— Patrick, 35, 108, 217, 240, 241, 247, 343.
— Patrick. Dr. Cameron Lee's *St. Giles'*.
Gap, Synod of, 291, 292, 293.
Garden, George, 58, 80, 81, 83, 86, 93, 98, 99, 105, 266, 269.
— Dr. George. Irving's *Lives of Scottish Writers*, 332.
Gardiner, 231, 232.
Garrow, Robert, 231.
Geneva, 208, 289, 290.
Gibson, George, 149.
— (Gybson), James, in Pencaitland, 52, 64, 346.
Gight, Laird of, 76.
Gilbert, Janet, 222.
Giles' (Geils') Church, Saint, 8.
Gladstanes (Gladstains), George, Archbishop of Saint Andrews, 84, 109, 169, 236, 240, 348.
— George, Bishop of Caithnes, 71.
Glames, Master of, 212, 221.
Glasgow, Bishop of, 169, 255.

Glasgow, University of, 82.
Glencairn, 212.
— Lord, 157.
Goodman, C., 350.
Gordon, Alexander, of the House of Huntly. Notices of in Keith's *Catalogue of Scottish Bishops*, 304, 347.
— Luke, 75.
— William, 64, 85, 86.
— William ; Last Popish Bishop of Aberdeen. See Keith's *Catalogue*, 324.
Gourlay, Robert, 200.
Gowrie (Gourie), John, Earl of, 150, 151, 152, 272.
Graham, George (Andrew), 109.
Grange, 295.
Gratian, 43.
Gray, Master of, 26.
Grayfreirs Kirk, Edinburgh, 173, 175.
Great Kirk, Edinburgh, 175.
Greenlaw, 260.
Greg, James, 59, 277, 278.
Gregory, John, 345.
Gunn, Dr., 342.
Guise, Duke of, 142, 145, 146.
Gutery, Janet, 221.
Guthrie (Guthry), 231, 232.
Guthry, Alexander, 272.
Guthrie, Janet, wife of James Lawson, 227, 228, 232, 234.

Haddington, Earl of, 169.
Hales, 125.
Hall, 108.
— John, 51, 75, 240, 241, 247, 343.
Hallyburton, James, 26.
Hamilton, Bishop of Galloway, 297.
— James, 52.
— John, 35.
— Patrick, 180, 348.
— Patrick. See Knox's *History*, Keith's *History*, and *Memoirs of Patrick Hamilton*, by Dr. Lorimer, 337.
— (Hamiltoun), Thomas, 26.
Hannay (Hanna), James, 175, 257.
Harlan, William, 347.
Harrison, Mrs., 232.
Hawick, Parson of, 38.
Hay, Andrew, Parson of Renfrew, 20, 35, 52, 59, 148, 154, 212, 217, 343.
— Andrew. Scott's *Fasti*, J. Melville's *Autobiography*, 313.
— George, Rector of Turriff, 12, 60, 90, 126, 184, 240, 241, 345.
— George, Notices of, in M'Crie's *Lives of Knox & Melville*, 303.
— John, 250.
— Theodore, 247.

356 WODROW'S COLLECTIONS.

Hay, Walter, 38.
Heeriot, Minister at Aberdeen, 66.
Heidelberg, 289, 290.
Helmstadt, 264.
Henderson, Alexander, 230.
— Janet, 222.
Henrieson, Robert, 155.
Hepburn (Stephen's ?), Andrew, 263.
— Adam, 347.
— George, 38.
— Thomas, 10, 346.
Herborn (Herbourg), 288.
Herries, 213.
— John, 34.
— or Hereis, John. Scott's *Fasti*, 312.
— (Harris), Lord, 151, 152.
Herriott, Adam, 7.
Herriot, Richard, 26.
Hiet, 232.
Hislop, Philip, 272.
Hogg, Thomas, 167.
Holland, 81.
Holt, 32, 33.
Holyrood (Hollyrood, Hallyrood), 6, 7, 54, 114, 169, 171, 176, 178, 195, 254.
Hornbie, 232.
Howeson, John, 52, 71, 346.
Howie (Howey), Robert, Professor of Divinity at Saint Andrews, 235-244, 295, 345.
Howit (Howat), Peter, 242.
Hume, 33, 213.
— Alexander, 38, 45.
— or Home, Alexander. M'Crie's *Life of Melville*, 311.
— David, of Coldingham, 51, 52, 231, 260.
— Daud, of Godscroft, 345.
— John, 51.
Hundson, 232.
Hunter, Andrew, 52.
Huntley (Huntlie), Earl of, 15, 34, 64, 72, 73, 129, 276.
— Marquis of, 76,
Huttoun, Laird of, 93.

Inverness, 78, 81, 278.
Ireland, 82.
Irvine, James, 278.
Irving, Dr., 299.
Irvings, 76.
Isla, 277.
Itlay, 2.

James IV., King, 1.
— VI. & I., 65, 81, 97, 106, 222, 252, 274.
— Mr., 277.
Jedburgh, Kirk of, 195.

Jedburgh, Minister at, 109.
Jerome (Jerom), 44.
Johnstoun, Adam, 38, 39, 51.
Johnston, Adam. Scott's *Fasti*, Calderwood's *History*, 314.
Johnstoun, John, Professor of Divinity in the University of St. Andrews, 148, 184, 236, 283-296, 345.
— Mrs., 232.
— Robert, 52.

Keith's *Catalogue of Scottish Bishops*, 298.
Keith, John, 182.
— Minister of, 80, 83.
— Parish of, 85.
Ker, Mark, 155.
Ker, Robert, 52.
Kerr, Walter, 26.
Kilconquhar, Laird of, 106.
— Lands of, 108.
Kincardin, Rector of, 90.
Kinghorn, 15.
King's College, Aberdeen, Principal of, 300.
— College, 97.
— College, Aberdeen, Principal of, 179.
Kinlowrie (Kinloghy), Patrick, 38.
— Patrick. Scott's *Fasti*, 315.
Kinneil, 145.
Kintyre, 270.
Kirkaldy, 195.
— William, of Grange, 295.
Knox, Andrew, 71.
— James, 272.
— (Knoxe), John, 1, 6, 7, 8, 9, 13, 20, 26, 52, 58, 71, 125, 136, 162, 164, 179, 182, 192, 193, 195, 208, 240, 349.
Kyle, 124.

Laing, Dr. David, 299.
Lamb, Bishop of Brechin, 297.
— Andrew, 55, 236.
— Andrew. See Keith ; Scott's *Fasti* ; Lee, 321.
— James, 51.
Lambeth, 117, 118, 120, 121, 122.
La Mott, 213.
Lanark, 57.
Lane, 232.
Laswade (Laswadd, Leswalt), 169, 170, 171.
Laud, Archbishop, 23, 116, 118, 119, 175, 241, 245, 253, 254, 265.
Lauder, Alexander, 38.
— Robert, 231.
Lauderdale, Earl of, 169.
Lauther, Minister of, 38.
Law, Bishop, 236.
— James, 55, 110, 343.

INDEX. 357

Law, James. See Dr. Sprott's *Introduction to Scottish Liturgies of James VI.*, 321.
Lawson, Christian, 228.
— James, sub-Principal of the College of Aberdeen, and Minister at Edinburgh, 31, 35, 62, 66, 67, 126, 139, 141, 142, 143, 144, 145, 148, 154, 155, 180, 183, 184, 192, 193-234, 343.
Leath, 87.
Lee, Dr., 298.
Lee's, Dr., *Lectures on the History of the Church of Scotland*, 307.
Le Fevre, 265.
Leighton, James, 247.
Leith, 14, 196, 197, 204, 254.
— Convention of. On this subject, see Church Histories of Cunningham, Lee, Calderwood, Grub, &c., 323.
Lennox, Earl of, 7, 20, 24, 25, 26.
— 59, 62, 144.
— Duke of, 145, 210, 212, 217.
Lesley, 76, 86.
Leswalt (Laswade), 169, 170.
Lethington (Lethingtoun), 8.
Levingstone, William, 346.
Leyden, 246, 289.
Leys (Leyes), Laird of, Burnet, 93.
Leythis, 76.
Libbertoun, 229.
— Minister at, 242.
Lik, 232.
Lindsay, Alexander, 71, 240.
— John, 227.
— David, 12, 31, 35, 52, 139.
— David, Bishop of Ross, 70, 145, 146, 148, 154, 262.
— David, Minister at Dundee, Bishop of Brechin, and then of Edinburgh, 165-178, 346.
— David, Minister at Leith, 183, 196, 197, 200, 211, 212, 217, 345.
— Lord, 19, 20.
— Robert, of Kirkton, 302.
Linlithgow, Minister of, 39.
Livingstoun, 55, 161, 213.
Livinsingston, John, See Wodrow Society's *Select Biographies.* Also, Scott's *Fasti*, 322.
Litle, Clement, 196, 201.
Lochleven (Lochlevin), 15, 142, 212.
Lochmaben, 243.
Logie, Rector of, 90.
Logy-Buchan, Minister of, 179.
London, 83, 120, 229, 231.
— Bishop of, 297.
Lorn, Lord (afterwards Marquis of Argyle), 176.
Lothian, Presbitery of, 91.

Lothian, Superintendent of, 9, 195, 205.
— Synod of, 32, 143.
— East, Commissioner for, 93.
— West, Commissioner for, 93.
Lousanus, 208.
Lowson, James, 34, 38.
Lundy, Laird of, 22.

Magdalen's Chapel (Edinburgh), 6.
Magdeburg, Protestant Council at, 186.
Maidment's Catalogues of Scottish Writers, 338.
Maitland, Sir John.
— Thomas, 190.
Makgie, Thomas, 51.
Malcome, John, 350.
Marischal College, 246, 267, 268.
Marishall (Marischal), Earl, 97.
Mar, 212.
— and Buchan, Churches of, 7.
Marjoribanks, Margaret, 221.
Mark, Robert, 221.
Marr, Earl of, 45, 52, 169, 221.
Martine, Alderman, 232.
Martin, Anthony, 224, 231, 232.
Martine, Mrs. Anthony, 232.
— James, 68.
— Sir James, 236.
Mary, Queen of Scots, 10.
Mauchline, 124.
Maxie, Doctor, 239.
Maximilian, Emperor, 6.
Maxwell, 118, 119, 212.
— John, 262.
M'Bryar, 349.
M'Crie's *Life of Melville*, 302.
M'Dowall, 349.
M'Keinzie, Dr., 179, 180, 182, 183, 185, 186, 187, 189, 190, 191.
M'Keson, George, 152, 153.
M'Naught, John, 248.
M'Ralzean, Thomas, 204.
Mearns (Mernes), 180
— Commissioner for the, 93.
Melvil, Andrew, 21, 34, 53, 57, 58, 59, 60, 62, 66, 67, 68, 69, 70, 82, 83, 84, 126, 150, 154, 164, 183, 184, 186, 189, 192, 200, 201, 206, 208, 210, 211, 212, 221, 229, 231, 235, 236, 237, 239, 240, 282, 283, 286, 287, 291, 292, 294, 295, 344.
-- James, 34, 45, 57, 59, 71, 74, 83, 155, 156, 158, 161, 234, 236, 283, 284, 350.
-- Robert, 113.
Merse, 51.
Methven, Paul, 350.
Milan (Millan), 4.
Mitchell, 88.

Mitchell (Mitchel), David, 173, 177, 253, 257, 262.
— Thomas, 89, 90, 91.
Mitchelson, John, 240.
Moncreif, Archibald, 52, 231.
Monkland (Munkland), 58.
Monnigill (Mannigil, Manningvill, Manningval, Menivil), 214, 215.
Monroe (Monro), John, Minister at Tain, 277, 278.
Montgomery (Montgommery), Robert, 30, 143, 144, 145, 210.
— Robert. See Scott's *Fasti*, Keith's *Bishops*, Calderwood, 309.
Montrose (Monross, Monros), 7, 20, 83, 124, 155, 156, 273.
— Marquis of, 222.
Monymusk (Munnimusk), 267.
Morison, 231.
Mornay Duplessis, Lord, 282, 291.
Mortingtoun, 232.
Morton (Mortoun), Earl of, 8, 21, 24, 25, 58, 60, 62, 93, 127, 141, 144, 163, 196, 197, 200, 210.
Murray, 81.
— Bishop of, 78, 255.
— David, 26.
— Dean and Chapter of, 182.
— Diocese of, 85.
— Earl of, 54.
— John, of Lochmaben, 243.
— John, Minister at Lochmaben, 348.
— Sir Patrick, 73.
— Synod of, 76.
— William, 26.
— William, Person of Dysart, 109.
Myln, Walter, 303.
Myrton, William, 257.

Nairn, James, 251.
Newbatle, 213.
Newbotle, Lord, 151, 276.
Newbottle, Minister at, 171.
New College, Saint Andrews, 82, 283.
Newton, Laird of, 76.
Nicholson, James, 55, 71, 89, 108, 165, 236, 345.
Nimmo, William, 248.
Nisbit, Henry, 211, 221.

Ochiltree, 127.
Ogilvy, James, Lord, 26.
O'Neil, Barron of, 80, 81.
Orkney, 277.
— Adam, Bishop of, 10, 13.
Ormestoun, Lady, 138.
Oswald, Archibald, 240.
— John, Minister of Pencaitland, 171.
Overtown, Mrs., 232.

Oxford, 222.

Paisley, 212.
Palatine Catechism, 320.

Parkhead, 35.
Paterson, Duncan, 93.
— Sir H., 301.
Paul, Seignior, 145.
— IV., Pope, 3.
Pencaitland, Minister of, 298.
Perth Articles, 308.
— 32, 73, 88, 91, 92, 93, 94, 193.
Peterkin, 298.
Peterkin's Edition of the *Booke of the Kirk of Scotland*, 340.
Petry, 23, 154, 179, 185, 186.
Pharnihurst, 213.
Philip, Henry, 240.
Philorth, Laird of, 273.
Piscator, Doctor J., 288, 289, 293.
Pittenweem, Prior of, 22.
Pius II., Pope, 6.
Poland, 283.
Pole (Pool), Cardinal, 2.
Polwart, Andrew, 35, 67, 212.
— Andrew. Scott's *Fasti*, Lee's *Memorial*, Calderwood, Melville's *Autobiography*, 313.
Pont, earlier Kynpont, Robert. His Publications, 310.
— Robert, 31, 35, 38, 39, 48, 51, 53, 58, 59, 70, 139, 144, 145, 148, 155, 156, 183, 184, 196, 199, 201, 204, 217, 232, 284, 343.
— Robert. M'Crie's *Life of Knox*, 314.
Pope, 232.
Porteous (Porteouse), James, 169, 170.
Porterfield, John, 71.
Potter, 232.
Pourie (Pury), William, 38.
— William. Scott's *Fasti*, 315.
Preston, Laird of, 93.
Primrose, Gilbert, 346.
Provand, John, 131.

Queensferry, 155.
Quick, 289, 293.

Raban, Edward, 308.
Ramsay, Andrew, Minister at Edinburgh, 171, 173, 175, 257, 347.
Ramsay, G., 38, 71.
Ratho, Minister of, 38.
Reid, John, 90,
Renfrew, 57.
— Commissioners of, 202.
Restalrig, Dean of, 38.
Rig, Bailie William, 251, 252.

INDEX. 359

Riross, William, 281.
Rizzio, 142.
Robertson, James, 46, 52.
— John, 283.
— Dr. Joseph, 301.
Rochelle (Rochell, Rotchell), 290.
Rollock, 56, 236.
— Harry, 175, 257.
— Robert, 236, 270, 271, 274, 284, 285, 343.
Rollock's *De Vocatione Efficaci*, 342.
Rome, 2.
Ross, Bishop of, 74, 169, 255.
— John, 277, 278, 346.
— Lord of, 120.
Rou, John, 346.
— William, 346.
Rough, John, 349.
Row, John, 1, 4, 5, 16, 22, 29, 55, 58, 163, 199, 245, 250, 253, 254, 260, 261, 270, 273, 295.
— John, Minister of Perth, 126, 206, 343.
Roxburgh, Earl of, 169.
Rutherford, 243, 244.
Ruthven, Lord, 19, 25, 26, 31, 142.
— William, of Bellenden.

St. Andrews, 1, 22, 23, 41, 48, 56, 68, 91, 92, 115.
Saint Andrews, Bishop of, 247, 248, 255, 262.
— Professor of Divinity at, 235.
— University of, 82, 91, 92, 180, 194.
Saint Cuthbert's Kirk, 171.
— — Minister of, 35.
Saint Giles' (Geils) Church, 8.
St. Giles' Kirk, 151.
Saint Johnstoun, 91.
Saint Leonard's College, Saint Andrews, 82.
Saint Nicholas Church, 79.
St. Nicholas, Parson of, 59, 65.
Saint Salvator's College, Saint Andrews, 82.
Saltoun, Lord, 85.
Sandilands, James, of Calder.
Sands, Patrick, 56, 272.
Saumure, 56, 274, 296.
Scot, George, 195.
— Robert, minister at Glasgow, 274, 348.
— William, 74, 87, 92, 167, 213, 240, 348.
— William. See Scott's *Fasti*, 327.
Scrimgeour, James, 26, 286.
— John, 348.
Scrimgeor, Henry, 346.
Seaton, Alexander, 26, 213, 215, 349.
— Lord, 135.
Sedan, 282.
Sharp, John, 207, 346.
— Patrick, 236, 240, 348.
Shaw, William, 26.

Sibbald, James, 98, 99.
Simson, Andrew, 38, 39, 48, 182, 194, 348.
— Archibald, 49, 166, 279, 348.
— Andrew. M'Crie's *Life of Knox*, Scott's *Fasti*, 315.
— Patrick, 38, 39, 51, 146, 236, 348.
— Patrick. Scott's *Fasti*, M'Crie's *Life of Melville*, 315.
Skeen, John, 142.
— or Skene, afterwards Sir John Skene of Curriehill. See *Memorials of the Family of Skene*, issued by New Spalding Club, 336.
Slezer, Captain, 301.
Smeton (Smeaton), 69, 67, 75, 212, 217.
— (Smeaton), James, 66, 67, 75.
— Thomas, 148, 164, 184, 187, 189, 192, 344.
Smith, 232.
Sohnes, 289.
Southesk, Earl of, 169.
Spain, King of, 19.
Spence, David, of Wermistoun, 83.
— Lucretia, 83.
Spotswod, Bishop, 1, 4, 6, 12, 20, 23, 24, 25, 55, 59, 60, 64, 71, 79, 118, 122, 123, 125, 145, 155, 161, 166, 189, 191, 192, 216, 221, 232, 297, 298, 346.
Spotswood, Archbishop, Primate of Scotland, 30.
— John, Superintendent of Louthian, 55, 195, 196, 205, 236, 240, 297.
Sprott, Dr. (*Scottish Liturgies*), 306, 340.
Stentoun, Minister of, 38.
Stephens, Andrew, 245.
Stewart, Captain James, 25, 26, 127.
— Colonel, 32, 33, 34, 209, 217, 221.
— Walter, 26.
— William, 139.
Stirling, 36, 51, 82, 143, 148, 149, 150, 151.
— Lord. See Rodger's *Memorials of Earl of Stirling and House of Alexander*, 335.
— Castle of, 132, 277.
— Provost of, 93.
— William, 71.
Storic, Thomas, 52.
Story, Rev. Dr., 300.
Strachan (Strauchan), 231, 232.
Strang, John, of Errol, 345.
Strathauchine (Strathauchin), John, 76, 92.
— or Strachan, John. Scott's *Fasti*, 330.
Strathern, Superintendent of, 195, 199.
Struthers, William, 241, 250, 345.
Sturt, 232.
Strype (Stryp), 208, 209.
Suddick, 232.

Surfleet, 232.
Sutherland, 75, 277.
— Elizabeth, 63.
Sydserf (Sidserfe, Sidserf), 118, 119, 168, 169, 247, 253, 255, 257, 262.

Tain Castle, 277.
Tay, 155, 222.
Teviotdale, 52.
Thomson, Alexander, 51, 174, 175, 255, 257.
Tolbooth Kirk, 173.
Tranent, Minister at, 38, 171, 279.
Traquair, Earl of, 121.
Travers, 232.
Trent, Council of, 29.
Trochrodge (Trockoroge, Trocherege, Trocherig), 52, 295, 296.
Tulchan, 21, 22.
— Bishops. See Melville's Diary; Calderwood's History, cited in Cunningham's Church History, 305.
Turriff, Rector of, 90.
Tylour, 231.
Tyrie, James, 196.

Udney, Minister of, 89, 90.
Udward, Alexander, 155.

Vannane, Mrs., 232.
Vannell, Mrs., 228.
Vantrellier, Mrs., 232.
Vienna, 5.

Waldgrave, 285.
Wales, Robert, 279.
Walgrave, 53.
Walsingham, Secretary, 232.
Walter, 138, 139, 141.
Waristoun, Lord, 55.
Watson, 74.

Wauchton, Laird of, 135.
Wedderburn, 128.
Weems, David, 58, 59, 346.
— See Scott's *Fasti*, 323.
— John, 240, 343.
Weemes, Easter, 26.
Welsh, 76.
— John, 276, 277.
Welch, or Welsh, John. See Scott's *Fasti*, M'Crie's *Life of A. Melville*, and *Melville's Autobiography*, 328.
Wermistoun (Wilmerstoun), 83
West Kirk, Edinburgh, 175.
White, Patrick, 232.
Whitebread, 232.
Whiteford (Whitford), Walter, 87.
Whitgift, 208, 209.
Whittinghame, 128.
Wilkie (Wilky), Robert, 68, 71, 236, 273.
Willock, John, 349.
Willocks, 16.
Wilson, 231, 232.
Winchester, Andrew, 52.
— Dean of, 92, 240.
Winram (Winrame) John, Superintendant of Fife, 12, 14, 15, 195, 349.
— or Wynram, John, brother of Mr. Robert Wynram of Ratho. Notices of in Lee's Church History, and M'Crie's *Life of Knox*, 303.
Winton, Earl of, 169.
Wishart, George, 303, 349.
Wisheart, William, 257.
Woodrow's Biographical Collection in the Library of the University of Glasgow, 343.

Young, John, 184.
— Peter, 26, 201.
Youngson, Robert, 277, 278.

Zetland, 277.

New Spalding Club.

REPORTS.

THIRD REPORT BY THE COUNCIL.

(Approved at the Third Annual General Meeting of the Club on Monday, 21st October, 1889.)

THE Council are again able to congratulate the Club on the condition of its affairs. The membership continues to reach the limit assigned by the rules, and, as will be seen from the appended Report by the *Interim* Treasurer, the finances could not be in a more satisfactory state, as no subscriptions are in arrears.

During the past year the Club has been deprived by death of seven of its members: The Rev. C. Elrington Bisset, younger of Lessendrum; Mr. P. H. Chalmers, the Honorary Treasurer; the Rev. Professor Christie; Mr. J. R. Cornwall; Mr. A. L. Pirie; Mr. J. F. Thomson; and Mr. H. J. Trotter, M.P. for Colchester.

It would be difficult to overestimate the loss sustained through the death of Mr. Chalmers. With him originated the idea of reviving the Spalding Club, and from none could that idea have come more appropriately, owing to his hereditary connection with the literary history of the district. It is to his enthusiasm and energy that we in large measure owe the successful start made by the new Society. His interest in its affairs never lessened.

Professor Christie was elected a Member of Council in 1888, and was entrusted with the editing of a volume of

Selections from the Wodrow MSS. The Council anticipated a full and painstaking treatment of the subject by Dr. Christie, but, unfortunately, at his death only a general plan had been sketched out.

Mr. Thomson, a young man of much promise, was, it will be recollected, associated with the Rev. Mr. Cooper in the editing of the St. Nicholas Chartulary. In losing him the Club has lost a valuable member, and one who bade fair to become an archæologist of note.

Mr. Trotter, a grandson of Andrew Philip Skene, of the Halyards (Fife) branch, took a lively interest in the appearance of the first volume issued by the Club; and shortly before his death printed for private circulation a Genealogical Tree, showing the descent of the Skene family (in a form to correspond with the volumes issued by the Club). His sister, Miss Trotter, has courteously placed a limited number of copies in the hands of the Secretary for distribution to members of the Club that may be specially interested in the family.

Among the new members admitted to fill up vacancies in the ranks of the Club, the Council are glad to note two Scottish peers, who have not merely done much for the study of Scottish Archæology in general, but have especially deserved well of printing societies. These are the Marquis of Bute, to whose munificence the Grampian Club owes the sumptuous edition of the Chartulary of Cambuskenneth, and the Ayr and Galloway Society a Collection of the Charters of the Friars Preachers of Ayr; and the Earl of Rosebery, the founder and president of the Scottish History Society, and the donor to its members of a volume of Papers connected with the Forty-five.

Since the last annual meeting, two volumes have been issued to the members of the New Spalding Club:—

I.—LACUNAR BASILICAE SANCTI MACARII ABERDONENSIS. The Heraldic Ceiling of the Cathedral Church of St. Machar, Old Aberdeen, described in Historical and Heraldic detail by William Duguid Geddes, LL.D., and Peter Duguid. With twenty-four coloured armorial plates, two photogravures from sketches by George Reid, R.S.A., and four other illustrations. (Pp. xix. + 172, with 40 pp. of Club Reports.)

II.—FASTI ACADEMIAE MARISCALLANAE ABERDONENSIS. Selections from the Records of the Marischal College and University, edited by Peter John Anderson, M.A., LL.B. Vol. I., Endowments. With four photogravures from portraits (by Jamesone) of early benefactors, and one coloured armorial plate. (Pp. xxxi. + 577.)

The publication of the Selections from the Wodrow MSS., referred to above, was contemplated by the original Spalding Club so far back as 1844. From the Annual Report of that year, it appears that "the Council have resolved to apply for permission to have transcripts made, from the manuscripts of the industrious Wodrow now in the Library of the University of Glasgow, of such portions of his Collections upon the lives of the Reformers and most eminent Ministers of the Church of Scotland, as refer to persons connected with the ecclesiastical history of the North-Eastern Counties" (*Notices of the Spalding Club*, p. 32). From entries in the Account Books of the old Club it would seem that the transcripts had actually been made, but these the Secretary has been unable to trace. Accordingly renewed application was made to the Senate of the University of Glasgow, who readily allowed the MS. to be again copied.

The selected portions of the Collections (which in all fill twenty volumes) treat of the lives of the following Divines :—

I.—MINISTERS AND BISHOPS :—

John Craig, second reformed minister at Aberdeen (1573-79), previously colleague of Knox, and afterwards chaplain to James VI.;

David Cunningham, first reformed Bishop of Aberdeen (1577-1600), previously sub-Dean of Glasgow;

Peter Blackburn, second Bishop (1600-16), previously Regent at Glasgow University;

Patrick Forbes of Corse, fourth Bishop (1618-35);

Adam Bellenden or Ballantyne, fifth Bishop (1635-38), previously Bishop of Dunblane, and afterwards Rector of Portlock;

John Forbes, minister at Alford (1593-1606), and afterwards at Middelburg and Delft;

John Durie, minister at Montrose (1585-1600), previously at Edinburgh;

David Lindsay, Bishop of Brechin (1619-33), previously minister at Dundee, and afterwards second Bishop of Edinburgh.

II.—PRINCIPALS AND PROFESSORS :—

Alexander Arbuthnot, first reformed Principal of King's College (1569-83);

James Lawson, sub-Principal of King's College (1569-72), afterwards minister at Edinburgh;

Robert Howie, first Principal of Marischal College (1593-98), afterwards Principal of St. Mary's College, St. Andrews;

William Forbes, fourth Principal of Marischal College (1620-21), afterwards first Bishop of Edinburgh;

Charles Ferme, Principal of Fraserburgh College (1598-1605), previously Regent at Edinburgh University;

John Johnston of Crimond, Professor of Theology at St. Mary's College, St. Andrews (1592-1611).

After the death of Professor Christie, it became the duty of the Editorial Committee to select another editor. They unanimously agreed to request the Rev. Robert Lippe, Chaplain to the Royal Infirmary, &c., to undertake the work. That gentleman has consented to act, and the Committee are confident that at his hands the book will receive careful and scholarly treatment. A considerable portion of the Collections is already in type. As it is wished, where possible, to give portraits of the above divines, members of the Club aware of the existence of such will confer a favour by communicating with the Secretary.

Together with the Wodrow Biographies it is proposed to issue a volume of Miscellanies, the materials for which are being collected by the Committees on Family History, Burgh Records, and Church Records. The Council would welcome further contributions suited for such a volume.

It is matter of regret to the Council that, owing to the departure for Canada of the Rev. Dr. Gammack, the progress of the Collections towards a History of Angus and the Mearns has been temporarily suspended. The Editorial Committee have found it no easy task to discover an editor at once competent and willing to undertake a work for which Dr. Gammack's qualifications were peculiarly great.

A similar difficulty has been experienced in connection with the projected History of the Gordons. The family papers of the Marquis of Huntly have been freely placed at the disposal of the Club, but as yet no editor has been found bold enough to venture on so wide a field.

The Council are assured that satisfactory progress is being made in the preparation of the other works promised in former

Reports: the Register of the Scots College at Rome; the Diary of the Scots College at Douai; the History of the Family of Burnett; the Annals of Banff; the Folklore and Place Names of the North-Eastern Province; the translation of Boece's Lives of the Bishops; the History of the Family of Forbes; the Book of Bon-Accord, revised edition; the Bibliography of the Shires of Aberdeen, Banff, and Kincardine, &c. Volumes dealing with the History of Agriculture in the three counties, and with the Rise of Natural Science in the same district, are also in contemplation.

The Council would remind the Club, that by Rule I. its objects are defined to be, "to promote the study of the History, Topography, and Archæology of the North-Eastern Counties, and to print works illustrative thereof". The Society, therefore, is not purely a book club, but is interested in all matters affecting local Antiquities. A suggestion has been made, which commends itself to the Council, to assume, in connection with the Act of 1882 for the better Protection of Ancient Monuments (45 and 46 Vict. cap. 73), some practical duty of surveillance over the ancient monuments belonging to the district.

The proposal has arisen in consequence of an application made to one or more gentlemen interested in Archæology, who happened also to be members of the Club, by General Pitt Rivers, the Inspector of Monuments under the Act, requesting them to take steps towards the formation of a Local Committee for such surveillance: a small grant from the Treasury being available towards any outlays that might be necessary. Considering the circumstance that one of the most notable works of the former Spalding Club, and one amongst the most remarkable single contributions to Archæology made by any Club, consists of the work known as "The Sculptured Stones of Scotland," the duty or function thus suggested seems both apt in itself and appropriate to the Society. It is proper to state that the Ancient Monuments Act has in view only the remains generally regarded as prehistoric, "dolmens, ancient forts, and similar monuments," and not "more recent historic and ecclesiastical ruins, such as castles, abbeys, or churches".

Of such prehistoric remains only three are at present scheduled in Aberdeenshire (the Bass of Inverurie, the vitrified fort on Tap o' Noth, and the Newton stone), one in Morayshire (Sueno's stone, near Forres), two in Forfarshire (the cross slab at St. Vigeans, and the so-called British forts on the Black and White Catherthuns), and none in either Banffshire or Kincardineshire. But, under the 10th Section of the Act, provision is made whereby other monuments of like character may, on due representation, have extended to them a similar protection. In the two volumes of the "Sculptured Stones" are chronicled no fewer than 39 ancient monuments in Aberdeenshire, 4 in Banffshire, 12 in Morayshire, 3 in Kincardineshire, and 53 in Forfarshire. During the twenty-two years that have elapsed since the appearance of the second volume, many other remains have been brought to light, and it has been suggested to the Council by more than one member of the Club that it would be a fitting task for the present Society to carry on the work of its predecessor by preparing a Supplementary Volume. This matter is referred to the Editorial Committee.

In conclusion, the Council have to tender their thanks to Mr. F. T. Garden, Advocate, for the efficient manner in which he has discharged the duties of *Interim* Treasurer since the death of Mr. Chalmers.

GEORGE GRUB, C.

REPORT BY THE INTERIM HONORARY TREASURER.

ABSTRACT of Account of the intromissions had by the Treasurer with the funds of the Club, for the period from 30th October, 1888, to 10th October, 1889, prepared by Mr. F. T. GARDEN, Advocate, Aberdeen, *Interim* Honorary Treasurer.

THE CHARGE.

	£	s.	d.			
Assets at close of last account,	358	3	8			
Subscriptions for year 1888—						
16 members in arrears at close of last account,	16	16	0			
10 new members, taking the place of others, dead or resigned,	10	10	0			
Subscriptions for year 1889—						
493 members,*	517	13	0			
Subscriptions for year 1890—						
4 members,	4	4	0			
Bank Interest,	9	14	6			
Amount of the Charge,				£917	1	2

THE DISCHARGE.

1888.   I. MISCELLANEOUS ACCOUNTS PAID.

			£	s.	d.
Nov. 14.	D. Wyllie & Son,		0	9	0
,, 27.	A. King & Co.,		2	0	0
Dec. 12.	The Secretary, expenses visiting Glasgow,		2	10	0
,,	T. & R. Annan & Sons,		21	3	4
,, 17.	J. Malcolm Bulloch,		2	2	0
,, 21.	A. Gibb & Co.,		45	0	9
1889.					
May 9.	Grosvenor, Chater, & Co. (per A. King & Co.),		79	15	3
,,	A. King & Co.,		59	4	7
	Forward		£212	4	11

* *Note.*—At the close of the account the membership of the Club stands as follows:—

Life members,	3
Members that paid for year 1889 during period of last account,	4
Do., do., during period of present account,	493
Total,	500

1889.		Brought forward	£212	4	11	
May 10.	Rev. R. Kilgour, Glasgow, .		16	10	8	
,, 17.	D. Wyllie & Son, . . .		4	1	6	
,, 31.	T. & R. Annan & Sons, . .		31	0	6	
Sept. 17.	Edmond & Spark, . . .		41	13	5	
,,	A. King & Co., . . .		2	13	5	
,, 30.	A. Gibb & Co., . . .		3	5	0	
,,	T. & R. Annan & Sons, . .		10	6	3	
Oct. 8.	A. King & Co., . . .		144	8	7	
,, 10.	Edmond & Spark, . . .		44	12	2	
						£510 16 5

II. SECRETARY AND HONORARY TREASURER.

Secretary's salary, 1888-89, . . .	£26	5	0
Secretary's postages, &c., 28th October, 1888, to 10th October, 1889, . .	4	16	6
Hon. Treasurer's postages, &c., do., do., .	2	19	7
Hon. Treasurer's sundry outlays, . .	3	16	0

37 17 1

III. ASSETS AS AT 10TH OCTOBER, 1889.

Three Deposit Receipts with Town and County Bank, Limited, dated 10th October, 1889, for £100 each, .	£300	0	0
Balance at Credit of Treasurer's Bank Account, ex int. from 31st Jan., 1889,	68	7	8

368 7 8

Amount of the Discharge, equal to the Charge, . £917 1 2

F. T. GARDEN, *Interim Hon. Treasurer.*

ABERDEEN, *10th October,* 1889.

The foregoing abstract has been framed from the annual accounts prepared by the *Interim* Hon. Treasurer, audited by us, and approved of.

JAMES AUGS. SINCLAIR, C.A., *Auditor.*
GEORGE COOPER, C.A., *Auditor.*

ABERDEEN, *16th October,* 1889.

Note.—The Miscellaneous Disbursements above are allocated as follows:—

I. "Ceiling of St. Machar's Cathedral."

	£ s. d.	
Printing 232 pp., per estimate, by A. King & Co.,	39 17 6	
,, corrections and extras,	19 7 1	
Illustrations: A. Gibb & Co.,	45 0 9	
,, T. & R. Annan & Sons,	*21 3 4	
Indexing: Mr. J. M. Bulloch,	2 2 0	
Binding: Edmond & Spark: cases, &c.,	22 1 8	
,, facing paper for plates,	4 12 3	
,, brass stamp for lettering,	0 10 6	
Packing,	2 3 9	
Carriage,	10 2 6½	
		£167 1 4½*

II. "Records of Marischal College," Vol. I.

	£ s. d.	
Paper: 38¼₀ reams (54 lbs.),†	79 15 3	
Printing 610 pp., per estimate, by A. King & Co.,	104 16 10	
,, corrections and extras,	39 11 9	
Illustrations: A. Gibb & Co.,	3 5 0	
,, T. & R. Annan & Sons,	41 6 9	
Binding: Edmond & Spark: cases, &c.,	22 1 8	
,, extra folding, &c.,	6 12 6	
,, brass stamp for lettering,	0 11 6	
Packing,	2 3 9	
Carriage,	13 2 9	
		313 7 9‡

III. "Wodrow Biographical Collections."

	£ s. d.	
Secretary's visit to Glasgow,	£2 10 0	
Transcripts: Rev. Mr. Kilgour,	16 10 8	
		19 0 8

IV. Club Library.

Works of reference purchased,	4 10 6

V. Sundries.

	£ s. d.	
Printing reports and circulars,	£4 13 5	
Stationery, &c.,	2 2 8½	
		6 16 1½
Amount of Miscellaneous Disbursements as above,		£510 16 5

* Together with £47 18s., as per former Statement of Accounts. Total, £214 19s. 4½d.

† A small portion has also been used of the paper set apart, as per former Statement, for the "Chartulary of St. Nicholas," Vol. II.

‡ Together with £14 19s. 9d., as per former Statement. Total, £328 7s. 6d.

www.ingramcontent.com/pod-product-compliance
Lightning Source LLC
Chambersburg PA
CBHW032002300426
44117CB00008B/864